Fast Ethernet

LIAM B. QUINN
RICHARD G. RUSSELL

WILEY COMPUTER PUBLISHING

John Wiley & Sons, Inc.
New York • Chichester • Weinheim • Brisbane • Singapore • Toronto

Executive Publisher: Katherine Schowalter
Senior Editor: Marjorie Spencer
Managing Editor: Brian Snapp
Text Design & Composition: North Market Street Graphics

Designations used by companies to distinguish their products are often claimed as trademarks. In all instances where John Wiley & Sons, Inc., is aware of a claim, the product names appear in initial capital or ALL CAPITAL LETTERS. Readers, however, should contact the appropriate companies for more complete information regarding trademarks and registration.

This text is printed on acid-free paper.

Copyright © 1997 by John Wiley & Sons, Inc.

All rights reserved. Published simultaneously in Canada.

This publication is designed to provide accurate and authoritative information in regard to the subject matter covered. It is sold with the understanding that the publisher is not engaged in rendering legal, accounting, or other professional service. If legal advice or other expert assistance is required, the services of a competent professional person should be sought.

Reproduction or translation of any part of this work beyond that permitted by section 107 or 108 of the 1976 United States Copyright Act without the permission of the copyright owner is unlawful. Requests for permission or further information should be addressed to the Permissions Department, John Wiley & Sons, Inc.

Library of Congress Cataloging-in-Publication Data:

ISBN: 0-471-16998-6
Printed in the United States of America
10 9 8 7 6 5 4 3 2 1

Contents

ABOUT THE AUTHORS vii
ACKNOWLEDGMENTS ix
INTRODUCTION xi

PART I How Fast Ethernet Works 1

Chapter 1 Fast Ethernet Basics 3

LOCAL AREA NETWORKING: A DEFINITION 3
FAST ETHERNET TOPOLOGY 6
TRANSMITTING AND RECEIVING FRAMES 9
PROTOCOLS: RULES OF THE ROAD 12

Chapter 2 Anatomy of a Node 23

APPLICATIONS 24
NETWORK PROTOCOLS 26
NETWORK INTERFACE 27
NETWORK INTERFACE DRIVERS 28
DRIVER SOFTWARE INTERFACES 29
PROTOCOL SOFTWARE INTERFACES 29

Chapter 3 Fast Ethernet Repeaters 31

TOPOLOGY RULES 31
WHAT REPEATERS DO 33
CLASS-II FAST ETHERNET REPEATERS 41
CLASS-I FAST ETHERNET REPEATERS 43
NODE-TO-NODE OPERATION 50
MORE ON 100BASE-TX AND -FX 52
AUTONEGOTIATION 53

Chapter 4 Frames: The Basic Unit of Communication 57

FRAME ADDRESSING 58
ADDRESSES AND THE MAC 61

LENGTH/TYPE FIELD   63
DATA FIELD   65
FRAME CHECK SEQUENCE   65

Chapter 5   MAC and CSMA/CD: Fast Ethernet's Heart and Soul   69

HOW CSMA/CD WORKS   71
COLLISIONS   74
WHY COLLISIONS HAPPEN   76
COLLISION DETECTION AND RECOVERY   92

Chapter 6   The Fast Part of Fast Ethernet: Network Performance   95

MAXIMUM THROUGHPUT   96
NETWORK UTILIZATION   98
OFFERED LOAD AND NETWORK PERFORMANCE   100
NETWORK MANAGEMENT   103

Chapter 7   Frame Switching, Routing, and Protocols   109

BRIDGES   110
FRAME SWITCHES   122
INTERIM CUT-THROUGH SWITCHING   130
STORE-AND-FORWARD SWITCHING   132
MIXING NETWORKING SPEEDS   134
HYBRID DESIGNS   134
CONGESTION   135
FULL-DUPLEX LINKS   138
ROUTING AND PROTOCOLS   140

PART II   HOW TO SET UP A FAST ETHERNET LAN   149

Chapter 8   Determining Network Requirements   153

PLANNING THE NETWORK   154
WORKGROUP LANs   160
DEPARTMENTAL NETWORKS   166
BACKBONE NETWORKS   168
ENTERPRISE NETWORKING   170
ENTERPRISE-LEVEL NETWORK MANAGEMENT   172

Chapter 9   Fast Ethernet Network Interface Controllers   175

PRICE AND PERFORMANCE   176
DRIVERS   178
TECHNICAL SUPPORT   180
EASE OF INSTALLATION   181
WARRANTY   182
NIC NETWORK MANAGEMENT   183
TYPES OF NICS   183
NIC ARCHITECTURES   189
PHYSICAL INTERFACE (PHY)   190
ADAPTER BUS ARCHITECTURES   192
PCI BUS   192
NIC FEATURE SET   206

Chapter 10   Designing the Cable Plant   209

PLANNING A STRUCTURED NETWORK   210
ELEMENTS OF A STRUCTURED CABLING SYSTEM DESIGN   213
SYSTEM-LEVEL DESIGN AND THE CABLE PLANT   222
SELECTING THE CABLE PLANT MEDIA   224

Chapter 11   Selecting Repeaters   227

STACKABLES   227
CHASSIS-BASED HUBS   230
CLASS-II REPEATERS   234
COMMON REPEATER FEATURES   234
SECURITY FEATURES   236
SMART UPLINK MODULES   242

Chapter 12   Fast Ethernet Switches   245

OVERCOMING TOPOLOGY LIMITATIONS   245
PERFORMANCE AND SEGMENTATION   247
SINGLE NODE PERFORMANCE   248
CATEGORIES OF SWITCHES   249
SWITCH PERFORMANCE   253
PROBLEMS WITH SWITCHING   258
COMMON SWITCH FEATURES   264

Chapter 13 Routers 267

TO ROUTE OR TO SWITCH? THAT IS THE QUESTION 268
CONNECTING TO THE INTERNET 274

Chapter 14 Using Network Management 277

USING MIB-II INTERFACE-BASED MANAGEMENT 278
MIB-II EXTENSIONS 285
ETHERNET-SPECIFIC MIB 288
MEASURING SWITCH CONGESTION 291
USING RMON NETWORK-BASED MANAGEMENT 291
BASELINING AND NETWORK PERFORMANCE 310
MIB BROWSERS 314

Appendix A Ethernet and Fast Ethernet Compared 317

Appendix B Fast Ethernet Topology Rules 321

MODEL-1 RULES 322
MODEL-2 RULES 324

Appendix C Online Resources 329

Appendix D Performance RFCs 331

Appendix E Fast Ethernet Media Specifications 361

100BASE-TX MEDIA 362
100BASE-FX MEDIA 365
100BASE-T4 MEDIA 370

Appendix F EIA/TIA Twisted-Pair Cable Specifications 377

EIA/TIA STANDARD CHOICES 378
OTHER FAST ETHERNET CABLING 380
INSTALLATION AND MAINTENANCE 381
EIA/TIA WIRING GUIDELINES 383
CABLE PLANT TESTING 384

GLOSSARY 385
INDEX 411

About the Authors

LIAM B. QUINN is an engineering manager for NIC hardware development with Compaq Computer Corporation in Austin, Texas. Prior, he was a principal design engineer with Thomas-Conrad Corporation, where he designed Ethernet, Fast Ethernet, and Token Ring NICs for the ISA and built PCI bus architectures. He worked with Digital Equipment Corporation for six years developing simulation environments and LAN hardware products for high-speed networking platforms including the FDDI Gigaswitch. He has lectured for over four years at the Dublin Institute of Technology in Ireland and has given numerous technical presentations and talks on LAN networking. He is a member of IEEE and IERE and is a registered Chartered Engineer.

RICHARD G. RUSSELL is a senior software engineer and engineering group leader for firmware development Compaq Computer Corporation in Austin, where he works on Ethernet and Fast Ethernet repeater and switch products. Prior, he was a senior software engineer with Thomas-Conrad Corporation, where he developed 100Mbps managed repeaters and high performance FDDI adapters. He has been developing embedded communications products for industrial and commercial use for the past 15 years.

vii

Acknowledgments

To my wife Tanya for your love, patience, and encouragement, and for being my best friend. For my daughters, Ashley, Sarah, Meghan, and Jennifer; your love, support and understanding made this project so much easier. The education, discipline, and dedication imparted to me by my mother, father, and family has once again proved invaluable. I would also like to thank my friend and partner Richard for your dedication and tenacity during the development of this book and other projects.

—Liam

To my wife Jenny for all your support (and proofreading); I couldn't have done this without you. To my mother who taught me the value of books and instilled in me a desire to learn. She also sent me to typing and ballroom dancing classes. Mom, the typing has really paid off. Of course, this book wouldn't be possible without Liam, a true friend and a great engineer.

—Richard

We would also like to thank all the people at John Wiley & Sons who made this book possible, especially Marjorie Spencer, our senior editor; Margaret Hendrey, her editorial assistant; and Brian Snapp, our managing editor. Thanks also to Carol McLendon at Waterside Productions for helping us put this project together.

Introduction

Network performance seems to be everybody's hot button. Magazines hype it, vendors promise to deliver it, users gripe about the lack of it, and accountants gripe about the cost of it. One of the questions most frequently asked by network managers and planners is, What's the best way to increase the capacity of our networks? More and more often the answer is *fast ethernet*. Our purpose is to help you understand why by:

- Explaining **how fast ethernet works.** The technology will be thoroughly described in everyday terms. Covered are all the components of a Fast Ethernet system, from NICs and repeaters to switches and routers.
- Helping you to **plan a Fast Ethernet network** by analyzing your current network or new needs, and determining which of your problems Fast Ethernet can solve.
- Exploring **concise examples of network configurations** using Fast Ethernet, and illustrating how they apply to real-world scenarios.
- Discussing the ins and outs of **equipment selection,** while taking stock of common features to look for and problems to avoid.
- Surveying **network management** strategies that will keep your Fast Ethernet system running well.
- Providing in-depth **appendices** that contain important technical information for those users who need or are interested in the nitty-gritty.

More News than We Can Print

In short we've tried to give readers not just the principles, but also all the groundwork they'll need to implement the Fast Ethernet solution. But no book can have all the answers. Fast Ethernet technology is advancing at a rapid rate and Gigabit Ethernet is right around the corner. So, to help readers further, this book has a companion website at **www.wiley.com/compbooks/fastethernet,** containing online information about the technology, late-breaking news, and pointers to other relevant sites. This site will be updated regularly as new information becomes available. Please visit often.

Behind the Hype

Fast Ethernet is able to solve many of today's performance problems, because it's fast, relatively inexpensive, easily understood, robust, and well supported by a large number of equipment manufacturers. Understanding how it works is crucial to successful implementation. In 1991 the top-end machine in most organizations was a 33MHz Intel '386 running DOS in text mode. By 1997 166MHz and faster machines running 32-bit operating systems, such as Microsoft Windows 95, Windows NT, Novell NetWare 4, OS/2, and powerful versions of UNIX, such as Solaris, SCO, and Linux, had become the norm. Today's standard Ethernet and Token Ring networking technology cannot handle the demands of a growing user population, increasingly sophisticated software, and new categories of applications—all of which escalate demand for network bandwidth. The widespread use of graphics, multimedia, Internet access, e-mail, groupware, and client/server databases now pervades almost all levels of corporate activity.

In this bandwidth-hungry world, most of us are still struggling to use technologies developed in the early '80s, such as 10Mbps (megabits per second) Ethernet technology and 16Mbps Token Ring, to support powerful new workstations and applications. Some leading-edge networks have installed solutions such as FDDI or ATM to provide backbone connectivity and move data around a campus or a large building. However, these high-speed solutions are too expensive to extend readily to every desktop in the workplace. Today's computing needs require high-speed, low-cost, networking power directly to the user.

High-speed networking has been around for many years and is usually defined as anything that runs at or above 100Mbps. The most common examples are FDDI (Fiber Distributed Data Interface) and ATM (Asynchronous Transfer Mode). However, several factors have limited their market acceptance: FDDI has an unpersuasive cost-benefit ratio, and ATM, which is even more expensive, presents interoperability problems.

Fast Ethernet is a very different story. Recent standardization of the technology and broad product availability have drastically lowered the entry barriers to high-speed networking for most organizations. Fast Ethernet is both an open system and an increasingly cost-effective one, making implementation efficient. There are two reasons for this. First, like its 10Mbps predecessor, Fast Ethernet is relatively simple (especially when compared to token passing technologies) and fundamentally reliable. Second, and most importantly, the Fast Ethernet standard (IEEE 802.3u) is a true international open standard neither developed nor owned by a single company. This is in direct contrast to IBM's Token Ring and Hewlett Packard's 100VG AnyLAN technologies. Open standards protect a company's technology investment by ensuring a flexible and competitive marketplace. The rights to develop, manufacture, and sell Fast Ethernet products do not have to be purchased or licensed. Any company can develop Fast Ethernet products. These are the same factors that enabled 10Mbps Ethernet to become the overwhelmingly dominant networking technology of the '80s and early '90s.

How Fast Is Fast?

At 100Mbps, Fast Ethernet is obviously 10 times faster than regular Ethernet. To say this, however, is to say very little until you can specify how this relates to network performance. How Fast Ethernet works, what makes Fast Ethernet fast—and what this means to users—is what this book is about.

Bottom-Lining It

Properly implemented, Fast Ethernet can greatly increase the power and usefulness of your LAN for a relatively low cost. It operates at a baud rate of 100 megabits per second over both copper and fiber cabling. Although parts of the technology have been evolving for some time, Fast Ethernet is new in that the IEEE 802.3u standard, which defines it, was ratified on October 26, 1995. Yet one of the most attractive things about it is how much is *not* new. Fast Ethernet has much in common with its Ethernet predecessor, and this commonality means that many of the lessons learned over the years about today's Ethernet systems are applicable to tomorrow's.

Of course, there are distinct limitations to the similarity between Ethernet and Fast Ethernet, and there are some surprises when it comes to the precise nature of their differences. Speed creates more than incremental difference. Imagine what driving would be like if your car suddenly ran like a fighter jet. This circumstance alone would dictate new driving habits and destinations.

Also, Fast Ethernet has different configuration rules than Ethernet. For example, 10Base-T Ethernet hubs can be cascaded together in many different ways, but Fast Ethernet hubs can only be stacked and not cascaded. These are called **Class-1** repeaters. A **Class-2** Fast Ethernet repeater can be uplinked to *one* other Class-2 repeater. Most of the technical differences between Ethernet and Fast Ethernet fall into these two categories, which together yield many of the more dramatic differences between regular and high-speed Ethernet.

Properly utilized, Fast Ethernet is perhaps a great technology to use at many levels of a network infrastructure. It can furnish high-speed connectivity to the desktop, function as a backbone, and provide high-speed, high-capacity links for today's superservers. We hope that reading this book will give you a solid understanding of Fast Ethernet, and how to make it work well for you.

PART I

HOW FAST ETHERNET WORKS

To make smart decisions about implementing Fast Ethernet, you first must know how Fast Ethernet works. The amount of information on the topic is scattered and only semidigestible. One of the hardest parts for a newcomer to the field to master is sorting out good information from bad, and separating what you need to know from what you don't. We originally conceived this book as a pathway through the information thicket. For example, experience suggests that you'll need to understand what collisions are and why they happen, but you're much less likely to use the fact—however intriguing—that Fast Ethernet 100Base-TX uses 3-Level MLT-3 signaling with 4B5B data encoding. If you are interested in the bits and bytes, you'll be happy to know we didn't omit it—we just put it in Appendix E.

Part 1 first describes the individual components of a Fast Ethernet LAN, and how they relate to each other. Once the terrain is mapped, we discuss how each component functions in sufficient detail for you to start problem-solving on your own. Several sections describe not just what collisions are, but also why they occur, and how they affect network performance. Finally, we pull everything together in an analysis of the basic performance characteristics of Fast Ethernet.

The idea is to translate information into knowledge. If you can fully understand how Fast Ethernet operates and how all its components fit together, you can design a functional network that meets your needs. We don't assume that you are an Ethernet network expert (many readers will be migrating to Fast Ethernet from Token Ring or

FDDI), so we won't define Fast Ethernet by explaining it in terms of its predecessor. Nonetheless, the relationship between Ethernet and Fast Ethernet is often revealing. When it is important to the discussion, information about 10Mbps Ethernet is included. If you are interested in a really detailed comparison between Ethernet and Fast Ethernet, Appendix A is dedicated to this analysis.

While you won't need to know Ethernet in order to succeed with Fast Ethernet, it's important to note for research and documentation purposes that Fast Ethernet is an extension to the IEEE 802.3 standard commonly called the *Ethernet Standard*. These standards are written as a set of *clauses*, which resemble chapters in a book. The Fast Ethernet standard is specified as the *u* addendum to the 802.3 standard, and specifies changes to the first 20 clauses and adds 10 new clauses (numbers 21 through 30) to the original. In practical terms, all of this implies that Fast Ethernet is simply a faster implementation of 10Mbps Ethernet technology. To think of it that way is not wrong but *is* something of an overgeneralization. Fast Ethernet is at least as different from Ethernet as it is similar.

As you might expect, most of these differences derive from the magnitude of increase in speed. The chapters to come will explore all the ways in which higher speeds generate technology that is not merely faster, but in many ways also genuinely new.

CHAPTER 1

Fast Ethernet Basics

Networking can be a complex topic, but it is grounded on some basic, simple concepts. This chapter covers these networking basics with a focus on Fast Ethernet. It describes a few key network terms, and introduces the components that make up a Fast Ethernet LAN and some key concepts on how it all works, including the following:

- The definition of the term LAN
- The difference between LANs and WANs
- What a topology is and how it applies to Fast Ethernet
- The concept of repeaters and nodes
- An introduction to frames and protocols

If you are familiar with networking, you can easily skip this section. If not, you may find it valuable to spend some time reading this chapter.

Local Area Networking: A Definition

Fast Ethernet is a **Local Area Network** (LAN) technology and is designed to connect computers over a small area, such as an office, a building, or small campus. Fast Ethernet is not designed for use over a wide area, such as a large campus or city, in contrast to **Wide Area Networks** (WANs), which are systems designed to connect devices or LANs to each other over a wide area.

A simple definition of a LAN is *a system for directly connecting multiple computers.* Some would say this is not an academically precise definition, but it is a *practical* one, and suitable for our purposes. Of course, this definition needs some explaining. Four of the words bear closer examination: *system, directly, connecting,* and *multiple.* Networks are systems because they are made up of several components, such as cable, repeaters, network interfaces, nodes, and protocols. You may have often heard the term *hub.* The terms *hub* and *repeater* are often used interchangeably, but for Fast Ethernet there are differences. All of these elements work together and function as a network. If any one of these elements is missing, there is no LAN system.

The *connecting* part is easily explained. Networks provide connectivity, a way for computers to exchange information and/or data. (We could get into an abstract discussion of the difference between information and data, but we'll leave that to the database folks.) This is the primary purpose of a LAN or of any network. More importantly, the LAN imposes no restrictions on the type of data that nodes can exchange except that it be in digital form. At first, this seems like a minor technical point but it has profound implications. Most LANs are used to share files and printers. Almost all of us have used a LAN like this. However, LANs (and other networks) can carry video, telephone conversations, and any other data or information that can be carried in digital form.

One of the most interesting and controversial things that happened on the Internet in 1995 was Internet Telephones. The first software written by enterprising college students was free. It allowed voice to travel over the Internet. At first this was very crude. It functioned just like walkie-talkies: Only one person could talk at a time and the sound quality was crude. Moreover, it worked between only two people. It was free (no long-distance charges), however, and required only a sound card and a microphone. It also worked for people with only modem (i.e., slow) connections to the Internet.

Software companies such as Netscape, Microsoft, and Intel (among others) quickly saw the commercial opportunities of this technology and developed software that worked almost as well as a regular telephone. Of course, some small, long-distance telephone companies were threatened by this and asked the Federal government to outlaw such technology. Fortunately, the Federal Communications Commission didn't regulate this technology. Interestingly enough, big companies such as MCI, AT&T, and Sprint did not object. They carried most of the Internet traffic, so they made money either way!

Explaining *multiple* isn't difficult, either. A network isn't a network without two or more computers. Of course, there can be other devices on a network, such as printers. We generally call the devices connected to a network, **nodes.** A node is connected to a LAN via a **network interface.** In short, LANs directly connect **multiple** nodes.

The word *directly* is an extremely important word in the LAN definition. This is really what makes a LAN local. *Directly* means that any given node on a LAN can communicate with any other node on the *same* LAN without having to use a third node or other device as an intermediary, in contrast to a WAN, which uses **gateways** to connect LANs or other devices (see Figure 1.1).

Figure 1.1 shows three LANs connected together over two WAN links. The nodes on each of the LANs can communicate directly to each other. However, when a node on LAN 1 communicates with a node on LAN 3, the data that travels between them must go through two gateways. The nodes on the different LANs must also be aware of, and communicate with, the gateway connected to their LAN. Another common term for a gateway is *router*. A router is a gateway, but not all gateways are routers. For more information on routers, see Chapter 13.

On a single, Fast Ethernet LAN (or any other LAN), any two devices can talk directly to each other because they share the same media. Media is generally the cable and/or devices that physically connect all the computers on the LAN. Another way to say this is that Fast Ethernet is a **shared media technology.** All the nodes on a LAN share the same media and use the same basic rules for transmitting data on the LAN. The key thing about a LAN is that *any* two nodes that need to communicate with each other do not have to explicitly communicate with, or be aware of, any intermediate devices. (An example of this direct communication, or *any-to-any* [usually said *many-to-many*] communication, is the **Peer-to-Peer Networking** support in Microsoft Windows 95.) Thus any two computers on a network can share resources. The classic example of this is often called **drive mapping** or **drive sharing.** One person could make drive letter

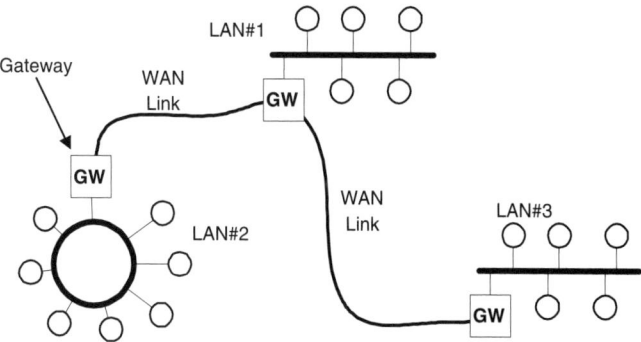

Figure 1.1
LANs and WANs.

K: access the disk drive on someone else's computer. For example, if Bob's K: drive was connected to Karen's computer, then when Bob saved a word-processing file to his K: drive, it would actually be written to the disk drive in Karen's computer. The important thing to note is that this occurs without any other computers being involved: Karen's and Bob's computers communicate directly with each other.

Several other common LAN technologies—Ethernet, Token Ring, FDDI, 100VG AnyLAN, and ArcNET—are all LAN technologies and meet the preceding definitions. All are LANs, but each is significantly different from the others, and has different operational rules and different Topologies.

Fast Ethernet Topology

LANs are local because all the computers on a LAN are essentially tied together by the same media. Every network type has a set of rules, called **topology rules,** that dictate how the components of a network are physically connected to one another. There are three basic network topologies: the *Hub and Spoke* (often just called *Star*), *Ring,* and *Bus* (see Figure 1.2). Physically, Fast Ethernet uses a Hub and Spoke, or Star, topology just like 10Base-T Ethernet. We will usually use the term Star in this book to name the Hub and Spoke topology because it is the term most commonly used.

However, Fast Ethernet and its Ethernet predecessor both operate as bussed networks. In other words, Fast Ethernet uses a physical Star topology but logically operates as a bussed system due to Fast Ethernet's long family history. On early Ethernet networks, from which Fast Ethernet was derived, all the nodes were literally attached to a single segment of cable with T connectors. The first Ethernet cable was a thick coaxial cable. Each end of the cable ended in a device called a *terminator* (see Figure 1.3). This is called 10Base-2 Ethernet or often *thin net*. There are other Ether-

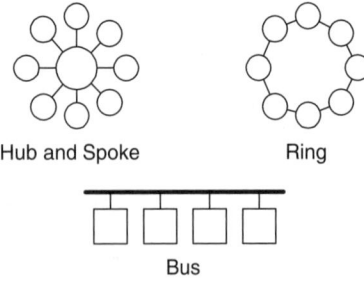

Figure 1.2
Network topology types.

Figure 1.3
A 10Base-2 bussed Ethernet network.

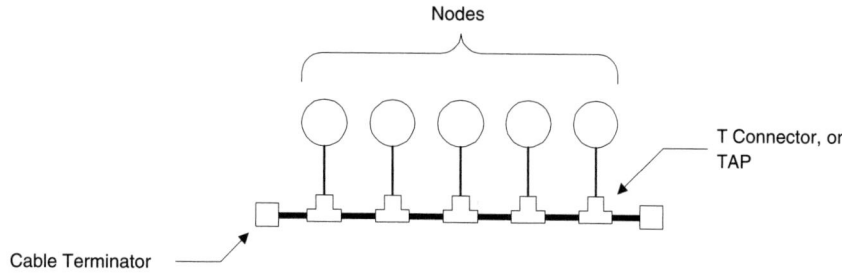

net bussed technologies, such as 10Base5, often called *thick net*, which used a thick, yellow wire.

As you can imagine, this connection scheme has some limits. The biggest problem is snaking a single piece of cable throughout an entire building. Another problem is that if there are any breaks or other problems anywhere on the cable, the entire LAN quits working. Early Ethernet LANs could not get very big due to these cable limitations, so the concept of a repeater was introduced to allow networks to grow (see Figure 1.4). The first repeaters were devices that tied two cable segments together to form one LAN.

These repeaters did more than just connect two pieces of cable; they also cleaned up the electrical signals between each cable segment. These early repeaters had another advantage: If one cable segment had a problem (e.g., was shorted out), the nodes on the other cable segment could still communicate with each other. This is called **partitioning** and is still used by modern Ethernet and Fast Ethernet devices to isolate network components which are causing problems. While these repeaters are physically connected to pieces of cable, they are *low-level* electrical devices and are invisible to the nodes. Therefore, the entire system still operates as a single LAN.

Newer technologies (here we're referring to 10Base-T) improve on the idea of early repeaters by introducing the concept of a **repeater hub**

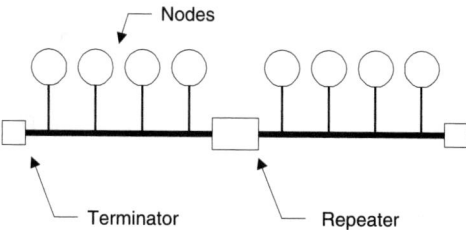

Figure 1.4
Early repeaters.

(usually just called a hub or repeater). A hub is a device that each node on the network plugs into instead of having a T connection to a common cable (see Figure 1.5).

A hub takes the place of the cable and T connections of the bussed network but behaves just like the shared cable in Figure 1.3. Each node connects to a hub via a cable. Only one node can be on a cable. Inside the hub is a digital bus to which each node is connected via a repeater port. The internal digital bus takes the place of the coaxial cable in a bussed network. The repeater ports do exactly the same thing as the cable-to-cable repeater in Figure 1.4, the difference is that instead of having just two ports, a repeater hub has many, often up to 24 or 32. For Ethernet, this hub technology is called 10Base-T. For Fast Ethernet, it is called 100Base-T.

From a cabling perspective, using a hub has some advantages and makes wiring a whole lot easier. First, a hub is much simpler to wire. Cable runs are made from a central location, the hub, to each node on the network. This is a common technique, as all telephone systems are wired like this. Secondly, inexpensive, unshielded twisted-pair wiring can be used to connect the nodes to the hub. 10Base-T was even designed to use regular telephone cable, which made putting 10Base-T networking in an existing building very easy. Often no new cable needed to be installed at all, as 10Base-T could run over the same cable that was used for a telephone. Twisted-pair cabling can be used for Fast Ethernet as well (see Appendix E and F for more information on cabling).

Using cheap, centrally wired cable really cuts costs. However, the biggest advantage with repeater hubs is that a repeater is an intelligent digital device that controls each connection to the network, and manufacturers have built a multitude of innovative features into Ethernet and Fast Ethernet repeaters. While Ethernet supports two physical topologies, the Bus and Star, Fast Ethernet supports only the Star topology. Fast Ethernet networks cannot be run over coaxial cable.

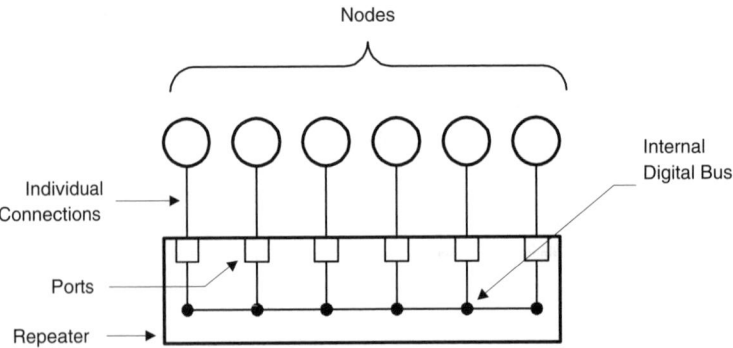

Figure 1.5
Basic repeater.

> One feature common to both Ethernet and Fast Ethernet is that the nodes and repeaters test link integrity. If the cable is plugged in and has a proper connection, the fact that the link is up is indicated. This is usually done by turning on an LED. As mentioned before, many hubs will autopartition (disconnect) nodes that are causing too many problems on a network.

Frequently you will see the terms *hub* and *repeater* used. For Ethernet and Fast Ethernet, these terms are interchangeable. For other technologies, these terms are often ambiguous and may mean two different things. A hub is usually a central device to which all the wires from a set of nodes are connected. Hubs are often just mechanical wiring blocks that are used to terminate the ends of cables. You have probably seen telephone punch-down blocks, which are a form of wiring hub. Other networking technologies use different terms. FDDI uses the term *concentrator*, Token Ring uses *MAU* (Media Access Unit), while 100VG AnyLAN and ARCNet use the term *hub*.

For Ethernet and Fast Ethernet, a repeater is a device that copies (repeats) electrical signals between two or more devices. Early two-port repeaters merely connected two coaxial cable segments together. Fast Ethernet repeater hubs perform both of these functions: They are both a wiring hub and a repeater. For convenience, in this book we generally call the repeater hubs simply repeaters, because this is the term used in the Fast Ethernet specification. A repeater can be a single, stand-alone box, or a plug-in card for a larger chassis. Sometimes a single repeater is made up of individual devices called **stackable hubs.** For more information on Fast Ethernet repeaters, see Chapter 11.

Transmitting and Receiving Frames

Once nodes are connected to a repeater, they communicate by sending **frames** to each other. For Fast Ethernet, the frame is the basic unit of communication—any information sent between nodes is placed in the data payload portion of one or more frames. To send a frame from one node to another, there must be a way to uniquely identify each node on the LAN. This is done by assigning each node an address. Every node on a LAN has an address, usually called its **MAC address.** This address is unique: No two nodes on a LAN can have the same MAC address. In fact, for all LAN technologies (except ARCNet), no two nodes in the whole world have the same MAC address. In other words, *all* MAC addresses are unique. For more information on addressing, see Chapter 4. All frames contain at least

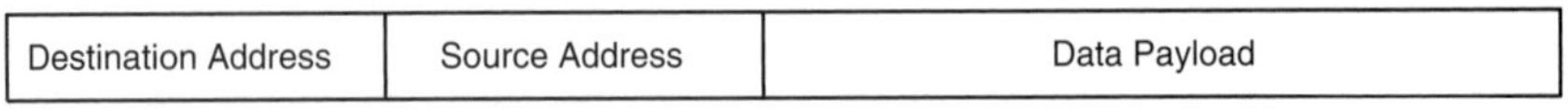

Figure 1.6
Frame elements.

| Destination Address | Source Address | Data Payload |

three basic pieces of information: a destination address, a source address, and a data payload. Some frames have other fields, but these three are the critical pieces (see Figure 1.6).

For example, take two stations, Alpha and Beta, on a LAN. When station Alpha needs to send data to station Beta, Alpha creates a frame containing a destination address (Beta's address), a source address (Alpha's own address), and a data payload (the data it wants to send to Beta). Alpha then transmits the frame. Beta will then receive the frame because Alpha and Beta are both connected to the same physical media. The Ethernet 10Base-2 cable bus network is a perfect example. When a node transmits a frame on the cable, *all* nodes on the network *hear* or receive the frame because they are all attached to the same cable (see Figure 1.7).

Sharing the cable like this has an important requirement: Only one node can talk (transmit) at a time. If a node tries to transmit while another node is transmitting, the signals on the wire become garbled and the data that both nodes transmitted becomes lost, a situation very much like the old telephone party lines. All LAN technologies use shared media and have this problem, and Fast Ethernet is no exception. On a shared media LAN, something must control when a node can transmit. If there were no controls, then the LAN would be like a room full of people all trying to talk at once, which would never work. To solve this problem, each type of LAN technology has a set of rules that govern when each node can transmit. These rules are called **Media Access Rules.** For Fast Ethernet, these rules are called CSMA/CD and are fully described in Chapter 5. This behavior is *exactly* mimicked by a repeater. The nodes as pictured in Figure 1.8 are connected to a repeater. This system behaves just like the network in Figure 1.7.

The data transmitted by Alpha is received by port 1 and repeated (copied) to all the other repeater ports. This means that *all* nodes on a Fast

Figure 1.7
Each node receives all frames.

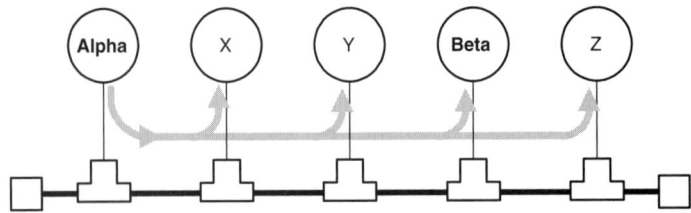

Figure 1.8
A repeater works like a cable bus.

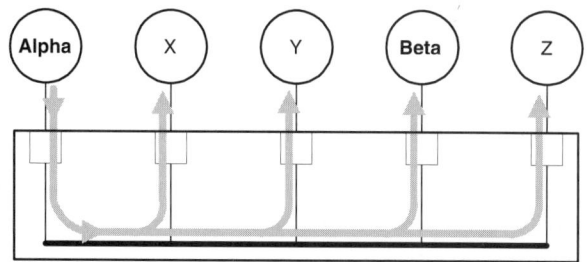

Ethernet LAN receive *all* frames transmitted on the LAN, no matter what. This is an important and fundamental characteristic of both Fast Ethernet and Ethernet, as devices, such as switches and bridges, depend on being able to hear all the frames that are transmitted on a LAN. The behavior of the repeater means that nodes X, Y, and Z receive the frame that Alpha sent to Beta. Of course, nodes X, Y, and Z are not really interested in this, but the repeater doesn't know that. To the repeater, a frame is just a train of bits which are received on one port and repeated to all the others. In other words, bits go in one port and go out to all the other ports.

To solve this problem, nodes use a mechanism called **filtering.** When a node receives a frame, it compares the destination address to its own address. If the addresses are different, then the node ignores, or discards, the frame. If the addresses match, then the frame is kept and processed. This is sometimes called **copying,** since the frame is actually copied from the LAN to the node's memory.

With all LAN technologies, there is a special address called a **broadcast address.** If any node transmits a frame with a destination address set to the broadcast address, then all nodes will copy and process the frame. For Fast Ethernet the broadcast address is an address with all 48 bits set to a 1. (See Chapter 4.) This broadcasting technique is fundamental to all LAN technologies and is widely used for a variety of purposes. Broadcasts are most often used for searching for other resources on a LAN. This is often called **discovery.** For example, when using the peer-to-peer networking in Windows 95, your computer will use a broadcast to find other computers on the LAN.

A node can also operate in a special way called **promiscuous mode.** When a node is in promiscuous mode, it turns off filtering and copies *all* the frames received, regardless of the frame's destination address. This is usually used for diagnostics. As you can imagine, this can be quite handy. One computer attached to a LAN can monitor all network traffic. This is a common practice used to measure performance and gather error statistics and other useful information. Other devices, such as bridges, switches, and RMON probes, operate in promiscuous mode.

Protocols: Rules of the Road

Exchanging frames is the basic method used to communicate over a network, but by themselves, frames are not structured enough to be useful. For nodes to have meaningful conversations, there must be rules governing when they should send frames to one another, and what is in the data payload of each frame. A set of rules governing how computers communicate is called a **protocol**. Any time two computers communicate over any kind of network, they use at least one protocol and often more than one.

Let's take opening and reading a file as an example. This is an activity that takes place frequently on a conventional network. If you use your word processor, spreadsheet, or database program to open and read a file over the network, the two computers involved will exchange a series of frames. Basically, this process will require four different types of frames.

- Open command
- Open response
- Read command
- Read response

The process works like this: First, node Alpha (your computer running the word processor) sends an Open File command to node Beta (the server). The Open command has one piece of data: the name of the file to open. This frame tells Beta to open the file and return an answer (response) to Alpha (see Figure 1.9).

The Open response is very important. It tells Alpha if the command sent to Beta was successful. For example, if the user specified the name of a file that did not exist, then Beta would return an error indication to Alpha (see Figure 1.10). In this example, we will assume that the file **letter.txt** actually exists and Beta returns a success indication to Alpha.

There is something subtle but very important to notice in Figures 1.9 and 1.10. Beta knows the node to which it should send the response by looking in the source address field of the frame, which contains the Open command. This is a fundamental networking activity and happens all the time.

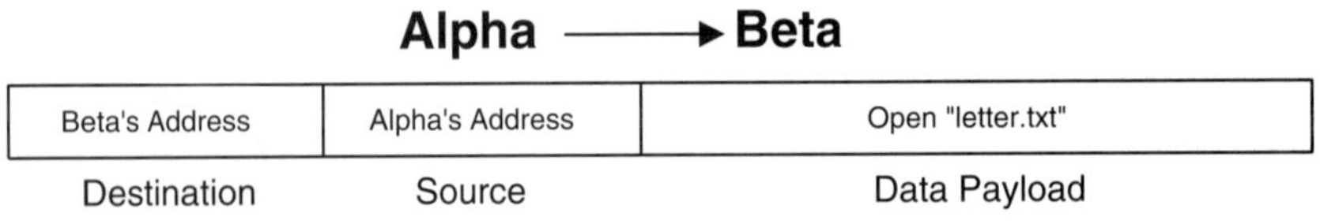

Figure 1.9
Open command.

Alpha ⟶ Beta

Beta's Address	Alpha's Address	Open "letter.txt"
Destination	Source	Data Payload

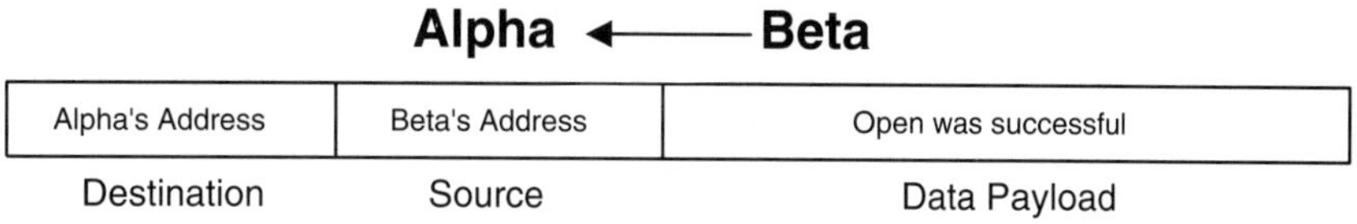

Figure 1.10
Open is successful.

```
                    Alpha  ←——— Beta
| Alpha's Address | Beta's Address | Open was successful |
   Destination       Source            Data Payload
```

Now that Alpha has opened the file, it must read it. To do this, Alpha sends the Read command with two pieces of information, where to start reading and how many characters to read. As with the Open command, Beta will respond to Alpha's request to read the file. It could be an error message, but in this case, it is the first 200 characters of the file **letter.txt** (see Figures 1.11 and 1.12).

This is a very simple example and leaves out many technical details, but it does illustrate the crucial command/response pattern of network protocol operation. Almost all network communications take the form of a command and response. Some network protocols are very complex; others are really quite simple. For example, the networking features in Microsoft Windows, Windows 95, and Windows NT are presented to the user in a very simple way but are actually built on a very complex set of protocols (the 802.2 LLC Type-2 protocol, a protocol called **NetBEUI** (pronounced net-boo-ee), and Microsoft's **Server Message Block** (SMB) protocol). These complex protocols were derived from protocols developed at IBM in the mid to late 1980s, when Microsoft was still a partner with IBM.

The **Hyper Text Transport Protocol** (HTTP) is used to read Web pages by World Wide Web browsers, such as Netscape's Navigator, Mosaic, and Microsoft's Internet Explorer. Amazingly, this is a very simple protocol, really only a little more complex than the concept just illustrated. One reason the Internet works so well and so successfully is that it is based on simple networking protocols. Protocols like TCP/IP and HTTP are quite uncomplicated. Networking is one of those wonderful systems where the simpler solution is often the fastest, the most reliable, and the easiest to implement.

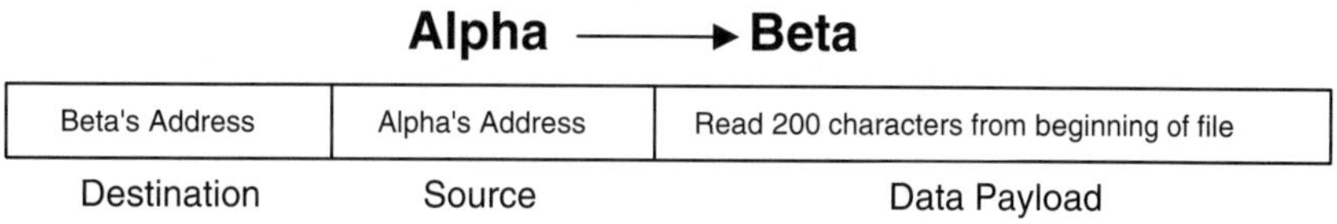

Figure 1.11
Read Data command.

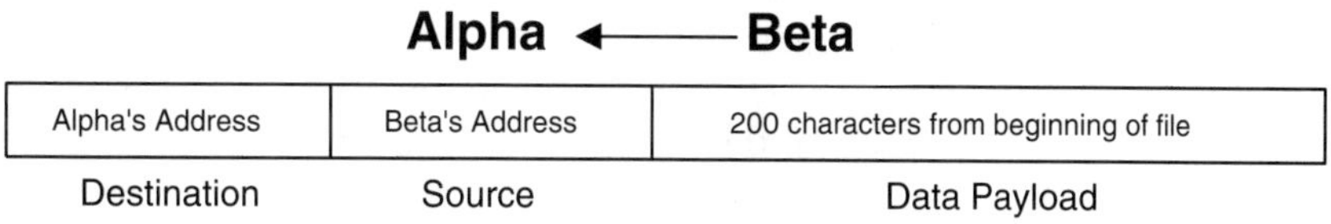

```
                    Alpha  ———→ Beta
| Beta's Address | Alpha's Address | Read 200 characters from beginning of file |
   Destination       Source            Data Payload
```

Figure 1.12
Read response.

```
                    Alpha  ←——— Beta
| Alpha's Address | Beta's Address | 200 characters from beginning of file |
   Destination       Source            Data Payload
```

Protocols and frames are different logical levels of communication components. Frames are a low-level mechanism and are tied to specific hardware technology, like Ethernet or Fast Ethernet. The frame format for Ethernet and Fast Ethernet is the same, but differs from the format used for other technologies such as Token Ring and FDDI. Network protocols are a higher-level mechanism than frames and are independent of the lower-level technology being used. For example, the TCP/IP and HTTP protocols can function over almost any kind of low-level frame type or networking technology. How higher-level protocols and lower levels of a system fit together is often called a **hierarchy**.

These basic examples illustrate the fundamentals of all LAN technologies. The concept of a system of components is applicable to Fast Ethernet in particular, as repeaters, media, nodes, network interfaces, and protocols all work together to make Fast Ethernet a functional networking system.

The concepts of levels and hierarchy are also fundamental and reflect a systems approach to networking. These ideas are extremely important and permeate all networking technologies. Often the most important thing about Fast Ethernet and other LAN technologies is not how each component works, but how it interacts with other components to form a networking system.

Components of a Fast Ethernet Network

The components of a Fast Ethernet system can be categorized in several ways. Most manufacturers describe Fast Ethernet in terms of its physical components, such as network interface cards and repeaters, switches, and routers. There is also a standard network model, called the *OSI Reference Model*, that is often used to categorize and describe network components for all kinds of technologies.

For our purposes, these are the components of the Fast Ethernet system:

Physical Components	*Logical Components*
Nodes	Frames
Repeaters	Media Access Rules
Network Interfaces	Network Protocols
Cables (Media)	

All of these components are necessary to create a functioning Fast Ethernet system. The physical components are what most advertisements and magazine articles focus on. Manufacturers also focus heavily on these pieces of the system because they make the money. The logical components are just as important as the physical pieces, but since these are things that are not usually purchased they are often overlooked. Frames and

Media Access Rules are never purchased; they are just definitions of how things work. Protocols are definitions, too, but must actually be implemented as software. Often protocols are part of an operating system, such as Windows 95, Windows NT, or Novell Netware.

Three other optional components are often used in constructing Fast Ethernet LANs. In fact, it's difficult to build all but the smallest Fast Ethernet LANs without them:

Physical Components	*Logical Components*
Switches	Network Management
Routers	

Physically, a Fast Ethernet LAN is pretty simple. A simple network consists of nodes, network interfaces, cables, and a repeater (see Figure 1.13). A node can be many things: computer, printer, router, or bridge. A repeater is the central component in a Fast Ethernet network, and is the device that all the nodes must connect to; in other words, the central point of the Star topology, or the cabling hub. Nodes, of course, are connected to repeaters by cable—just like today's Ethernet 10Base-T repeaters. A **network interface** is what actually connects a node to the repeater via a cable. Nodes can have one or more network interfaces, but a network interface belongs to a single node.

> It's often useful to distinguish between a node and a network interface. Generally, the term *node* encompasses the entire device connected to the network, such as a computer, printer, or some other computer-like device. A node is connected to the network via its network interface, and uses that interface to send and receive frames. Network interfaces are usually called **Network Adapters** or **Network Interface Cards**. Usually network interfaces are plug-in cards; however, it is common for network interfaces to be built into motherboards or other devices, such as printers or workstations.

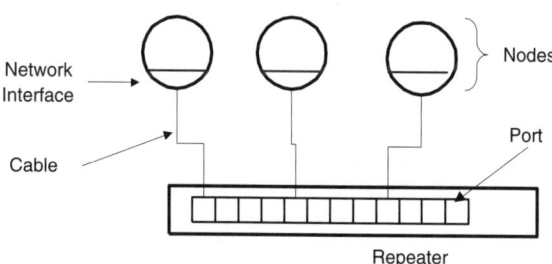

Figure 1.13
Basic components.

Fast Ethernet can use three different types of cable: high-quality Category-5 cable, lower-quality Category-3 cable, or fiberoptic cable. The most common type of cable used is Cat-5. 100Base-TX and 100Base-FX are very similar and really differ only in the specific electronics used to transmit and receive low-level signals. 100Base-TX (or just TX) has electronics specific to transmit and receive over Cat-5 copper cable, and 100Base-FX (or just FX) is specific to fiberoptic cable. Except for these small differences, TX and FX are the same and are often referred to as just 100Base-X. 100Base-T4 is very different and is designed to use lower-quality Cat-3 cable.

Fast Ethernet has some strong similarities to regular old Ethernet. Fast Ethernet uses the same 802.3 frame format that Ethernet does. This format consists of a destination address, source address, length field, data field, and frame check sequence. Fast Ethernet also uses the same media access rules that Ethernet uses, called **Carrier Sense Multiple Access with Collision Detection** (CSMA/CD). These are the rules that govern when a node can transmit on the network.

The fact that Fast Ethernet uses the same media access rules and frame format as Ethernet is why some people say that Fast Ethernet is just like Ethernet. This is only partially true. Fast Ethernet is a lot like Ethernet, but there are some significant differences, which will be explored in detail in later chapters. The most important thing about Fast Ethernet is its transparency to protocols, such as TCP/IP or IPX. These protocols run over Fast Ethernet quite well. No new software needs to be written, no translation or encapsulation layer introduced. Fast Ethernet is designed to be fully compatible with its older Ethernet cousin. The diagram in Figure 1.13 is a complete representation of the Fast Ethernet system.

Figure 1.14 shows all the physical components in a Fast Ethernet network, and how they are related. The components of a node will make a little more sense when we look at how they correspond to the pieces of a Windows 95 or NT computer system. For example, when Netscape Navigator needs to send a message to read a page from the Web, it does so via the TCP/IP protocol. TCP/IP breaks the message into frames and sends it to the Driver (the LLC) for transmission. The Driver then works in conjunction with the NIC (a network interface) to actually transmit the frames on the network (see Figure 1.15).

In general, the upper layers in a network system deal with application data, such as Web pages, files, e-mail, and printing. The middle layers deal with translating application layer information into a format suitable for sending and receiving on the network. The middle layers also manage how nodes on a network find each other and have meaningful conversations. The lower layers deal with physically sending and receiving data on the network itself. Data flows up and down through the layers. Each layer uses well-defined interfaces to communicate to adjacent layers (the ones above

Fast Ethernet Basics

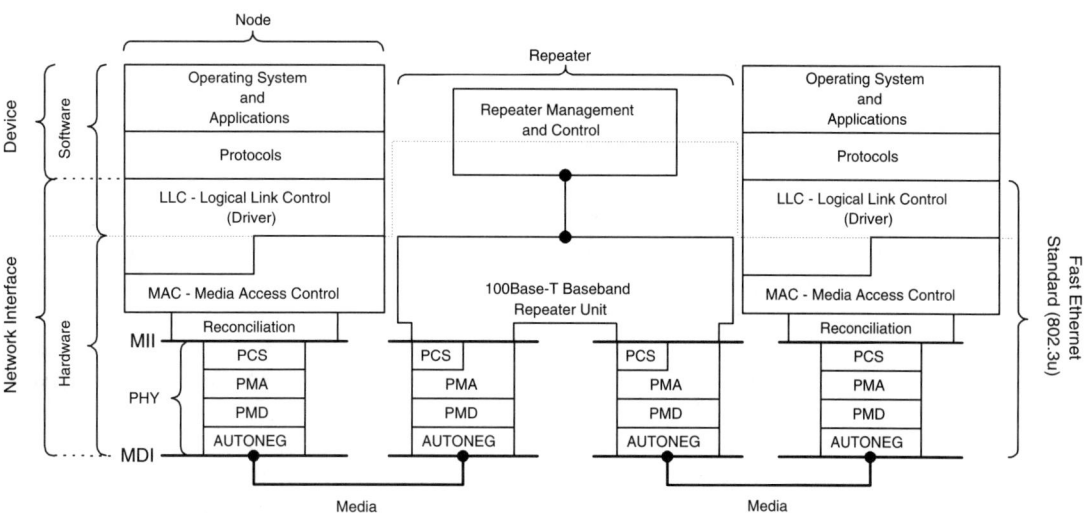

Figure 1.14
The Fast Ethernet System.

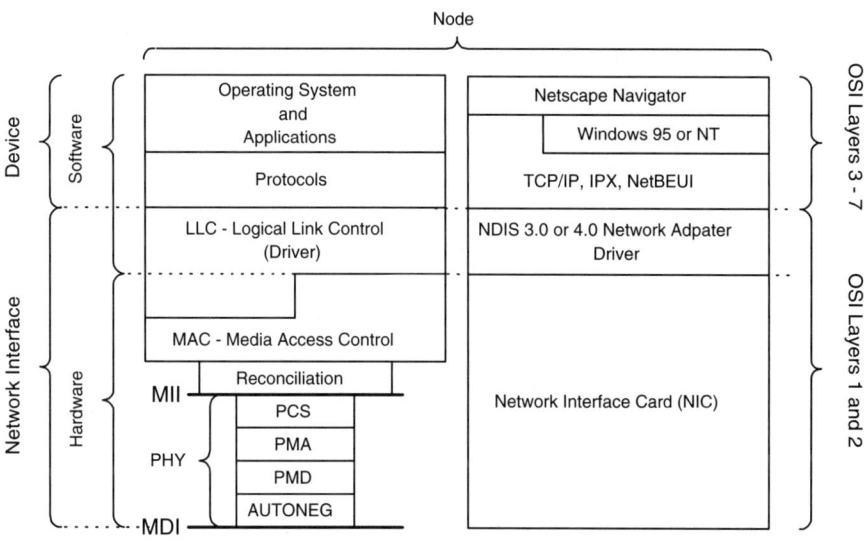

Figure 1.15
Node details.

and below it). In Microsoft terms, these interfaces are called **Application Programming Interfaces** (APIs). You may be familiar with two of these, NetBIOS and WinSock.

Three other important components are often used when building a Fast Ethernet LAN: network management, frame switching, and routing. While not absolutely required like the other components, these are often indispensable when building all but the smallest Fast Ethernet LANs.

Network management consists of a protocol called the **Simple Network Management Protocol,** or SNMP, and a method of describing data called the **Abstract Syntax Notation 1,** or ASN.1 format, which is used to describe data objects and structures in a networking device or component. These descriptions are stored in a simple ASCII text file called a **Management Information Base,** or MIB. A device or component's data objects and structures can be retrieved and/or modified using the SNMP protocol. When a device supports data described by an MIB and the SNMP protocol, it is said to be **managed.**

For example, using SNMP, the number of frames transmitted and received on any given port can be retrieved from a repeater. Devices can also be controlled. For example, any port on a managed repeater can be turned on or off. These are very simple examples but quite useful by themselves. Managed devices often support extremely complex MIBs that provide very detailed information about their operation, and allow a fine degree of control over the device.

A **frame switch,** or just a switch, is a device that is used to connect single Fast Ethernet LANs, often called **segments,** into a larger system called a **Switched LAN** (SLAN). Switches can be used for many reasons, but their primary purpose is to provide higher network performance for a set of nodes than could be provided by a single Fast Ethernet LAN. A SLAN is more complex than a simple LAN, but from a node's perspective, a SLAN operates just like a regular LAN. Switches can be used for other reasons as well, such as connecting to other network types or allowing a Fast Ethernet LAN to become physically very large. These devices are called frame switches because they process Fast Ethernet and Ethernet frames and not higher-level protocols.

Routing is similar to frame switching and is also used to connect LANs together. Unlike frame switching, which works at a low frame level, routing works at a higher network protocol level. While routers are also used to connect LANs, they are used in different ways than switches. Routers can be used to connect different types of LAN; for example, Fast Ethernet and Token Ring. They can also be used as gateways to connect systems over wider areas, such as a city or country. The Internet itself is a truly huge routed network. When you open a Web page, the information is delivered to you by routers and may traverse a myriad of systems, technologies, and interfaces to get from its source to your computer.

OSI Reference Model

Developed in 1977 by the International Organization for Standardization, this model is a framework for defining how communications and networking systems are described and fit together. It describes a formal hierarchy and system of seven layers, and defines the function of the layers, each of which corresponds to a logical communications function. Each layer performs a defined set of tasks and relies on the next lower layer to perform a more primitive (closer to the hardware) task. Each layer also provides a set of services to the next higher layer. For example, the TCP/IP protocol uses the network interface to send and receive network frames. TCP/IP is a protocol that works at OSI layers 3, 4, 5, and 6. The seven layers of the OSI model are usually drawn as shown in Figure 1.16.

The seven layers can be defined in many ways. A search on the Web for "OSI Reference Model" will yield over 200 pages, each describing the model in a different way. If you would like to learn more about the model, researching using the Web is a great way to do it. One reason the model is so popular is that it is extremely flexible and subject to interpretation. For Fast Ethernet, the model can be defined in the following way:

- 7—The **Application** layer provides high-level network services to the users of a system or application software. Examples of such services are file and print services, Web services, FTP services, and network server log-on and log-off services.

- 6—The **Presentation** layer provides data translation services to higher levels of software in the system. Early Presentation layer functions provided such services as conversion between character sets such as EBSDIC and ASCII. Newer Presentation layer functions provide data encryption and decryption services. Examples of such services are Netscape's Secure Socket Layer and Microsoft's PCT API.

- 5—The **Session** layer provides a mechanism to set up, maintain, and tear down connections between nodes on a network. A connection

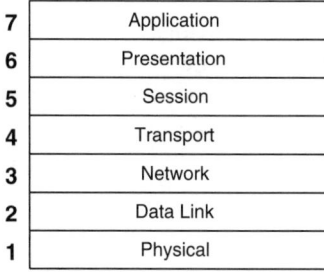

Figure 1.16
The seven OSI layers.

is often called a session or conversation. Sessions are used by most higher-layer networking software, and provide a framework and context in which to exchange information.

> The preferred way to access a network on Windows 95 and NT, especially for Internet (TCP/IP)-aware applications, is WinSock 2.0. WinSock provides layers 4, 5, 6, and 7 services to programs such as Netscape Navigator or Microsoft Internet Explorer.

- **4**—The **Transport** layer provides a mechanism to reliably exchange data between two (or more) nodes on a network. This layer ensures that data is transferred from node to node, error free and in sequence, with no data loss or duplication. For example, if your computer sends messages A, B, and C to a server, the Transport layers at each end make sure that the server receives messages A, B, and C, in that order. This may seem to be an obvious requirement of any communications system, but it is harder to ensure than it seems. Think of how much equipment data must go through every time you open a new Web page. Much of the protocol work in a node is done at the transport layer.
- **3**—The **Network** layer is extremely important. It provides a mechanism that allows the upper layers to be independent of the data transmission technologies in layers 1 and 2. It also hides the specific path data may take to reach its destination (routing). For example, all three protocols widely supported by Windows 95 and NT (TCP/IP, IPX, and NetBEUI) will work over Ethernet, Fast Ethernet, Token Ring, ARCNet, FDDI, ATM, ISDN, and XDSL (all the common networking technologies). The network layer for some systems, such as Ethernet and Fast Ethernet, is pretty simple, but for ATM and ISDN, it is very complex. For example, a network layer for ISDN must know how to dial another ISDN number, when to dial, and when to hang up.
- **2**—The **Data Link** layer provides access to the physical network for the upper layers. For Fast Ethernet, these are the LLC, MAC, and PHY layers in Figure 1.14. Fast Ethernet's frame structure is also a Data Link element. The Data Link layer controls when information can be transmitted by a node and what information is received for the node. Much of the design of Fast Ethernet revolves around the Data Link layer.

- **1**—The **Physical** layer defines the mechanical connections, electrical signaling, and media type that are used to move data from one point to another. For Fast Ethernet, the physical layer standards are 100Base-TX, 100Base-T4, 100Base-T2 and 100Base-FX. The Fast Ethernet 802.3u standard corresponds to layers 1 and 2 of the seven OSI Reference Model layers. In other words, Fast Ethernet is a Physical and Data Link standard. It defines only how nodes are connected and the basic (lowest level) way data is transferred, and is only a part of a networking system.

CHAPTER 2

Anatomy of a Node

A network (or LAN) node is a complex device consisting of many components, each of which provides part of the system-level functionality that enables a node to communicate with other nodes on the LAN. The major components of a node are

- Applications (Clients and Servers)
- Network Protocols
- Network Interface Card (NIC)
- Network Interface Drivers
- Software Interfaces

Figure 2.1 shows how these components work together in a node on a Fast Ethernet LAN. Note that the transmitting and receiving paths in a node are separate and independent of each other. This is true all the way to the repeater. Almost all components in a Fast Ethernet have both a transmitting side and a receiving side.

These categories are not the only way to describe the components of a node. For example, the OSI model places applications in one layer, but splits network protocols into layers 3 through 6 and lumps network interface drivers and NICs into layers 1 and 2. The OSI model doesn't really address software interfaces much at all other than to say that layers use them to communicate with each other. In the real world, interfaces are extremely important. If you don't have the right ones, nothing will work.

While the OSI model is an excellent framework for discussing networking, it categorize things in an abstract way. The previous list is

Figure 2.1
The anatomy of a node.

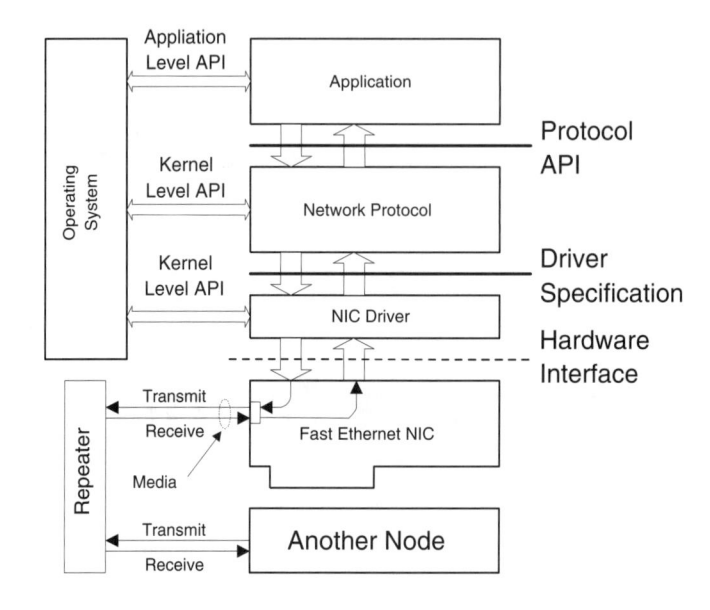

more practical and will mirror network setups that you will see in such products as Windows 95, Windows NT, UNIX, and on the Macintosh.

Applications

From a networking standpoint, applications software can be divided into three categories:

- Client/Server
- Peer-to-Peer
- Network Independent

Client/server applications require two pieces: a client application and a server application. Client software makes requests for information or services, and server software satisfies these requests. This is an extremely broad definition, but one that works very well. Clients and servers tend to be on different computers and must communicate over a network. They communicate using application-level protocols. Hundreds, if not thousands, of application protocols are in use today. Some are well documented and understood, such as HTTP and FTP. (HTTP is the Hyper Text Transport Protocol and is used to read Web pages, among other things. FTP is the File Transfer Protocol and is used to move files between computers.) Many other protocols are proprietary and only used by the software from a single vendor. The key element about these application-specific protocols is that they are designed for a specific and narrow purpose. They have detailed, specialized, and often private rules and vocabularies.

Common examples of client software are Web browsers, such as Netscape Navigator; e-mail programs, such as Microsoft Mail; and client programs for online services, such as CompuServe and America Online. These clients have corresponding server software, such as Netscape Enterprise Server, Microsoft Back office, and the huge programs that run on CompuServe and America Online's giant computers. These applications each support one (or more) application-specific protocols.

Some network-aware software falls into a category called peer-to-peer (PTP). PTP software communicates via application protocols, just like client/server (C/S) software. However, while C/S software has one program (or set of programs) that makes up a server and a different set that makes up the client, the PTP architecture runs the same software, or software with the same capabilities, on each node.

A good example of peer-to-peer software is Intel's Video Teleconferencing systems called ProShare, which allows two computers to have a video teleconference between them. The software at each end does the same thing, and if both systems are the same (for example, Windows 95 machines), they could run the exact same software. The nodes could also be very different (for example, one could be a Windows NT machine and the other a Macintosh).

Some applications are not network aware but work well with networks. For example, your word processor is probably not a network-aware application. When you open a file, it could be on your local hard disk or on a server. The word processor doesn't know how the file is physically accessed. Actually, accessing the file is something handled by the operating system. For example, Microsoft Word doesn't know the difference between a drive letter that is local and one that is on a network server. Word just asks Windows 95 to open the file. It's up to Windows 95 to figure out how to do it. This is the first example of an interface.

Operating systems such as Windows 95 and Windows NT provide a set of Applications Programming Interfaces (APIs) to applications. Opening, reading, writing, and closing files is one set of APIs. From the application's point of view, it uses APIs to ask the operating system for information or to perform services. The relationship between application and operating system is a client/server one. As long as these APIs are well designed, the operating system can hide how the services are performed. The services can happen locally or over a network.

There is actually a fourth kind of software: the kind that is network hostile. These are usually legacy (old) applications that depend on very low-level operating system services, such as direct disk access. In the old days, before we had Windows 95 and Windows NT, DOS and Windows 3.x software often bypassed the application-level APIs and accessed low-level APIs such as the BIOS. The hardware was accessed directly to obtain high performance or to provide features that were not provided by these early, and sometimes primitive, operating systems. Of course, these programs won't work over networks.

Network Protocols

Network-layer protocols are the key components in any network architecture, and receive a lot of focus in networking-related literature. Protocols are the standard rules by which applications communicate to each other over a network. These protocols are like standard English, German, or French—extremely standardized, documented, common, and well understood—and are used to transport application-specific protocols over networks (such as Fast Ethernet) between applications on different nodes.

There are a huge number of application-level protocols but only a handful of commonly used Network Protocols, and only two are really in widespread use:

- **TCP/IP** (Transmission Control Protocol/Internet Protocol)
- **IPX/SPX** (Internet Packet Exchange/Sequenced Packet Exchange)

TCP/IP and IPX/SPX are by far the most commonly used protocols today. Of course, TCP/IP is the basis for the Internet, and is used to transfer everything from Web pages and files to real-time voice and video. IPX/SPX is the core protocol used by both Novell's Netware and Microsoft's Windows 95 and Windows NT. (All three of these operating-system products can use other protocols: For example, all of them use TCP/IP equally well and the Microsoft products also support a protocol called NetBEUI.)

Other commonly used protocols, such as Apple Talk from Apple, IBM's SNA (System Network Architecture), and Digital Equipment Corporation's DECNet, are mostly used with a specific vendor's equipment and operating systems. These vendor-specific protocols do not have the widespread use of TCP/IP and IPX/SPX.

Network-layer protocols define the message formats and rules by which nodes communicate with each other. All of these protocols, especially TCP/IP can be transported using an extremely wide variety of networking technologies. TCP/IP can be transported over traditional networks, such as Ethernet or Token Ring, and new technologies, such as Fast Ethernet. TCP/IP is also easily transmitted over serial links on PCs, satellite links, radio links, and just about anything else that will transport digital data.

This is one of the key features about protocols: They are transport independent. An application using TCP/IP or IPX/SPX operates independently of the networking technology used. This allows general-purpose applications to work over any network technology that supports these protocols. For example, you can upgrade your Ethernet LAN to Fast Ethernet, and all your applications will continue to work as before, but much faster.

Network Interface

Any device that needs to be connected to a network must have at least one network interface. For PCs and workstations, the network interface is usually an add-in card called a Network Interface Card, or NIC (see Figure 2.2). A NIC is the hardware device that physically connects a node to the network. Sometimes a NIC is built directly into a system, usually as part of a motherboard, or system baseboard.

Though they are conceptually simple devices, NICs come in an extremely wide variety of types. Manufacturers have devised many clever and useful features that differentiate their products from each other. Some NICs are optimized for workstations and are inexpensive and easy to install; others are designed to be plugged into a network server and are optimized for performance. Some NICs have multiple network interfaces on them, allowing a single card to connect the host computer to two or four separate LANs. Any given NIC is also specific to a networking technology, such as Ethernet or Token Ring, and also to an expansion bus type, such as ISA, EISA, or PCI.

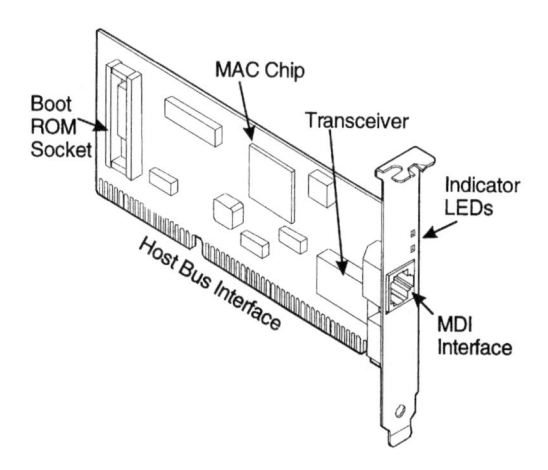

Figure 2.2
A typical NIC.

Besides physically connecting the device to a LAN, a NIC is also responsible for transmitting and receiving data over the LAN. It does this using the rules of the LAN technology for which it was designed. For example, a Fast Ethernet and a Token Ring NIC use very different rules for transmitting and receiving data. NICs are key components of any network architecture. Often a network manager will choose a NIC based on price alone, feeling that since all NICs for a given technology meet the standard, they all work the same. This could not be further from the truth. Performance, reliability, and ease of installation are just a few of the things to consider when selecting a NIC. An entire section of this book (see Chapter 9) is dedicated to NICs.

Network Interface Drivers

A network interface driver is the software that connects a NIC to the network protocols used in the system. While seemingly mundane, drivers are key components in networked systems, and other than the actual speed of the network, the driver is a component that can significantly affect or determine the performance of your network. A well-written NIC driver is small, fast, efficient, and bug free. Once you install it, you should never have to think about it again. On the other hand, a poorly written driver is big, slow, inefficient, and can have subtle bugs that are extremely hard to diagnose and can cause all kinds of weird problems.

Believe it or not, a NIC with a high-quality driver can be hard to find. Writing and testing a NIC driver is often the bulk of the work in designing and manufacturing a NIC, especially with today's highly integrated NICs. For example, many of today's Fast Ethernet NICs are based on the Texas Instruments Thunder LAN device (T-LAN). The T-LAN chip is practically an entire network adapter on a single chip. With the addition of a connector and a few components, a manufacturer can quickly build a Fast Ethernet NIC. TI even sells a basic set of NIC drivers for the T-LAN. Using hardware and software purchased from TI, almost any company could build and sell a Fast Ethernet NIC; and some companies do just that.

It would seem that hardware and software like the T-LAN would quickly make Fast Ethernet NICs a commodity device. Indeed, the T-LAN and other chips like it from DEC and other manufacturers have been leading factors in the continually falling cost of Fast Ethernet NICs. However, there is still a lot of room for differentiation between manufacturers' Fast Ethernet NICs, especially when it comes to drivers. Companies like Compaq spend a great deal of time and effort designing, developing, and testing the drivers for all their NICs, including their Thunder LAN-based devices.

The performance of Compaq's NICs and drivers is significantly better than that of a stock T-LAN card, which might come from a small company that just glued the pieces together.

Reliability is another area where drivers can be very different. Drivers from companies like Compaq are also extremely well tested. They go through rigorous certification tests from companies like Microsoft and Novel. A common problem with many cheap adapters from overseas is that their drivers do not go through these certification tests.

Driver Software Interfaces

NIC drivers allow protocols to work with a NIC to send and receive data on a network. The interface between the driver and the protocol is defined by the operating system. For Microsoft systems, this interface is called the Network Driver Interface Specification (NDIS). Any NIC that has an NDIS drive can be used with a Microsoft product. Over the years, the NDIS specification has evolved, and now, to be fully compatible with all Microsoft operating systems, a NIC vendor must develop and test at least three drivers. Windows for Workgroups 3.11 requires NDIS 2.0 drivers, Windows 95 requires NDIS 2.0 or 3.0 drivers, and Windows NT requires NDIS 3.0 or 4.0 drivers. Some modern NICs come with only NDIS 3.0 drivers, which allows the card to be used with Windows 95 or Windows NT.

Other companies have designed driver specifications as well. Novell's specification is called the Open Data Link Interface (ODI) specification. ODI drivers can be used under Novell Netware, DOS, Windows 3.x, Windows 95, and Windows NT. Most NICs also come with ODI drivers for use with Novell-oriented networks. Novell also has multiple versions of the ODI specification, so a NIC will usually come with separate ODI drivers for servers and workstations.

The critical thing to note about NIC drivers is that a protocol such as Microsoft's TCP/IP protocol in Windows 95 can work with *any* NIC that has an NDIS 2.0 or 3.0 driver. The software interface between a protocol and driver is standard, while the interface between the driver and the NIC is designed by the manufacturer of the NIC.

Protocol Software Interfaces

NIC drivers and network protocols work together to provide the ability for applications to send and receive data over the LAN. Applications must communicate with protocols, and protocols must communicate with drivers, which in turn work with a NIC to send and receive data.

Operating systems such as Windows 95 and Windows NT define standard interfaces and APIs for such protocols as TCP/IP and IPX/SPX. Applications use these interfaces and APIs to send and receive data using a specific protocol.

For Windows 95 and Windows NT, the most useful API is called WinSock. The WinSock 2.0 API allows application programs to communicate over TCP/IP, IPX/SPX, and other protocols using only the WinSock 2.0 API. Before WinSock 1.0, there were *multiple* APIs for TCP/IP, another for IPX/SPX, another for NetBEUI, and others for DECNet and IBM's SNA. If an application program needed to use multiple protocols (often a big marketing advantage), it had to be written and tested using several APIs. As you can imagine, this was a lot of work.

WinSock 1.1 (WinSock 1.0 was quickly updated to WinSock 1.1 and was never really used) provided a single interface to the TCP/IP protocol on Windows 3.x, Windows 95, and Windows NT. This encouraged an explosion of TCP/IP-enabled applications that helped fuel the rapid acceptance of the Internet by PC users. WinSock 1.1 meant that a program could use *any* vendor's TCP/IP protocol to communicate over a LAN or the Internet. WinSock 2.0 expanded on this concept by providing a common interface for other protocols besides TCP/IP. WinSock 2.0 also supports the IPX/SPX, DECNet, and OSI protocols.

CHAPTER 3

Fast Ethernet Repeaters

A repeater is the central point to which all nodes on a Fast Ethernet LAN are connected, so when you are designing your LAN, much of your time will be spent on selecting repeaters. Unlike network interface cards, which tend to be low-cost commodity items, repeaters are generally the most expensive devices on a LAN. They come in many price ranges, from a few hundred to several thousand dollars, and with a wide array of creative features.

Repeaters have two pieces: the standard part, defined by the 802.3u standard; and the proprietary part, designed by the manufacturer. As we'll see, the standard part really doesn't do much; its functionality is very basic and low level. However, since all the nodes on the LAN are attached to a repeater, and all the network traffic passes through them, a tremendous number of features and flexibility can be built into a repeater (see Figure 3.1).

The 802.3u Fast Ethernet standard describes two types of repeaters: **Class I** and **Class II**. Both do the same thing, but in slightly different ways. The differences between the two types of repeaters are subtle, technically detailed, and important to the engineers that design them. However, the differences do affect how they are used and how Fast Ethernet LANs are implemented. The most important of these effects is the Topology Rules for connecting nodes and repeaters.

Topology Rules

Sometimes repeaters can be connected together. The rules governing how these connections are made are called **topology rules,** and these

Figure 3.1
Parts of a repeater.

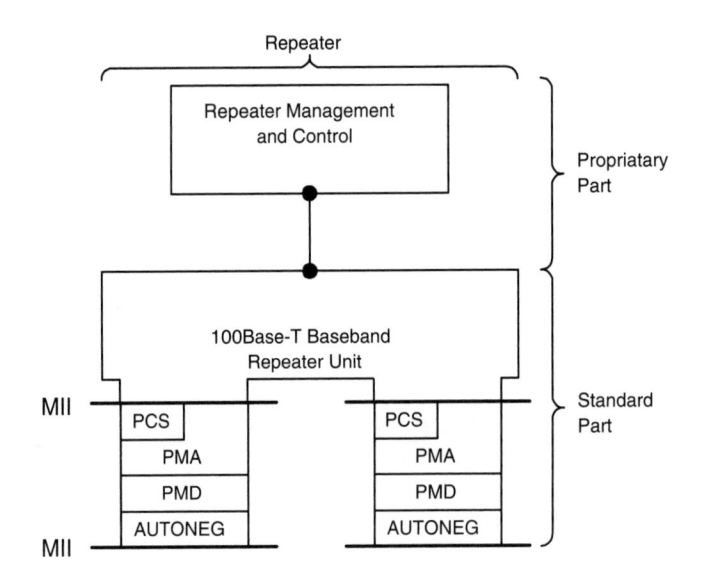

rules are among the significant differences between Fast Ethernet and 10Base-T Ethernet. The Fast Ethernet specification defines two types of topology rules: **Transmission Model 1** and **Transmission Model 2.** The Model-1 rules are simple. When copper cable alone is used, they are as follows:

- The copper cable (Cat-3, -4 or -5) between a node and repeater can be a maximum of 100 meters (328 feet) in length.
- A single Fast Ethernet network (or segment) can have one or two Class-II repeaters.
- Connecting three or more Class-II repeaters is not allowed.
- The **uplink cable** connecting Class-II repeaters must be 5 meters (16.4 feet) or less in length.
- A single, Fast Ethernet network (or segment) can have exactly one Class-I repeater.
- Class-I and Class-II repeaters cannot be used in the same Fast Ethernet network.

The Model-1 rules get a little more complex when using fiberoptic cable. The Model-2 rules involve calculations using data from equipment manufacturers and can get quite involved. Detailed information on both sets of rules is covered in Appendix B.

Fast Ethernet's topology rules (both models) are the only significant drawbacks to Fast Ethernet and, other than speed, are the biggest differences between Fast Ethernet and Ethernet. The limitation that there can be *only* one or two repeaters on a single Fast Ethernet LAN not only differentiates Fast Ethernet from 10Base-T Ethernet, but also from other LAN technologies, such as 100VG AnyLAN, Token Ring, ARCNet, and FDDI. These all allow several repeaters, concentrators, MAUs, or hubs on a LAN.

These topology limitations keep Fast Ethernet LANs from becoming physically large in terms of **network diameter.** (The diameter of a LAN is the maximum cable distance between any two nodes.) With Class-I repeaters, the maximum network diameter is 200 meters; with Class-II repeaters, it is 205 meters. This is one of the biggest problems when moving from Ethernet to Fast Ethernet. It is relatively common for a 10Base-T Ethernet LAN to have a network diameter of more than 205 meters. This makes it difficult (or impossible) to upgrade these LANs to Fast Ethernet by just swapping out the old Ethernet for new Fast Ethernet equipment.

Of course, there are ways around these topology limitations. The most common solution is to use frame switches (see Chapter 7). Also, fiberoptic cable runs can be longer than copper runs. Some manufacturers, such as Compaq, have implemented proprietary links between hubs, which overcome many of these topology limits.

What Repeaters Do

While Fast Ethernet is *physically* wired in a Star topology, it *functions* as if it were a Bus topology. On a bussed network, all nodes are physically connected to the same media, so any data transmitted by one node is received by all the other nodes. When Ethernet runs over coaxial cable, it operates this way. Fast Ethernet cannot run over coaxial cable, so a repeater takes the place of the cable, just like 10Base-T Ethernet. A Fast Ethernet repeater is an OSI Layer-1 device and operates only with the electrical signals defined at this layer. Repeaters do not operate on or decode frames. When a node transmits a frame, it converts it to a stream of bits called a **packet.** These bits are then transmitted to the repeater using electrical signals appropriate to the type of media used to connect the two. The repeater then takes the signals transmitted by the node and *simultaneously* repeats them to (or out of) all the other ports (see Figure 3.2). A side effect of this is that if bad signals are received on one port, they will be repeated out on all the other ports. Repeaters actually have rules embedded in them to minimize the propagation of bad signals.

There is very little delay between the time signals received on one port and repeated to the other ports. A repeater will retransmit a signal received on one port to all the other ports just as soon as it can, and will not wait until an entire packet is received before sending it to the other ports, which is usually called **buffering.** The time delay between when a signal is

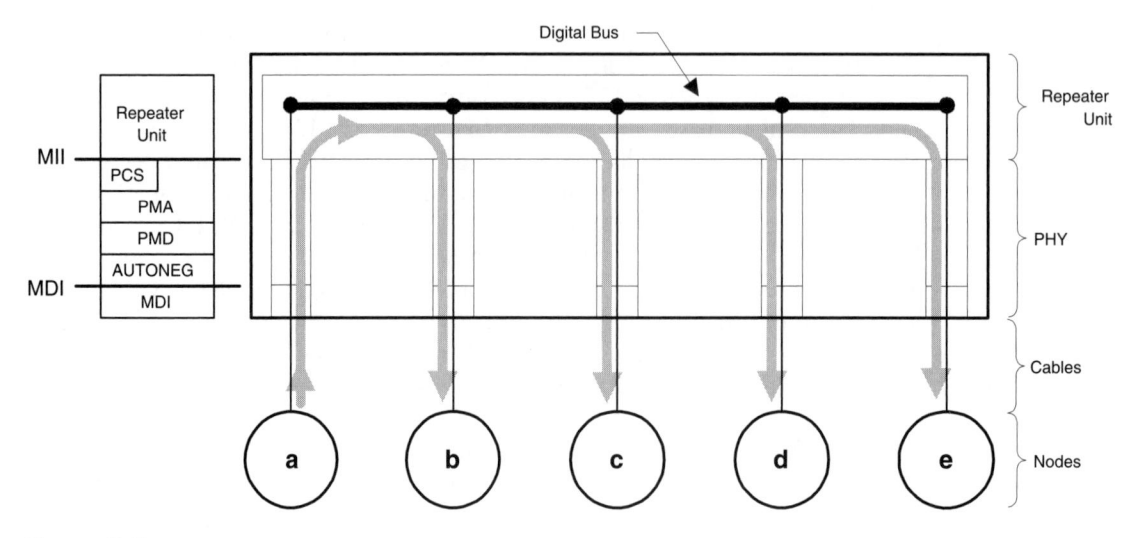

Figure 3.2
Fast Ethernet repeater.

received and when it is retransmitted is called a repeater's **start-of-packet propagation delay** and is precisely specified by the Fast Ethernet standard. Another way to define this is the time delay between when the first bit of a packet is received on one port (the **incoming port**), and when the first bits of the repeated packets begin to leave the repeater on the **outgoing ports.**

Repeaters tie each port together using an internal digital bus inside the repeater unit. This bus is independent of the type of PHY on each port, is extremely fast, and is often inside a single chip.

Repeater PHY

Each port on a repeater has a PHY, which contains the electronics in the repeater unit to the cable (the media) used to connect a repeater with nodes. The PHY layer in a repeater converts between the electrical or optical signals on the cable, and a standard digital form used internally by the repeater unit. Fast Ethernet supports three types of Media (or cable) and describes three types of PHYs.

PHY	Media
100Base-TX	Category-5 twisted-pair copper cable (uses two pairs)
100Base-T4	Category-3 and -4 twisted-pair copper cable (uses all four pairs)
100Base-FX	For fiberoptic cable

> Usually, 100Base-TX, 100Base-FX, and 100Base-T4 are just abbreviated TX, FX, or T4. Since TX and FX are extremely similar, they are often collectively called 100Base-X.

These PHYs are an important part of the Fast Ethernet standard and are used by both repeaters and nodes. The most important feature about all three PHYs are that the connection between the PHYs and the upper layers are the same. A 100Base-FX and 100Base-T4 PHY connect to a repeater unit or MAC reconciliation layer in exactly the same way. Also important is that repeaters and network interfaces (nodes) use *exactly* the same PHY layer electronics.

The PHY layer not only handles packets, but also provides some other useful information and capabilities for the repeater unit.

Link Status	The PHY can detect if there is an operational link between a repeater port and a node.
Collision Sense	When a collision is detected, the PHY indicates it to the repeater unit.
Jabber	When a node transmits for longer than allowed, this is called a *jabber*. This is detected by the PHY.
Autonegotiation	Allows the PHYs at both ends of a link to negotiate the connection type.

The PHY also provides the mechanical connection used to connect the media to the repeater (or node). For 100Base-TX and -T4 these are standard 8-pin RJ45 telephone-type connectors. Repeaters and nodes have RJ45 sockets and the copper cable uses RJ45 plugs. Fiberoptic connections (100Base-FX) are made with either MIC FC, or SC type connectors. As with RJ45s, the connectors on nodes and repeaters are sockets; those on the cable are plugs (see Figures 3.3 and 3.4).

The specification and design of the PHY are probably the most important things ensuring that Fast Ethernet components from different manufacturers interoperate with each other. In the 802.12u Fast Ethernet specification most of the attention is given not only to specifying how

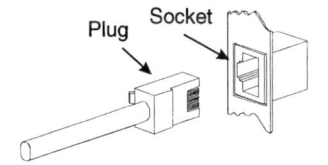

Figure 3.3
RJ45 connectors.

Figure 3.4
MIC, SC, and ST fiberoptic connectors.

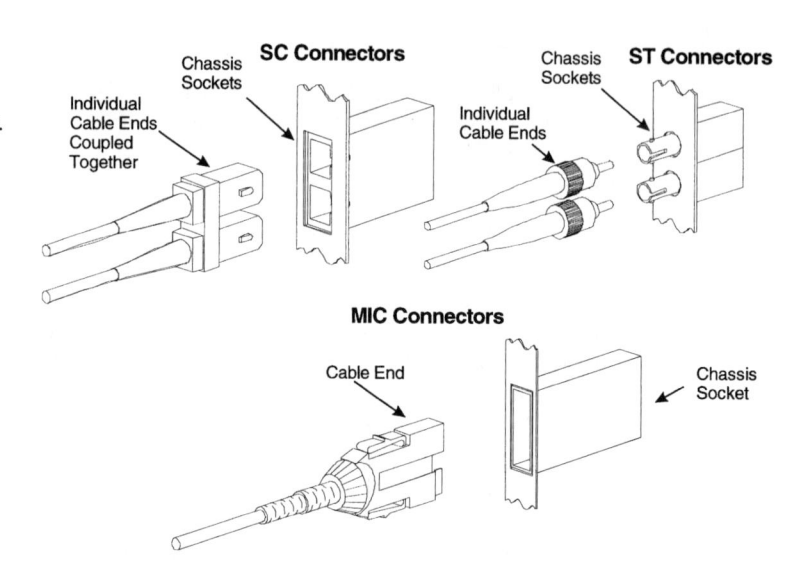

PHYs should work, but also to how they should be tested. The Fast Ethernet standard has a set of **Protocol Implementation Conformance Statement** (PICS) tests that any supplier of Fast Ethernet components must pass before they can say they meet the specification.

Packets: How Data Travel on the Wire

When a node transmits a frame, it converts it into a series of bits called a **packet,** or sometimes a **MAC frame.** Packets are then transmitted by the PHY on the media. A packet has the format shown in Figure 3.5.

Just as the data payload is encapsulated in a frame, frames are in turn encapsulated in packets. The data frame portion of the packet is the standard Ethernet frame format, consisting of a destination address, source address, length/type field, data field, and frame check sequence. For example, the preamble for 100Base-TX and -FX is a series of 7 bytes (56 bits) with the following values:

10101010 10101010 10101010 10101010 10101010 10101010 10101010

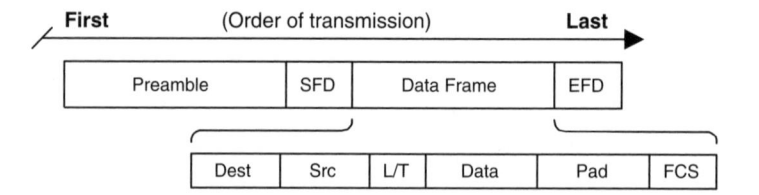

Figure 3.5
Packet format.

This preamble is transmitted, as shown, from left to right. The Start of Frame Delimiter (SFD) is a single octet and indicates the start of the frame and has the value:

10101011

For 100Base-TX and -FX, the end of frame delimiter is not a bit pattern at all, but merely the end of the data. The Fast Ethernet PHY layer signals the layer above it (the Reconciliation and MAC layers) that the end of the packet has been reached when data stops being received. The state when no data is on the wire is called the **idle state.**

The 802.12u Fast Ethernet standard describes two types of packets: one used for 10Base-TX and 10Base-FX, and another used for 100Base-T4.

Repeater Functions in Detail

The job of the repeater is to see that nodes on the LAN can communicate reliably. This may seem like a trivial requirement, but real-world network installations are rarely ideal. Some cable may be substandard, connections could be poorly terminated, there can be electrical noise and interference, nodes may behave improperly, or users may connect the wrong device to the repeater, such as a telephone. Believe it or not, it's a common error to plug a telephone into a network connection! The repeater must do all it can to keep the network (or most of it) running in spite of all these things. The Fast Ethernet 802.12u standard says that a repeater must provide the following:

- *A Transmit function.* A repeater must be able to output signals in the appropriate format for the media attached to each port. This may sound like a simple requirement, but the specification is extremely precise about how this occurs. If a repeater meets the specification, it will work properly with any other device that also meets the specification.
- *A Receive function.* Much like the Transmit function, a repeater must be able to receive signals that are transmitted in the standard way.
- *A Data Handling function.* This is the function of the repeater that *repeats*. A repeater must be able to transfer signals between each port in the absence of a collision (or other error).
- *Received Event Handling function.* A repeater must be able to detect when a node is transmitting data. This is in contrast to when a node is idle. This is called **carrier sense.**
- *Signal restoration.* When a signal is received by a repeater, it may be distorted or noisy but still adequate enough to be received by the

repeater. When the repeater resends signals to the other ports, they should be restored to their normal (clean) state.

- *An Error Handling function*. A repeater must be able to detect when a link to a node (or the node itself) is causing errors, and prevent these errors from interfering with other links. These types of errors are usually caused when a cable is connected or disconnected, or when a node powers up or down. Certain kinds of errors can also be caused by bad cables and improperly terminated connectors.
- *A Partition function*. If a node causes an excessive number of consecutive collisions, it must be partitioned (isolated) from the rest of the nodes by shutting off its repeater port.
- *A Receive Jabber function*. If a node transmits for too long a time, the repeater must be able to interrupt the node's transmission. This is called a jabber.

Signal restoration is easily accomplished and occurs naturally in a Fast Ethernet repeater. When electrical signals come into a port, they are converted by the PHY into a standard digital form and passed to the repeater unit. The repeater then sends the digital signals to the PHYs on the other ports for transmission, which reconverts the signals back into the form appropriate for the media. The PHYs for Fast Ethernet are designed to receive even very distorted or noisy electrical signals and still interpret them correctly. Only extremely bad electrical or noise problems will result in data being lost. Detecting some of these problems is also part of the repeater's job.

The Receive, Transmit, and Data Handling functions are just a more detailed way of specifying that a repeater must receive and retransmit data. Simply put, a repeater must repeat.

The Received Event Handling function of a repeater refers to how it cooperates with nodes in the context of the CSMA/CD media access rules. If more than one node is transmitting at a time, the repeater sees this and transmits a JAM signal to all its ports. The JAM tells the transmitting nodes that a collision has occurred and everyone should back off. For more information on how this works, see Chapter 3.

As you can see, the biggest part of a repeater's job is to detect, contain, and isolate errors. Repeating, while essential, is only a small part of a repeater's job.

Packet Level Error Handling

If for any reason a link is causing too many errors, the repeater will shut off that port until the link is working properly again. When the repeater detects an error condition on a port, that port's PHY will be isolated from the other ports. While the port is isolated, the repeater will continue to monitor it. When the error condition goes away, the port will be reconnected to the other ports via the repeater unit. This prevents link problems on any given port from disrupting the communications between devices on other ports for any length of time, and is one of the main strengths of Fast Ethernet technology. Many other LAN technologies also depend on an active repeater or hub; for example, FDDI, 100VG Any-LAN, and, of course, 10Base-T Ethernet. Token Ring and ARCNet can also have active hubs, but allow the use of passive hubs that do not perform error detection, error isolation, and signal retiming. Active hubs do not guarantee that problems with a node will not disrupt a LAN, but the chances of it doing so are greatly decreased.

A Fast Ethernet repeater will partition (turn off) a port when the following error conditions are detected:

- False carrier events
- Excessive collisions
- Receipt of a jabber

When a port is partitioned, no packet data or other signals will flow between the PHY and the repeater unit. After a port has been partitioned, it will be reenabled when the repeater believes the error condition has gone away. This kind of partitioning can happen extremely quickly, and a port may be partitioned for only a short period of time. For example, a jabber can be detected in as little as 400 microseconds (0.0004 seconds). The port will be enabled immediately after the jabber has cleared, which is detected when the repeater sees an idle condition on the port.

> Microseconds are normally indicated by the symbol μs after a number, as in 400μs. 1μs is 0.0000001, or 1 millionth of a second.
> Nanoseconds (1 billionth of a second) are even shorter than microseconds. Nanoseconds are indicated by the symbol **ns**. Each bit on a Fast Ethernet network is transmitted in 10ns. This is usually called the **Bit Time** and is Fast Ethernet's Baud Rate. Bit time is usually abbreviated BT.

False Carrier Events

A False Carrier Event (FCE) is detected when a repeater receives data on a port without a proper start-of-stream delimiter (bit sequence) for a specific media type. This will usually be caused by physical cable problems, electrical noise, or a PHY on either end of the link that is not working properly.

When a repeater receives two False Carrier Events in a row on a port, it will partition the port *and* send a JAM signal to all the other ports on the repeater. An FCE is also detected if a single data stream is received by a repeater that lasts longer than 5µs and did not have a valid start-of-stream delimiter. The JAM signal will last for 5µs, or until the end of the invalid data stream that caused the FCE.

When the FCE is detected, the repeater will put the port into the LINK UNSTABLE state and partition the port. This effectively isolates the problem port from all the other ports on the repeater.

After an FCE occurs, the repeater will continue to monitor the problem port so that it can clear the LINK UNSTABLE state and allow the port to operate normally again. (If you are really interested in how this works, it is described in great detail in section 27.3.1.5 of the 802.3u specification dated October 26, 1995.) This will happen under two circumstances:

- The repeater has detected no activity (idle) on the port for more than about 331µs.
- The repeater detects a valid incoming packet after the line has been idle for the interpacket gap time of 640µs.

Of course, a power cycle of the repeater will also clear this LINK UNSTABLE condition for a port.

Excessive Collisions

A repeater will partition a port when excessive collisions occur. An Excessive Collision Error (ECE) occurs when more than 60 collisions in a row occur on a port. Note that the spec says that this value must be at least 60. It could be more, depending on the manufacturer of the device. Some devices might even allow this value to be programmed by the user. Note also that these collisions must be consecutive. The repeater maintains a collision counter for each port and will reset it to zero when a packet is received by the port without a collision. Like FCE errors, excessive collisions can be caused by physical cable problems, electrical noise, or a PHY on either end of the link not working properly.

When an ECE occurs, the port is partitioned just as it is when an FCE occurs. However, this condition will be cleared when:

- The repeater detects activity on the port, without a collision, for more than 5µs.
- On power up or reset.

Jabbering

A node is considered to be jabbering when it transmits data for more than about 400µs. The largest packet is transmitted in only 120.56µs, so anything which takes longer is an error. The jabber time is set over three times longer than the largest packet transmission time to make sure that only true jabber conditions are detected. When the repeater detects a jabber, it partitions and waits for the condition to clear. The jabber condition will be cleared and the port reenabled when the data ceases to be received on the port (the jabber stops). There is no time delay.

> Most of the time durations listed in this section are discussed in terms of microseconds or nanoseconds to be precise and indicate a sense of scale. In other words, a port can be partitioned and reenabled extremely quickly. However, in the spec most of these times are specified in terms of a range of bit times. For example, the false carrier timer must have a duration of between 450 and 500 bit times.

Class-II Fast Ethernet Repeaters

Class-II repeaters are one of two types of repeaters specified in the standard. The distinguishing characteristic of Class-II repeaters is that two of them can be connected together to act as the central point, or hub, of the Star topology for a single Fast Ethernet LAN. Class-II repeaters are connected together using a special port, called an **uplink port.** A cable is plugged into the uplink port of one repeater and into any regular port on the other repeater (see Figure 3.6).

Unlike stackable hubs and chassis hubs (see the following sections), an uplink connection between two Class-II repeaters does not directly connect the repeater units internal to the repeaters. The repeater units are indirectly connected through the PHYs in the connected ports (see Figure 3.7).

The Fast Ethernet standard says that on a Fast Ethernet LAN only two Class-II repeaters can be used this way, while only a single, Class-I repeater can be used. On the surface, it may seem that using Class-II repeaters would be the most common choice. However, using Class-II repeaters has some disadvantages:

- When using the Transmission Model-1 topology rules, the connecting cable between the Class-II repeaters can be only 5 meters long.

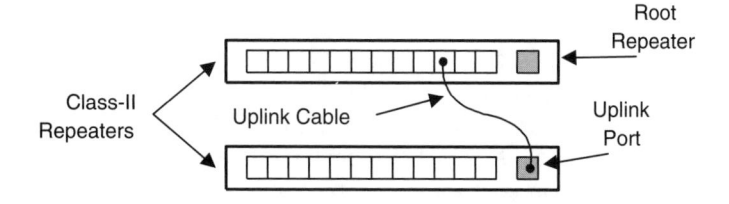

Figure 3.6
Connecting two Class-II repeaters.

Figure 3.7
Class-II repeater connection detail.

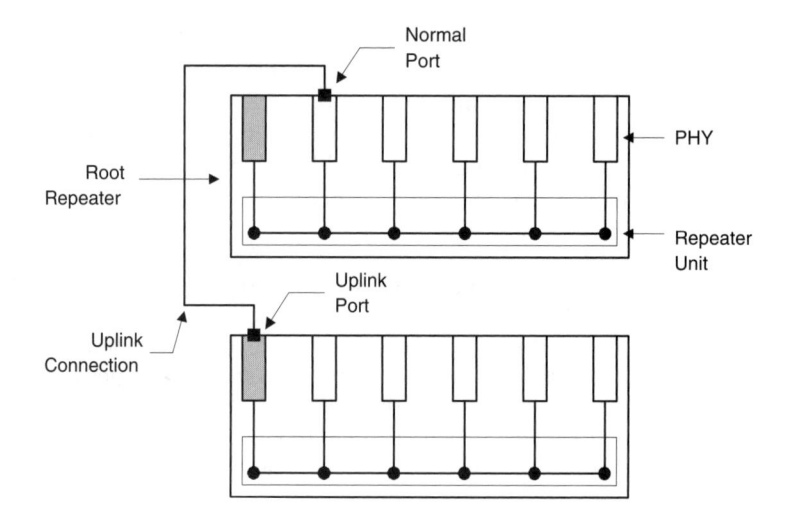

This is in contrast to most other technologies (e.g., Ethernet, Token Ring, FDDI, and 100VGAnyLAN), which allow much greater distances between repeater-like devices. (The repeater-like device for Token Ring is called a MAU; for FDDI, a concentrator; and for VG, a hub.)

- Using Class-II repeaters limits the network interfaces on the *entire LAN* to either TX and FX PHYs or T4 PHYs.
- Only two Fast Ethernet Class-II repeaters can be connected in this way on a single Fast Ethernet LAN.
- Unlike Class-I repeaters, the design tolerances for Class-II repeaters often prevent them from being combined into stacks or chassis. Again, most other technologies allow many more than two hub type devices to be used on a single LAN.

> Class-II repeaters exist for one reason: The IEEE 802.3u Standards Committee had to specify at least one method for connecting repeaters. The uplink port method was chosen because it is very similar to the way 10Base-T Ethernet repeaters are connected.

Class-II repeaters are allowed to be uplinked because the IEEE limited their maximum internal collision and JAM propagation delay (see Section 27.3.1.4.3 of the October 26, 1995 802.3u spec) to 46 bit times for 100Base-TX and -FX repeaters, and 67 bit times for 10Base-T4 repeaters. This is in contrast to 140 bit times for a Class-I repeater. Even with this restricted maximum delay, only two Class-II repeaters can be uplinked. This short delay also makes it almost impossible to build a Class-II repeater that stacks, thus making the practical limit for the number of ports on a Class-II repeater about 24 to 36 ports. (It is possible that a Class-II repeater with more ports could be built.) So, even with a large Class-II repeater the maximum number of ports on a Fast Ethernet network is not very large.

Problem number two is a result of the differences between the propagation delays for 100Base-TX/FX and 10Base-T4 repeaters, and is a serious disadvantage. Because of this limitation, Class-II repeaters must have all 100Base-TX and -FX or all 100Base-T4 ports. Class-II T4 repeaters cannot have FX ports.

Not being able to use fiberoptic cable with Class-II T4 repeaters is a serious drawback. Fiberoptic cable runs for Fast Ethernet can be longer than copper runs (up to 134 meters). This makes fiber useful for connecting different buildings or for longer runs inside larger buildings. It is also common to use fiberoptic cable to connect to switches or servers.

In reality, Class-II repeaters are also more difficult to build. They have much tighter internal timing tolerances than Class-I repeaters. Some Class-II products are available, but most of them have 100Base-TX and -FX ports. Few, if any, Class-II T4 products are marketed.

In most instances, stackable or chassis-based Class-I repeaters will be more flexible to use than Class-II repeaters.

Class-I Fast Ethernet Repeaters

Today's Fast Ethernet repeaters are almost always Class-I devices. Class-I repeaters differ from Class-II repeaters in two respects: *T4 and TX/FX ports can be on the same repeater.* Class-II repeaters can only be TX/FX or T4, while Class-I repeaters allow each port to be TX, FX, or T4. This is very useful when existing Cat-3 cable plants need to be used. Many cable installations of 10Base-T Ethernet in the late '80s and early '90s were Cat-3 installations instead of Cat-5, as Cat-3 cable supported a telephone and an Ethernet connection over the same 4-pair cable.

The other big difference is that there can be only one Class-I repeater in a Fast Ethernet network. (Remember that a collision domain is a single Fast Ethernet network.) At first glance this sure seems like a *huge* limitation, even worse than the limitation of having only two Class-II repeaters.

From the standpoint of the Fast Ethernet specification, this *is* the case, but manufacturers have been extremely clever in designing Class-I repeaters. As mentioned before, Class-II repeaters are difficult to build because they have a tight collision and JAM propagation delay. However, Class-I repeaters have looser (though still precisely defined) propagation delays that give the designers much more flexibility in how Class-I repeaters are built. This has allowed engineers to design repeater devices that can be combined to form a single Class-I repeater. Two common designs allow this:

- Stackable repeaters
- Chassis-based repeaters

Stackable and chassis-based repeaters are covered in detail later in this chapter and in Chapter 11.

Media Types and the PHY

Like other networking technologies, Fast Ethernet can operate over different types of cable or media. Usually, cable means copper wire, while media is a broader term that covers anything that connects network components. The most common media types are coaxial, twisted-pair, and fiberoptic cable. Other media are radio waves, cellular digital packets, microwaves, or lasers for wireless communications.

Most LAN technologies, Fast Ethernet and Ethernet in particular, are **media independent,** which means that their basic operation does not depend on any particular media type. For Fast Ethernet and Ethernet this means that a network interface's Media Access Controller (MAC), which implements the CSMA/CD media access rules, operates independently of the type of media to which the network interface is attached.

As mentioned before, Fast Ethernet is a modular system and is built using a system of layers. The diagram of the Fast Ethernet system bears repeating and is shown in Figure 3.8.

As Figure 3.8 shows, the MAC in each network interface and the repeater unit all connect to the media through a layer called the PHY. The PHY is the *media-dependent* part of these components and is considered to be in Layer 1 of the OSI model, the Physical layer.

Unlike Ethernet, which supports both the Star (hub and spoke) and Bus physical topologies, Fast Ethernet supports only the Star topology. Nodes must be directly connected to a repeater by a single cable. Fast Ethernet cannot run over coaxial cable. This is not a significant limitation, as the use of coaxial cable has dropped off in recent years in favor of unshielded twisted-pair wire installed in a Star configuration. Fast Ethernet can operate over four types of media. Following are the names of the 802.3u standard clauses that define the PHYs and their associated cable types:

802.3u Standard Clause	*Cable Type*
100Base-TX	Category-5 UTP copper cable using two twisted pairs

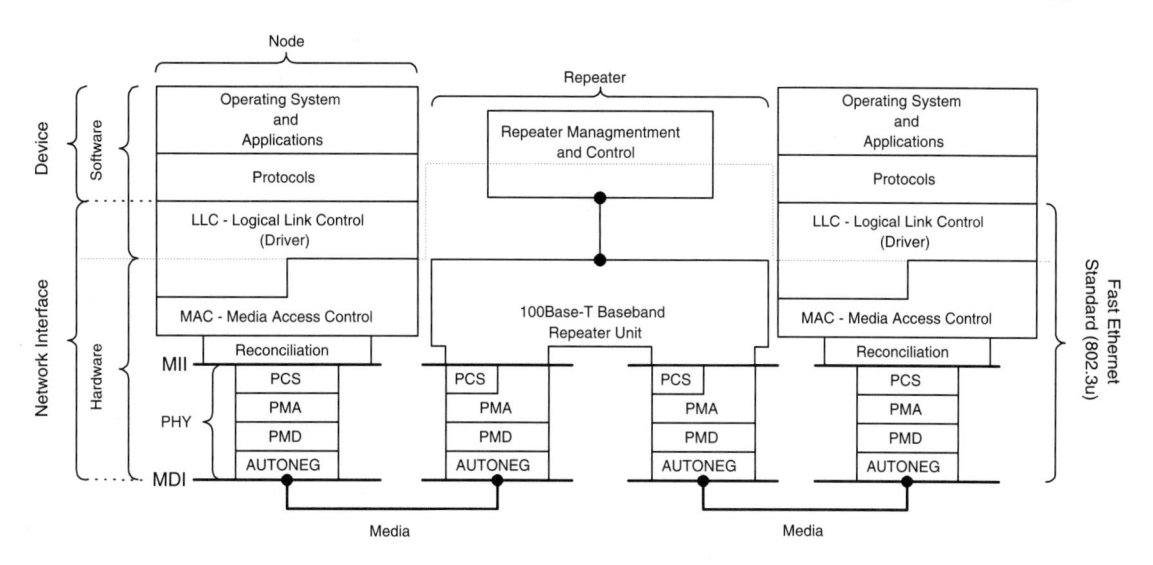

Figure 3.8
The Fast Ethernet system.

100Base-T4	Category-3 and 4 UTP copper cable using two twisted pairs
100Base-T2	Category-5 UTP using one twisted pair. (The 100Base-T2 standard has not yet been ratified by the 802.3u committee. It should be ratified sometime in late 1997.)
100Base-TX	Fiberoptic cable

UTP stands for Unshielded Twisted Pair. All copper cable used for networking is manufactured in pairs of wires that are twisted together. Some network cabling is shielded and has a woven metal jacket or metal foil jacket around each pair of wires in the cable. As you can imagine, shielded cable is significantly more expensive than unshielded cable. In even small networks, with 30 to 40 users, cable installation costs can be quite expensive. For unshielded data-grade cable, a single cable drop or run can cost anywhere from $80 to $150 or more. The designers of Fast Ethernet wanted it to become a very widely used technology, and knew that it needed to be as inexpensive to implement as possible. To this end, they designed PHYs that would run over unshielded cable.

A common question is, Can Fast Ethernet run over shielded cable? The long answer is, Fast Ethernet copper cabling does not require shielding, and there is no specification for using shielded cable with Fast Ethernet. The short answer is a *qualified* Yes. It is highly recommended that shielded cable *not* be installed in order to run Fast Ethernet (or Ethernet, for that matter). It's not necessary and has no advantage. Also, there is no standard for connectors for STP wire, and you can't buy adapters or repeaters with 9 pin shielded connectors. However, there is nothing inherent in the electrical characteristics of shielded cable that will keep it from working with 100Base-TX PHYs.

Fast Ethernet and Ethernet are often called **half-duplex** systems. This term is usually used to mean a network interface that is connected to a repeater using the CSMA/CD media access rules, not the full-duplex rules. The reasoning usually is that CSMA/CD is not full duplex, so it must be half duplex. While half duplex is a convenient term, it is both ambiguous and technically inaccurate. Unfortunately, it is a term that has crept into manufacturers' literature, magazine articles, and even other books on Ethernet and Fast Ethernet. In the context of Fast Ethernet and Ethernet, it has been used frequently enough to come to mean CSMA/CD operation.

The terms full and half duplex originated with low baud rate, point-to-point serial channels and modem technology. A full-duplex serial link is one in which there are separate communications paths for both transmitting and receiving data. In other words, both ends can simultaneously transmit and receive data to and from each other, which is exactly how full-duplex Fast Ethernet works. For serial channels, half duplex means that the transmitter and receiver share the same physical channel, and only one can transmit at a time. For Ethernet systems that use coaxial cable, this is actually the case and the term half duplex applies pretty well. Fast Ethernet and 10Base-T Ethernet are not really half-duplex systems at all, because of the way the PHY uses the media.

For 100Base-TX and -FX, the physical connections between a network interface and a repeater are truly full duplex. There are separate transmit and receive paths between the PHYs on each end of the cable. 100Base-TX uses two pairs of a four-pair, Category-5 cable. One pair is used for data from the network interface to the repeater; the other for data from the repeater to the network interface (see Figure 3.9).

Figure 3.9 shows how the node's network interface is connected to a repeater using 100Base-TX. Note how the node's transmit and receive paths are completely separate. In other words, the 100Base-TX connection is inherently full duplex. Note also that the transmit side and the receive side of the PMD, PMA, PCS, REC, and MAC are also separate. From a node's perspective, transmitting and receiving are completely different operations. This is true up through the driver and protocol layers as well. All that physically ties nodes together is the digital bus in the repeater unit. In other words, the repeater itself is the shared media.

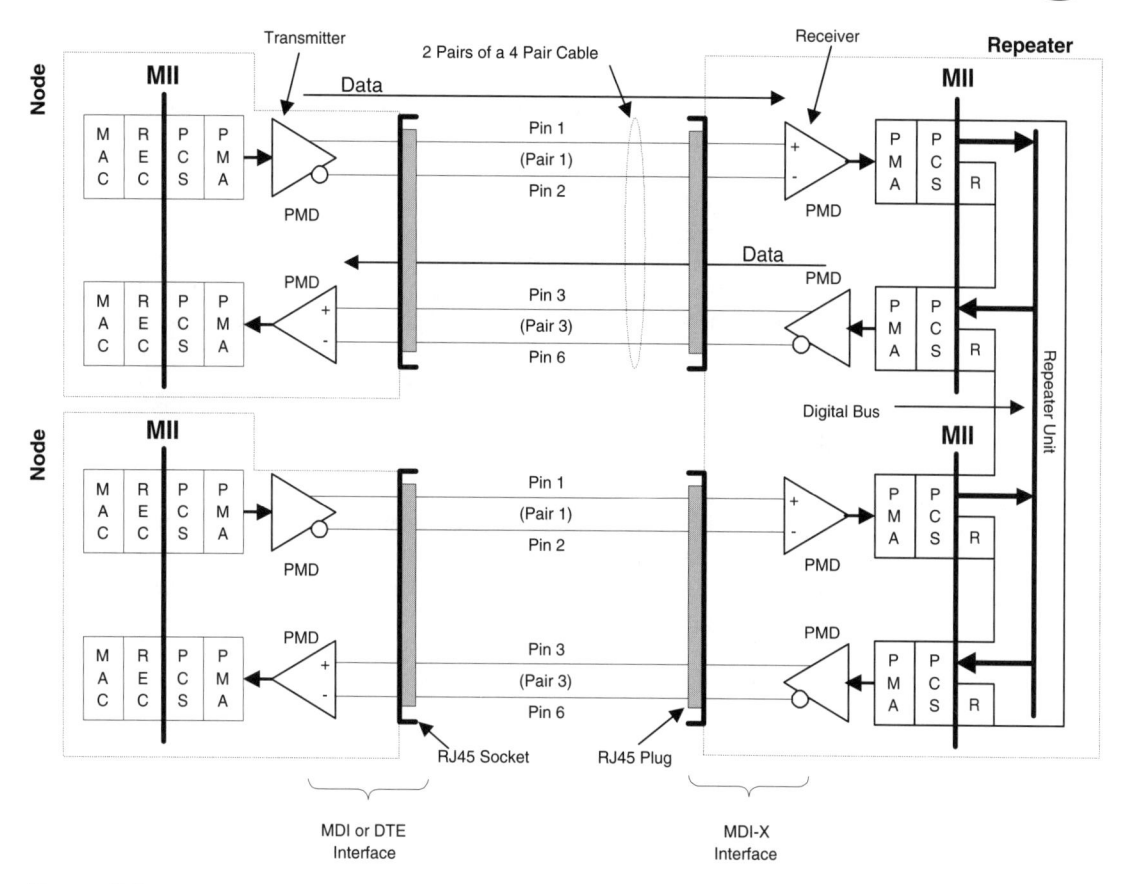

Figure 3.9
100Base-TX connections.

For 100Base-TX, the PMD, usually called a **transceiver,** has a transmitter and a receiver, each using a single twisted pair to communicate to the other end. These devices transmit **balanced signals,** in which the signal in one of the wires of the pair is the opposite of the signal in the other wire. Balanced signals over twisted-pair wire are very immune to noise and can travel long distances. Both are necessary characteristics to meet the 100-meter distance requirement for copper cable. In contrast, many unbalanced signals, like those used for RS232 serial ports are useful only at distances from 50 to 100 feet.

On the repeater side, the RJ45 socket is called an **MDI-X** port. On an MDI-X port, pair 1 of the RJ45 plug is connected to the PHY's receiver, and pair 3 to the transmitter. On the network interface or node side, the plug is most often called a **DTE** or **MDI** port. On a DTE port, pair 1 of the RJ45 socket is connected to the PHY's transmitter, and pair 3 to the receiver. (For more information on cabling and connectors, see Appendix E and F.)

> An interesting twist on this is how Class-II repeaters are connected together. Figure 3.7 shows that two Class-II repeaters are connected by a cable between one repeater's uplink port and any normal port on the other repeater. There is really nothing special about a Class-II uplink port, which is simply an MDI-configured port. In fact, some repeaters even have a little switch by one port that allows it to be configured as an MDI or MDI-X port. Using this switch allows an uplink port to be used as a normal port if it isn't used to connect to another repeater.

The TX PHY on the network interface and the TX PHY on the repeater are exactly the same, except that the socket on the network interface is connected to the PHY backward from the PHY on the repeater. This allows a **straight through cable** to be used to connect a node to a repeater. This kind of cable is called straight through because connector pins 1 through 8 on one end of a cable are connected to their corresponding pins

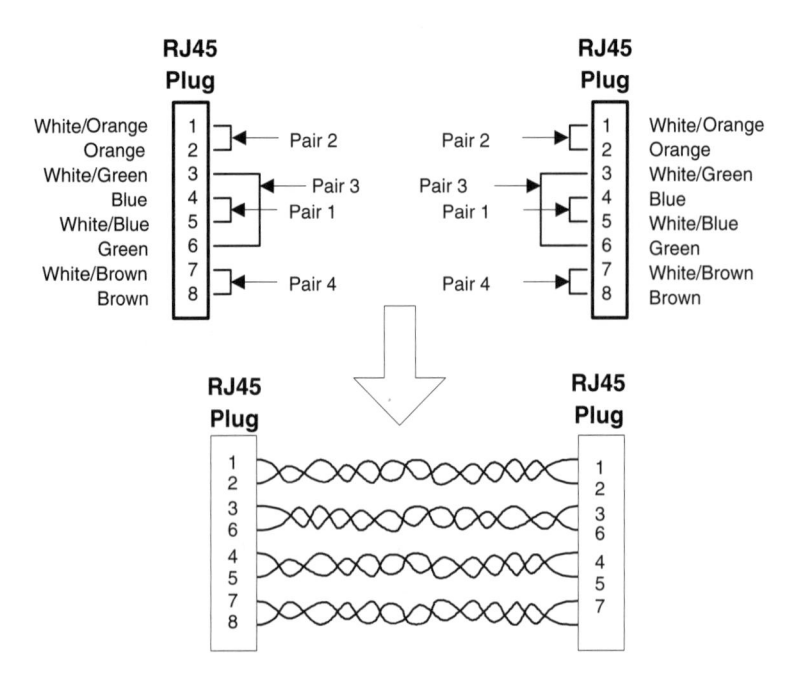

Figure 3.10
Straight through cable.

on the other end by terminating both ends of the cables with RJ45 plugs the same way on each end of the cable, as shown in Figure 3.10.

The 100Base-FX PHY for fiberoptic cable functions in a very similar way to 100Base-TX. In fact, the only difference between a 100Base-TX PHY and a 100Base-FX PHY is the PMD itself. A 100Base-FX connection is shown in Figure 3.11.

Instead of a balanced transmitter and receiver at each end, an FX connection has an LED or a laser diode emitter at the transmit end, and a matching detector at the other end. TX and FX use exactly the same signaling method. The only difference is the physical way the signals are transmitted and received on the media: TX uses a balanced electrical signal; FX uses pulses of light. The similarity between the TX and FX PHYs is why a Class-1 repeater can have both TX and FX ports.

100Base-T4 is completely different from TX and FX. Besides allowing the use of Category-3 and -4 cable, which cannot be used with TX, T4 uses four pairs of wires instead of two. T4 also uses a completely different signaling method than TX. In fact, the use of balanced electrical signaling is about the only thing that T4 has in common with TX. A T4 connection is shown in Figure 3.12.

A T4 connection uses pairs 2 and 3 for dedicated transmit and receive just as TX does. However, T4 also uses pairs 1 and 2 in a bidirectional way, making a T4 node to repeater connection inherently half duplex. When the node is transmitting, it uses pairs 2, 1, and 4. When the repeater is transmitting, it uses pairs 3, 1, and 4. The half-duplex nature of T4 is its big drawback.

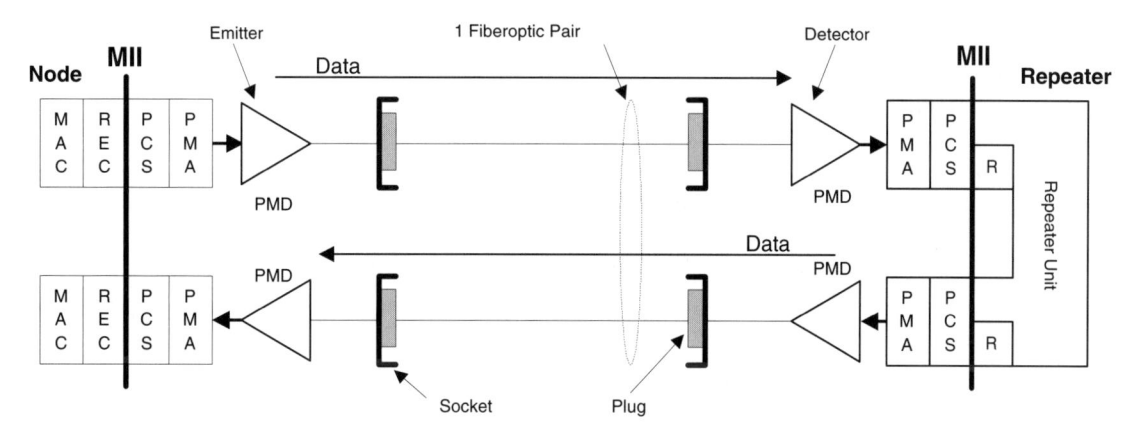

Figure 3.11
A 100Base-FX connection.

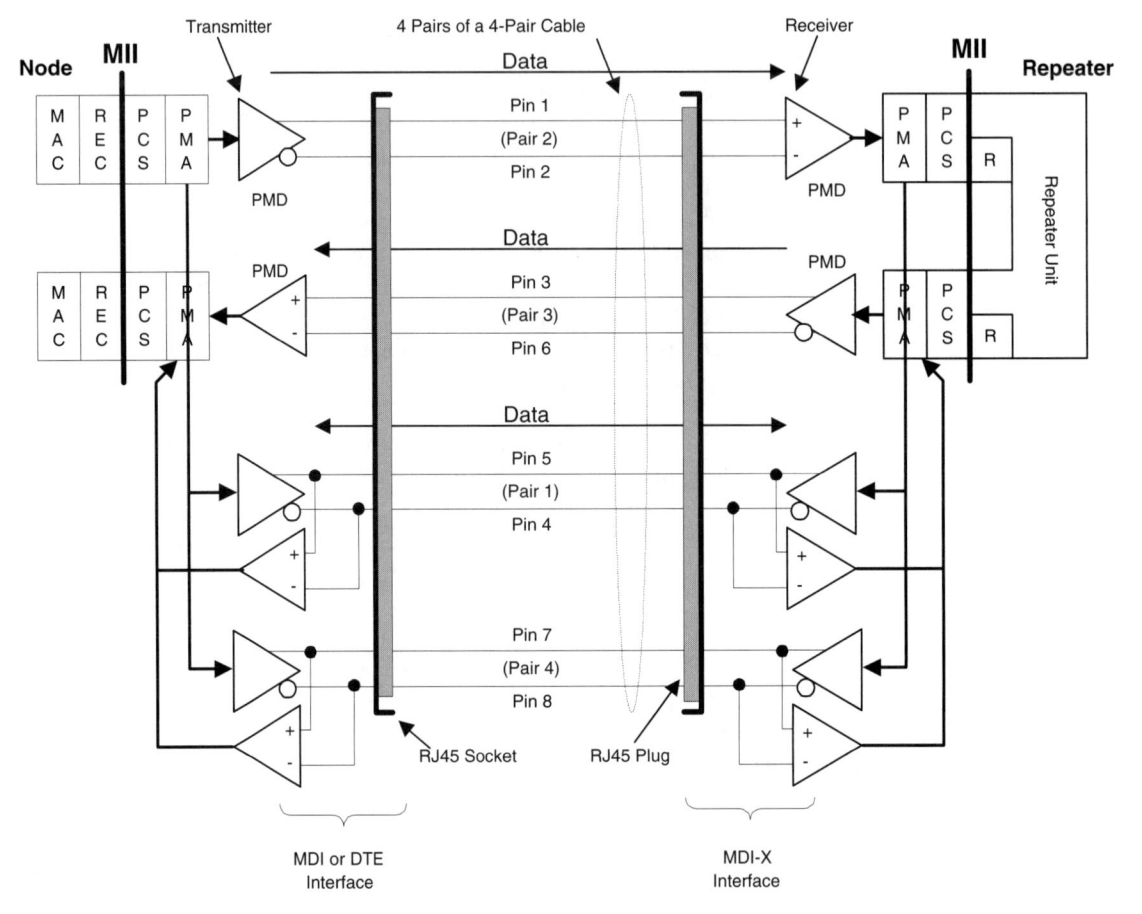

Figure 3.12
A 100Base-T4 connection.

T4 works this way because Cat-3 cable just cannot run at the high data rates (100Mbps) that Cat-5 cable can. For T4 to have an effective baud rate of 100Mbps, all three transmit links run at one-third the rate of TX.

Node-to-Node Operation

One of the advantages of Ethernet is that two 10Base-T cables can be directly connected to each other without a repeater. The same is true for Fast Ethernet. This is possible because nodes and repeaters use the same PHYs, and all a repeater does is repeat signals sent by nodes. Connecting two FX-based nodes is easy: Just connect the TX ports to the RX ports on the two nodes, just like a fiber connection between a repeater and a node.

Connecting two TX or T4 nodes is less straightforward but still pretty simple. It requires a **crossover** or **null repeater** cable. A crossover cable is not wired in a straight-through manner but crosses pairs 2 and 3. One of the ends is terminated just like a normal straight-through cable; however, in a crossover cable, the other end is terminated differently (see Figure 3.13).

Either end of a crossover cable can be plugged into either node. All that is required is that a crossover cable connect the two nodes. A direct connection between two 100Base-TX nodes is shown in Figure 3.14.

When a crossover cable is used to connect two FX nodes, they are simply connected with fiberoptic cable. Since fiberoptic cable comes in simple pairs, with fiber at each end of the cable, no special fiber crossover cable is required.

In all cases, when two nodes are connected directly together, both communicate using the same CSMA/CD media access rules, as if there were a repeater between them. In addition, two nodes connected by TX or

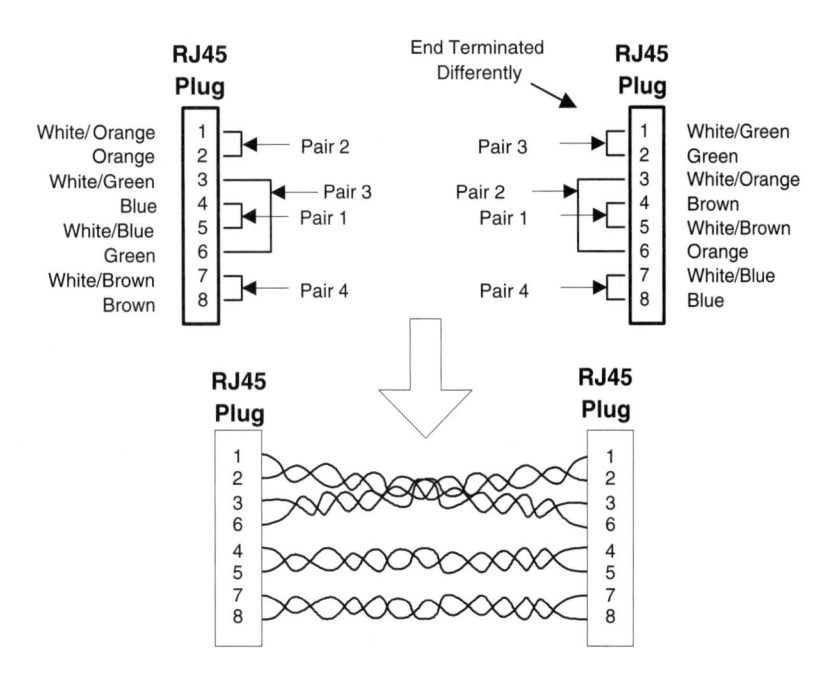

Figure 3.13
Crossover cable.

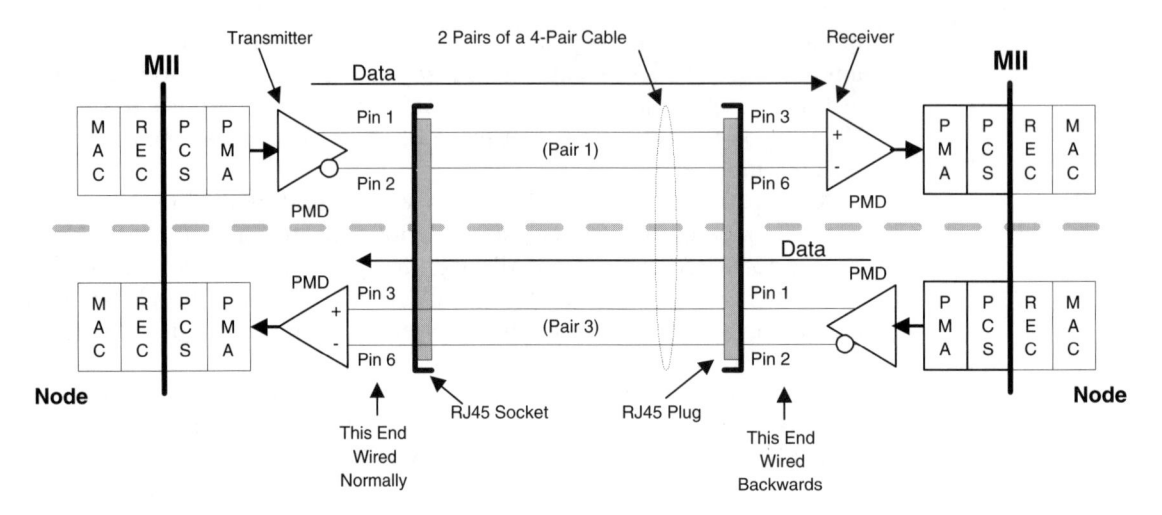

Figure 3.14
Node-to-node connection.

FX can also communicate in full-duplex mode and can transmit up to 12 megabytes per second in each direction simultaneously. For more information on full duplex operation see Chapter 7.

More on 100Base-TX and -FX

The goal of the 802.3u standards body that developed Fast Ethernet was to develop a new 100Mbps networking standard that was very similar to Ethernet. They recognized that developing new Fast Ethernet hardware would happen more quickly, and the standard would be better accepted if existing technology could be used or leveraged as much as possible. Of course, the most obvious example of this is the CSMA/CD media access method used by Fast Ethernet. Another example is the frame type, which is exactly the same as 10Mbps Ethernet. One of the biggest questions the designers had was how to develop a PHY. It was not practical to use the 10Base-T PHY, as it would not scale up to 100Mbps.

FDDI is a 100Mbps networking technology that has been around for several years. It is well known, widely accepted and, more importantly, considered to be robust and reliable. Another important fact is that the FDDI standard and currently shipping hardware support both fiberoptic cable and Category-5 copper cable. The Fast Ethernet committee made a wise choice and decided to use the PMD from the FDDI standard. The 802.3u Fast Ethernet standard references the FDDI PMD standard explicitly and lists a few minor details that need to change to make it work with Fast Ethernet. The Fast Ethernet PHY uses only the very lowest layer of the FDDI PHY (the PMD), and does not use any of the other FDDI techniques, such as tokens or station management. Some things changed, such as the RJ45 connector assignments: 100Base-TX uses the 10Base-T pins, while FDDI has a different pin out.

Using the FDDI PMD allowed the 802.3u committee to standardize Fast Ethernet more quickly: Few decisions had to be made, since a PHY did not have to be argued about and specified. More importantly, it allowed manufacturers to develop and bring to market Fast Ethernet equipment much more quickly than if a new PHY had to be developed from scratch. This is exactly what happened to the 100Base-T4 PHY. The first T4 products were available many months after the first TX and FX products were already in widespread use.

While a good idea, T4 just hasn't worked out very well and only a few manufacturers sell it. T4 was initially more expensive than TX because the PHYs are more complex. T4 was also not available as early as TX because it was completely new and also more difficult to get working. T4 is also often criticized as being much less resistant to noise and less tolerant of cabling problems.

However, T4 was developed for a reason. Often it is impractical or too expensive to install new Cat-5 cable in order to upgrade to TX. T4 allows Fast Ethernet to operate over the Cat-3 cable installed in most buildings. In many cases, this is cable installed to support voice telephones and 100Base-T network connections. This type of cable plant is in place in many organizations. If TX and FX were the only solutions, Fast Ethernet would not be suitable for such installations. The Fast Ethernet designers recognized that this was a problem and that without a solution like T4, Fast Ethernet would have a much smaller market.

Autonegotiation

Many newer 100Base-TX and 100Base-FX PHYs support a feature called **Autonegotiation,** which allows two PHYs to automatically detect layer-1 and -2 features of the device at the other end. Often called NWAY Autonegotiation, this feature allows each end of a link to query the features on the other end so that they may determine a compatible mode of operation. For example, if a node is plugged into a switch, and both support full-duplex operation, then the node and the switch can determine this and operate in this mode. When a link becomes active, an Autonegotiation-capable PHY will find the highest priority mode of operation common between the two devices. The following list shows the priority, from highest to lowest:

100Base-TX or -FX Full-Duplex Mode
100Base-T4
100Base-TX
10Base-T Full Duplex
10Base-T

When an Autonegotiation PHY starts up, it will send out a special link integrity pulse, in which its capabilities are encoded. This pulse is fully compatible (and derived from) the signal used by all 10Base-T nodes. It will also listen for a corresponding pulse from the other end. When an NWAY PHY receives the other end's link pulse, it detects the other end's capabilities and selects the highest priority mode of operation present on both ends of the link, which allows a node to be compatible with one, some, or all of the possible modes of operation. For example, a network interface card (NIC) for a workstation may support 10Base-T, 100Base-TX, and 100Base-TX full-duplex operation. If this NIC is plugged into a 10Base-T repeater, it will see the 10Base-T link integrity pulse and operate in that mode. Of course, the 10Base-T repeater has no idea what Autonegotiation is and runs in only one mode, but since the NIC is *smart* everything works fine. If this same NIC is plugged into a 100Base-TX repeater, the same thing will occur, but the link will end up operating at 100Mbps. Finally, if this same NIC is plugged into a switch that supports full-duplex mode, this will be the negotiated mode of operation.

Autonegotiation is very useful for NICs and allows true plug-and-play operation. However, its real value comes when this feature is implemented in switch ports. Many new switches support all five modes of operation on each port. This allows them to support any CSMA/CD device, from regular 10Base-T links all the way to full-duplex Fast Ethernet links, in true plug-and-play fashion.

The real value of Autonegotiation is its ability to correctly configure links with no intervention from the user. When using Autonegotiation, there are no dip switches, configuration files, or system setup screens that users have to properly configure before their networks will run properly. While fully automatic configuration is usually very desirable, the 802.3u standard requires that the Autonegotiation feature can be disabled, allowing a user to explicitly configure a device for one mode of operation.

The implementation of Autonegotiation is also very simple and happens at the PHY level, which allows it to be built into any device, even low-cost NICs and switches. Similar features in other networking technologies often require that an expensive processor be present to properly implement such features.

Autonegotiation-capable devices are also fully compatible with 10Base-T and 100Base-T devices that do not support it. When a device at the other end of a link doesn't support Autonegotiation, a smart PHY can still detect the device's type from its signaling characteristics, and determine if it is a compatible mode. Autonegotiation will become more important as new capabilities and features are added to the Fast Ethernet standard over the next few years, because it is specifically designed to support new features that have not yet been designed, and will allow devices purchased today to interoperate correctly with devices purchased years from now.

CHAPTER 4

Frames: The Basic Unit of Communication

Chapter 1 described frames as the basic units of network communication. The frames used in the earlier examples are a little simpler than the actual frames used by Fast Ethernet, which have the structure shown in Figure 4.1.

The first thing to note about the frame is that there is a minimum and maximum frame size.

- The **minimum** frame size is 64 octets, or 512 bits (the term octet is synonymous with the term byte).
- The **maximum** frame size is 1518 octets, or 12,144 bits.

The basic purpose of the network is to move data from one computer to another. The purpose of the frame format is to provide an envelope to contain the data. The frame contains four key pieces of information:

- The **destination address** for the node receiving the frame
- The **source address** of the node sending the frame
- The **L/T** or **Length/Type** field, which is the type of data being sent
- The **FCS** or **Frame Check Sequence** field, which verifies that the frame has been correctly received by the destination node.

Destination Address	Source Address	L/T	Data Payload	FCS
6 Bytes	6 Bytes	2 Bytes	46 to 1,500 Bytes	4 Bytes

Figure 4.1
Fast Ethernet frame structure.

Frame Addressing

Each node on a Fast Ethernet network has a unique number assigned to it called its **MAC address,** or sometimes its **node address,** a 48-bit (6-byte) number that is assigned to a network interface when the device is manufactured and programmed into the network interface's MAC at initialization time. So, all LAN network interfaces, except for ARCNet, which uses an 8-bit address that is assigned by the network administrator, have a built-in, unique MAC address that is guaranteed to be different from any other MAC address on the planet, assigned by the manufacturer in cooperation with the IEEE.

This is one of the most important ideas and standards to come out of the IEEE, which recognized early on that there would eventually be gazillions of networked devices, and that maintaining node addresses by hand would be a significant impediment to the acceptance of networking in general. So, they devised a way to assign unique node addresses to network interfaces.

Of course, the simplest way to accomplish this would be to just assign a unique number to each network interface when it is manufactured. Since IEEE network addresses are 48 bits in size, there could be about 280 trillion different network interfaces built, each with a unique address. Unfortunately, this would be extremely difficult to keep track of. To make administering unique network interfaces manageable, the IEEE divided the 48-bit address field into four parts, as shown in Figure 4.2. The first two bits in the address (bits 0 and 1) are the address type flags. The value of these flags determines how the address portion (bits 2 through 47) is interpreted.

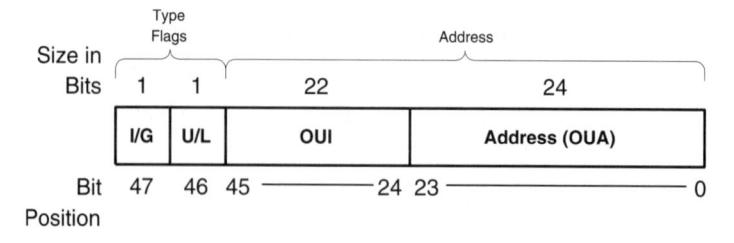

Figure 4.2
MAC address format.

The I/G bit is the **individual or group address flag** used to indicate if the address is an individual or group address. Individual addresses are assigned to one, and only one, interface (or node) on a network. Addresses with the I/G bit set to zero are **MAC addresses** or **node addresses.** When the I/G bit is set to one, the address is a group address, usually called a **multicast address** or a **functional address.** A group address can be assigned to one or more network interfaces on a LAN. Frames sent to a group address are received, or copied, by all the network interfaces on a LAN with that group address. Multicast addresses allow a frame to be sent to a subset of nodes on a LAN. If the I/G bit is a one, then all the bits 46 through 0 are treated as the multicast address, and not as the U/L, OUI, and OUA parts of the address. The U/L bit is the **universal or local administration flag.** The U/L bit determines how the address was assigned to the network interface it represents. If both the I/G and the U/L bits are zero, then the address is the unique 48-bit identifier discussed earlier.

The basic tool that the IEEE uses to administer addresses is the **organizationally unique identifier.** The IEEE assigns one or more OUIs to each manufacturer of network adapters and interfaces. This way, all the IEEE has to track is a few numbers per manufacturer (often just one), not individual node addresses; 22 bits of OUI allow for just over 4 million OUIs. Each manufacturer is then responsible for keeping track of the **organizationally unique addresses** that it assigns to each node it manufactures. The 24 bits in the OUA allow a manufacturer to build over 16 million network interfaces before it needs another OUI.

> OUIs are assigned by the IEEE Registration Authority. A list of OUIs or new OUI assignments can be requested by contacting:
>
> IEEE Standards Department
> 445 Hoes Lane, P.O. Box 1331
> Piscataway, NJ 08855-1331
> Phone: 908-562-3813
> Fax: 908-562-1571
>
> There are several lists of OUIs on the Web. For some pointers, see our Web page at www.wiley.com/compbooks/fastethernet.

A combination of an OUI and an OUA make up a **universally administered address** (UAA), also called an **IEEE address.** The I/G and U/A bits of a UAA are always both zero. Each manufacturer must guarantee that each OUI/OUA pair it uses is assigned to one and only one network interface it manufactures. So, even if the OUA portions of two (or more) network cards are the same, their MAC addresses will still be different because their

OUIs will be different. This method ensures that each IEEE network node, no matter what LAN type or manufacturer, has a unique address.

The IEEE has standardized several local area network technologies that use IEEE network addresses under the 802 series of standards. The primary standards are:

802.3	CSMA/CD-based network Ethernet standard
802.3u	CSMA/CD-based network Fast Ethernet standard
802.4	Token Passing Bus standard
802.5	Token Passing Ring standards (Token Ring)
802.12	Demand Priority-based network 100VG AnyLAN

The Fiber Distributed Data Interface (FDDI) also uses standard IEEE network addresses. FDDI is an ANSI (American National Standards Institute) standard.

If the U/L bit is set, then the address is a **locally administered** address. This means that someone besides the network interface's manufacturer sets the address. For example, an organization could set the MAC address on a network interface to a value of its own choosing by setting the U/L bit to a one, and then setting bits 2 through 47 to some value. Of course, that organization would have to keep track of them. Since all network interfaces come with a universally administered address, locally administered addresses are rarely used. There are no modern networking protocols or other software in wide use that require you to set network addresses by hand. Actually, we are not aware of *anything* that requires, or that is even helped by, using locally administered addresses. There is usually a way to override the UAA of a network interface, normally an entry in a configuration file, or registry. This method is often obscure and poorly documented, or undocumented altogether.

Universally or locally administered individual MAC addresses are sometimes called **unicast addresses**. Broadcast addresses and multicast addresses are very similar in that both have the G bit set. Together, they are often just called **group addresses**.

Frames are often typed by their destination address. For example, a frame with a broadcast address as its destination is usually just called a **broadcast frame**. This idea is extended for multicast and unicast addresses as well, with the terms **multicast frame** and **unicast frame**, respectively. A frame with a unicast address is also sometimes called a **directed frame** because it is directed at a single node, and the term **directed packet** is also sometimes used.

The I/G bit is *much* more useful than the U/L bit. When set, it indicates that an address is a group address rather than an individual address. While the Fast Ethernet standard defines how multicast addresses work, it does not define what they are used for. The use of multicast addresses is defined by the designers of network protocols such as TCP/IP, IPX, and NetBIOS.

When a network interface receives a frame, the first thing it decodes is the frame's destination address. If the I/G bit of the destination address is set, then the MAC will receive the frame only if the destination address is in a list kept by the node. This allows a node to transmit one frame and have it received by multiple nodes.

There is a special multicast address called the **broadcast address.** The broadcast address consists of a 48-bit IEEE address with all of the bits set to a one. If a frame is transmitted with a destination address set to the broadcast value, then *all* nodes on the network will receive and process the frame.

> There is another IEEE address format that has 16 bits—a 1-bit I/G field and a 15-bit address field. As you can imagine, this format is not very useful. Indeed, it is not supported on any Fast Ethernet equipment or any modern Ethernet equipment, and is in the spec to provide backward compatibility with old technology. The 16-bit format does not support multicast addresses, but it does support the broadcast address (all bits set to a one).

Addresses and the MAC

From the MAC hardware's point of view, an address is a much simpler thing. The I/U, OUI, and OUA fields of the MAC address exist only to help humans administer MAC addresses. The hardware does not use these fields. From the hardware's perspective, a MAC address looks like that shown in Figure 4.3.

As you can see, the MAC hardware treats an address as either a group (multicast) or individual (unicast) address. The hardware does not need to interpret the U/L or the OUI fields.

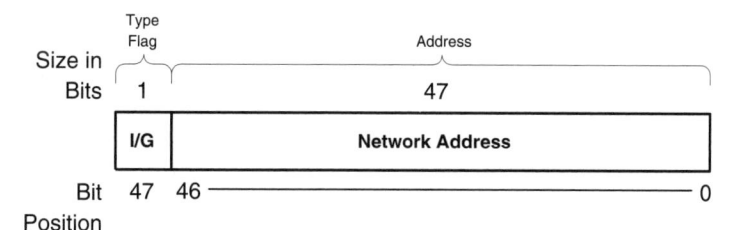

Figure 4.3
Hardware addresses.

How MAC Addresses Are Used

Unicast addresses are used when a node wants to send a frame directly to another node. This is how the bulk of network traffic is sent. Almost all data transfers and application-level data is transferred between nodes using unicast frames. For example, workstations send unicast frames to servers, and servers send back unicast response frames.

On the other hand, broadcast frames usually make up only a small percentage of total network traffic, and are generally not used for transferring application-level data. Broadcasts are usually used for a process called **discovery.** The discovery process occurs when a node needs to communicate with another node and does not know its MAC address. The searching node broadcasts a special packet, requesting a response from the node it's looking for. If the node it is searching for hears the broadcast, that node will respond with a unicast frame to the original sender. This is an essential and fundamental function and is used by every protocol and many applications.

Multicast addresses are used in much the same way and usually for the same purpose. The advantage of multicast addresses is that only a subset of machines on the network will actually receive the multicast frame. This means that stations that do not provide the service being searched for will not receive, and therefore will not copy and process, the multicast discovery frames in which they are not interested.

A good example of this is Windows 95 and Windows NT Server. Let's say Alfred E. Neuman logs his Windows 95 machine onto the NT Server \\GIGEM every morning. When Alfred's machine starts up, it has no idea what \\GIGEM's address is. To find the server, Alfred's machine will broadcast a special frame called a FIND NAME message. The name it is looking for is \\GIGEM. If the server \\GIGEM is up and running, then it will send back a unicast frame to Alfred's machine answering the FIND NAME request. Alfred's machine now knows \\GIGEM's MAC address and can then communicate with \\GIGEM using unicast packets. Not all machines on the LAN need to respond to FIND NAME requests. For example, the LAN may also have Netware and UNIX servers. Since they use a different mechanism for discovery, they ignore any messages sent to the multicast address that NT uses.

Another example is the diskless workstation. In the UNIX world, workstations often have no local floppy disk or hard disk drives and must boot over the network. All the system files that would normally be loaded off a local disk drive are loaded over the network. When a diskless workstation first starts up, it must find a boot server. It does this by broadcasting a BOOTP request. If a boot server is up and running, it will respond to the BOOTP request with the name of the initial startup files the workstation needs.

Broadcast and multicast frames are used for many other purposes as well, such as address resolution and service discovery. Without broadcast frames, almost nothing on a network could happen automatically, and everything would have to be configured by hand.

Length/Type Field

The Length/Type (L/T) field is a little strange. Due to historical (some say hysterical) reasons, the L/T field is used in two different ways:

- to indicate the length of the data field of the frame, not including any padding; and
- to indicate the type of data in the data field.

The interpretation is simple: If the L/T field is between 0 and 1,500, then it is the length of the data held in the frame's data field. If the L/T field is 1,500 or greater, then it is a protocol-type indicator. The reasons for this are rooted in how Ethernet became a standard. Xerox did the original design work for Ethernet in 1973. In 1979, Xerox got together with DEC and Intel to take Ethernet to the IEEE to get it standardized. This group of companies became known as the DIX group. They initially released the famous DIX Blue Book. The DIX group took this to the IEEE in February, 1980, to get the Blue Book spec endorsed by the IEEE. The DIX group wanted, and expected, to have the IEEE accept the Blue Book standard as it was presented. Of course, this didn't occur. The IEEE has never liked companies dictating standards. Since the IEEE 802.3 committee was (and is) made up of representatives from many companies, they were not going to let the DIX group push a standard without input from the other IEEE members. While the IEEE did adopt most of the Blue Book spec, they did change several things. One of the most contentious was the L/T field.

The Blue Book spec defined the 16 bits just after the source address to be a protocol-type field. After all, the length of the frame was determined by the MAC when the packet was received, so there was no need to encode the length explicitly in the frame. However, the 802.3 committee disagreed, and here's why. The data field of the frame must be at least 46 bytes long, so the minimum frame length is met. However, many protocols need to send only a few bytes, sometimes as few as three or four. If the LLC (just above the MAC) is told to send less than 46 bytes of data, it will add enough bytes to the end of the data field so that it is 46 bytes in length. Simply put, the 802.3 committee decided there needed to be a way to easily (and quickly) determine the length of the data in the frame, without including any additional padding, so they changed the type field to a length field.

Unfortunately, a lot of work had already been done with Ethernet using the L/T field as a type field. In the early days, these values were all less than 1,500, which conflicted with the L/T field being a length field. This was a real pain in the mid to late 1980s. Networking software and hardware that had been designed and manufactured before Ethernet was standardized in 1983 often did not work with hardware and software that conformed with the 802.3 specification. Early hardware and software used the L/T field as a type, and hardware and software that conformed to the new standard used it as a length.

This caused a great deal of confusion and consternation. There was a lot of criticism of manufacturers that didn't conform to the standard. Usually, this criticism was directed at DEC, Intel, and Xerox, who, ironically enough, actually invented and perfected Ethernet.

On the other hand, somebody realized that the L/T fields could be used as length *and* type fields if types could be distinguished from lengths, which would be easy if type values were always greater than 1,500. As you can imagine, this is exactly what occurred.

This system works well because Ethernet and Fast Ethernet *hardware* never uses the L/T field. It is there strictly for the convenience of the frame-processing software (protocols). Using the L/T field in this manner is *not* standard. The only true standard way to use the L/T field is as a length field, not a type field. In fact, the 802.3 specification doesn't even mention its use as a type field. The standard says: "Frames with a length field value greater than those specified in 4.4.2 may be ignored, discarded, or used in a private manner. The use of such frames is beyond the scope of this standard."

Is using the L/T field as a type evil? No, not at all. Lots of systems and protocols use this field as a type field and not a length field. Fortunately, this isn't a problem, as this field's use as a type field is a universally accepted convention, and the type values that are less than 1,500 were purged from common usage a long time ago. There is even a group at Xerox that keeps track of these values, which are known as **Ether Types**.

Ether Types are assigned and managed by Xerox Systems Institute. A list of Ether Types or new Ether Type assignments can be requested by contacting:

Xerox Systems Institute
3400 Hillview Avenue
PO BOX 10034
Palo Alto, CA 94303
Phone: 415-813-7164
Contact: Fonda Lix Pallone

There are several lists of Ether Types on the Web. For some pointers, see our web page at www.wiley.com/compbooks/fastethernet.

All of this means that the L/T field is the primary mechanism by which a frame's **frame type** is determined. A frame's type is essentially the way the frame's data field is structured. Fast Ethernet and Ethernet frames with an L/T field used as a length (L/T ≤ to 1,500) are called **802.3** frames. Frames using the L/T field as a type field (L/T > 1,500) are called **Ethernet-II,** or **DIX,** frames.

Modern operating systems, such as Windows 95, Windows NT, NetWare, and OS/2 2.0, work quite well with either basic frame type. However, older software, such as Microsoft LAN Manager, OS/2 1.x, and many versions of UNIX, are quite picky about the frame type used. Using frame types is discussed more fully in the chapters on setting up a Fast Ethernet network.

Data Field

The **data field** carries the information being sent from one node to another. Unlike the other fields, which contain very specific information, the data field can contain almost anything, as long as it is physically between 46 and 1,500 bytes in length. How the contents of the data field are formatted and interpreted is defined by protocols.

As discussed earlier, the data field cannot be shorter than 46 bytes, but it is often necessary to send data that is less than 46 bytes in length. When this occurs, the LLC adds bytes containing data of an unknown value, called **pad data,** to the end of the data to make the field 46 bytes long.

When a frame's type is 802.3, the L/T field holds the actual length of the data in the data field. For example, when a 12-byte message is sent, the L/T field will contain the 12 bytes and 34 additional bytes of padding, which is added so that the data field will be 46 bytes long. This padding is the responsibility of the LLC part of the Fast Ethernet spec, and is usually done in hardware.

Unlike any data field padding, the MAC (hardware) does not set the contents of the L/T field, the software does. Setting the L/T field is almost always done by the Network Interface Driver.

Frame Check Sequence

Fast Ethernet hardware is extremely reliable and designed to deliver data from one place to another without error. However, nothing is perfect. Occasionally, a frame will be corrupted as it travels from one node to another. These corruptions are called **transmission errors** and can occur for several reasons, the most common of which are:

- Random bit errors (these happen very rarely)
- Bad cables
- Flaky network interfaces
- Electrical interference (noise)

When a frame is corrupted, its data is actually changed or lost as the frame travels on the network. As you can imagine, this isn't very good. If a bad frame were actually passed to a protocol or other software on a node, that protocol or software could operate incorrectly or even crash.

The Frame Check Sequence (FCS) is used to make sure that frames are properly received. When a node transmits a frame, the MAC uses a special mathematical formula, called a **CRC**, to calculate a 32-bit value. The CRC is placed in the frame's FCS field. The input to the MAC's CRC engine are the frame's byte values from the first byte of the destination address to the last byte of the data field.

The way the CRC value is calculated gives it a very valuable property: The CRC is practically unique for that frame. In other words, the chances that any other frame will have the same CRC is 1 in 4,294,967,296, or 1 in 2^{32}. This is a pretty small number. There is a better chance of winning the lottery or getting hit by lightning than of finding two different frames with the same CRC.

When a frame is received, the receiving MAC calculates another CRC value for the frame. If the new CRC, usually called the **receive CRC**, differs from the value in the frame's FCS field, then the frame has most assuredly been corrupted. Corrupted frames are usually ignored and discarded. Errors detected this way are usually called **CRC errors.**

The FCS field is the primary, and most important, mechanism that Fast Ethernet has for detecting and handling errors. This is all done in hardware and is very fast. All modern MAC chips also keep a counter that is incremented each time a CRC error occurs. This value can be extremely valuable to a network administrator. During normal operation, few CRC errors should occur (a few a week are normal). However, if a cable or Network Interface fails, then CRC errors can skyrocket. Looking at the CRC errors of the nodes on a network can help to quickly pinpoint problems.

Other MAC-Level Frame Errors

Besides CRC errors, there are other errors that a MAC detects. A **run-on frame** is any frame that is too long. It doesn't matter if the CRC is good or not. No MAC should ever transmit a frame that is longer than 1,518 bytes. These are almost always caused by a faulty network interface, but a buggy driver could also cause this problem.

Framing errors are caused when a packet is received that contains a frame that is not an integral number of octets in length. Frames are made up of octets (bytes); therefore, the number of bits in the frame must be evenly divisible by 8. If some bits are lost during the transmission of the frame, then this won't be true. Note that the CRC will almost always catch framing errors, but the MAC both detects and counts framing errors separately.

Length errors occur when the Length/Type field does not agree with the physical length of the frame. Length errors can be used only if the node is set up to handle 802.3-type frames. If the node is using Ethernet-II frames, then the L/T field cannot be used to look for frame errors. For nodes using only the 802.3 frame type, this lets a node check the value of the L/T field as follows:

- If the L/T field is greater than 1,500, then the frame is invalid.
- If the L/T field is between 46 and 1,500, and is also not equal to the frame length minus 18, then the value in the L/T field is inconsistent with the length of the frame and the frame is invalid.
- If the L/T field is between 1 and 45, then the length of the entire frame should be exactly 64 bytes. If it is not, then the frame is invalid.

Most modern systems, such as Novell NetWare, Microsoft NT, and Windows 95, can handle both frame types. If an L/T field is greater than 1,500, it's an Ethernet-II frame. If an L/T field is less than 1,500, it's an 802.3 frame. This is important because multiprotocol networks are now common. For example, the native protocol for NetWare, Windows 95, and Microsoft NT is IPX, which runs over 802.3 frames. It is also common for Microsoft Systems and IBM OS/2 systems to use a protocol called NetBEUI, which also uses the 802.3 frame type. However, TCP/IP networks, such as the Internet and UNIX-based networks, usually use Ethernet-II frames because TCP/IP and UNIX have been around longer than the 802.3 standard.

CHAPTER 5

MAC and CSMA/CD: Fast Ethernet's Heart and Soul

Each node on a Fast Ethernet network has a **Media Access Controller.** The MAC is really the heart and soul of Fast Ethernet, and has three purposes:

- Determine when a node can transmit a packet
- Send frames to the PHY for conversion into packets and transmission on the media
- Receive frames from the PHY and send them to the software that processes frames (protocols and applications)

While all three of these purposes are essential, the most important is the first one. For each shared media technology, the rules that govern when a node can transmit, called **media access rules,** are its defining characteristic. Indeed, entire IEEE committees revolve around defining media access rules. The 802.3 committee, often just called the Ethernet committee, defines LAN standards that use the rules called **CSMA/CD,** which stand for **Carrier Sense Multiple Access with Collision Detection.**

CSMA/CD are the media access rules for both Fast Ethernet and Ethernet—one area where Fast Ethernet and Ethernet are exactly the same and one reason why many people say that Fast Ethernet is compatible with or the same as Ethernet.

Since all the nodes on a Fast Ethernet LAN share the media, nodes cannot transmit whenever they need to. Nodes can transmit only when it is their turn. The CSMA/CD rules define what a turn means. The MAC also fits into the network model in a very important place: OSI Layer 2 (see Figure 5.1).

The MAC is the interface between a device and the network. It takes frames from the higher layers and uses the media access rules and the PHY to transmit them on the LAN. It also receives frames from the PHY and passes them to the higher layers.

One of the most important things about the MAC is that while it controls a node's access to the media, it is media independent. The MAC has no features that are tied to the type of media used on the LAN. To access the media, the MAC uses the PHY. For example, Fast Ethernet supports four types of media: 100Base-TX, 100Base-FX, 100Base-T4, and 100Base-T2. Ethernet also supports several types of media: 10Base-T, 10Base-2, 10Base-5, 10Base-F, 10Broad-36, and 1Base-5. In all these cases, there is a PHY specific to each media type. The PHY provides an interface between the MAC and the media, and allows the MAC to be media independent. A Fast Ethernet MAC could use any type of media for which a PHY could be built. For example, some manufacturers, such as Compaq, build Fast Ethernet adapters that have a modular PHY. By changing the PHY, the same Fast Ethernet adapter card can function using 100Base-TX, 100Base-FX, or 100Base-T4.

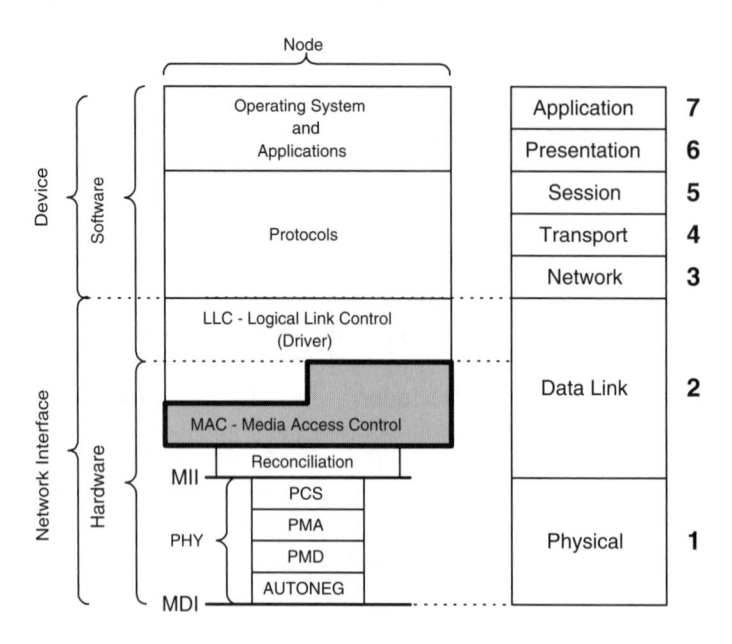

Figure 5.1
The MAC and the OSI model.

MAC and CSMA/CD: Fast Ethernet's Heart and Soul

Determining if one set of media access rules is better than another is extremely difficult. Arguments about media access rules are as serious, emotional, and heated as any religious argument. People tie their careers and company profits to the success of particular media access rules. The reason is simple. A LAN technology is defined by its media access rules. These rules determine how well a LAN technology works. For example, these rules determine its overall performance, how efficient it is, how well it recovers from errors and problems, how robust it is, how easy it is to troubleshoot, and even how expensive its components are.

A good example of this is the age-old battle between proponents of Ethernet and of Token Ring. Token Ring people say that CSMA/CD has too many problems when network traffic gets heavy and that you can't predict the behavior of Ethernet LANs because of their random behavior. Token Ring networks are extremely predictable and behave very well when network traffic gets heavy. This position is quite correct.

On the other hand, Ethernet people say that Token Ring is too complex. They say that the simplicity of Ethernet makes it cheaper to install and easier to troubleshoot, and that in all but a few uncommon circumstances, Ethernet will perform better than a Token Ring network. This position is also quite correct. About the only thing that everyone agrees on (usually) is that Ethernet is less expensive (by about a half to three-quarters) than Token Ring to install. Even then, the Token Ring folks will point out that Token Ring is so much more reliable and robust that it ends up being significantly cheaper to operate.

All this sounds very contradictory but it's really not. The comments made by both camps are actually correct, as far as they go. Both talk about the strengths of the technology they champion; both have the annoying habit of ignoring its faults. Briefly put, the two technologies are simply different; neither is better or worse than the other. The type of LAN you install should be dictated not by emotion, but by what the application needs and, to a lesser extent, what you know about the technologies. Indeed, the reason we wrote this book was so that you could make intelligent and informed decisions about Fast Ethernet. In the bigger picture, the marketplace will decide which technology is better. In the case of Ethernet and Token Ring, there are probably 10 (or more) Ethernet nodes in the world for every Token Ring node.

Fast Ethernet products have been on the market for only a short time, but this technology is already vastly more popular than other high-speed technologies, such as 100VG AnyLAN, FDDI, and ATM.

How CSMA/CD Works

Fast Ethernet is a lot like old-time telephone party lines that were used up through the 1960s (and 1970s in a few backwoods areas) to help keep telephone lines inexpensive. Back when telephones were first being installed in rural areas, it was much too expensive for everyone to have their own line, so several families often shared. It was not uncommon for four or five families to share a single telephone line. Today everyone has an individual telephone line, which is literally a pair of copper wires that go from your house to the telephone company.

This party-line example illustrates exactly how Fast Ethernet works, because all the nodes on the network share the same medium, which in the Fast Ethernet's case is the digital bus in the central repeater (or repeaters).

One of the most popular activities on party lines was gossip. Several people on the same line would pick up the phone and chat. Great fun for them, and for us, a good analogy of how Fast Ethernet works. As you can imagine, gossip parties required some amount of cooperation between each person on the line. Since the operator didn't force everyone to behave, everyone had to know the rules.

This illustrates an important and fundamental concept about Fast Ethernet: *The media access rules are implemented in each node's MAC.* There is no central controlling device on a Fast Ethernet LAN. The nodes themselves cooperate to keep the network operating in an orderly fashion, just like a party line.

Take the case of five people on a party line. Not everyone can talk at the same time. If two or more people try to talk simultaneously, their messages become garbled and nobody can understand them. The basic rule everyone used was to *listen before talking*. There had to be silence before something was said. Fast Ethernet has exactly the same rule.

A Fast Ethernet MAC does this by listening for a carrier before transmitting. A carrier exists only when another node is transmitting. The PHY detects the carrier and generates a carrier indication to the MAC. The presence of a carrier indicates that the medium is in use and the listening node (or nodes) should defer to the currently transmitting node.

A person with something to say on a party line would usually wait a second or two before talking to make sure that the other person was finished. A Fast Ethernet MAC does the same thing. A MAC that has a frame to transmit (sometimes called a **pending frame**) must wait for a minimum period of time after the end of the last transmitted frame before transmitting its next frame. This time is called the **interpacket gap** (IPG) and is 0.96μs long, exactly 1/10 the time for 10Mbps Ethernet (the IPG is the only time period always specified in μs [a μ equals one millionth of a second] and not bit times). For an example, see Figure 5.2.

After the end of frame 1, all nodes on the LAN must wait the IPG time before they can transmit. In Figure 5.2, the time intervals between packets 1 and 2, then 2 and 3, are the IPG time. However, after packet 3 is finished, nobody has anything to transmit for a while, so the time between packets 3 and 4 is longer than the IPG.

All nodes on the network must comply with this rule. Even if a node has multiple frames to transmit and is the only node that needs to trans-

Figure 5.2
Interpacket gap.

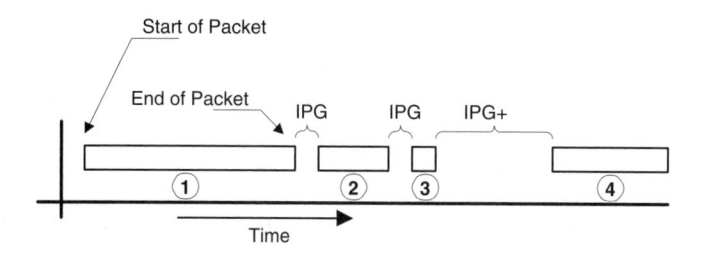

mit, it must ensure that there is at least the IPG time between each packet that it transmits.

This rule is the CSMA part of the Fast Ethernet media access rules. In short, *multiple* nodes have *access* to the medium and use a *carrier* to *sense* when the medium is busy.

Very early experimental networks used just these rules and worked pretty well. However, using only CSMA resulted in a problem. Frequently, two nodes would both have a packet to transmit, and after waiting the IPG time, both would begin to transmit, which caused both transmissions to be corrupted and unreceivable. This was (and still is) called a **collision.**

To overcome this, early protocols used a simple command response mechanism. Packets were divided into two categories: commands and responses. Each command transmitted by a node needed a response. Even modern protocols work this way. Some, like SNMP, are actually this simple; others, like the 802.2 LLC protocol used by NetBEUI, are more complex.

If a command was transmitted and a response was not received in some period of time (called the time-out period), then the original command was retransmitted. This could happen some number of times (the time-out limit) before the transmitting node would give up and declare that an error occurred.

This scheme worked, but it didn't work very well. As long as there were no collisions, everything worked fine, but even a small number of collisions would cause performance (usually measured in bytes per second) to suffer, because nodes were often sitting around waiting for responses to come in for commands that never reached their destination. If the network became very busy or node count increased, so did the number of collisions, which caused network performance to slow to a crawl.

Early network designers quickly figured out a way to solve this. Each node would detect the loss of a transmitted packet by detecting the collision when it happened instead of waiting around for the response, which would never come. This means that transmitted packets lost due to a collision could be retransmitted immediately, instead of after the time-out period. This also means that if a node transmits the last bit of a packet without a collision, then it knows it successfully transmitted the packet.

Carrier sensing coupled with collision detection worked very well. Collisions still happened, but nodes were quick to recover from them, and network performance did not degrade badly in the presence of more collisions. In fact, this worked extremely well. The DIX group that initially invented the Ethernet CSMA/CD media access rules refined them into the simple algorithm used by both Ethernet and Fast Ethernet today. The flowchart shown in Figure 5.3 is a complete illustration of the CSMA/CD media access rules.

This simple algorithm is executed independently by each node needing to transmit a frame. If a node doesn't need to transmit, it just monitors the network for end of frames so that the decision at point ❶ in the flowchart can be made.

The nodes that share an Ethernet or Fast Ethernet LAN using the CSMA/CD rules are said to be in the same **collision domain.** Webster's defines a domain as "1: the set of elements to which a mathematical or logical variable is limited: specifically the set on which a function is defined. 2: a region distinctively marked by some physical feature (the domain of rushing streams, tall trees, and lakes)."

The first definition is precise and mathematical. For Fast Ethernet and Ethernet networks, the function is CSMA/CD and the set to which it is applied are all the nodes on a single LAN. Definition 2 actually works better as a working definition for collision domain. In this case, the domain is defined by the physical repeater, or set of repeaters, that connects a set of nodes.

The terms *LAN*, *segment*, and *network* are often used somewhat interchangeably. Usually their meaning must be derived from the context in which they are being used. The acronym LAN and the word *network* are usually used to mean a set of one or more interconnected collision domains. For example, people often say, I'm connected to the company LAN. Or, The network is down. When people use these terms, they don't refer to the single collision domain to which they are connected, but to the networking system in general. On the other hand, the term *segment* almost always means a single Ethernet or Fast Ethernet collision domain, and this is how we use the word in this book.

Collisions

Collisions are probably the most misunderstood facets of the two CSMA/CD LAN technologies, Fast Ethernet and Ethernet. Discussions have raged for years about collisions. Are they bad? How many are too many? When will they occur? How can we predict them?

The most important thing to note is that *CSMA/CD LANs are designed to have collisions.* Collisions will happen during the normal operation of properly functioning networks. It's somewhat unfortunate that the

MAC and CSMA/CD: Fast Ethernet's Heart and Soul

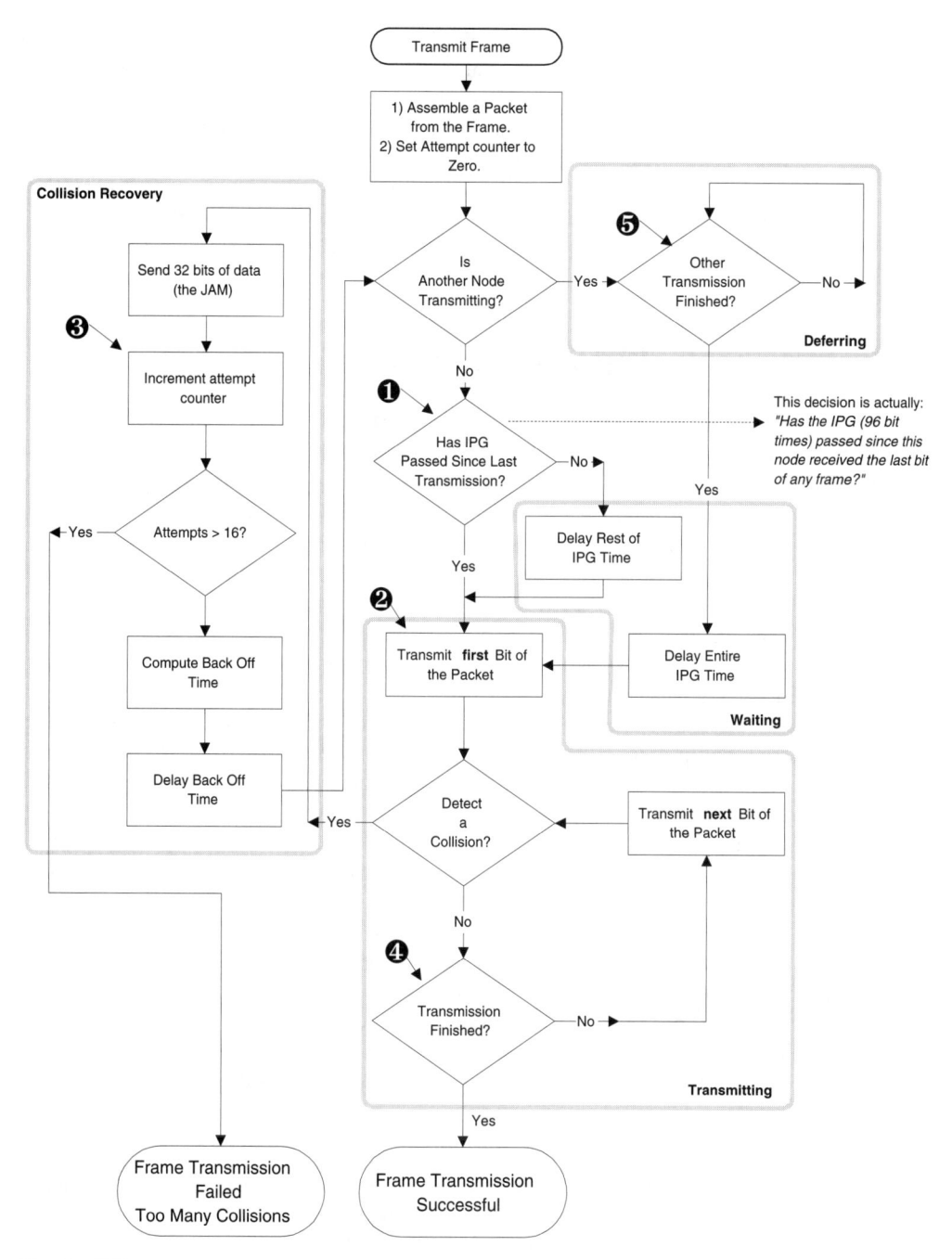

Figure 5.3
CSMA/CD flowchart.

original designers of Ethernet didn't call a collision something else, because in the real world a collision is almost always a bad thing (cars colliding is rarely ever good), and many people think the same thing about collisions on Ethernet and Fast Ethernet networks. Some folks think that if their network is having collisions then something must be wrong. This couldn't be further from the truth. Collisions are part of how nodes on a CSMA/CD LAN arbitrate for the ability to transmit packets. Collision detection is actually an *improvement* on early CSMA only networks.

Why Collisions Happen

Collisions occur on a Fast Ethernet LAN when two or more nodes attempt to transmit at the same time. This happens when multiple nodes all have packets to send and have been listening for the end of the packet currently being transmitted. They will all see the end of the current packet at *about* the same time, but not at *exactly* the same time, which means that two or more nodes on a LAN can reach ❷ in the CSMA/CD flowchart together. Of course, the nodes with pending transmissions don't know about each other, so each begins to transmit and a collision results. This situation is called **contention,** as the nodes are contending for the network, instead of deferring to an already transmitting node.

Contention occurs because of the signal **propagation delay** inherent in each component of the LAN. Propagation delay is the time it takes for an electrical or optical signal to travel through a component. In human terms, electrical (or optical) signals travel instantaneously, essentially at the speed of light. However, at the speeds at which electronic network equipment operates, the time it takes for a signal to travel through a component is not only measurable, but significantly long.

For example, when Category-5 cable is being used, a node can be a maximum of 100 meters from its repeater. In the worst case, signals travel at just over half the speed of light on Cat-5 cable. It takes 57μs for a signal to get from one end of the cable to the other. The bit rate (baud rate) for Fast Ethernet is 100 million bits per second. One bit takes 10μs to transmit (a bit time). So, in 57μs *just over 5 bits* can be transmitted.

> The propagation delay for cable is specified using a measurement called the **Nominal Velocity of Propagation** (NVP). This is the speed (in percent), relative to the speed of light, at which signals travel through the cable. For unshielded twisted-pair cable (Cat-3, Cat-4, and Cat-5), this value

is nominally 0.59 to 0.65. While not a standard, Cat-5 cable will generally never have an NVP worse than about 0.5852. This translates to 0.570 bt/m. (Propagation delays for Fast Ethernet (and Ethernet) are specified in bit times (bt)—1 bt is 10 μs or 10 millionths of a second; the speed of light is 3.34 ns/m.) We use this value as a worst case for Cat-5 cable propagation delay. Using this value, a 100m Cat-5 cable run will have a propagation delay of 57 bit times. The accepted nominal value of NVP for Cat-5 cable is about 0.60 or 0.556 bt/m. In the real world, NVPs tend to be much better. In a recently installed Cat-5 cable plant, the propagation delays were precisely measured and averaged about 4.66 ns/m (an NVP of 0.72) for all 185 runs of Cat-5 cable.

While there is no specified worst-case propagation delay for cable in the Fast Ethernet spec, there are maximum allowable propagation delays for the other components in a Fast Ethernet LAN. The PHYs in a node's network interface, as well as in Class-I and Class-II repeaters, both have maximum allowable propagation delays. The delay through the PHY on a network interface cannot exceed 25 bt. The delay between any two ports cannot exceed 70 bt for a Class-I repeater, 46 bt for a Class-II repeater with all 100Base-TX and/or 100Base-FX ports, or 33.5 bt for a Class-II repeater with one or more 100Base-T4 ports.

While cable is usually the largest source of propagation delay, it isn't the only one. It also takes time for bits to travel through the PHYs in each node and repeaters. The maximum allowable propagation delays of every component on a Fast Ethernet LAN (and also Ethernet) are each *precisely* defined in the standard. Proving that components have propagation delays that are equal to, or less than, those specified is a big part of meeting the specification.

The time difference, in terms of propagation delay, between two particular nodes on the Fast Ethernet LAN is called the **Path Delay Value** (PDV). Each pair of nodes on a Fast Ethernet LAN has a PDV. The PDV for two particular nodes is calculated simply by adding up the individual propagation delays of each component between the MAC at each node to get the **Simple Path Delay** (SPD) time, then multiplying the SPD by 2. The PDV is twice the SPD because it is a measure of the round-trip time between two nodes, or the time it takes for a signal to get from the MAC at one node to another MAC and back again. Note that the term SPD is only a term used in this book. You will not find it in the standard. The term PDV is used in the standard and other literature about Fast Ethernet.

The maximum PDV for any given Fast Ethernet segment is extremely important. Called the **collision window,** it is the time between when a MAC transmits the first bit of a frame and when it can detect a collision with *any node* on the LAN. A Fast Ethernet segment's collision window is directly dependent on the segment's network diameter. The bigger the network diameter, the bigger the maximum propagation delay between any pair of nodes.

The Fast Ethernet specification defines the maximum allowable collision window for Fast Ethernet to be 512 bit times. This value is called the **slot time.** A configuration of Fast Ethernet components that has a collision window larger than the slot time is an invalid configuration and will not function properly. This rule can also be stated like this: The worst-case SPD on a Fast Ethernet must not be more than half the slot time.

Two important values are derived from the slot time: the minimum frame size and the maximum network diameter. The **minimum frame size** is directly derived from the slot time, and is 512 bits (64 bytes). The **maximum network diameter** is determined by the slot time. A segment's network diameter must be small enough that a signal can start from one MAC and travel to any other MAC and back inside the slot time. The time this trip takes is often called a segment's **round-trip time** and is synonymous with its collision window size.

To see why there is a maximum collision window size and a minimum allowed packet size, we really need to look at an example of how propagation delay determines when each node on a segment sees the end of a transmitted packet. The network in Figure 5.4 is an example of why there is a collision window and how propagation delay effects the LAN. In this example, nodes A, B, and C are connected to a repeater. Nodes A and B are close to the repeater, and node C is at the maximum 100-meter distance from the repeater.

Figure 5.4 shows all the components and their propagation delay in bit times. The length of the cables is also indicated. Note that there is a propagation delay in each node. These are the delays inherent in the node's PHY. The propagation delay of the repeater takes into account the delays of two PHYs and the repeater unit itself. The following shows the path delay value for each pair of nodes on the LAN:

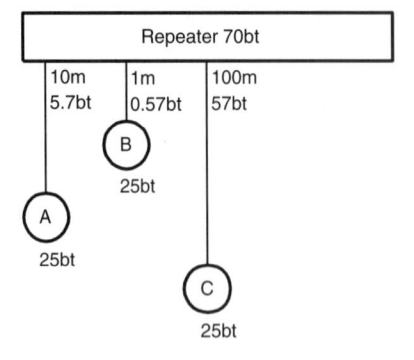

Figure 5.4
Basic collision detection.

Node-to-Node	Path Delay Value (rounded to the nearest whole bit time)
	[All times are rounded to the nearest whole bit time]
A → B	25 + 5.7 + 70 + 0.57 + 25 = 126
A → C	25 + 5.7 + 70 + 57 + 25 = 183
B → C	25 + 0.57 + 70 + 57 + 25 = 178

Let's say that node **A** transmits a packet and both nodes **B** and **C** have packets pending transmission. While **A** is transmitting, nodes **B** and **C** have sensed the carrier and will defer transmission to node **A**. All is fine and good until node **A** stops transmitting.

Of course, when nodes **B** and **C** see the end of **A**'s packet, they will start their IPG timers. However, their timers (and **A**'s timer) will not start at the same time due to propagation delays on the segment. Note that node **A** also starts its IPG timer when it finishes transmitting, and like all the other nodes on the segment, it must also ensure that there is a valid IPG between any packets it transmits.

Figure 5.5 shows when the important events occur. All times are in bit times.

Since node **A** knows exactly when it finishes transmitting, its IPG timer starts first at time zero (T-0). Node **B**'s timer will start next, at T-126, as it is closer to node **A** than node **C** and therefore sees the end of **A**'s frame sooner than **C**. Node **C**'s timer will start last, at T-182, because it is the furthest from node **A**.

Node **B** will start to transmit at T-222 after its IPG timer is finished. At this time, **B** is the only node transmitting, as **C**'s IPG timer is still running, 57 bit times later, **C**'s IPG timer times out and will begin to transmit. It can do so because it still sees an idle segment. At this time, although **B** and **C** are now contending for the media, a collision has not yet occurred because the start of **B** and **C**'s packets haven't reached each other yet.

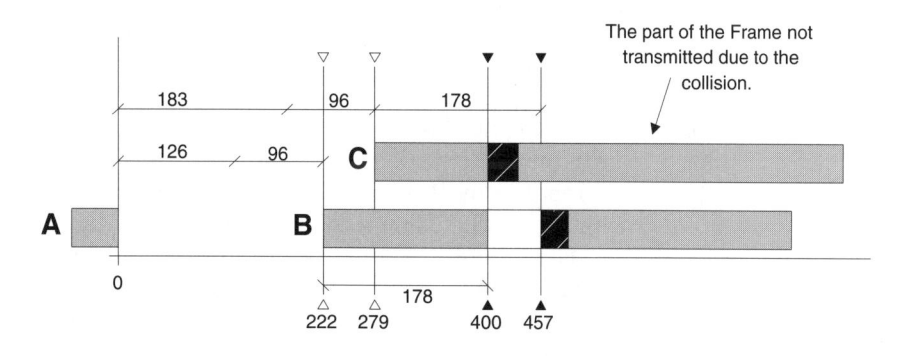

Figure 5.5
Collision timing.

It takes 178 bit times for the first bits in the packets from **B** and **C** to reach the other node. Since **B** started transmitting first, **C** will detect the collision first. This occurs at T-400. When **C** detects the collision, it will continue to transmit for the JAM time and then stop transmitting. The data transmitted during the JAM time (usually just called a JAM) ensures that enough data is transmitted after the collision so that the repeater will detect the collision.

Meanwhile, **B** is still happily transmitting away, as the beginning of **C**'s packet still hasn't gotten to it yet. Finally, 57 bit times after the collision at node **C**, **B** detects it too and sends its JAM signal.

> The JAM is 32 bit times worth of transmission. The spec says that the data sent during the JAM by the MAC is unspecified, but the MAC shall *not* be intentionally designed to send the 32-bit CRC of the data transmitted before the JAM (the partial frame) as the JAM itself. This may seem like an odd thing to specify, but since the MAC has to transmit something which is 32 bits long, and the CRC is 32 bits long and is already contained in the MAC, it would be natural for a hardware designer to just send the CRC as the JAM data. If the CRC was intentionally sent, then as long as a collision occurred 32 bits into the packet or later, the partial frame would actually end up being a valid frame. As you can imagine, this is not a good idea. While the frame would look like a valid frame, it would not be what was originally transmitted.
>
> This poses the question: Why doesn't the spec say *never* transmit any data such that the JAM would be the valid CRC for the previous fragment? The answer is that this would be much more complex to implement and has only about 1 chance in 4.2 billion of happening anyway.

The collision window for a particular Fast Ethernet LAN is a function of its network diameter—the larger the network diameter, the larger the collision window. Fast Ethernet networks that only use Cat-5 (or Cat-3) cable will never have a collision window size that approaches 512 bit times, because the Fast Ethernet specification limits copper cable lengths to 100 meters. For copper cable, electrical factors—such as noise immunity, signal attenuation, and near end crosstalk—are the limiting factors, not propagation delay.

Figure 5.6 shows a Fast Ethernet LAN using a Class-I repeater that has a maximum network diameter of 200 meters. Both nodes are connected to the repeater by 100 meters of Cat-5 cable (the maximum allowable length). This LAN has a collision window of only 472 bit times.

The values in Table 5.1 show how this value was derived. Note that we have added a safety margin of 4 bit times to our calculation. This is not required, but it is recommended. In a real LAN, connections aren't usually

Figure 5.6
Maximum size network.

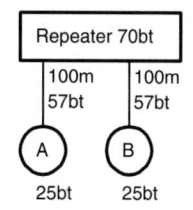

```
      Repeater 70bt
      ┌──────┬──────┐
      │100m  │100m  │
      │57bt  │57bt  │
      │      │      │
     (A)    (B)
     25bt   25bt
```

made by a single cable from a node to a repeater, but by two or three cables connected by wall jacks and patch panels. The Fast Ethernet specification suggests that a safety margin from zero to five bits should be used and recommends a value of 4, which is used in these examples.

If the maximum length of a Cat-5 copper cable run were not limited by electrical characteristics, then Cat-5 cable runs could be up to 170 meters in length when using Class-I repeaters. However, the 100Base-TX and 100Base-T4 PHYs are designed to work with a maximum length of 100 meters. This 100-meter value comes from the **EIA/TIA 568** structured cabling standards. (The EIA is the Electronics Industry Association, the TIA is the Telecommunications Industry Association.)

This is the big advantage of using fiberoptic cable in a Fast Ethernet LAN. Fiberoptic cable is not susceptible to electrical interference or near-end crosstalk, both of which limit the practical length of copper cable. With fiberoptic cable, the only limiting factor for cable length is the cable's propagation delay. The nominal propagation delay for fiberoptic cable is 0.50 bt/m. If we replaced the copper cable in Figure 5.6 with fiberoptic cable, then both fiber runs can be 134 meters in length (see Table 5.2).

The key thing to note from Tables 5.1 and 5.2 is that the topology of a Fast Ethernet LAN is limited by the worst-case propagation delay between any two nodes on the LAN. This cannot be more than 256 bit times one way, or 512 bit times for a round trip (the slot time). As you can see from Table 5.1, any Fast Ethernet LAN configured using the Model-1 topology

Table 5.1 Worst-Case Cat-5 Collision Window Using a Class-I Hub and Copper Cable

Item	Prop Delay (In bt/m)	Quantity	×2 for Round Trip	Total Prop Delay
Network Interface PHY on each Node	25	×2	×2	100
Class-I Repeater	70	×1	×2	140
100 Meters Cat-5 Cable (Node A)	57	×1	×2	114
100 Meters Cat-5 Cable (Node B)	57	×1	×2	114
Safety Margin				4
Total Round-Trip Propagation Delay				472
Bit-Time Margin (512 − Total)				40

Chapter Five

Table 5.2 Worst-Case Cat-5 Collision Window Using a Class-I Hub and Fiberoptic Cable

Item	Prop Delay (In bt/m)	Quantity	×2 for Round Trip	Total Prop Delay
Network Interface PHY on Each Node	25	×2	×2	100
Class-I Repeater	70	×1	×2	140
134 Meters Cat-5 Cable	67	×1	×2	134
134 Meters Cat-5 Cable	67	×1	×2	134
Safety Margin				4
Total Round-Trip Propagation Delay				512
Bit-Time Margin (512 − Total)				0

rules (see Chapter 3) will always yield LANs that have collision windows well inside the slot-time limit. That's the idea behind the Model-1 rules. If you use them, you do not have to be concerned with the PDVs on your Fast Ethernet segments.

The Model-2 topology rules are still simple but are based on calculating the worst PDVs on a Fast Ethernet segment. To use the Model-2 topology rules, simply perform calculations like the preceding ones using the two nodes in your LAN that are on the longest cable runs from the repeater. If the worst-case PDV is less than or equal to 512, then everything will work fine.

The problem with designing a Fast Ethernet LAN (or an Ethernet LAN, for that matter) that has a collision window at or close to the slot time is that you can never be completely sure that the collision window is not greater than the slot time. If this occurs, then you are in for lots of LAN trouble.

To explore this, we'll use two examples. In the first example, shown in Figure 5.7, a LAN is configured with a collision window just under the slot time. In the second, shown in Figure 5.8, a LAN is too big, with a collision window larger than the slot time. In both examples, the LAN starts off idle, then node **A** decides to send a packet to node **C**. Later, but inside the LAN's collision window, **B** transmits a packet. In Figure 5.7, every-

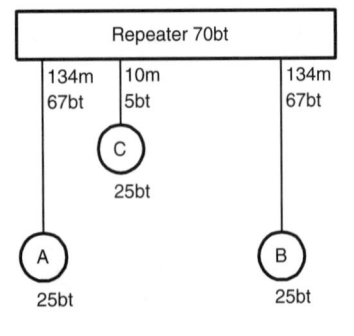

Figure 5.7
Max diameter fiber LAN.

Figure 5.8
Collision timing.

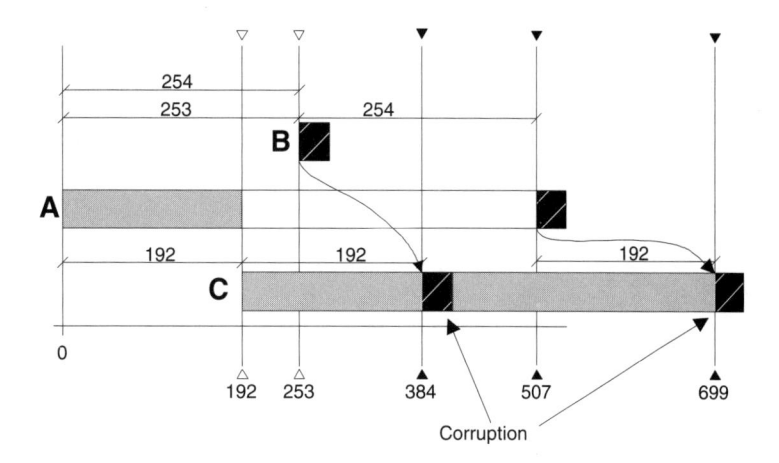

thing works fine because the collision window is smaller than the slot time. However, in Figure 5.8, node **A** cannot detect the collision because the collision window is too big.

The segment in Figure 5.7 has a large network diameter (264 meters), but is still a valid LAN because its collision window is 508 bit times, just under the 512 bit-time slot time.

The following shows the node-to-node propagation delays:

Node-to-Node	Path Delay Value (in Bit Times)
A → B	25 + 67 + 70 + 67 + 25 = 254
B → A	25 + 67 + 70 + 67 + 25 = 254
A → C	25 + 67 + 70 + 5 + 25 = 192
B → C	25 + 5 + 70 + 67 + 25 = 192

> The minimum frame size on a Fast Ethernet LAN is 64 bytes, the maximum 1,518 bytes. For more information on frames and packets, see Chapter 4.

A can transmit its packet immediately because the network has been idle for more than the IPG time. A T-0 node **A** decides to transmit a 64-byte packet to node **C**. At T-253 a packet becomes available for **B** to transmit. From **B**'s standpoint, the network has been idle for more than the IPG time, because the first bit of **A**'s packet has not yet reached **B**. Because of the propagation delay between the two nodes, this will not happen until T-254, which means that **B** will immediately transmit its packet at T-253.

The result is that **B** gets to transmit one bit and then will detect a collision as the first bit of **A**'s packet arrives at T-254. **B** detects the collision at T-254, then transmits a 32-bit JAM. The first bit of **B**'s packet followed by 32 bits of JAM are now heading for **A**. However, **C** is closer (in terms of propagation delay) to **B** than to **A**, so the data from **B** collides with **A**'s packet at node **C** first. This corrupts the packet that **C** has been receiving since T-192.

At T-507 **A** will finally sense a collision as the first bit of **B**'s packet arrives. This is *just 5 bits* before **A** would have successfully finished transmitting its packet. Even though it's close to the end of the packet, **A** sees the collision and retransmits the packet to **C**. The first packet that **A** sent to **C** was corrupted by the collision, just as **B**'s packet was. Figure 5.8 also shows when the packet **C** is receiving from **A** was corrupted, and that it actually happened twice: once at T-384 when the **B**'s first data bit and JAM reached **C**, and then again at T-699 when **A**'s JAM reached **C**.

If we had not used a 4-bit-time safety factor in designing this LAN, then **A** would have detected the collision only when it transmitted the very last bit of its packet. Since fiberoptic cable has a propagation delay of 0.5 bits per meter, a cable installation mistake that made the network diameter longer by just two meters (about 6½ feet) would cause **A** to miss detecting the collision, even though one had occurred. For this LAN, a two-meter mistake is only 1.2 percent of the network diameter—not very much room to work with.

As you can see from spot ❹ in Figure 5.3, once a node has sent the last bit of a frame without sensing a collision, then it believes that the frame was successfully transmitted. If a Fast Ethernet LAN's diameter gets too big, then nodes will be able to send packets that result in a collision and still believe that they sent the frame successfully. A missed collision means frames will not be retransmitted when a collision occurs. Remember the CSMA media access rules? The exact same thing happens when a missed collision occurs: The protocol must recover, which degrades throughput.

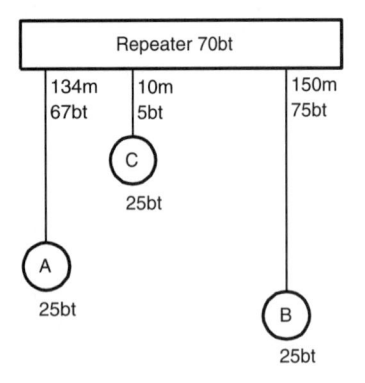

Figure 5.9
A network that is too large.

This is illustrated in Figure 5.9. Here, the network is just like the one in Figure 5.7 except that node **B** is on a 150-meter cable run instead of a 134-meter run (too long by 16 meters).

The following shows the node-to-node propagation delays:

Node-to-Node *Path Delay Value (in Bit Times)*
A → B   25 + 67 + 70 + 75 + 25 = 262
B → A   25 + 67 + 70 + 75 + 25 = 262
A → C   25 + 67 + 70 + 5 + 25 = 192
B → C   25 + 5 + 70 + 75 + 25 = 200

If the same transmit scenario in Figure 5.7 happens in Figure 5.9, then **A** will not detect the collision due to the overly long propagation delay between **A** and **B** (see Figure 5.10).

Figure 5.10 shows how the first bit transmitted by **B** doesn't get to **A** until T-523, 11 bit times after **A** has finished transmitting. **C** is able to properly receive the first 200 bits of **A**'s packet, then, at T-392, **C**'s reception gets corrupted by the 33 bits of data and JAM that **B** transmitted. As in the previous example, **C** ignores the packet from **A** because it has been corrupted by a collision. However, **A** believes the packet was successfully transmitted because it sent the last bit of the packet without sensing a collision. It is now up to the protocols to recover from the lost frame.

Note that both these examples assume that **A** is sending a minimum-sized, 64-byte frame. This is the shortest frame allowed on a Fast Ethernet (or Ethernet) LAN. In the latter example, if **A** had sent a frame longer by just two bytes, then everything would have worked fine, as **A** would have been transmitting long enough to see the collision. A collision that happens after the 512th bit of a transmission is still an error and is called a

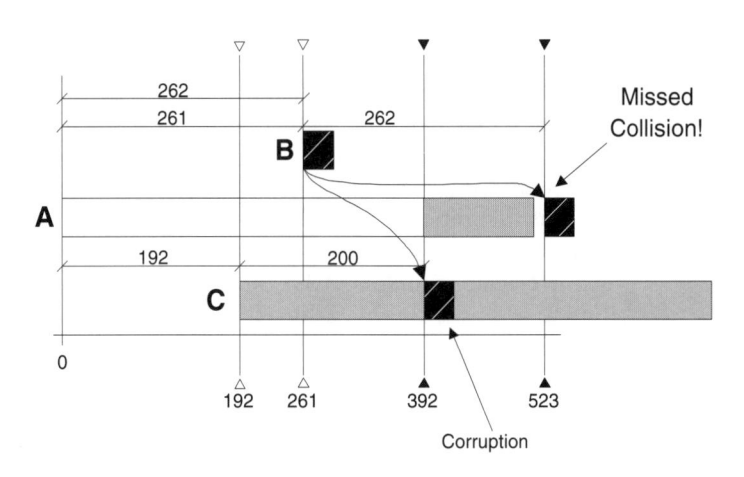

Figure 5.10
Missed collision.

late collision. Late collision errors are a strong indication that a LAN has a network diameter that is too large.

This is just one of the reasons why it is extremely important to ensure that your Fast Ethernet LAN is built correctly. If you use copper cable and keep all your runs at 100 meters or less, you will not have any problems associated with a collision window that is too large. However, if you need a Fast Ethernet LAN with long fiberoptic cable runs, you must be careful. A Fast Ethernet LAN that is too big will have intermittent problems that are extremely difficult to diagnose and fix.

In short, because of the propagation delays inherent in the components of the segment, collisions happen because end-of-packet events do not arrive at each node on a Fast Ethernet segment at the same time. This means that the IPG timers on each of the nodes will start at different times. If no data arrives at a node before the IPG timer times out (indicating that the network is busy), then that node can transmit a packet. This can happen at two or more nodes at the same time, resulting in a collision.

Slot Time and Collision Windows

As mentioned before, the minimum frame size (measured in bits) must be equal to the slot time (measured in bit times). Since the Fast Ethernet slot time is 512 bit times, the minimum frame size must be no smaller than 512 bits. The reason for this is illustrated in Figures 5.7 and 5.9. In Figure 5.7, node **A** transmits a frame of minimum size (512 bits, or 64 bytes). The first bit transmitted by **A** gets to **B** 253 bit times after **A** transmits it. At this time, **A** is just transmitting its 254th bit, exactly when **B** detects the collision and starts to send its JAM. The first bit (followed by the JAM) takes another 253 bit times to travel back to **A** and arrives there just as **A** is transmitting its 507th bit, just barely in time for **A** to detect the collision.

In Figure 5.9, the exact same thing happens but the propagation delay between **A** and **B** is just long enough that **A** has already finished transmitting when the data from the collision reaches it, which is too late.

There is a minimum packet size for Fast Ethernet because a node must transmit long enough for its first bit to reach the node furthest away from it, and then for a collision with that node to get back to it. Both of these events must occur before a transmitting node sends the last bit of a frame.

It is theoretically possible to allow a Fast Ethernet LAN to have a minimum frame size equal to its collision window. For example, a small LAN with a collision window of 100 bit times could allow operation with a minimum frame size of 13 bytes, which is 104 bits. All frames must be an integral number of octets (bytes) in size. This would also allow Fast Ethernet segments to get large. If the collision window were 8,000 bit times, the minimum packet size would be 1,000 bytes, allowing fiberoptic drops from a single, Class-I repeater to be up to 880 meters each. Of course, having a huge minimum packet size is extremely inefficient. Some protocols need to send only a few bytes to each other, some as few as 3, and therefore waste 997 bytes in a minimum-sized frame.

Of course, there is another reason why this would be *extremely* impractical. Every LAN installed would have to have its maximum propagation delay accurately measured, and then the minimum packet size would have to be adjusted on all the nodes. If the measurement were off, even a little bit, then the LAN wouldn't operate properly because collisions would be missed. Even worse, when the LAN configuration changed, the maximum propagation delay would have to be measured again and the minimum packet size adjusted again on all the nodes. This would be extremely difficult and prone to error.

Instead of this, the designers of Ethernet and Fast Ethernet wisely decided to define a practical maximum propagation delay for an Ethernet LAN of 512 bit times. Fast Ethernet kept this same value. The minimum packet size is, of course, 512 bits (64 bytes). The result is that as long as a Fast Ethernet LAN has a collision window less than or equal to the slot time, collisions will always be detected by the transmitting stations and all will be well, and the Earth will continue to spin smoothly on its axis.

Slot Time and Network Diameter

Specifying the slot time has another side effect besides determining the minimum frame size: It also puts a maximum bound on the physical size of a Fast Ethernet LAN. As mentioned in Chapter 1, there are two sets of rules for determining if your Fast Ethernet LAN has a valid topology: **Transmission Model 1** and **Transmission Model 2.**

Model 1 is simple and doesn't need to be repeated. However, Model 2 is more involved. It consists of calculating the worst-case PDV value for a LAN. If the worst-case PDV is no more than 512 bit times, the LAN is a legal Fast Ethernet LAN. If the worst-case PDV is more than 512 bit times, the LAN must be reconfigured.

Transmission Model 2 has no application for Fast Ethernet LANs, which use only copper cable. When copper cable is used, a Fast Ethernet segment cannot be built that is too big. The Model-2 rules come into play only when fiberoptic cable is used. Figure 5.7 shows a Fast Ethernet LAN using fiber cable to connect nodes and repeaters. Nodes **A** and **B** are both on 134 meter fiberoptic runs. Since fiberoptic cable distance is not limited by electrical characteristics, we could shorten one of the runs and lengthen the other by the same amount and still have a legal Fast Ethernet LAN.

In general, most 10Mbps Ethernet installations do not run into problems with network diameter. A 10Base-T LAN can span a maximum of about 500 meters (1,640 feet), which is plenty for most installations. However, with fiberoptic cable and a Class-I repeater the maximum is 272 meters (892 feet). This can be a serious problem for people with large 10Base-T Ethernet LANs wanting to upgrade to Fast Ethernet.

Another implication of using Transmission Model 2 is that it is possible to have more than two Class-II repeaters in a Fast Ethernet LAN. However, doing this requires careful attention to calculating the worst-case PDV. For example, the LAN in Figure 5.11 shows a maximally sized Fast Ethernet LAN with three Class-II repeaters.

Table 5.3 is an example of calculating the cable bit-time budget for the preceding segment. The round-trip propagation delays for the components, except for cable, are subtracted from the slot time (the total bit budget). What's left over are the round-trip bit delays for *all* the cable in the worst-case delay path on the LAN.

Since our worst-case propagation delay for Cat-5 Cable is 0.57 bt/m and we have 163 bit times for cable, the cable length connecting **A** and **B** to their repeaters is limited to a *total* of 142 meters, or 71 meters each if we divide it evenly. This is significantly less than the maximum 100-meter cable length for copper cable. Note that in this case, **A** and **B**'s cables don't have to both be 71 meters; they just have to total 142 meters. One could be 50 meters and the other 92 meters. Even though we are using Transmission Model 2, a copper cable run still can't be over 100 meters in length, so the most lopsided split is 100 meters for one node and 42 meters for the other node.

More nodes can be added to the LAN in Figure 5.11 as long as the PDV between the new node and each existing node on the LAN doesn't exceed the slot time.

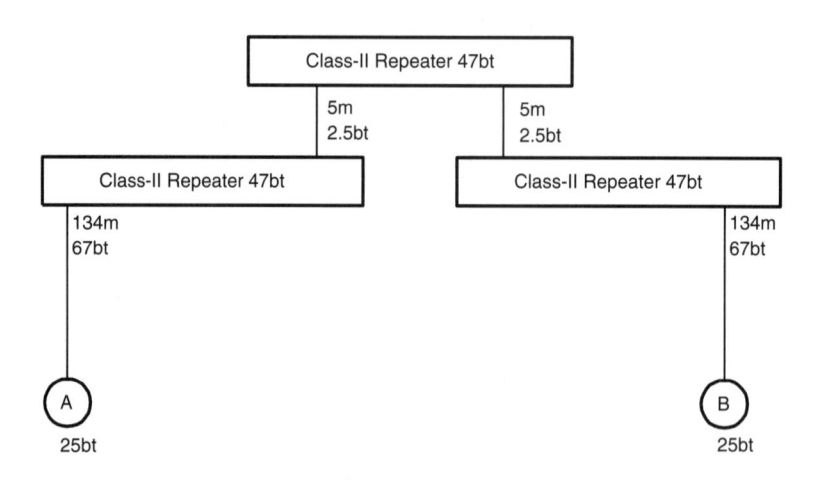

Figure 5.11
Three Class-II repeaters.

Table 5.3 Class II Bit-Budget Calculation

Slot Time (Total Bit-Time Budget) — 512

Item	Prop Delay (in bt/m)	Quantity	×2 for Round Trip	Total Prop Delay
Network Interface PHY on each Node	25	×2	×2	−100
Class II Repeater	47	×3	×2	−235
Intra Repeater Patch Cables	2.5	×2	×2	−10
Safety Margin				−4
Cable Bit-Time Budget				**163**

Collision Window and Network Performance

The size of the collision window on Fast Ethernet also has an effect on network performance. A Fast Ethernet segment with a smaller collision window will tend to have fewer collisions than one with a larger collision window, because a Fast Ethernet LAN's collision window is an upper bound on the time it takes for a node to **acquire** the network for transmission.

A node is said to acquire the network when it has transmitted the nth bit, where *n* is the size of the collision window. Figure 5.12 will help illustrate this, as it shows a LAN with 6 nodes and a collision window of 498 bit times, which comes from the PDV between nodes **A** and **C**.

Following are the PDVs for all the nodes with respect to node **A**:

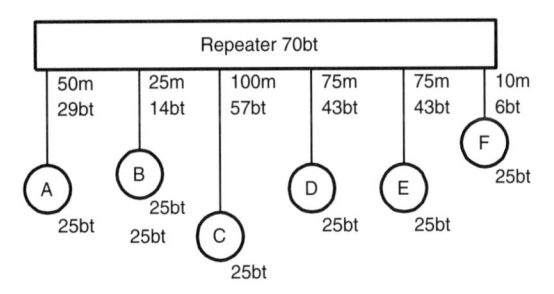

Node-to-Node	Propagation Delay (in Bit Times)	PDV
A → B	25 + 29 + 70 + 14 + 25 = 163	326
A → C	25 + 29 + 70 + 100 + 25 = 249	498
A → D	25 + 29 + 70 + 43 + 25 = 192	384
A → E	25 + 29 + 70 + 43 + 25 = 192	384
A → F	25 + 29 + 70 + 6 + 25 = 155	310

Figure 5.12 A LAN with several nodes.

If node **A** starts to transmit a 100-byte frame (800 bits) at time zero (T-0), a collision can occur anytime inside half the collision window time (at T-249). Remember that the collision window time, the slot time, and the PDV are round-trip times, not point-to-point times like the SPD (see Figure 5.13).

The first bit that **A** transmits takes 155 bt to get to node **F**. It reaches this node first because **F** is nearest to **A** in terms of propagation delay (**A** and **F** have the smallest SPD on the LAN). If **F** hasn't transmitted anything *before* T-155, then it won't for the duration of this frame plus the IPG time. Once **F** sees **A**'s transmission (it senses a carrier), it will defer transmission until **A** has finished transmitting (see spot ❺ in the CSMA/CD flowchart).

If **F** *does* start to transmit before T-155, it will cause a collision, which **A** will sense before T-310. This same pattern exists for nodes **B**, **C**, **D**, and **E**, but with times dependent on the PDV between them and node **A**. We know that in the worst case, all collisions must happen by T-249 and be detected by T-498 for any node on the LAN.

Once node **A** has transmitted 498 bits of a frame, it is said to have *acquired* the network. At this point we know that enough time has passed for a collision to occur with any other node on the segment which will be detected by **A**. If no collision has happened by T-498, then node **A** is guaranteed that its transmission will finish successfully. The slot time is an upper bound on the acquisition time for any Fast Ethernet segment. Actually, we could make a chart like the preceding one and a timing diagram like Figure 5.13 for each of the node pairs in Figure 5.12, resulting in 15 combinations in all. Of course, this would be extremely impractical to do with a real segment. A segment with 50 nodes has 1,225 node-pair combinations. Instead of worrying about each one, we need to know only that the LAN's collision window is not bigger than the slot time. If this is true, then collisions will always be properly detected, regardless of the value and distribution of PDVs on the LAN.

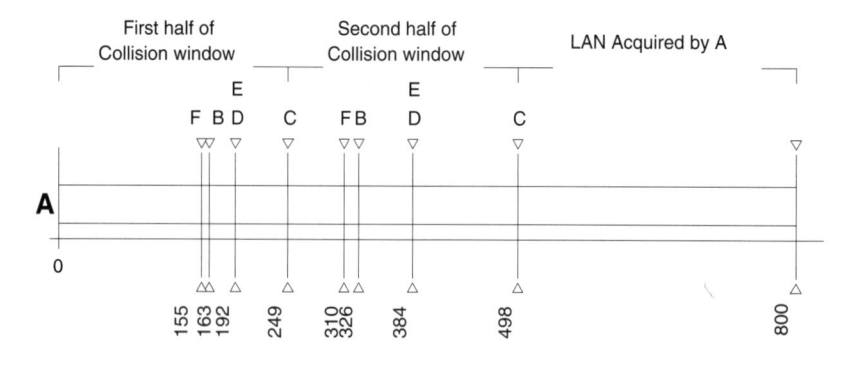

Figure 5.13
Collision window timing.

A network designer can use this knowledge to build a better Fast Ethernet LAN. When nodes with the highest traffic are placed nearest to the repeater, the average number of collisions over time will be lower than if those nodes were on the longest cable drops. For example, placing a server on a short drop to a repeater is better than placing it on a long drop.

Runt Frames

An interesting side effect of collisions is that they usually result in **runt frames.** If you look back at Figure 5.5, nodes **B** and **C** collide with each other. Both were attempting to transmit 512 bit frames. Due to the collision, **C** transmits only 153 bits and **B** transmits only 267 bits. All of the other nodes on the LAN will receive between 153 and 267 bits of junk. This junk is a runt frame.

The common definition of a runt frame is any frame that results from a collision. This isn't precisely true, but it is a widely accepted definition nonetheless. A more accurate definition of a runt frame, and the one we prefer, is any frame that is shorter than 512 bits (64 octets) in size. This definition is more accurate because not all runt frames are caused by collisions. A faulty MAC can send frames that are too short but have valid CRCs and meet all the other rules for valid frames—a common problem with early Ethernet network interfaces. With modern MACs this is a very rare problem but still a possibility.

We prefer the term **collision frame** as the name of any frame that results from a collision. Note that this isn't a widely used or accepted term, just one we made up because we find it useful.

The common definition of runt frame has a problem because, contrary to popular belief, by the precise definition, not all collisions will result in a runt frame. If a collision happens at bit 480 (the 60th byte) or later, the transmitting node will stop sending after another 32 bits (the JAM). This will result in a frame between 512 and 544 bits in size, which are valid frame lengths.

Fortunately, collision frames are not a problem. In fact, they must be repeated. A collision frame will always violate at least one rule that is required for valid frames. Frames resulting from a collision will have one, some, or all of the following problems. First, they are often too short. A valid Fast Ethernet (or Ethernet) frame must be at least 512 bits in size. By definition, runt frames are always shorter. Any frame that is less than 512 bits in size is considered to be the result of a collision. As mentioned before, a faulty MAC can generate runt frames, but this is very rare.

Second, runt frames will practically never have a valid frame-check sequence, because a MAC immediately stops transmitting and sends a JAM when it detects a collision. It never calculates or transmits a CRC for the corrupted frame. The odds that the 32 bits of the JAM signal are a valid CRC for the previously transmitted part of the frame are 1 in 4.2 billion (2^{32}—the CRC is 32 bits in size).

Third, runts will often not be an even number of octets (8 bits) in size, which is also a requirement for a valid frame (because a collision can happen at anytime during a frame's transmission, not just on octet boundaries). A collision only has a 1 in 8 chance of resulting in a frame that is an even number of octets in size.

Since a repeater's job is to repeat everything it hears, it will propagate runt frames around a segment. If it didn't, then the collision mechanism wouldn't work properly. Collision frames are handled by the receiving logic in each node.

Collision Detection and Recovery

The first thing to know about collision detection is that only transmitting nodes and repeater(s) can detect collisions. Nodes that are not actively transmitting cannot detect a collision between two (or more) other nodes. A node is actively transmitting only if it has gotten to spot ❷ in the CSMA/CD flowchart. A node that has one or more packets to send, but is waiting for the IPG to be satisfied or is deferring to another node, has only pending transmits and is not actively transmitting.

Collisions are detected in a very simple way. If a node is transmitting and begins to receive any kind of data, then there is a collision. It's that simple.

How Repeaters Help Collision Detection

Repeaters play an active role in detecting collisions. A repeater knows when each node connected to it is transmitting. If it sees two nodes transmitting at the same time, it knows there is a collision. When a repeater detects a collision, it immediately sends a 32-bit long JAM pattern out to *all* its ports. This guarantees that all transmitting nodes will sense a collision and that all receiving nodes (all other nodes) will end up with a corrupted packet.

One side effect of this is that an intelligent repeater can count the number of collisions on each port. These values can be extremely useful in helping to tune network performance and troubleshoot problems. Collision and other statistics are usually gathered from a repeater by management software. For more information on this, see Chapter 14.

Transmission Collision Recovery

When a transmitting node senses a collision, it must recover by retransmitting the frame. The simplest way to accomplish this would be to merely jump to the beginning of the transmit flowchart in Figure 5.3 and start over. However, this would mean that all the transmitting nodes that were interrupted by the collision would resend their packets within 256 bit times of each other, or half the slot time. Since this time is half the minimum packet size in length, another collision would be sure to occur when the stations attempted to retransmit. As you can imagine, this is not a workable solution.

To avoid this, the MAC increments the transmit attempts counter (see Figure 5.3, spot ❸) and waits a random period of time (called the **back-off time**) before attempting to retransmit the lost packet. After the back-off time has passed, the node can attempt to retransmit the packet. It does this the normal way, deferring to a currently transmitting node and maintaining the IPG. If the packet is successfully transmitted (with no collision), this fact is indicated to the higher layer (the protocol). On the other hand, if another collision occurs, the attempt counter is incremented again, another back-off time calculated, and the process starts over.

This continues until the packet is successfully transmitted or until the attempt counter reaches 11, at which point the **too many collisions** error counter is incremented, the packet is discarded, and the higher layer protocol is informed of the error. It is then up to the protocol to recover from the error in some other way.

Calculating the Back-Off Time

The back-off time is calculated by each node, independent of any other node. The back-off time is always an integer multiple of the 512 bit slot time (i.e., 512, 1,024, 1,536, 2,048, etc.) but never more than 4,096 bt. The back-off time can also be zero. This back-off time is calculated using a formula called **truncated binary exponential back off,** which goes as follows: Back-Off Time = RAND(0, $2^{\min(N, 10)}$), where N is the transmit attempt counter.

The first time the collision-recover algorithm is executed (see Figure 5.3), the back-off time can be one of three values: 0, 512, or 1,024 bit times. After the second consecutive collision, it could be 0, 512, 1,024, or 4,096 bit times. This progresses until 16 attempts have been made to retransmit the frame due to collisions.

The maximum back-off time is 524,288 bit times (5.2 milliseconds). This is quite a long time when the bit time is 100 million bits per second (520,000 bt to be precise). However, the chances of this happening are small (1 in 1,024 to be exact), and it would occur only on the 10th or subsequent retry attempts. Generally, frames are successfully retransmitted after a collision on the first or second retry attempt, even on a busy LAN. On an extremely busy LAN, it might take three or four retry attempts. If a LAN is experiencing packets being dropped due to excessive collisions, then there is probably some kind of problem with the LAN, such as a network diameter that is too large, a cable problem, or possibly a repeater that is malfunctioning.

Having a random back-off time increases the odds that contending stations will not try to retransmit in the same collision window and have another collision. It also provides time for the contending stations to sync up with the other transmitting nodes on the LAN and defer to them, instead of colliding with them.

Receiving Collision Recovery

All nodes on a LAN that are not actively transmitting are classified as receiving nodes. These nodes don't actually recover from a collision, as they never know a collision even happened. Only the MACs in actively transmitting nodes and repeaters can detect collisions.

A node's MAC handles runt frames and invalid frames generated by collisions by rejecting frames that don't meet very specific and rigid rules. A receiving MAC discards any frame that:

- Is shorter than the minimum frame size of 64 bytes (512 bits)
- Has an invalid frame check sequence
- Is not an integral number of octets in length

A collision is guaranteed to cause at least one of these errors. When a frame is received by a MAC, it first checks to see if the frame is shorter than 512 bits. If it is, then it is discarded. This is not considered an error, as runts are normal results of collisions, and collisions are normal and expected events. In other words, runt frames happen.

On the other hand, a frame that is 512 bits in size or longer, and has an invalid FCS or is not an integral number of octets in length, *is* considered an error and is counted as such. In any case, any frame not meeting the preceding rules is discarded by the MAC and not passed up to the protocol layers.

CHAPTER 6

The Fast Part of Fast Ethernet: Network Performance

Of course, the most important thing about Fast Ethernet is the *fast* part. Fast Ethernet transmits bits at a rate of 100 million bits per second (megabits per second or Mbps)—a full 10 times the speed of regular old Ethernet. It's 781 times faster than an ISDN line, and 3,000 times faster than a 33.3k baud modem. The extremely high speed of Fast Ethernet is reflected in *everything* about it, from the way a Fast Ethernet LAN will operate, to what kind of cable needs to be installed, to how the network adapters and repeaters are designed by the manufacturer.

It's kind of funny to use the term *baud rate* when describing Fast Ethernet, but that is exactly what 100Mbps is—Fast Ethernet's baud rate. Fast Ethernet runs only at 100Mbps. This is an important distinction, because you will find Fast Ethernet equipment that operates at both 10 and 100Mbps. For example, there are many 10/100 Ethernet NICs on the market. These adapter cards have only one socket for a cable connection but can be plugged into either a Fast Ethernet repeater or a 10Base-T Ethernet repeater, have two PHYs, and can run at two speeds. If plugged into a 10Base-T repeater, they behave like regular old 10Mbps Ethernet cards. When plugged into a 100Base-TX repeater, they operate in Fast Ethernet mode. For more information on adapter cards, see Chapter 9.

Maximum Throughput

The most important thing to note about Fast Ethernet's 100Mbps baud rate is that it does not directly translate into a data throughput number such as bytes per second. The most useful number we can have for Fast Ethernet is its maximum possible throughput measured in bytes per second. Unfortunately, this cannot be derived directly from the 100Mbps baud rate. Fast Ethernet and all other LAN technologies are not 100-percent efficient because there is overhead associated with transmitting data. Not every bit that travels on the network is useful (or significant) to the higher-level application that is using the network, such as a word processor or Web browser. This isn't to say that some transmitted bits are wasted; they aren't. Some are just overhead and used for running the LAN. For example, the destination address bits in a frame determine which node receives the frame, but contain no data useful to an application. Lots of transmitted bits fall into this category, such as the packet preamble, the frame check sequence—anything that is not part of the data payload of a frame is overhead.

The 100Mbps baud rate, media access rules, and the frame format all must be considered in order to compute Fast Ethernet's maximum throughput. When application data is transmitted on the network, it is first packaged into frames, then transmitted on the LAN using the CSMA/CD media access rules.

Both the maximum throughput and maximum efficiency of Fast Ethernet are directly derived from the maximum number of packets that can be transmitted per second. This is a very easy number to calculate. Figure 6.1 shows the bit times for each part of a transmitted packet. While not strictly part of the packet, the IPG is included because another frame cannot be transmitted until that amount of time has passed. If only a single node were transmitting, it could transmit packets back to back, each only separated by the IPG.

The data payload for a maximum-size frame is 12,000 bits (1,500 bytes), giving us a total of 12,304 bits per transmitted packet. Dividing

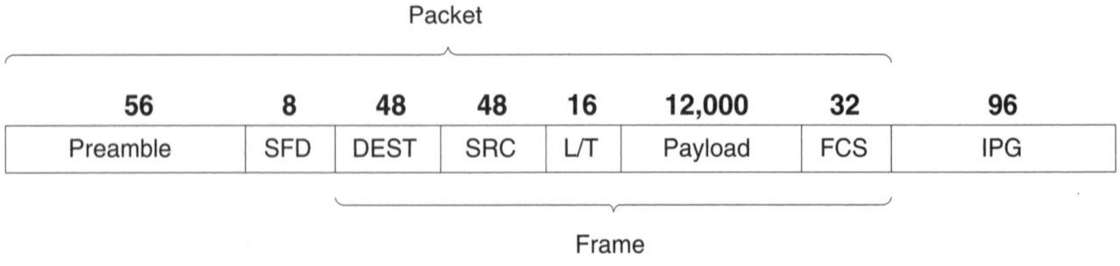

56	8	48	48	16	12,000	32	96
Preamble	SFD	DEST	SRC	L/T	Payload	FCS	IPG

Figure 6.1
Transmission bit times.

this into 100,000,000 bits per second gives us a maximum packet rate of 8,127.44 maximum-size packets per second.

When the useful data payload of 1,500 bytes is multiplied by 8,127.44, we get the maximum throughput of Fast Ethernet, which is 12,191,157 bytes per second! That is why Fast Ethernet is called *fast*.

The other interesting number is Fast Ethernet's efficiency, which is the percentage of total bandwidth (100Mbps) that is used to transmit useful data. This number is also easy to calculate: 8,127.44 packets containing 12,000 bits of useful payload can be transmitted per second for a total of 97,529,258 useful bits of data per second. If we divide this by 100Mbps, we get an efficiency of 97.53 percent (about 98 percent).

However, not all packets transmitted are maximum-size packets. A node often needs to send pieces of data that are smaller than 1,500 bytes, so it's useful to calculate the same numbers when the frame is the minimum size of 64 bytes with a data payload of 46 bytes (368 bits). Table 6.1 summarizes this data.

Table 6.1 shows the maximum frames per second, throughput, and efficiencies for various frame sizes and data payloads—note that a high frame rate at a low frame size is the least efficient way to send data. 148,810 frames per second sure sounds fast, but it isn't very efficient. All of the frame rates in the Max Frames Per Second column in the table are what are commonly referred to as **wire speed** frame rates. Wire speed traffic is simply network traffic where the frames are all separated by only the IPG. Figure 6.2 shows this same data in graphical form. Note how the efficiency of the frame size really starts to drop off for frames less than 256 bytes in size.

Table 6.1 Throughput and Efficiency

Frame Size (in Bytes)	Data Payload (in Bytes)	Max Frames Per Second	Throughput (Bytes/Sec)	Efficiency
1,518	1,500	8127.44	12,191,157	97.53%
1,280	1,262	9615.38	12,134,615	97.08%
1,024	1,006	11973.18	12,045,019	96.36%
512	494	23496.24	11,607,143	92.86%
256	238	45289.86	10,778,986	86.23%
128	110	84459.46	9,290,541	74.32%
64	46	148809.52	6,845,238	54.76%
64	32	148809.52	4,761,905	38.10%
64	24	148809.52	3,571,429	28.57%
64	16	148809.52	2,380,952	19.05%
64	8	148809.52	1,190,476	9.52%
64	3	148809.52	446,429	3.57%

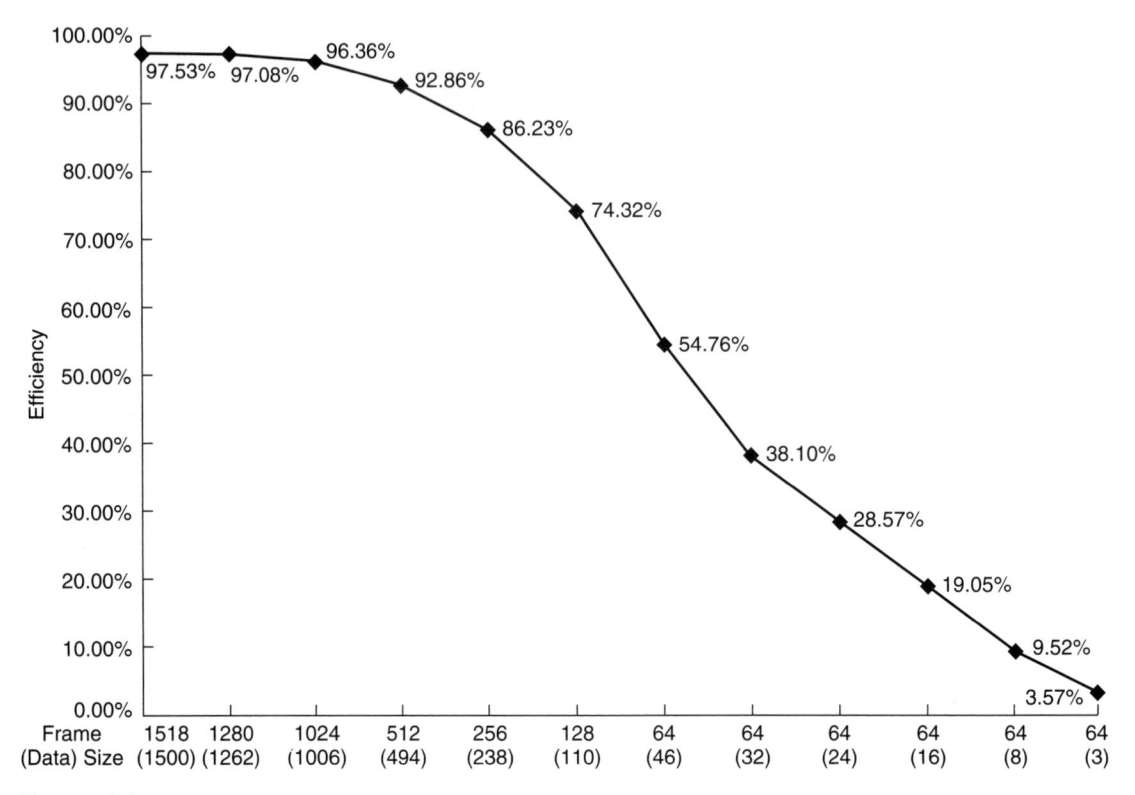

Figure 6.2
Frame size versus efficiency.

As Table 6.1 indicates, Fast Ethernet has the potential to carry a lot of information. This level of performance, coupled with its low cost, makes it ideal to service today's high-performance workstations and servers.

Network Utilization

The throughput numbers in the previous section are maximums. A Fast Ethernet LAN will rarely operate at these data rates for any length of time. Protocols such as TCP/IP, IPX/SPX, and NetBEUI usually transmit packets in bursts of from 2 to 64 frames at a time. After transmitting a burst, they will wait for an acknowledgment from the receiving end. This takes time. If there were only two stations on a LAN, this time would be completely wasted and total network efficiency would be low, because the LAN would often be idle. However, the two stations would have a dedicated 100Mbps LAN all to themselves.

If we add a few stations to our little LAN, things get better. It becomes possible for stations to transmit frames when other stations are busy waiting for incoming data, waiting for acknowledgment, or processing data they have already received. With just two stations, there will rarely be any collisions, but as we add stations, it is inevitable that there will be a few. However, the number of collisions will remain small in proportion to the number of frames successfully transmitted.

As the LAN starts to become populated, contention and collisions will begin to occur more often as more nodes are trying to share the LAN. The percentage of collisions in relation to successfully transmitted frames will go up. This isn't bad. It's just a natural result of many nodes sharing the same LAN. This measure is called the **collision percentage.** The collision percentage of a Fast Ethernet LAN is an extremely poor measure to use for network performance and has very little correlation to how well your LAN is operating. Fortunately, there is another, much better performance metric.

Over any given period of time on any particular Fast Ethernet LAN, some number of data bytes will be transmitted. When this number is divided into the maximum possible throughput of Fast Ethernet, we get a number called **network utilization,** which is a ratio that indicates how efficiently the LAN is being used over a given period of time. This is a much better way to measure how well a Fast Ethernet LAN is operating, for it takes into account all the operational factors, not just collisions. Another way to define network utilization is as the amount of bandwidth actually used for useful data transfer over a given period of time.

Network utilization is a good measure of total LAN performance. For busy Fast Ethernet and Ethernet systems, a network utilization of 30 percent is considered to be a good target. Some LANs may run higher than this; some may run a little lower. There is no absolute value of network utilization that is good or bad. However, using network utilization as a measure of network performance has another problem: It depends on the time frame over which it is measured.

For example, if you measured your network utilization during the busiest time of day, let's say about 10:00 A.M. to 11:00 A.M., you may find that it averages about 30 percent. However, as lunch rolls around, it may fall off to 10 percent to 15 percent. This isn't bad, but merely because everyone has gone to lunch and the LAN is idle much more of the time. In this case, network utilization is low because there is a low offered load to the LAN.

A network manager must know the system and understand the usage patterns of the LAN. Network performance can then be measured in relation to historical data. For example, a network manager may know that late afternoon is a LAN's busiest time because the sales team is updating the sales database. In other words, this is the time with the highest offered load. When the network is first set up, the network manager has no idea what the network utilization should be, though the 30-percent target is a good start.

Over the first week or two of the network's operation, the network manager will use network management tools to measure utilization during the peak network usage times. The first day may be 31 percent and the second 32 percent. This looks good, but on the third day it jumps to 38 percent, then 37 percent, 36 percent, 39 percent, and finally 38 percent on the seventh day. It turns out that the initial 31 percent and 32 percent numbers were low and 37 percent to 38 percent network utilization is a good target, not 30 percent.

This technique is called **baselining** and is discussed in Chapter 14. The best way to monitor network utilization is to track it over time and watch for changes. Any significant changes in network utilization should be correlated with changes in users' behavior or changes in network configuration. For example, adding two salespeople may cause network utilization to fall a little bit. This is to be expected. However, if nothing changes and network utilization falls significantly, there may be a network problem that needs to be discovered.

The key idea here is that networks are often complex and very dynamic, and should be monitored on a regular basis. Small changes in configuration or user behavior can cause large changes in network utilization.

Offered Load and Network Performance

Offered load is the amount of data, or frames, that the network is being asked to carry. Another way to look at it is: The offered load is the demand for throughput that the users are currently placing on the LAN, or simply how much traffic needs to travel over a LAN at any point in time. This is in contrast to network utilization, which is a measure of how much traffic is actually traveling over a LAN over a given period of time. It's important to realize that these two things are entirely different.

Unfortunately, it is very difficult to exactly measure offered load. There is no such thing as an offered load meter or offered load MIB, or any other way built into workstations or servers to measure offered load. This is really too bad, because if we had a direct measure of offered load then designing networks would be much easier. We could just build networks that would handle the offered load 80 percent of the time and everyone would be happy. While it is almost impossible to measure, it is pretty easy to illustrate the concept: For example, at night, a single server with a tape backup may back up itself and three other servers. Of course, backing up itself doesn't take up much bandwidth if the tape drive is attached directly to the server, but backing up the other servers must be done over the Fast Ethernet network. This can take a long period of time, easily four to five hours. More importantly, it can really make network utilization, gross throughput, and frames per second skyrocket because the network is being used by only two machines. The server with the tape backup will be reading data from the other servers as fast as they can deliver it over the network.

In this case the offered load is 12.2 megabytes per second, as the source server is asking the network to transmit as much data as it can. The source server is simply transmitting data as fast as the CSMA/CD mechanism and 100Mbps baud rate will allow. Most of the data is also going one way, from the source server to the backup server. In this situation there will be very few collisions and network utilization will be extremely high—network utilizations of 60 to 80 percent are achievable.

In contrast, several graphics art designers may come back from lunch at the same time and each sit down and load the large graphics files they were working on before lunch. Instead of one server, there are three, one for each small design group. When each user opens its file, its workstations are in essence telling the server, Hey! Send me that file as fast as you can! Now three servers are trying to fulfill multiple file load requests. Each one will attempt to transmit multimegabytes of data to users' workstations as fast as they can. They will be limited only by the speed of the Fast Ethernet LAN.

In this scenario, *three* servers are each trying to send files to several workstations as fast as possible, making the offered load 3 × 12.2Mbps or 36.6Mbps. Of course, a Fast Ethernet LAN can deliver data only at an absolute maximum of 12.2Mbps at 100-percent network utilization. If there are six users, each trying to open 5-megabyte graphics files (small ones) and network utilization was running 30 percent, it would take just over eight seconds for everyone's files to be loaded, as shown in the following equation:

$$8.33 = \frac{5 megabytes' \ 6 users}{30\%' \ 12.2 Mbps}$$

This scenario assumes that the servers are big Pentium boxes with lots of RAM, fast SCSI disks, and PCI Fast Ethernet NICs, which make the network the bottleneck, not the servers.

Of course, both of these examples are extreme and were contrived to illustrate the point of offered load. Most of the time, the offered load will not be so obvious. Users do different things all the time in patterns that are not obvious or consistent. The point is that network performance is a function of both network utilization and offered load. If a network is not busy, it will be fast, because the offered load is less than the capacity of the network. Believe it or not, this is the usual range in which most networks operate, and the range in which you want your network to operate. There is a simple rule that takes all of this into account: A network is operating well when both its offered load and network utilization are high. The point at which utilization no longer rises with increasing offered load is called **full utilization.** This definition takes all factors into account: capacity, collisions, protocol efficiency, and user demands for bandwidth. Figure 6.3 illustrates this point.

As offered load starts to increase from 0, network utilization will rise correspondingly. At some point, the LAN will reach full utilization. If the offered load continues to increase, network utilization on the LAN will drop due to contention. If it increases even further, the LAN will reach its saturation point and utilization will fall off sharply, a phenomenon called **Ethernet collapse** and something for which Ethernet was criticized by purveyors of other technologies, such as Token Ring and 100VG AnyLAN, which do not collapse. (However, they do have similar problems.)

Ethernet collapse is like the bogeyman; it is used to scare people. Statements like, It is easy to make a CSMA/CD network collapse, or, I've seen Ethernet networks collapse all the time! are very common in the gray world of news groups, users' groups, and poorly written magazine articles. The fact of the matter is that collapsing a CSMA/CD LAN is actually pretty hard to do for any length of time. On really huge collision domains it is possible and may happen sometimes, but it is not a disaster and it does not plague most, or even many, CSMA/CD LANs.

Ethernet collapse is another way of saying that any network has a performance limit. This is true for all networking technologies, not just Fast

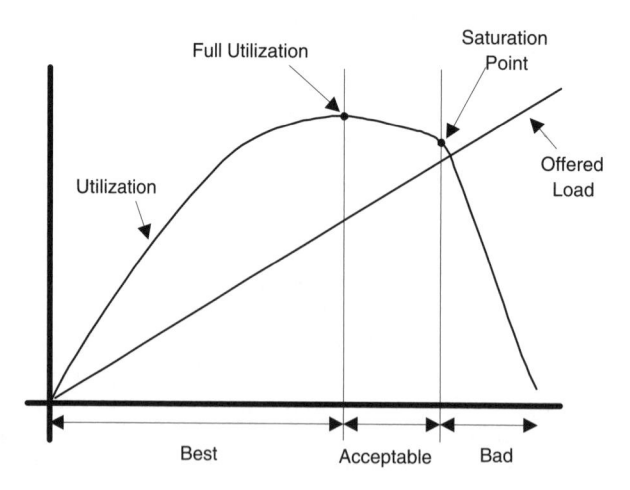

Figure 6.3
The peak-performance point.

Ethernet. When a CSMA/CD network is presented with an overwhelming load, it will saturate. It's that simple.

Another interesting term that is commonly used is **overload.** Often people will say, My network is overloaded. This is a really fuzzy term that isn't well defined. We like to define this term like this: A CSMA/CD LAN is overloaded if it can't run at full utilization or better at least 80 percent of the time.

This definition for overload is not commonly used but it is a good *practical* definition because it fits in with the phone-call metric. If your network isn't overloaded, then you probably won't get too many phone calls from unhappy users.

Often, people on the Usenet group comp.dcom.lans.ethernet will ask, When does a CSMA/CD network become overloaded? The honest answer is: It depends—and it really does. It depends on the offered load, which is a value that is practically impossible to measure (with today's tools). There will be a point on every CSMA/CD LAN where it becomes saturated.

A good goal for network design is to build a system that runs in the best range most of the time and in the acceptable range some of the time, and rarely becomes saturated. This is also the idea behind measuring network performance by baselining. For more on this topic see Chapter 14 on baselining.

Network Management

Network management is a critical tool that is essential to keeping anything but the smallest networks running at peak efficiency. Without network management, such statistics as collision counts, bytes transferred, frames transmitted and received, and other information could not be easily obtained from such devices as repeaters, switches, and network interfaces.

Many early networking devices, such as repeaters, were just simple hardware devices and didn't collect any statistics at all. Later devices were smart and had a small microprocessor, often called a **device controller** or just a controller, which was interfaced to the hardware. Controllers in early repeaters could gather statistics from the hardware and make them available to a network manager. By communicating to the controller, a network manager could both review statistics and control the device. For example, repeater ports could be enabled and disabled.

Some devices, such as routers and bridges, inherently relied on a CPU. In these devices, the CPU performed double duty: It not only performed the device's function, such as routing or bridging, it was also the device's controller.

This was all well and good except for one problem. The user interface for the devices was often extremely crude. Most had only a simple command-line interface that made even early versions of DOS look sophisticated by comparison. To communicate with these devices, a dumb terminal was usually connected to a serial port. This was better than nothing, but had the disadvantage that the network administrator had to physically go to the device and plug in the terminal in order to gain access, which made the regular gathering of network statistics a real pain. This kind of access is often called **out of band** access because it is not done over the network.

Later devices could be communicated with via a remote terminal session over the network using a program and protocol called Telnet, which allowed a network administrator to communicate with devices over the network from one central location—a big advantage. After the first Telnet-enabled devices hit the market, this feature became standard. This kind of access is often called **in band** access, as it is done over the network.

A couple of problems still existed, the first being that each manufacturer had a different interface. There were no standards. Many manufacturers didn't even have consistent interfaces on all their own devices. As you can imagine, this didn't make the network manager's job any easier.

In 1988 a protocol for communicating to devices and a standard for defining data objects, called the **Simple Network Management Protocol,** or SNMP, was proposed by the Internet Activities Board (IAB). The first document was RFC 1067 (RFCs are documents published by the IAB, which both propose and define Internet standards), which was later updated by RFC 1098 and then RFC 1157. (There are numerous repositories of RFCs on the Web. For more information see our Web site (www.wiley.com/FastEthernet). The IAB also defined a method of describing data called the **Abstract Syntax Notation 1,** or ASN.1, format.

SNMP is a standard and open protocol used to read statistics and other information from a device. It can also be used to send data to a device. SNMP is an application-level protocol that commonly runs over IP but can also be used with IPX and other network-level protocols.

Data objects and structures in a networking device or component are described using the ASN.1 format. These descriptions are stored in simple ASCII text files, each called a **Management Information Base,** or MIB. An MIB describes the data objects and structures in a device or component, which can be retrieved and/or modified using the SNMP protocol. When a device supports data described by an MIB and the SNMP protocol, it is said to be **managed.**

For example, when using SNMP, the number of frames transmitted and received on any given port can be retrieved from a repeater. Devices can also be controlled; any port on a managed repeater can be turned on or off. These are very simple examples but quite useful by themselves.

Managed devices often support extremely complex MIBs that provide very detailed information about their operation and allow a fine degree of control over the device.

When a device, such as a repeater, is managed, it runs some software internally on its controller, which is called an **SNMP Agent,** or often just an agent. A device's agent communicates with the hardware, maintains the device's data objects and structures, and responds to SNMP requests to either read or write data. Note that the agent doesn't directly use an MIB file, which is a description of the data objects supported by the agent itself.

Agents do not have to be in a device like a repeater or switch; operating systems for workstations and servers, such as UNIX, Windows NT, Windows 95, and NetWare, all support SNMP agents. These agents collect all kinds of data about the system on which they are running. UNIX vendors, Microsoft, and especially Novell have been very creative in the features that their agents support.

The term *MIB* can sometimes be confusing, as it is often used as an equivalent term for an agent. For example, Alfred E. Newman might say, I read the collision counts from the repeater's MIB and they don't look too good. What Alfred really means is that he read the collision counts from the device itself, not the ASCII MIB text file. However ambiguous, this kind of usage is common and is well accepted as normal.

The other piece to any network management system is the **Network Management Station** (NMS). Often these are called Network Management Applications or Consoles. An NMS is usually a software package that runs on a workstation running Windows NT, Windows 95, or UNIX. NMSs use SNMP to communicate with managed devices and provide a graphical interface that allows a user to easily read and interpret data read from managed devices. NMSs also allow the user to control managed devices.

The SNMP protocol is really very simple. It consists of commands and responses. An NMS sends a command to a device, and the device responds (see Figure 6.4).

The SNMP protocol supports only three types of commands. These are all that an NMS can use, or needs, to communicate with a device's agent:

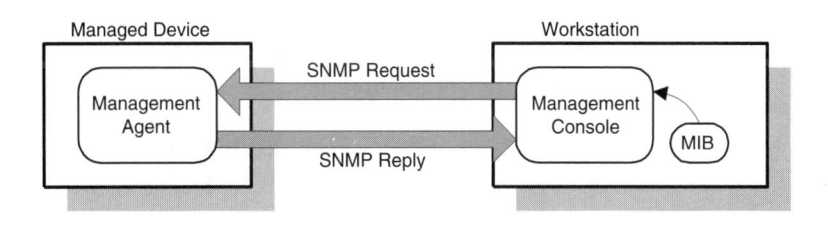

Figure 6.4
Network management.

Command	Purpose
GET	Reads the value of one or more data objects from a device. The GET command can get MIB values from a device in any order.
GET NEXT	Used to sequentially read the values of data objects in a device. The next value is the one after the last value retrieved using a GET or a GET NEXT command.
SET	Used to change the value of data objects in a device. It's essentially a write command.

SNMP commands and responses are encoded into a **Protocol Data Unit** (PDU). A PDU is the definition of the data portion of an IP datagram used to carry an SNMP command or response. (For more information on datagrams, see Chapter 13 on Routers and Protocols.) An SNMP PDU can be transported over other protocols as well, such as IPX, DECNet, and SNA.

SNMP also has another purpose, device independence. Not all devices or computers store data in the same format. SNMP solves this problem by defining how data values are encoded in PDUs. The SNMP encoding method is truly device independent and allows any two devices or computers to communicate with each other using SNMP, which is one of the reasons that the use of SNMP has become so widespread.

Often, protocols, interfaces, and other technological standards get to be standards because a manufacturer had the vision to create and promote them. Often the first company to do something is the company that defines the *de facto* standard, which is often less than ideal. Many *de facto* standards are specific to the equipment of the manufacturer that created it, which often makes it difficult for other companies to create compatible equipment or software. The IBM PC was a *de facto* standard, and it was several years before Compaq came along and created a PC which was truly compatible.

SNMP didn't happen this way. Engineers who were members of the IAB saw that a network management standard was necessary, and instead of waiting for a company to define it, they created SNMP. The SNMP protocol was rapidly adopted by almost everyone because it worked very well. It was easy to implement, small, and most of all, universal.

The other key component to network management is the MIB. Managed devices themselves do not use MIB files. An MIB is used (or read) by NMSs and are simply catalogs and concise descriptions of data objects supported by a particular device. An NMS cannot communicate to a managed device until it knows that data objects that device supports. It does this by reading in one or more MIBs. Once it knows what MIBs are supported by a device, the NMS can fully manage the device.

There are two types of MIBs: standard MIBs and enterprise MIBs. Standard MIBs are defined by the IAB. Enterprise MIBs are defined by the manufacturer of a device. The IAB has defined a few standard MIBs that most devices can or should support. Some of the more common are:

MIB Name	Purpose
MIB-II	Specified by RFC 1213, defines a set of data objects that can be used to manage a single network interface.
Repeater MIB	Specified by RFC 1516 and is a subset of MIB-II. It defines data objects that can be used to manage a repeater.
Bridge MIB	Specified by RFC 1493 and is also a subset of MIB-II. It defines data objects that can be used to manage a bridge.
RMON MIB	Specified by RFC 1271 and defines data objects that can be used to manage an entire network. For Fast Ethernet a network is a collision domain.

These MIBs contain a lot of useful data that can be retrieved about network interfaces, repeaters, bridges, and entire networks. The MIB-II, repeater, and bridge MIBs are closely related and contain objects specific to a network interface or device. For example, using MIB-II, an NMS can read the total number of frames transmitted by a network interface. Using the repeater MIB, an NMS can read the number of collisions on a port, and disable and enable individual ports. Using the bridge MIB, an NMS can actually read the bridge's address table and set aging parameters.

The RMON MIB is especially interesting. It contains data objects describing information about an entire network, not just a single device. For Fast Ethernet an RMON MIB will contain the data about a specific collision domain, so a network manager can find out the total number of broadcasts transmitted on a single segment or the total number of bytes of data transmitted on the segment. The RMON MIB also defines a method to keep historical data about a segment. For example, it can be used to calculate the network utilization for a segment over the last several hours.

The data objects in MIB-II and its associated MIBs are maintained by such devices as repeaters, switches, and routers. However, the data objects in the RMON MIB are often maintained by a device called an RMON probe. A probe is usually a device with one or more ports, where each port connects to a network segment and operates in promiscuous mode, allowing the probe to gather statistics about all the traffic that is transmitted on the segment to which it is attached. The entire purpose of the probe is to collect the data described by the RMON MIB. Often RMON probes are built into other devices, such as switches and repeaters.

Enterprise MIBs are defined in the same way as standard MIBs, by using the ASN.1 format. However, enterprise MIBs are defined and provided by the manufacturer of a device and not the IAB. Using an enterprise MIB an NMS can access data objects in a device not provided for in one of the standard MIBs. This lets manufacturers build powerful network management features into a device in a standard way. Many companies sell, or give away for free, very sophisticated graphical front ends for their managed devices. This completely hides the MIB and the SNMP protocol from the user, and makes managing them extremely easy. Often these graphical front ends, called **product interfaces,** will work with larger, enterprise-level NMS packages.

Enterprise-level NMS packages can be very powerful (and expensive). Companies such as Hewlett-Packard, Sun Microsystems, IBM, Intel, Novell, and Network General all sell enterprise-level software. These NMSs are designed to manage networks with hundreds and thousands of individually managed devices. Many of these can automatically baseline a network and calculate network utilization. Some even have artificial intelligence engines that can automatically detect and diagnose many common network problems.

Network management is an important tool for networks that reach any size at all. Standards bodies such as the IAB are adding new standard MIBs for such purposes as asset management, performance analysis, and control of Web servers. Network management can be used to both troubleshoot and monitor an active network. A well-setup network management system can make a network manger's life much easier and allow even a large network to be run and managed by a small number of people.

CHAPTER 7

Frame Switching, Routing, and Protocols

Frame switching (or just switching) is a technique that has been widely used in Ethernet networks and plays an extremely useful role in building Fast Ethernet systems. It is performed by devices usually called switches. A switch can be used for several purposes in a Fast Ethernet LAN to:

- Overcome Fast Ethernet Topology limitations
- Segment a Fast Ethernet network into smaller pieces
- Provide higher network performance for specific nodes

Switching can be a complex topic. A lot of industry lore surrounds this technology—some of it true and some of it pure FUD (fear, uncertainty, and doubt)—and much of it corporate salesdroid hype, marketeering misinformation, and specmanship. In short, lots of companies are trying to convince people that their switching solutions are the answer to their networking prayers.

As with Fast Ethernet, a good fundamental understanding of switching and how it works goes a long way to helping you decide if you need switching, and if you do, what to purchase and how to implement it. Understanding where switches came from and how they were initially developed is a good start in explaining how they work.

Switching is a technology that evolved directly from bridging, so understanding bridges is essential to understanding switches. The first switch was introduced in early 1991 by Kalpana Corporation, and quickly became a sensation. Early switches were simple devices and were extremely fast, but still simple, learning bridges. As time progressed, switches became more complex. Switches that began shipping in late 1995 were full featured, very fast multiport bridges. By late 1996, switches that reached the market had all the features and functionality of a bridge, but had additional features that were made possible only by innovative, high-speed switching architectures.

Bridges

10Mbps Ethernet systems often become overloaded. In other words, their offered load is high and their network utilization is low, usually due to having too many users on a single segment, which often causes excessive contention for access to the LAN, resulting in enough collisions to make network utilization (performance) suffer. Excessive collisions can also be caused by a change in the networked applications being used. For example, moving to a client/server database system or groupware package, such as Lotus Notes, can bring about new demands for network bandwidth, causing network performance to suffer.

Before switching technology was developed, the solution to this was to split the overloaded Ethernet segments into two or more separate segments, a technique often called **segmenting** or **partitioning**. Although this proved to be a straightforward solution, it was (and still is) rare that a single network could be segmented into separate unconnected individual LANs. When an Ethernet segment is partitioned, there almost always has to be some kind of connectivity between the new segments. Individual Ethernet segments can be connected to each other in two ways:

- With a router, or
- With a bridge.

In the 1980s to even the early 1990s, routers tended to be large, expensive devices that were difficult to set up and maintain. They also required that a routed protocol such as TCP/IP or IPX be used. In the PC world this was often not practical, because NetBEUI was the prevalent protocol and could not be routed. In addition, early routers were often slow. They didn't have enough bandwidth to keep up with normal network traffic. Due to these factors, routers were rarely used just to connect Ethernet segments at a local site.

Routers also have another characteristic that makes them less suitable for merely providing local connectivity between Ethernet (or Fast Ethernet) segments: They are not transparent devices. Each node must be aware of the routers that are used to connect it to other LAN segments or to a WAN. For the TCP/IP protocol, this means that each node must be set up by hand to support routing. Protocols such as IPX automatically discover routers and require no manual setup.

Bridges on the other hand are simpler devices specifically designed to solve these types of connectivity problems. Bridges have been around since the early days of Ethernet networking, and are the primary devices used to connect two or more Ethernet segments. Usually bridges are two port devices, each port connecting to an Ethernet segment. However, bridges can have more than two ports; counts of three and four are common. Figure 7.1 shows three segments connected by a bridge.

When two or more Ethernet segments are bridged together, each segment remains a separate collision domain. However, the bridge operates in a way that allows the nodes on the separate segments to communicate as if they were still on the same collision domain. In other words, from the node's perspective, the entire bridged network still looks and behaves like a single LAN. For example, in Figure 7.1 Node **A** can communicate with nodes **M** through **R** on segment Beta the same way it communicates with nodes **B** through **F** on its own segment. This is due to the singlemost important characteristic of a bridge—it is a *transparent device*, meaning the nodes on each segment are not aware that each exists.

A bridge is also a *Layer-2 device*, as it operates on *frames* and not *packets*. Unlike a repeater, which only operates on packets, which are merely streams of bits, a bridge receives and transmits frames, and interprets and operates on the elements in a frame.

Bridges allow a network manager to split a single Ethernet segment into two segments connected by a bridge without disturbing the users or

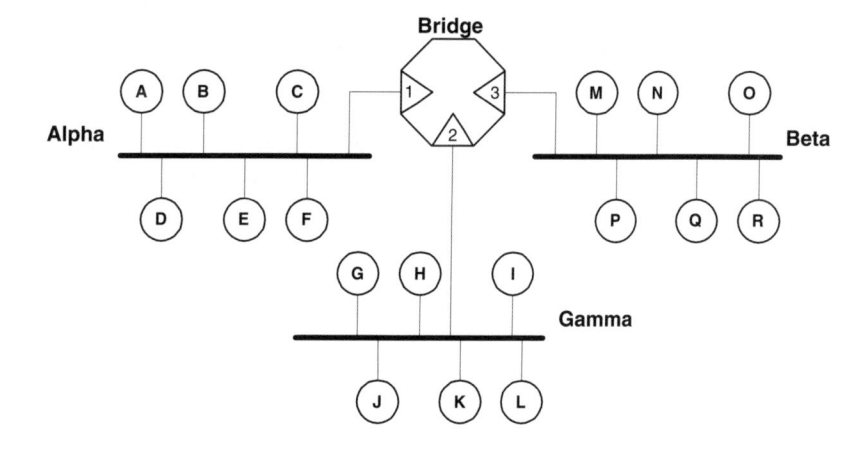

Figure 7.1
A three-port bridge.

reconfiguring or modifying the nodes in any way. As you can imagine, this is a really handy characteristic and allows a network's configuration to change over time with little if any impact on the users.

Conceptually, a bridge operates very simply. Let's take node **A** in Figure 7.1 as an example. Any frame that is transmitted by **A** with a destination address of a node on segment Beta (**Q**, for example) is received by the bridge on port 1 and transmitted out port 2, and thus can be received by **Q**. This is a process called **forwarding**. A frame is said to be forwarded when it is received on one bridge port and transmitted out another.

Conversely, a frame transmitted by **A**, with a destination address of node **B**, is naturally received by *both* node **B** and the bridge. However, the bridge knows that **B** is on the same segment as **A**, so it is not forwarded. This is a process called **filtering**. A frame is said to be filtered when it is received on one bridge port and *not* forwarded to another port.

> Note that we are using the term *frame* and not *packet*. A bridge is a Layer-2 device and operates on frames, not on packets like a repeater. A bridge is frame-aware and understands MAC addresses. On the other hand, a repeater is not frame-aware. It understands only packets, which encapsulate frames. The ports on a bridge are regular network interfaces with MACs, just like a node. In fact, a bridge is a node with multiple network interfaces.

Frame forwarding and filtering is the advantage and purpose of bridging. The only network traffic that needs to be forwarded are frames that are transmitted with a destination address of a node on a physical segment different from that of the sender. This kind of traffic is sometimes called **intersegment traffic**. Frames that have a destination and source address of nodes on the same bridge port (i.e., on the same physical LAN segment) can be filtered. This kind of traffic is called **intrasegment traffic.**

> For the sake of clarity, we have made up a couple of terms to replace the *inter* and *intra* phrases that somehow came into use. We call interlan traffic **off-segment** traffic, and intralan traffic **local-segment** traffic, which, if you think about it, is much easier to work with.

Segmenting an Ethernet system with bridges is effective when there is more, usually much more, local-segment traffic than off-segment traffic. This brings up one of the most common unwritten rules of thumb in networking: the **80/20 rule** (actually quite a lot has been written about the 80/20 rule but it's still considered a rule of thumb). The 80/20 rule says a network system should be designed and built so that at least 80 percent of the traffic is local-segment traffic. Of course this leaves 20 percent as off-segment traffic. When the 80/20 rule is met, bridges are very effective. Meeting the 80/20 rule is usually accomplished by merely putting the servers that users use most on the same segment as the users.

A bridge is able to filter and forward network traffic because it does two things:

- Each port runs in promiscuous mode.
- The bridge learns the address on each port.

Since each bridge port operates in promiscuous mode, it receives every frame transmitted on each connected segment. This is the key to the operation of a bridge. When a frame is received on a bridge port, the bridge decides whether to forward it or filter it. This choice is possible because a bridge learns the addresses that are on the segments connected to each port. Like CSMA/CD, this is more easily described with a flowchart, shown in Figure 7.2.

A bridge keeps a table, called the **MAC Address Table** (or just address table), of all the source MAC addresses and port pairs. When a frame is received on a port (the **inbound port**), the bridge looks to see if the frame's source address is in the table. If it is not, an entry containing the source address and the inbound port is added to the table. This process is called **Address Learning** (often just learning). The bridge will learn a network interface's MAC address and bridge port number from *any* frame that is transmitted by a node, because all frames (unicast, multicast, and broadcast) contain the unicast address of the network interface, and thus the node, that sent the frame. A bridge works by maintaining a one-to-one mapping of network interface addresses to bridge ports in a table. In other words, a bridge learns what port each node is either directly or indirectly connected to.

> It is common to use the terms *node* and *network interface* interchangeably. For example, it is easier to say (and type) *node address* than *network interface address*. This is usually not confusing because most nodes (like computers and printers) have only one network interface. Rarely do the network interface and the node need to be differentiated.
>
> Bridging is one case where this distinction can be important. A bridge strictly deals with MAC addresses and port numbers. That is all it knows about. Sometimes a node may have multiple network interfaces, but a bridge is completely unaware of this. For example, servers often have two (or more) network interfaces, each connecting to a bridged network. In this case, it's meaningless and often confusing to talk about the node address.

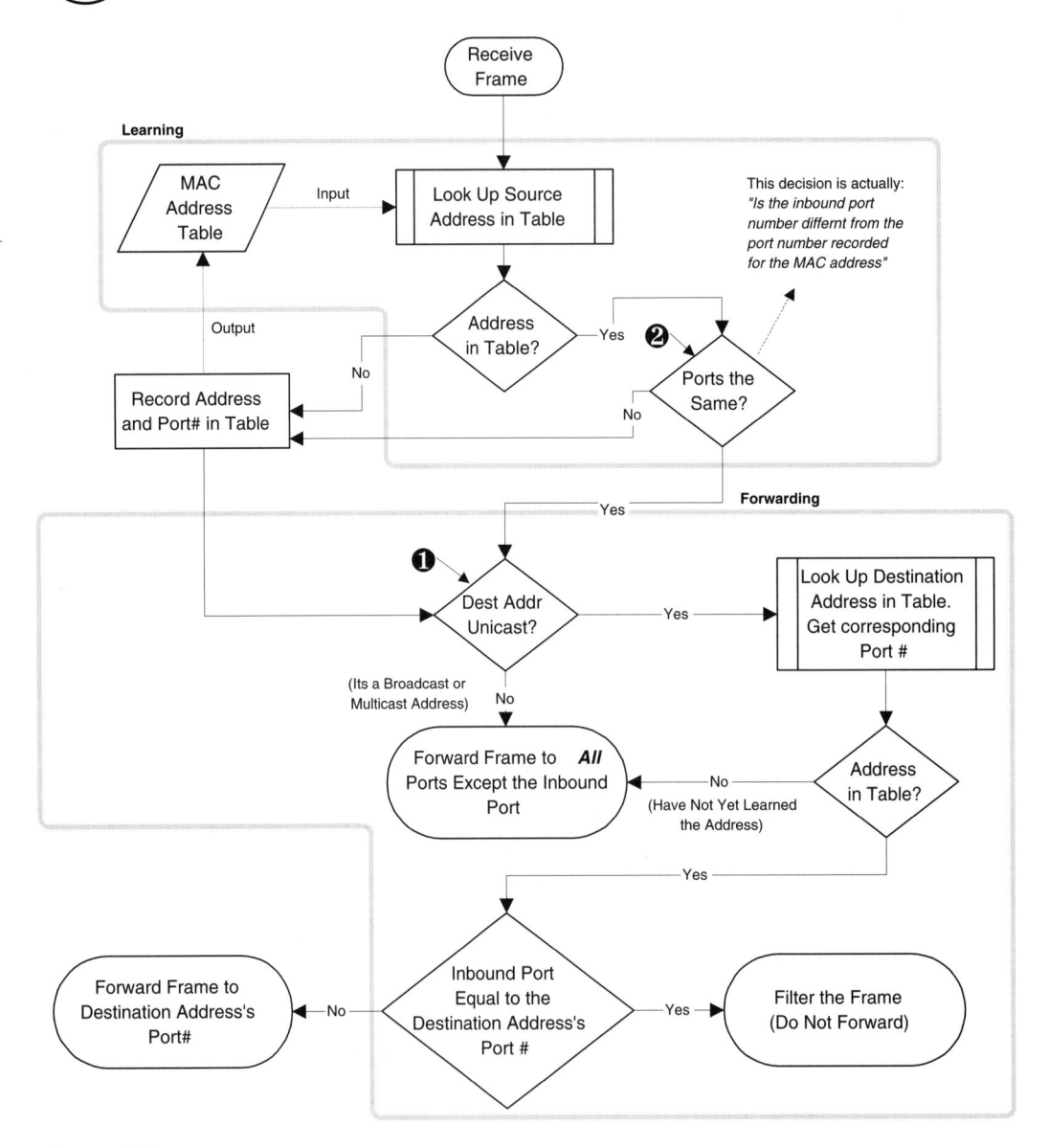

Figure 7.2
Basic bridge operation.

When the bridge is first turned on (or reset), its address table is empty, as it has not yet received any packets. Within a short period of time (usually a few seconds), a bridge will have learned most if not all of the active nodes on the segments to which it is connected. For the bridge in Figure 7.1, the MAC address table will end up looking like this:

Segment	Alpha	Beta	Gamma
MAC Address	A B C D E F	G H I J K L	M N O P Q R
Bridge Port	1 1 1 1 1 1	3 3 3 3 3 3	2 2 2 2 2 2
Age			

An address table has three fields per MAC address entry:

- The address itself
- The inbound port number on which the address was last seen
- The age of the MAC address

When a bridge learns an address, it records two things: the address itself and the inbound port number. It also sets the age of the MAC address to zero. Once per second, the age of the addresses in the table is incremented. If the age value gets to a certain value, called the **age limit,** the entry for that MAC address will be erased. This process is called **aging.**

A MAC address's age field is reset to zero anytime the bridge sees a frame with that source address. This keeps the addresses for active nodes in the table. All bridges have a maximum size for their MAC address table. If the address table fills up, then no new address can be added to it. The aging process ensures that if a node is disconnected from its segment, its entry is removed from the table. This also ensures that bridges will properly relearn the address of nodes when they are moved from one segment to another. The 802.1D specification for bridges recommends the default aging time of 300 seconds (5 minutes).

Generally, a bridge will learn all of the MAC addresses on its connected segments quite quickly, because most nodes do not sit passively on the network, never transmitting frames. This is especially true for today's Windows 95 and NT machines, which transmit quite regularly for many purposes, such as checking for new e-mail, updating directory lists for open windows, and keeping an active server session open.

All modern protocols, including TCP/IP, IPX, NetBEUI, AppleTalk, and DECNet, use broadcast (or multicast) frames for discovery. Since almost all network operations begin with a broadcast-based discovery process, a bridge will quickly learn the addresses on a LAN.

There is another interesting and important aspect to the learning algorithm: At spot ❷ in the flowchart (see Figure 7.2), the bridge has figured out that the address is in the table, but it still needs to check to see if the inbound port number for the source address is the same as the one recorded in the address table. If they are different, then the address and port number are rerecorded in the table, so a node can be moved from segment to segment, and the bridge (or bridges) can keep up with the location of the node.

The address table is used by the bridge's forwarding and filtering mechanism. When a frame is received, the bridge will go through the learning process for that frame, then figure out what to do with it.

The first thing to note about forwarding is that broadcast and multicast frames are forwarded out on *all* the bridge's ports except the inbound port. This is called **flooding** or **spraying.** When a frame is flooded, it is forwarded from its incoming port to all the other ports. Broadcast and multicast frames must be flooded because bridges are transparent devices: Their presence is (and must be) invisible to the nodes on the network. A bridge must forward broadcast and unicast frames, as the intent of the sender is that multiple stations should receive that frame. In short, a bridge will forward broadcast frames to all ports because they are destined for all nodes. A bridge will forward a multicast frame to all ports because there is no way for it to know what stations are listening for that address. This is why the nodes on a bridged network can't tell the difference between a bridged network and a single collision domain.

Often a bridged network is called a broadcast domain in contrast to a collision domain. A **broadcast domain** is the set of all nodes on a set of collision domains that will receive each other's broadcasts. For example, in Figure 7.1, nodes (A–F), (H–M), and (N–S) are on different collision domains, but are in the same broadcast domain. Since all the nodes on a bridged network are on the same broadcast domain, normal LAN services, such as server discovery and booting, work as if all the nodes were on a single collision domain.

Unicast frames are forwarded in a completely different manner. When a unicast frame is received by a bridge, the frame's unicast destination address is looked up in the address table. Based on the result, one of three forwarding decisions can be made, as follows:

Lookup Result	*Forwarding Decision*
1 The address is not found in the table.	The frame is forwarded to all ports (flooded), just like a broadcast.
2 The address is found in the table and its port number is different from the inbound port number.	The frame is forwarded only to the address's port.

3 The address is found in the table and its port number is the same as the inbound port number. — The frame is filtered. It is *not* forwarded to any port.

This process is called the **forwarding decision** and is made for every frame a bridge receives on an active port. The first forwarding decision is very important, and is one of the main reasons why a bridge is truly a transparent device. It is quite possible for a node to send a unicast frame to a node on another bridge port before the other node has been revealed by transmitting a frame. For example, node **A** may send a unicast packet to node **Q** before the bridge has learned that **Q** is on port 3. Until the bridge learns where **Q** is, it must forward all unicast packets from **A** to **Q** to ports 2 *and* 3. Usually this will happen very quickly, as **Q** will probably respond to **A**'s first packet.

Why would this happen? is a common question, and it has a simple answer. The aging process can remove entries from the address table while an active node is merely quiet. A networked printer is a good example. A printer is basically a passive device. As long as nobody needs to print, it is quiet and does not transmit any frames. If it's quiet for longer than the aging time, then the bridge will forget where it is. When someone needs to print, it is possible that the print server will send a directed frame to the printer. When this occurs, the bridge must flood that frame since it doesn't know on which port the printer is attached.

All bridges operate just like this, or in a very similar fashion. Some bridges have nifty features that allow the forwarding decision to be made using more complex rules. For example, it is common to set up a bridge to forward only some types of broadcast frames and always filter others. Many bridges also allow entries in the address table to be entered manually. These are called **static entries** and never age out of the table.

It's often the case that a single bridge is not sufficient to allow a large network to be segmented as needed. Since bridges are truly transparent devices, multiple bridges can be used in a bridged network. For example, two more segments, Epsilon and Delta, could be added to the network system in Figure 7.1 by bridging from segment Gamma (see Figure 7.3).

This network operates properly because frames can flow through multiple bridges to get from their sources to their destinations. A frame traveling from **A** to **X** is forwarded from bridge 1 to bridge 2 in order to get from segment Alpha to segment Epsilon. The following shows how the frame travels from **A** to **X**:

From	In	Out	In	Out	To
Node A	Bridge 1 Port 1	Bridge 1 Port 2	Bridge 2 Port 1	Bridge 3 Port 3	Node X

Figure 7.3
Multiple bridges.

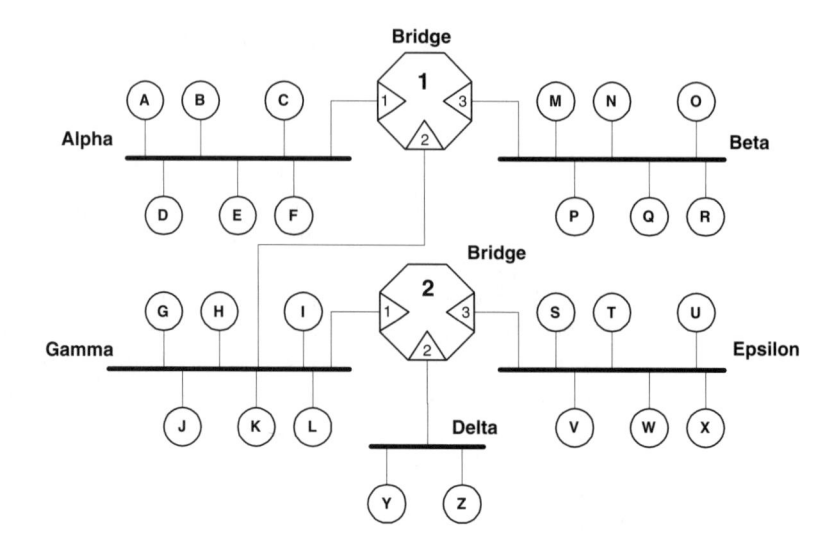

This works because bridges 1 and 2 both learn the network. From a learning and forwarding standpoint, the two bridges don't know about each other. From bridge 1's perspective, segments Gamma, Epsilon, and Delta are on port 2. From bridge 2's standpoint, segments Alpha, Beta, and Gamma are on port 1. Bridge 1 and 2's address tables look like this:

Segment	Alpha	Gamma	Beta	Epsilon	Delta
MAC Address	A B C D E F	G H I J K L	M N O P Q R	S T U V W X	Y Z
Bridge #1	1 1 1 1 1 1	3 3 3 3 3 3	2 3 2 2 2 2	2 2 2 2 2 2	2 2
Bridge #2	1 1 1 1 1 1	1 1 1 1 1 1	1 1 1 1 1 1	3 3 3 3 3 3	2 2

Broadcasts are not treated any differently. A broadcast from node **A** is forwarded out bridge 1 ports 2 and 3. This broadcast will reach bridge 2 port 1 and then be forwarded out bridge 2 ports 2 and 3. The propagation of frames with unlearned addresses works the same way.

The fact that bridges are transparent allows quite complex bridged networks to be built. Everything will work fine as long as the bridge network is configured as a *tree*. This means that there must be one, and only one, active (bridged) path between any two nodes on the bridged network. If a bridged network has multiple, active paths between some or all nodes, then it is *not* a tree. These multiple paths are called **loops,** which are very bad and will cause huge confusion and broadcast storms. For example, adding a bridge between segments Alpha and Gamma yields the LAN shown in Figure 7.4. In this network, there are multiple paths between the nodes on all the segments except Delta and Epsilon. This causes three really bad problems:

Figure 7.4
Loops in a bridged network.

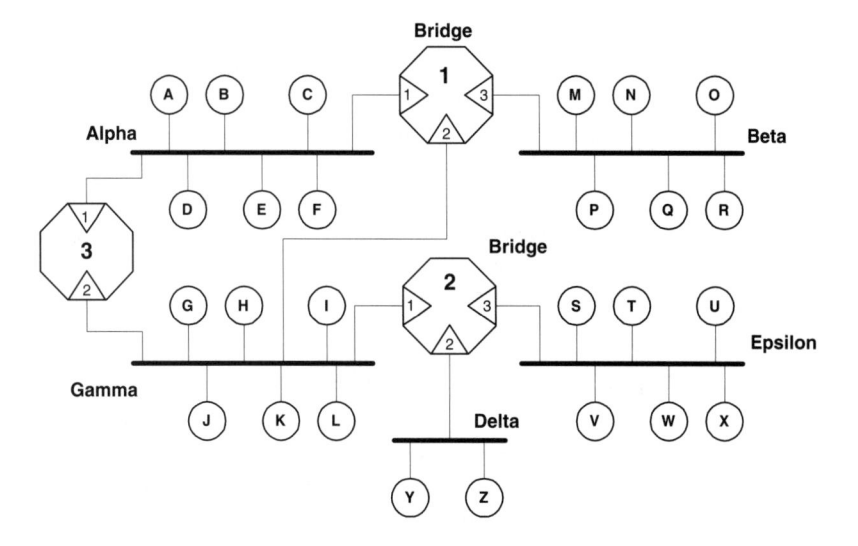

- Broadcast storms
- Learning problems
- Cloned unicast frames

The first problem (**broadcast storms**) is the worst one and will usually prevent the network from operating at all. For example, if **A** broadcasts a frame, it will be received and forwarded by both bridges 1 and 3. Both bridges will subsequently forward the frame onto segment Gamma. The problem exists when bridge 3 receives the broadcast that bridge 1 sent on its port 2. Of course, it doesn't know that and forwards the broadcast back out port 1. The broadcast that **A** originally sent is back on segment Alpha. We call this **frame cloning.** It gets worse. Bridge 1 will do the same thing with the original broadcast frame that bridge 2 forwarded. It gets worse yet. Each broadcast results in two more of the same frame being cloned. In the first round there will be 2 clone frames, then 4, then 8, then 16, and so on. This will rapidly increase until the bandwidth on all the segments is eaten up with the same broadcast frame. All this results from just one node transmitting a broadcast on just one loop.

Learning problems are almost as bad. As the broadcast frames move around the network, each bridge on the loop will see the same source address on multiple inbound ports and will continually take the Yes branch at spot ❷ in the bridge flowchart and update its address table. This makes things incredibly messy, as other unicast frames that manage to get through will be forwarded to the wrong port.

Unicast frames will also be cloned, but they won't be cloned more than once. This can also cause big problems. Network protocols are designed to receive each frame once and only once. If they receive cloned frames, they will consider it an error and attempt to recover by requesting the sending node to send the frame again. Since each unicast frame is cloned, the original sending node will get two retransmit requests and will retransmit twice.

In short, a network just cannot function when there are bridge loops. Fortunately, there is a simple, better, and *completely automatic* way to both detect and eliminate bridge loops. Besides learning and forwarding, all modern bridges have a feature called a **spanning tree.** This is an algorithm that will prune a looped network (technically called a graph) into a legal, loop-free tree.

The spanning tree algorithm is detailed in the IEEE 802.1D specification, together with the learning algorithm and a protocol that bridges use to communicate with each other. This protocol consists of a special set of multicast messages called **Bridge Protocol Data Units** (BPDUs). Bridges use BPDUs to communicate with each other and discover a network's bridged topology and detect loops. If the bridges find loops, they will cooperate to turn off selected bridge ports in order to eliminate the loops, while still maintaining a tree topology that reaches all the nodes. This type of tree is called the spanning tree (and thus the name of the algorithm). For example, the network in Figure 7.4 could be pruned as shown in Figure 7.5, in which Ports 1 and 2 on bridge 3 have been disabled. The links between bridge 3 and segments Alpha and Gamma become a backup for the links on bridge 1.

The spanning tree algorithm means that a bridged network can intentionally be built with loops. Loops are used in a network design to provide redundant backup paths between segments. Once the spanning tree is

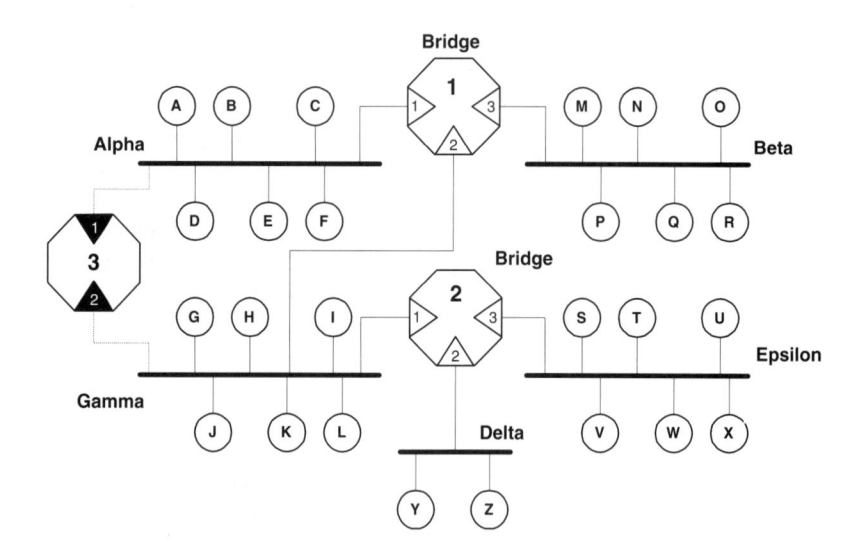

Figure 7.5
A pruned network.

computed and set up, the bridges will monitor the network to make sure that all the links of the tree are functioning. If any link that has a disabled counterpart (that would be a loop if enabled) goes down, then the backup link is enabled. This all happens fully automatically and transparently. In Figure 7.5, if either or both of the links from bridge 1 to segments Alpha and Gamma go down, the spanning tree algorithm will detect the problem and enable ports 1 and 2 on bridge 3.

> Most of the bridges available today fully support dynamic learning of addresses and the spanning tree algorithm. However, in the old days, these were considered advanced features. The earliest bridges had to have their forwarding table programmed by hand and had very low performance. Learning bridges soon became common but they were often difficult to implement, especially in larger networks. To correct this, the 802.1D standard for bridges was approved in May of 1990, and bridges supporting both address learning and the spanning tree algorithm soon became common.

Bridges are pretty conventional devices and have a simple architecture. Basically, bridges are embedded computers with two or more network interfaces. They have a CPU, some RAM, and some ROM (or Flash or EEPROM). Frames are received on each port (network interface) just as they are at any other node, such as a workstation or server. The only difference is that each port on a bridge operates in promiscuous mode. For every packet received on each active port, the CPU must examine the packet, maintain the address table, and make a forwarding decision as necessary (see Figure 7.6).

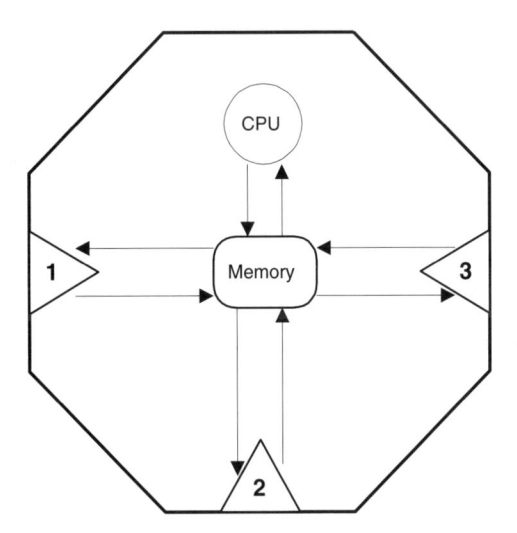

Figure 7.6
Bridge internals.

Most bridges have only one CPU, so they inherently process only one packet at a time. This is why most bridges have only two, three, or four ports. Bridges have been made with more but they are expensive and require a lot of memory and CPU processing horsepower. Bridges with multiple processors have also been built but while providing very high performance, they are extremely expensive.

By now you are asking, What does this have to do with switches? The answer is very simple. A switch is a bridge. Actually, a switch is much more than a bridge. Unlike a bridge, which has a central processor that must handle each packet one at a time, a switch has specialized hardware that allows it to handle multiple ports simultaneously. A switch provides all the advantages of a bridge with none of the drawbacks, and has significantly more performance, allowing networks to be built that were previously unfeasible at best.

Frame Switches

The first Ethernet frame switch developed by Kalpana (now a part of Cisco Systems) was a basic learning bridge. It didn't support spanning tree and it wasn't managed. It was also expensive. The Kalpana frame switch had one crowning virtue: Compared to a bridge it was very, very fast.

The Kalpana frame switch was an instant success because it gave network managers a way to segment their overloaded Ethernet networks without sacrificing performance. Even the best bridges were slow when compared to the networks to which they were attached.

> Frame switches are usually just called switches. In this book, when we talk about switches, we usually mean Fast Ethernet or Ethernet frame switches. There are actually many different kinds of switches for voice, video, ATM, and even such protocols as IP (the Internet Protocol).

Two of the common measures of bridging performance are **maximum forwarding rate** and **aggregate forwarding rate**. The maximum forwarding rate is the maximum number of packets per second that can be forwarded from one port to another. On bridges with more than two ports, this is usually measured on two ports only while the other port is idle. Most Ethernet bridges have a forwarding rate less than the maximum frame rate of Ethernet. This means that while providing connectivity, bridges can be a performance bottleneck between nodes on different segments. Some high-speed bridges have a forwarding rate that can keep up with the maximum Ethernet frame rates.

A bridge's aggregate forwarding rate is the maximum number of frames it can forward for all ports. For example, a four-port Ethernet bridge may have a maximum forwarding rate of 14,800 frames per second (the highest it can get), but have only an aggregate forwarding rate of 18,000 frames per second. This means that it cannot handle full packet rates on all its ports, but just on two. Bridges like this have a lower aggregate forwarding rate than the sum of the segments to which they are connected. These bridges are called **oversubscribed.**

The biggest problem with setting up a bridged network is arranging the bridges and the devices on the different segments so that the 80/20 rule is met. It can be a great challenge to set up a bridged network so the bridges are not a performance bottleneck. Often this is downright impossible.

Switches help solve this problem because they have a much higher aggregate forwarding rate than bridges. A switch connects multiple segments together as a bridge would, but without the performance penalties of a bridge. Early switches were only slightly oversubscribed and had high aggregate forwarding rates, which allowed them to forward frames on several ports as fast as the connected segments could deliver them. Since switches have a higher port density than bridges, they can also segment a network into smaller pieces. Switches allowed Ethernet network managers to put a smaller number of users on each segment. Fewer users on a segment means more average network bandwidth per user, so using switches can give a user on one segment access to resources on other segments with little or no performance penalty. The high port count and high aggregate forwarding rate make switching an almost perfect solution for segmenting an Ethernet LAN.

After the first Kalpana switch hit the market, switches quickly became more powerful. New switches began supporting more ports and having higher aggregate throughputs. Most modern switches support the spanning tree algorithm, and a large number of them are managed. Almost all modern switches have very high aggregate throughputs and provide the maximum possible forwarding rate on each port.

While switches function as true multiport bridges, a switch is really much more than just a bridge with lots of ports. There are three primary differences between switches and bridges:

- Switches usually have more ports than bridges. Early switches had only a few more ports than most bridges, with six or eight being common. As the technology improved, switches with 12 and 16 ports became prevalent, and switches with 24 ports were also common. Modern *enterprise-level* switches can support even more ports.

- Switches also have an internal architecture completely different from that of bridges. A switch is differentiated from a bridge because it can process multiple incoming frames at *the same time*. A switch examines frames, maintains the address table, and makes forwarding decisions for all its ports *simultaneously* or in parallel.
- A bridge's aggregate forwarding rate is determined by the horsepower of the CPU. This means there is really only one path between the ports on a bridge. In contrast, switches support receiving and transmitting multiple frames also in parallel. Switches logically have multiple paths for data flow and can receive and transmit frames on any, some, or all of their ports simultaneously.

As you can imagine, switches have huge amounts of horsepower. This frame processing power doesn't come from a big CPU, or even multiple CPUs. Some switches don't even have a CPU. Switches are specially designed devices that provide most if not all of the bridge functions using special chips, called ASICs. An ASIC is an **Application-Specific Integrated Circuit**. ASICs allow very complex, fast, and powerful electronic designs to be implemented as low-cost, high-density chips.

ASICs are wonderful devices. Ever wonder why computers get more powerful and less expensive at the same time? Remember when a 300-baud modem cost $1,200? ASICs are a big part of the reason for the ever increasing capability at lower and lower costs. ASICs are designed by a hardware engineer a lot like software is written by a software engineer. All of the logic design is done on a computer using a high-level language.

In the past, custom electronic chips were designed at the transistor level, which was a detailed, complex, and time-consuming process. To test one of these designs, the device actually had to be built, which was often very expensive. If any problems were found (and they usually were), the process had to start all over again.

The advent of ASICs changed all of that. ASICs are designed not at the transistor level, but at the logic level, using special hardware design languages. ASIC designs can also be thoroughly tested by simulation on a computer before a single physical device is created. Many ASIC designs are subsequently tested in real hardware by loading them into **Field Programmable Gate Arrays** (FPGA). An FPGA is a device consisting of a large number of logic devices (gates) that can be connected together in an almost infinite number of ways by loading an FPGA program into the device. To test an ASIC design, it is converted into an FPGA program and loaded into an FPGA that is part of an actual device, such as a switch. It can then be tested more rigorously, proving the ASIC design. The drawback to FPGAs is that they are expensive. A large FPGA can cost $10,000 or more. Many ASIC designs can be bigger than a single FPGA. An ASIC design that might fit into $50,000 of FPGAs can cost as little as $10 or $12 for the final ASIC chip.

Once an ASIC design is fully tested, it can then be turned into an actual ASIC chip. Again, this is done by an automated process, which further reduces the chance of errors and speeds up development. This process of designing with ASICs has four effects on the design of switches:

- It allows them to be designed more quickly.
- It allows more complex and powerful designs to be created.
- It allows more reliable designs to be created.
- It lets the cost of switches continually fall.

Not only do ASICs accelerate and improve the design process, ASIC technology itself is improving at a fantastic rate. The software and tools to develop ASICs get better every year. The actual electronic devices from which ASICs are created improve every few months, supporting faster, more complex designs for less cost than the previous generation. ASICs and other modern hardware and software design techniques have allowed companies to build switches that are ideal for solving many of today's network problems for both Ethernet and Fast Ethernet. There are even switches for Token Ring, 100VG AnyLAN, and FDDI; and ATM is a new technology that is only switched.

Like bridges, switches are Layer-2 devices and operate on frames, which is why they are called frame switches. A switch is a bridge and makes forwarding and filtering decisions based on a frame's destination address in the same way an old-style bridge does. However, a bridge is unlike a switch in how it physically forwards frames from one LAN segment to another. Switches provide multiple paths for frames to move from port to port, and these multiple paths are the keys to the operation of a switch. A six-port switch logically looks like the one shown in Figure 7.7.

Each port on the switch, like a port on a network interface or repeater, has a receive side and a transmit side. Each side of the ports is logically connected to a **crossbar matrix.** The receive side of each port is connected to a horizontal bar, and the transmit side to a vertical bar. When a receive bar is connected to a transmit bar, a path is created from the receive side of one port to the transmit side of another port. Any two ports can be connected in this way. For example, ports 5 and 3 are connected and ports 2 and 4 are connected. A frame can be received on incoming ports 2 and 5, and transmitted out ports 3 and 4 simultaneously.

When a frame is received on a port, the switch examines its destination address and makes a forwarding decision. If the frame needs to be forwarded, a connection is made to the appropriate port, and the frame is

Figure 7.7
A crossbar switch.

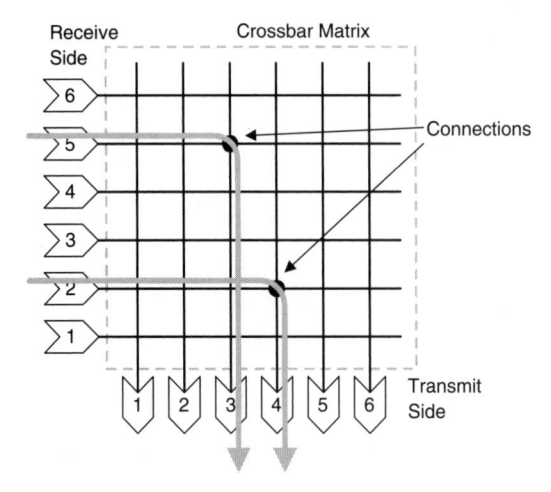

forwarded. Since there can be multiple logical paths between ports on a switch, multiple frames can be forwarded at the same time.

Figure 7.7 shows how unicast frames are forwarded from one port to another. Bridges must also forward broadcast, multicast, and unknown unicast frames to multiple ports. If a broadcast is received on port 2, then it must be forwarded to ports 1, 3, 4, 5, and 6. This is easily handled by a switch, as shown in Figure 7.8.

Figures 7.7 and 7.8 are both *logical* views of a switch in operation. All switches can be thought of as having a crossbar matrix connecting the receive and transmit sides of each port. Some switches, the first Kalpana switch among them, actually have physical crossbar devices in them. How-

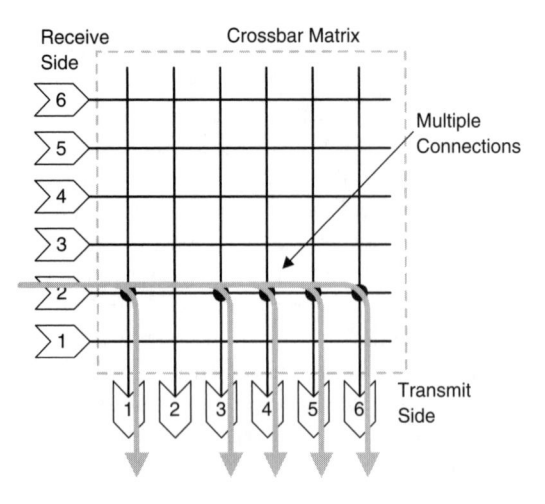

Figure 7.8
Handling a broadcast.

ever, many switches have completely different internal architectures. There are probably more switch architectures than there are companies that design and manufacture switches.

Each of these companies has designed its own architecture in an attempt to differentiate its switch from those of its competitors. The goal is to have a switch with more features and higher performance at a lower cost than the other guy. Most companies patent their switch designs and don't allow other companies to build switches the same way or charge hefty licensing fees to do so.

This, coupled with the huge demand for switches, has fostered an extremely competitive environment that has produced a truly mind-boggling array of switch designs. Due to the wide range of switch designs, it is not practical to cover switch internals in this book. Thoroughly covering two or three would give you some good insight into those designs, but none into the many other equally good designs. Discussing many designs, without getting into the details, wouldn't be much help either.

The best way to explore the internal design of switches is to begin by understanding what they must accomplish, which is, of course, bridging, and then to read manufacturers' literature and magazine articles. Most manufacturers tout the benefits of their designs and supply tutorials, white papers, and even short books on how their switches work. Most of this is available via the Web. Of course, you must take manufacturers' literature with a grain of salt, as it's often biased. After all, they are trying to convince you to purchase their product.

There are other resources as well. Many are online and accessible via the Web. For more on these, see Appendix C and the Web site associated with this book. Magazine articles are also a great source of information about switching. Often, a magazine will test several switches in head-to-head competition and report the results, usually accompanied by analyses of the switches' internal architectures.

It is impractical for us to discuss internal architecture, but it is very important to understand the three basic types of switching techniques. A switch can use one or more of three basic techniques to switch frames from one LAN segment to another:

- Cut-Through Switching
- Interim Cut-Through Switching
- Store-and-Forward Switching

All three techniques have their advantages and disadvantages. The good news is that many modern switches employ two, or even all three, of these switching methods.

Cut-Through Switching

Cut-through switching is used by many switches to provide an extremely low forward time latency. A switch's **forwarding latency** (or often just latency) is the time between two events: when the first bit of a frame is received on one port (the incoming port), and when the first bit of the frame is transmitted out another port.

Cut-through switches have extremely low forwarding latency, much lower than that of a regular bridge. Instead of waiting for a frame to be fully received, a cut-through switch will begin to actually forward a frame before all the bits of a frame are received. In other words, the bits in the front part of a frame are actually transmitted on the outgoing port while the bits in the tail end of the frame are still being received on the incoming port.

While the forwarding latency of a cut-through switch is very low, it is still much greater than the start-of-packet propagation delay in repeaters. Class-I Fast Ethernet repeaters have a start-of-packet propagation delay of about 40 to 60 bit times. A repeater always propagates an incoming frame to all the other repeater ports and does not need to examine an incoming frame in any way.

On the other hand, before a switch can make a forwarding decision, it must examine a frame's destination address. This means that it must buffer, or store, at least the first 120 bits of the frame before it can make its forwarding decision. Once the entire destination address has arrived, the switch can then make its forwarding or filtering decision (see Figure 7.9). This will also take some number of bit times (not even a switch can do things instantaneously).

Some switches can make a forwarding decision very quickly, sometimes in as little as 10 bit times (100ns). If a switch decides to forward the frame, it must construct a temporary path between the incoming port and the outgoing port. This can take another 5 to 10 bit times. In short, some switches have a forwarding latency as low as 140 to 150 bit times, or 1.4 to 1.5 µs.

After the switched frame path has been created, the switch can begin to transmit the first part of the frame that has been buffered. This means that the data portion of the frame is still being received while the preamble of the forwarded frame is being transmitted. Cut-through switching provides very low latency when frames are forwarded from one collision

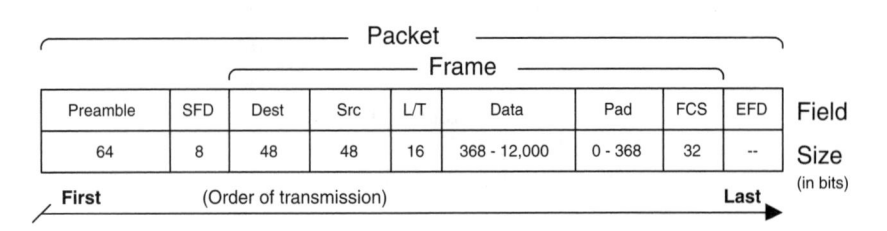

Preamble	SFD	Dest	Src	L/T	Data	Pad	FCS	EFD	Field
64	8	48	48	16	368 - 12,000	0 - 368	32	--	Size (in bits)

Figure 7.9
A packet's fields.

domain to another. As desirable as this is, cut-through switching has three major problems:

- It forwards run frames.
- It forwards error frames.
- It congests easily.

If a runt frame with at least 120 bits is received on a cut-through switch port, it may be forwarded to one or more ports. A normal bridge does not have this problem, as all frames are completely received and only frames with no errors will be forwarded. A cut-through switch forwards frames as soon as the forwarding decision can be made. Some runts may be too short and don't even contain a complete destination address. These very short runts will not be forwarded. However, if a runt is long enough to have a complete destination address and that address is on another port, then it will be forwarded.

Broadcast and multicast frames can also have collisions, which will result in broadcast and multicast runt frames. Unlike a unicast runt, these frames are flooded to all the other switch ports. Forwarding or, worse, flooding a runt is a complete waste of both time and bandwidth, since all nodes inherently discard runt frames. When a runt is forwarded from one segment to another, it will cause the nodes on the destination segment to defer transmitting until one IPG time after the end of the runt is seen. Even worse, a forwarded runt can cause a collision on the destination segment, causing the transmitting station(s) to back off and retry. Both of these events are an unnecessary use of bandwidth and cause network utilization to be lower.

Cut-through switches also forward frames with CRC errors, framing errors, and other errors. This is even worse than forwarding runt frames. Forwarding actual invalid frames causes the same problems that forwarding a runt will, but results in error frames from one segment being propagated to other segments, which can be a big problem. Often a single segment may have problems due to a bad cable, a fault repeater, or network interface. By forwarding error frames, a cut-through switch propagates errors from one segment to one or more of the other connected segments.

A cut-through switch can also easily suffer from a condition known as congestion. For example, take the case when two frames are simultaneously received on two ports and both of them need to be forwarded to the same port. Only one frame can be forwarded to the outgoing port. The *entire* other frame must be stored in the switch for transmission at a later time, or discarded. On a busy, switched LAN, this can happen frequently. Moreover, more than two frames can be destined for the same port at the same time, making the problem even worse.

Another form of congestion is when the segment connected to the output port already has a transmission in progress, and the outgoing switch port must defer to the transmitting node. Once again, the forwarded frame must be stored or discarded.

A similar form of congestion occurs when a forwarded frame has a collision on the destination segment. In this case, the normal CSMA/CD rules apply and the forwarded frame must be stored or discarded. In all of these cases, the switch has the option to store, or buffer, the frame for transmission at a later time, or to discard the frame. Storing requires that the switch be able to store the entire frame in a memory buffer, very much like a basic bridge would. Many early Ethernet cut-through switches did not have this capability and dropped frames when congestion occurred. Some had just enough buffer room in either the receive or transmit path to store one frame. This was better but congestion could still easily occur, as only one frame could be stored. Unfortunately, in the early days of switching, very fast buffers were quite expensive and engineers had to use them sparingly or their switch designs would be too expensive. As time progressed, it became clear that dropping frames when congestion occurred caused performance to suffer, because the protocols had to recover from the lost frames. To combat this, switch designs became more complex and large frame buffers became the norm. Although this solved some congestion problems, it had the unfortunate side effect of making these switches quite expensive.

Unfortunately, cut-through switching doesn't work very well by itself, as congestion just happens too easily and runts and errors are always forwarded. In modern Ethernet and Fast Ethernet switches, cut-through switching, when supported, is usually augmented by the store and forward method.

Interim Cut-Through Switching

Interim cut-through switching (ICS) is a simple improvement on the basic cut-through method. ICS avoids forwarding runt frames by forwarding only frames that are at least 512 bits (64 bytes) in length. Since all runt frames are less than 512 bits in length, they are always filtered.

To accomplish this, an ICS switch stores at least 512 bits of a frame in a special kind of buffer, called a FIFO which stands for first-in-first-out. In essence, bits go into one end and come out the other end in the same order. As a frame is received, it is stored in the FIFO. If the frame ends up being less than 512 bits in size, the contents of the FIFO (the runt) are simply discarded (see Figure 7.10). This is a very elegant solution to the

Figure 7.10
Input FIFOs.

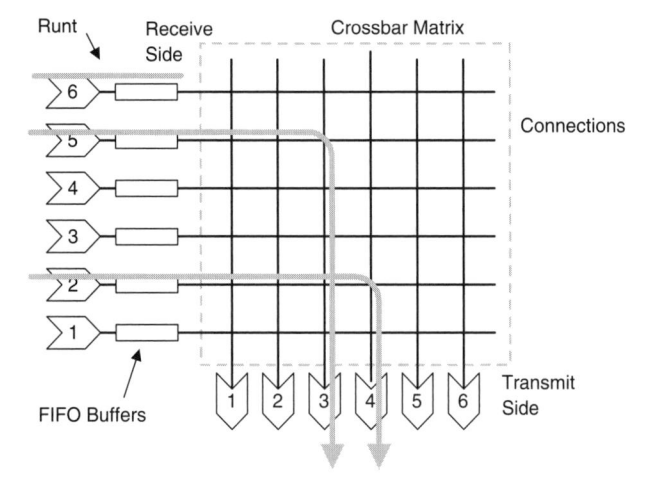

runt-forwarding problem that basic cut-through switches had, and almost all modern switches use ICS instead of the basic cut-through method.

The primary disadvantage of ICS is that it makes the minimum forwarding latency just over 512 bit times. However, this isn't really a problem. In the early days of switching, low forwarding latency was considered to be one of the most important performance characteristics of an Ethernet switch. Since repeaters have a very small start-of-packet propagation delay, it was believed that switches had to maintain very low forward latencies on the assumption that if they didn't, network performance could suffer.

This turned out not to be the case. The latency through a repeater or switch plays a negligible role in total network performance, even for multimedia applications, which generally require lower end-to-end latencies. Even larger latencies of more than 512 bit times are still very small when compared to the latencies that can be caused by deferring transmission to other nodes and from the back-off time due to collisions.

While avoiding forwarding runts, ICS switching still forwards some error frames. This simply cannot be avoided, since an ICS switch will make the forwarding decision and begin to retransit the frame before it can detect the error in the frame.

> Interim cut-through switching is often called **run-free cut-through** or **modified cut-through**. Some marketers have come up with other creative names for this switch feature, so it may not be readily apparent that ICS is what the switch supports.

Store-and-Forward Switching

Store-and-forward (SAF) switching is very different from both kinds of cut-through switching. Store-and-forward switches operate more like a conventional bridge: An entire frame is received and stored in a memory buffer before it is forwarded.

This solves all the problems with cut-through switching, because runt and error frames are *never* forwarded. SAF switches also have another big advantage, as they do not get congested as easily as most cut-through designs because frames are inherently buffered, which is the biggest advantage of the store-and-forward method when compared to cut-through switching.

Compared to both kinds of cut-through switching, this method has the disadvantage of a much greater forwarding latency, which will often be proportional to the frame size but can sometimes be significantly greater than the 12,144 bit times of the largest allowable frame size. This occurs for two reasons. First, the entire frame must be stored in a buffer (or a FIFO) before it can be forwarded, which simply takes time. A high-performance SAF switch will have forwarding latencies proportional to the forwarded frame size—the longer the frame, the longer the time it takes to forward it. In older SAF designs, the forwarding latency is simply large for all packets. However, in most modern switch designs, forwarding latency is directly proportional to frame size. This is very desirable and means that the time it takes to make a forward or filter decision doesn't depend on the size of the frame. As mentioned before, the forwarding latency in a switch will generally not be the limiting factor for performance on a Fast Ethernet network (or an Ethernet network, for that matter).

Compared to cut-through switches, SAF switches usually have lots of buffer space in which to store frames. The more buffer space there is, the better the switch will handle congestion. The downside to this is that more buffer space costs more money.

One of the architectural design decisions a switch engineer has to make is where to put the buffer memory. Buffers can basically be placed in any of three locations in a switch:

- At the input ports
- At the output ports
- Shared between all ports

Buffer memory placed at the input ports provides a place for frames to be stored as they arrive. A frame will not be removed from its input buffer until it is successfully forwarded or the switch decides it needs to be filtered. Input buffering is very effective and, from a switch design standpoint, one of the more elegant designs.

Buffer memory placed at the output ports provides a place for frames to be stored before they are forwarded to the outgoing port. In this case, only frames that need to be forwarded are placed in the output buffers. Switches with output buffers will filter frames before they are placed in an output buffer. This usually requires a small amount of input FIFO buffer, which provides enough time for the switch to examine the frame and decide where it needs to forward or filter it.

Some switches use a shared memory architecture and have a single, large pool of buffer space that is used by all the ports. This is very much like a regular bridge: Frames are placed in the shared buffer and the switch makes forward/filter decisions. If the frame needs to be filtered, it is simply discarded by making its buffer free for newly received frames. If the frame needs to be forwarded, it is transmitted to the proper outgoing port. The big difference between a shared memory switch design and a bridge is that the flow of frames is controlled by an ASIC and not by a CPU, and the aggregate bandwidth between the shared memory and the ports is extremely high.

These three basic, frame-buffering methods are often used in various combinations. Engineers have been extremely inventive when designing methods for efficiently using all three methods. Their design goals are to minimize the amount of memory needed, and use it efficiently while maximizing their switches' ability to handle congestion. For example, frame buffer memory does not necessarily operate in a first-in-first-out manner. The switched network in Figure 7.11 shows a four-port switch that uses shared memory.

If node **A** transmits two frames (the first destined for **C** and the second destined for **G**), both frames will end up in the switch's shared memory. However, the first packet cannot be immediately forwarded to

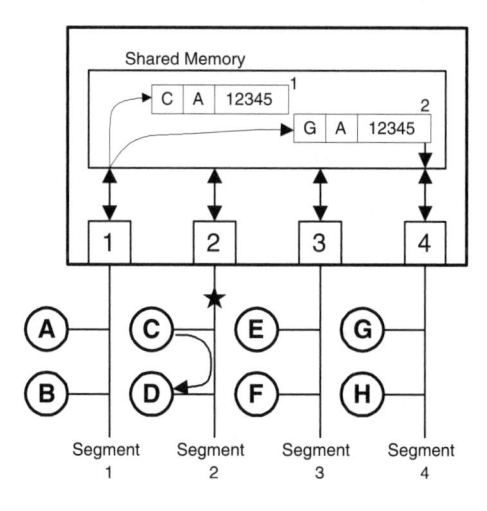

Figure 7.11
Multiple destinations.

segment 2 (and thus to node **C**) because segment 2 is busy with a transmission between **C** and **D**, and port 2 must defer to that transmission. This does not prevent the second frame from **A** to **G** being forwarded to segment 4 even though it was received by the switch after the first frame.

A switch does not have to maintain FIFO transmission for all frames, but it must ensure that frames transmitted between two nodes arrive in the same order as they were transmitted. The switch in Figure 7.11 can forward frame 2 before it forwards frame 1, because they go to different nodes. If another frame is transmitted by **A** to **C** (a third frame), then the switch would have to ensure that it was forwarded after frame 1.

Mixing Networking Speeds

Some SAF switches also have another extremely useful feature: They support both 10Mbps Ethernet and 100Mbps Fast Ethernet in the same device. In short, this means that some ports can operate in Ethernet mode and others in Fast Ethernet mode. This allows the fully transparent integration of existing 10Base-T Ethernet segments with Fast Ethernet segments.

Moreover, some switches support either 10 or 100Mbps operation on *each port* and will *automatically* detect at what speed each port should run. If a port is attached to an Ethernet repeater or node, it will run at 10Mbps. If it is attached to a Fast Ethernet segment or node, it will run at 100Mbps.

As you can imagine, these types of switches are very useful when upgrading an existing Ethernet system to Fast Ethernet. Many devices can even remain connected to Ethernet segments. For example, network printers will usually not need to be connected directly to a Fast Ethernet segment. Some types of legacy equipment, such as UNIX workstations, have built-in network interfaces that cannot be upgraded to Fast Ethernet. Attaching such devices directly to a switch port will provide them with dedicated 10Mbps links to the Fast Ethernet switch in a fully transparent manner.

These dual speed devices can operate because the slow ports are completely decoupled from the high-speed ports by the store-and-forward mechanism, in contrast to the cut-through method that requires that the input and output ports run at the same speed.

Hybrid Designs

Many of today's modern Fast Ethernet and Ethernet switches combine both interim cut-through switching and store-and-forward switching. Often a switch will operate in cut-through mode when there is no congestion and the error rate is low. However, if congestion occurs or the number of error packets per second becomes too high, then a hybrid switch can switch to store-and-forward operation.

On some switches, the entire device operates in cut-through or store-and-forward mode. On more sophisticated switches, the decision to cut through or store and forward can be made on a frame-by-frame basis. Often this is called **adaptive switching** and provides the very low latency of cut-through switching when the network is running smoothly, and the reliability of store-and-forward when congestion or errors occur. Most switches that use cut-through in this way use interim cut-through, as the difference in forwarding latency is not that much and the benefits of filtering runt frames is great.

Many switches also have very complex internal buffering schemes that help to avoid congestion in all but the most extreme cases. Some switches use a combination of buffering at the port, both for input and output and shared buffering. While more expensive, these switches can forward huge amounts of traffic without congestion.

Congestion

The term *congestion*, as it is applied to switches and routers, is frequently used and one you will read and/or hear on a regular basis. Vendors will claim to have sophisticated congestion management schemes. Some have even claimed that their device can never become congested. Both of these comments imply that congestion is a problem that is caused by some entity external to the vendor's device. This sounds nice, but these kinds of comments are the result of an overactive imagination.

In short, congestion occurs in a switch or router (we'll just call them devices for this discussion) when there are not enough resources inside the device to handle the offered load to the device. The result of congestion is that a device must discard, or drop, frames. This means that a frame that would normally be received and properly processed by the device is not properly processed.

Usually the proper processing of a frame consists of forwarding it. However, congestion can affect other functions as well, such as making statistics incorrect and preventing SNMP traffic from reaching the device's management engine, or spanning tree BPDUs from being processed. Losing BPDUs can be especially problematic, as the congestion that caused them to be dropped could be a result of bridge loops, which can only be fixed when BPDUs are properly processed.

There are other definitions of congestion but we feel this one is best. While doing research for this book, we found a particularly atrocious definition on a vendor's Web page. It doesn't make much sense and is a good example of the misinformation about networking prevalent on the Web. It reads: "Congestion is the point at which the overall throughput on a link reaches zero because the bandwidth does not have the capacity to transmit data at a rate which does not result in error or retransmission."

You should ignore such definitions when you see them. In short, all devices are subject to congestion, but not always for the same reasons. In general, devices can become congested due to the lack of one, some, or all of three resources:

- Buffer memory
- Internal bandwidth
- CPU processing power

For switches, lack of buffer memory is the most common reason for congestion. Often, there is simply a large amount of traffic that needs to go to a particular port. If the traffic is coming in faster than it can be transmitted, then the switch must buffer the incoming data. Since the incoming rate is faster than the outgoing rate, the buffers will slowly (or not so slowly) fill up. If the switch runs out of buffers, it must discard further incoming frames.

This kind of traffic load is called an **asymmetric load,** as illustrated in Figure 7.12.

In Figure 7.12 frames are coming in on ports 1 through 4 at an average utilization of 30 percent. Ten percent (or one-third), as measured by utilization, of the traffic needs to be forwarded to port 5. This means that the network utilization forwarded to port 5 is 40 percent. If the average network utilization on port 5 is also 30 percent, then the asymmetric load on port 5 is 10 percent.

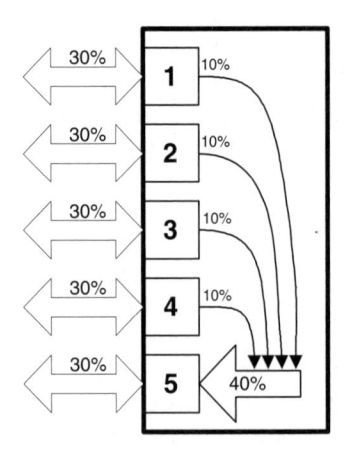

Figure 7.12
Potential congestion.

Everything will be fine as long as the switch can buffer the frames that cannot be forwarded to port 5. However, if the asymmetric load condition lasts long enough for the switch to run out of buffers, congestion will occur and the switch will start to discard frames received from the other ports. The ability of a switch to handle asymmetric loads is what most vendors are talking about when they discuss congestion management. Their schemes usually revolve around clever and efficient ways of handling buffer resources. Better switch designs will handle larger asymmetric loads for longer periods of time before congestion occurs.

Another important thing to note about congestion is that *it is impossible to avoid asymmetric loads.* These kinds of loads are normal and will happen all the time. Most switches will handle normal asymmetric loads for reasonable periods without congesting, but may drop some frames at peak busy times on a network. This is usually okay and can be monitored using network management. Baselining your network and monitoring for congestion problems is the best way to stay on top of this. If you design your network well, this type of congestion will rarely be a problem.

Some kinds of network connections are inherently asymmetric, such as switches that handle both Ethernet and Fast Ethernet. Traffic that needs to travel from a Fast Ethernet segment or node to an Ethernet segment is naturally asymmetric. For example, 5-percent utilization on Fast Ethernet translates to 50 percent on an Ethernet segment. Most switches that handle both speeds are specifically designed to handle this type of loading well. Often they will have extra buffer space to store frames destined for a 10Mbps Ethernet link.

Another kind of congestion is caused by lack of internal bandwidth. For example, a Fast Ethernet switch that has eight ports must have a minimum internal bandwidth of 97.6 megabytes per second in order to keep up with six 12.2 megabyte-per-second ports. If an eight-port switch had only 50Mbps internal bandwidth, then it would be **oversubscribed.** In other words, its internal bandwidth would not add up to the total bandwidth that could be connected to it. Many early switches were built this way, as it was too expensive or impossible to make them faster.

Some devices, especially routers, are not designed to handle large traffic loads; doing so would make the device too expensive. Often these kinds of devices can become congested, because they have too much work to do and simply cannot process the offered load.

The lack of CPU horsepower can also cause congestion. With modern devices this rarely occurs, as most of the critical frame processing is done in hardware. However, many low-end routers still can become congested simply because their CPU runs out of steam.

It's important to note that there is some level of asymmetric offered load that will cause *any* device to become congested. The more asymmetric the load is, the quicker a device will become congested. Some devices will simply handle it better than others.

Full-Duplex Links

Most Fast Ethernet and many newer Ethernet switches support a type of operation called **full-duplex mode.** A full-duplex mode connection is supported only when two network interfaces, such as two nodes or a node and a switch port, are connected directly together. This is often called a **point-to-point** link.

When two Fast Ethernet nodes are connected by a 100Base-TX or 100Base-FX point-to-point link, an interesting thing can happen: The entire CSMA/CD mechanism can be *turned off!* In other words, they can communicate without any collisions ever occurring and never having to defer if the other is transmitting. This apparent bit of magic can happen because of the nature of the point-to-point link.

As explained in Chapter 2, the underlying connection between a TX or FX node and a repeater is inherently a full-duplex one, as the transmit and receive paths are completely separate. Usually a node is connected to a repeater and must use the CSMA/CD access rules. A repeater port can never support a full-duplex link and always operates in CSMA/CD mode. However, when two nodes are connected directly together using a TX or FX connection, they have two completely independent transmit paths between them (see Figure 7.13).

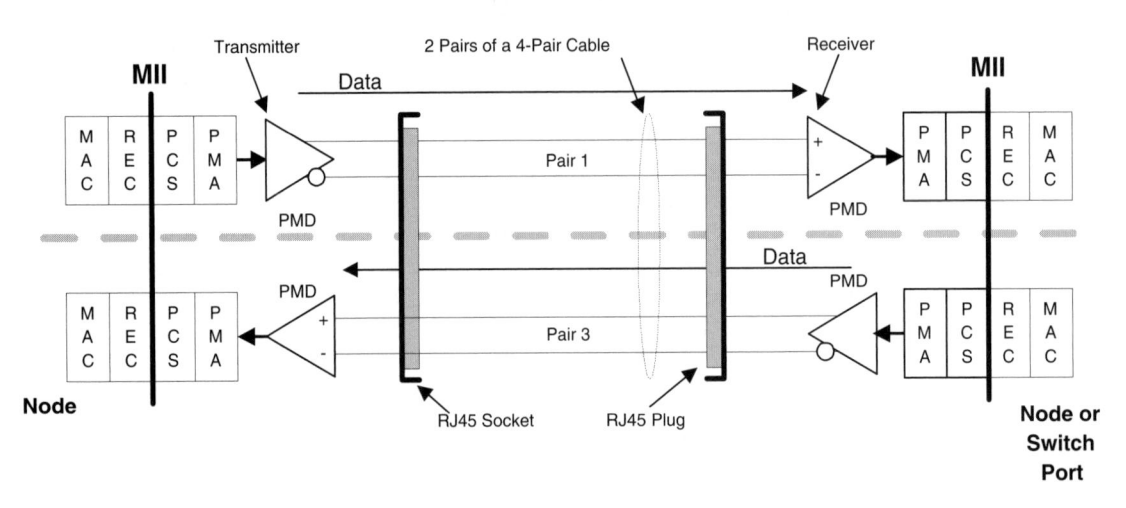

Figure 7.13
A full-duplex 100Base-TX link.

As Figure 7.13 illustrates, frames flow from the node on the left over Pair 1 of the cable to the right-hand node. Frames flow from right to left over Pair 3. Since the frames flow between the nodes on completely different paths, a collision can *never* occur. This allows the CMSA/CD mechanism to be turned off on each end. The only rule that is still used is the IPG rule. For full-duplex links, the transmit flowchart becomes very simple (see Figure 7.14).

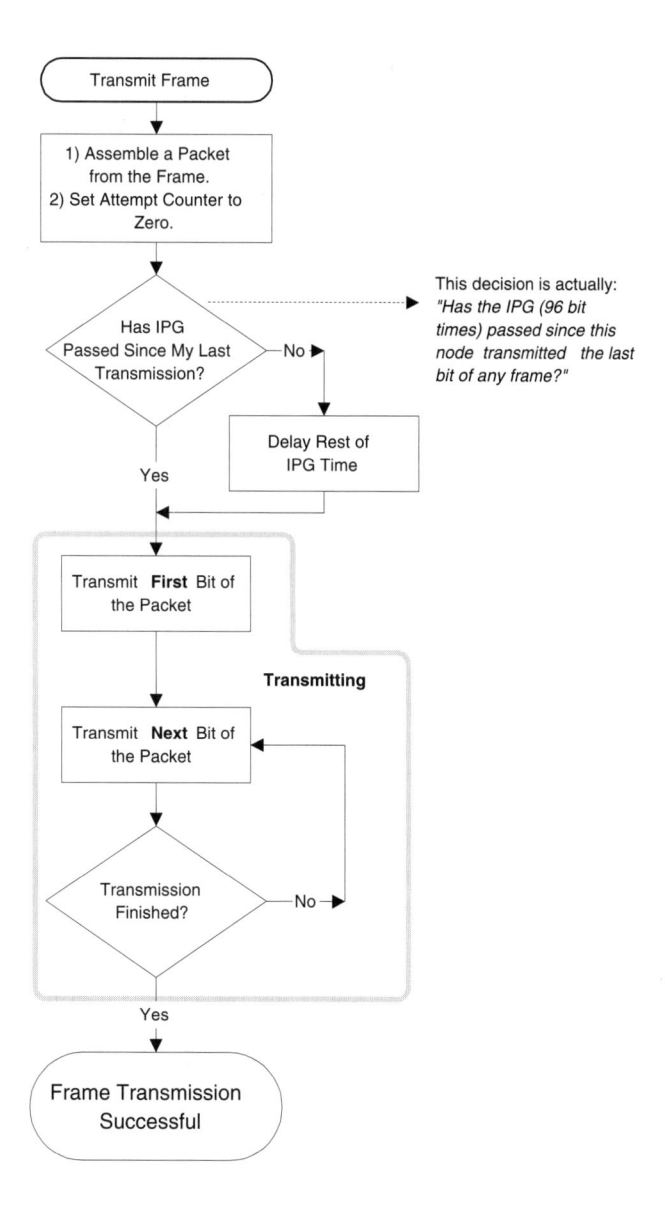

Figure 7.14
Full-duplex transmissions.

The most obvious advantage of a full-duplex link is that one node never has to defer to another node to transmit. As long as they satisfy the IPG rule, both nodes can transmit whenever they want. This means they can both be sending at the same time. This leads us to the next and most important advantage of full-duplex links. Instead of sharing a single, 100Mbps medium via a repeater, the nodes have a 100Mbps channel going both ways between them for a total bandwidth of 200Mbps.

Another way to look at it is that a full 12.1 megabytes per second can flow in each direction. Without collisions, the network utilization on a full-duplex link can easily approach the theoretical 98-percent maximum, and it is not uncommon to see full-duplex links run at 80-percent utilization for extended periods of time.

Of course, there is not much advantage to just connecting two nodes together—for example, two computers or a computer and a printer. It might be convenient at home or in a lab, but there is little practical application for it. The real advantage is when one of the nodes is a Fast Ethernet or an Ethernet switch. Since there are no collisions between the device and the switch, it is much more difficult for that link to become congested, and much more data can flow between them than if the link were still operating in CSMA/CD mode.

Not all nodes need to be on a full-duplex link to a switch, especially such devices as low-end workstations and printers. However, high-end workstations and especially servers really benefit from a full-duplex link. The use of full-duplex links can really boost the performance of a Fast Ethernet LAN with high-performance workstations and servers. For more information on using full duplex links in a network design, see Chapter 12.

In summary, from a logical standpoint, a switch is simply a bridge. All modern Ethernet and Fast Ethernet switches are full learning bridges and support the spanning-tree algorithm and protocol, fully conforming to the 802.1D specification. While switches function as transparent learning bridges, their internal architectures are *very* different from old CPU-based bridges. For more information on selecting switches, how they perform, and what feature sets to look for, see Chapter 12.

Routing and Protocols

Some folks may argue this point, but believe it or not, routing is very similar to bridging. Both technologies forward frames from one network segment to another. Early routers were built just like bridges: They had two or more network interfaces, a CPU, some RAM, and some ROM. The only difference was the software that ran on them. Like switches, sophisticated

ASIC-based hardware has been used in routers to give them more performance at a lower cost.

There are three big differences between routers and bridges:

1. Routers make their forwarding decisions *completely* differently. They do not use a frame's destination MAC address to make forwarding decisions. Instead, they use a similar but different address called a **network address.** Routers forward only information sent directly to them. Unlike a bridge, they do not forward broadcast frames.

2. Routers are *not* transparent devices and do not run in promiscuous mode. Each node that needs to communicate to another node across a router must be aware of, and communicate with, the router.

3. Routers support networks that are meshed. A **meshed network** is allowed to have multiple, active transport paths between any two nodes on the network. In contrast, a bridged network must be configured as a tree. There can be only one active transport path between any two nodes on the network.

Items one and two are important but the most significant difference is item number three. Routers support multiple paths between nodes on a routed network. For example, the network shown in Figure 7.15 is completely valid. This network is identical to the illegal bridged network in Fig-

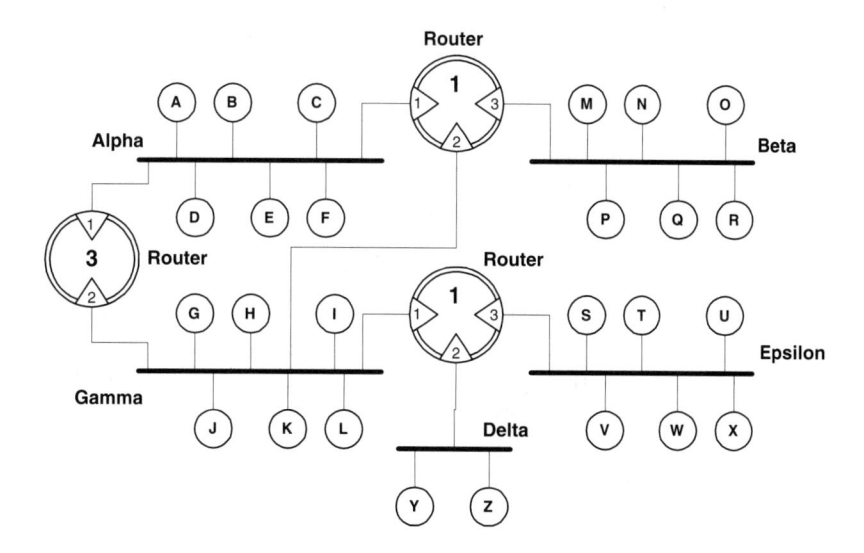

Figure 7.15
A routed network.

ure 7.4, except that the bridges have been replaced by routers. Unlike the bridges, the routers can easily handle the multiple paths between segments.

Routers are often differentiated from bridges and switches, as routers often support network interfaces of very different types. For example, a router may have some Ethernet ports, some Fast Ethernet ports, a couple of Token Ring ports, and a WAN interface port. It can easily route information between these different technologies. In contrast, bridges almost always support only the same type of interface on each port. Many switches support two types of interfaces: their primary interface, such as Fast Ethernet, and an uplink interface such as FDDI. In this case, bridging still occurs and a translation takes place between the different frame types.

Lots of people have asked the question: Why bridge when you can route? In fact, many router vendors want you to ask just that. The answers are simple:

- Switching is almost always cheaper than routing. A 12-port Fast Ethernet switch will be much less expensive than a 12-port Fast Ethernet router. Ethernet switching can be 10 times cheaper than routing.
- Switching is fully transparent to the attached devices and is thus easier to design, set up, and maintain.
- Switches are faster than routers, offering much more bandwidth per port. (Actually, some routers are very fast, so a better way to say this is that switching provides a much better price-performance ratio than routing.) Almost all of today's Fast Ethernet switches run at wire speed on all ports at a relatively low cost.
- Fast Ethernet routers which can run at close to wire speed are quite expensive with a *per-port* cost often running in the tens of thousands of dollars.

The primary difference between a router and a bridge isn't performance, but how they make forwarding decisions. Routers use a protocol header instead of a frame header to route information. As we've seen before, various networking technologies work at different layers of the OSI reference model. Repeaters are layer-1 devices, bridges are layer-2 devices, and routers are layer-3 devices.

Repeaters operate on packets and do not depend on the contents of a packet's data field that contains a frame. Bridges operate on frames and do not depend on the contents of a frame's data field, which usually (but not always) contains a **datagram.** Routers operate on datagrams, sometimes called **data packets** or messages. Basic routers do not depend on the contents of a datagram's data field, either, although some sophisticated routers do peek in there in order to implement very sophisticated forwarding and filtering decisions.

Datagrams are encapsulated in frames, just like a frame is encapsulated in a packet. It is often said that the lower layer structures provide an envelope to contain the higher-level structures. The two most prevalent layer-3, or datagram, protocols are IP and IPX. In examples, we'll usually use IP and include information on IPX where necessary.

Figure 7.16 shows how an **Internet Protocol** (IP) datagram is encapsulated in a Fast Ethernet frame. IP is a layer-3, or network-layer, protocol and can be transported over almost any type of layer-2 service. Most often, IP is used with the TCP protocol, and called TCP/IP. TCP is a layer-4 and -5 (the transport and session layers) element and operates over the IP protocol.

The IP header shown in Figure 7.16 is a little simplified, as we have omitted detail in the IP Info fields that isn't germane to this discussion. The important pieces are the Destination and Source Network Addresses. A MAC address uniquely identifies a node on a LAN, and a network address uniquely identifies a node on a routed network.

Both the IP and IPX protocols use a network address divided into two fields: a network number, or link number, and a station identifier. IPX addresses have only one format, while IP addresses come in three formats: class A, B, or C (see Figure 7.17).

IP addresses are always 32 bits in size and consist of 4 groups of 8 bits each, called **octets** (bytes). All IP addresses have two pieces, a **network number** (often called a link number), and a **host number** (or station identifier). The difference between the three classes of addresses is how the 32 bits are divided between network number and host number. The first one, two, or three bits determine what class an address is.

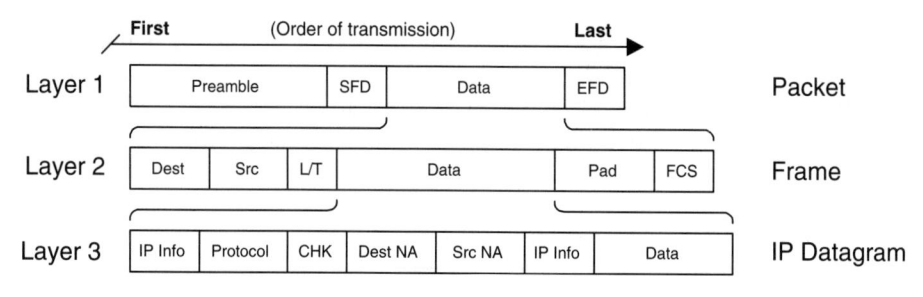

Figure 7.16
Encapsulation of layers.

Figure 7.17
IP address classes.

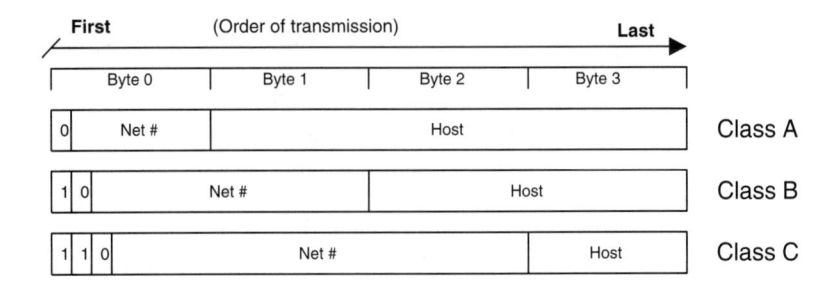

	Byte 0	Byte 1	Byte 2	Byte 3	
0	Net #	Host			Class A
10	Net #		Host		Class B
110	Net #			Host	Class C

An IPX address is a little simpler. It is 80 bits in size and consists of two fields: a network number and a node address. Unlike an IP address, the fields in an IPX address are of fixed size (see Figure 7.18).

The network number is always 32 bits in size, and the station ID is always 48 bits in size. Unlike an IP address, which has no relationship to a node's MAC address, an IPX address uses a node's MAC address as the station ID. Both protocols have different network address formats, but they both have one thing in common: A network address has two parts, a network number and a station ID. Unlike a bridge, which uses an entire MAC address to make its forwarding decision, a router uses only a network address's network number.

The network number is just that, a number that uniquely identifies a network. For most LAN technologies, including Fast Ethernet, a network is defined as a single *broadcast domain*. This means that from a routing standpoint, multiple collision domains tied together with switches (or bridges) are treated as a single network. It's the router's job to move datagrams between networks. Often, the term LAN is used in this way, meaning a single network from a routing standpoint.

Both bridges and routers are connected to a network by a normal network interface. However, unlike a bridge, which runs in promiscuous mode, a router does not. Each node that needs to communicate on a routed network must also cooperate in the routing process by sending datagrams that need to be routed directly to the router. This is unlike a bridge, which receives all frames on a network, regardless of their destination, and forwards only the ones destined for other segments.

Figure 7.18
IPX network address format.

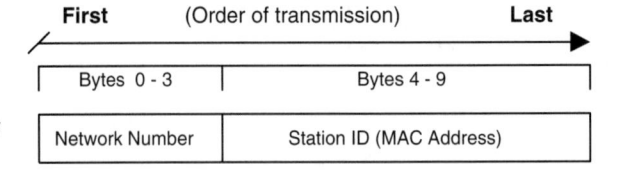

Bytes 0 - 3	Bytes 4 - 9
Network Number	Station ID (MAC Address)

When a node sends a datagram, it places its own network address in the source field, and the network address of the destination node in the destination field. Before a node sends the datagram, it must figure out if it can send it directly to the destination, or if the datagram must be routed. A node can transmit a datagram directly to the destination without using the router if its network number and the destination's network number are the same. For Fast Ethernet, this means that both nodes are in the same broadcast domain. In this case, the node merely fills in the MAC address in the frame of the node identified by the destination network address. If the source and destination network numbers are different, then the sending node must transmit the datagram in a frame that is addressed to the router. The router will then take care of delivering the datagram to its ultimate destination.

Earlier the question was raised, Why bridge when you can route? The answers really seem to favor bridging and switching over routing. The big advantage of routing versus bridging is that *routing scales well*. What we mean by scale is that a routed network can get arbitrarily big and complex and still function properly, provide adequate performance, and remain manageable, in contrast to a bridged network, which does not scale well.

Routed networks can be extremely complex and orders of magnitude more complex than bridged networks. For example, the Internet is a colossal, actually gargantuan, routed network connecting millions of host computers throughout the world. Routed networks scale well because that is what routers are designed to do. Switched (bridged) networks don't scale up past a certain point for two main reasons:

- Broadcasts will take up too much bandwidth.
- The network must always maintain a spanning tree.

Switches are great at segmenting individual collision domains. In a switched network, unicast frames are propagated only to exactly the segments necessary to get the frame from its source and to its destination. However, in a bridged network, or LAN, a broadcast frame sent by one node must be transmitted to all nodes. As a bridged network gets bigger, a larger percentage of the total traffic on the entire network will be broadcast, leaving less bandwidth for frames useful data carrying. In other words, the more broadcasts, the lower the network utilization. This puts a practical limit on the size of any particular bridged or switched network.

A switched network must also maintain a spanning tree. This means that one switch must be the primary or **root bridge**. If the root bridge becomes broken, then all the bridges must renegotiate the spanning tree. For large bridged networks, this can take time and is also a single point of failure, as bridged networks cannot have active redundant links. Imagine having the Internet depend on a single device!

Since routers do not propagate broadcasts and support multiple active links, they are the solution to these dilemmas. Just as bridges and switches are used to connect collision domains, routers are used to connect broadcast domains. Figure 7.19 shows five broadcast domains (LANs) connected together by three routers. The FAST links are Fast Ethernet. The slow link between router 1 and 2 is an Ethernet link. The WAN links are even slower.

All of the nodes in this routed network can communicate with each other, but broadcasts never leave the LAN on which they originate, so they do not use up bandwidth in any of the other LANs. Unlike a bridged LAN, routed networks support multiple active paths between LANs. Routers do this by always sending a datagram along the *best* path. How the best path is determined can be quite complex. For example, some links may be fast and therefore preferable. However, if one of these fast links gets congested, a router may choose an alternate path for a datagram. Routers also avoid the looping problem that bridges have, because they learn and keep track of the routed topology.

Routers also have different delivery characteristics than bridges do. Bridges will guarantee that frames sent by one node are received by their destination node in the same order in which they were transmitted. On a routed network, datagrams are not guaranteed to arrive in the same order in which they were transmitted. For example, if node **A** sends three frames to node **B**, they may not arrive in their transmitted order, because each

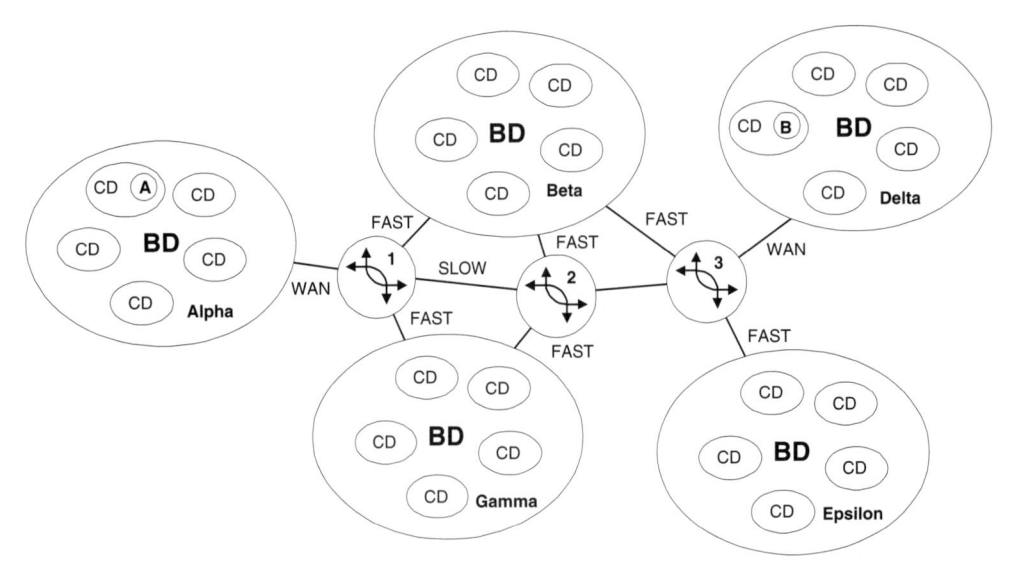

Figure 7.19
Routers and LANs.

datagram may take a different path through the routers to get from **A** to **B**. If the first datagram is sent via a slow link or one that is congested, a datagram that is transmitted later may get on a speedy link and arrive at **B** before the first one. There is nothing wrong with this—in fact, it can be a desirable behavior. Routed networks are often designed with redundant active paths for just this reason.

Redundant routed paths can be set up for a couple of reasons. The first is usually to provide a backup path in case the primary path is down or congested. Another common reason is to provide more bandwidth between two LANs. For example, routers 1 and 2 connect LANs Beta and Gamma using Fast Ethernet links. Since datagrams can flow through either router 1 or 2 to get between these LANs, twice as much traffic can travel between these LANs as could if there were just one link.

Contrast this to a bridged network, in which redundant links can be used only as passive backups, not as truly redundant links. With bridges, redundant links are kept in a disabled state until a failure occurs that destroys the spanning tree.

In summary, basic routers merely move traffic based on a datagram's network number and are certainly useful for managing the size of broadcast domains. For more information on how to select a router, see Chapter 13.

Several major topics regarding routing are not covered in this book. For example, routers use a set of protocols to communicate with each other in order to learn the routed topology and figure out the best path to forward datagrams, nodes must also communicate with routers in order to send datagrams, and many routers support sophisticated features designed to further control how traffic flows between LANs. Our Web page, www.wiley.com/FastEthernet, lists some other good books on routing and the TCP/IP protocols.

The key thing to remember about routing and Fast Ethernet is that routing is used primarily for connectivity, connecting broadcast domains and keeping them at manageable sizes, in contrast to switching, which is used to connect collision domains and provide high performance.

PART II

HOW TO SET UP A FAST ETHERNET LAN

Networking today is more complex then ever before and getting more so every day. In the past, most Local Area Networks (LANs) were installed to service a small number of users by connecting them to a file server and a printer, or perhaps provide a connection to a corporate network for e-mail. In the past four or five years, this has all changed. LANs have become a central and critical infrastructure supporting an entire organization and its core business processes. As time progresses and applications become more sophisticated, integrated networking will become correspondingly more complex. This requires that today's LAN be more flexible, robust, reliable, and above all have more performance.

This complexity requires planning before setting up any kind of network. Small networks will need only a little planning: perhaps only a few notes taken ahead of time, and a diagram or two. Large networks for an entire company can take weeks to plan and even longer to install and get running. Planning your network ahead of time:

- Helps in the selection of proper equipment
- Allows for more accurate prediction of the installation costs
- Ensures that the installation will result in a minimum disruption to existing network users
- Results in good documentation on how your network is put together

- Helps in future troubleshooting
- Helps to ensure that network performance meets user needs
- Gives you a plan for expanding your network in the future

Often people have only one consideration when planning a network: performance. Everybody wants a fast network. But performance isn't the only desirable attribute in a network. There are probably some other criteria for special applications but, in general, all networks should:

- Cost a reasonable amount
- Provide good reliability
- Be robust
- Allow predictable growth without sacrificing the other goals

Cost is always a consideration. Most companies do not have a budget that allows a dedicated, switched Fast Ethernet connection for every user. Wouldn't that be nice. Most companies require that any new network plan be justified, and costs kept to a reasonable level. The more planning you do, the greater your chances of purchasing new equipment at low cost while still meeting performance and other requirements.

Reliability is another important factor, but one that is easy to come by. Today's highly integrated electronics are extremely reliable. Repeaters and switches are available with redundant power supplies. Some repeaters support redundant links. Often switched paths between segments can have redundant backup paths. Many people put all network equipment (servers, repeaters, and switches) on UPS power. All in all, reliability is a fairly easy criterion to meet.

Robustness is a more difficult term to define, as there is no objective technical measure for it. We define robustness as the ability of a network to function well in the face of unpredicted changes and problems. For example, a critical backbone switch may have a cheaper, low-performance switch connected in parallel in order to provide redundant links for certain segments, such as between a group of servers and a router. If the primary switch goes down, the backup switch will detect the change and activate backup links. This is *automagically* taken care of by the spanning tree feature. Some repeaters support backup links to servers. Using this feature, two adapter cards can be installed in a server. If one link goes down for any reason, the other will be automatically activated. Redundancy isn't the only way to build robustness into a network, just the most obvious and expensive way. Other factors can make a network robust, such as using high-quality NICs with fully certified drivers, or using RMON to automatically detect problems and page a network manager when they occur. These can all contribute to a system's robustness.

As you plan your Fast Ethernet LAN, keep one thing constantly in mind: Your network will need to change and grow. A large percentage of a budget for maintaining a networked system often goes to what are known in the industry as **adds**, **moves**, and **changes**. Almost every network installed will need to be modified over time. This can happen for any number of reasons. Most often it is to add new users or more network resources, such as servers or printers. The adoption of high-powered applications, such as client/server systems, videoconferencing, groupware, the Internet, and intranets will require more network resources. Whatever the reasons, you should plan your network so that it can be expanded or modified to suit changing needs.

Planning and installing your Fast Ethernet LAN can be broken down into several activities. These steps aren't the only way to categorize them, but they are practical:

> **Determining network requirements** is the first step. This involves determining how many users will be on the LAN, what kind of applications will be in use, and how your network will be partitioned. Other factors can come into play, such as connecting to remote sites and connecting to the Internet. Often, baselining your existing network is a good first step.
>
> **Selecting the adapter cards** to be installed in each machine is more important than most people think. Many people make the decision on price alone. As you will see, this is only one measure of the value of a network adapter.
>
> **Designing your cable plant** is one of the few things actually simpler for Fast Ethernet than for other network technologies. However, there are a few decisions you must make and, above all, it is a disaster having a Fast Ethernet network that is too big.
>
> **Selecting repeaters** is a critical decision. Manufacturers have designed a multitude of repeaters with many different features, capabilities, and prices. Like network adapter cards, there is more to a repeater than just its price per port.
>
> **Selecting Fast Ethernet switches** can be difficult. Switching is a topic that is sure to come up as you talk to anyone who sells networking equipment. It has been promoted as the great cure-all for many networking problems, and it can be of great benefit in many installations, increasing bandwidth and allowing a LAN to grow. However, switching can also be a snake-oil cure; you could spend a lot of money for

little or no benefit. In the worst case, a switch can actually cause performance problems.

Selecting routers is a topic about which volumes could be (and are) written. Routers are a critical component for any sizable network and can be preferable to switches in many instances. You will use routers to connect to the Internet, remote offices, or people who work at home. Routers can also be used in a smaller area to divide a network into manageable pieces.

Integrating with existing networks will be the norm for most people installing new Fast Ethernet equipment. Most network installations are not brand-new, and rarely can a company afford to upgrade an entire organization or site to Fast Ethernet in one fell swoop. Usually it will be done in pieces, which means the new Fast Ethernet installations will probably need to communicate with other networking technologies, such as Ethernet or Token Ring.

Managing your network is an important part of setting up your Fast Ethernet LAN. Once your LAN is in place, you will want to keep it running at peak efficiency and troubleshoot problems quickly. Network management provides the tools to do this.

Installing new LAN equipment can be an extremely painful experience if not well planned. Once you have figured out how your network will be structured, what adapter cards you will need, and how your cable plant will be configured, you must get it installed. Paying attention to a few details will make your actual installation go smoothly.

These steps don't have an inherent order, although planning your network will usually come first and installing your equipment will usually come last. The other steps can be done in any order; designing your cable plant before selecting adapter cards is perfectly reasonable. The important thing is that completion of all of these steps is critical in setting up a Fast Ethernet LAN successfully.

CHAPTER 8

Determining Network Requirements

Not much work can be done to build a new network or expand an existing one until the requirements for the new system are known, so collecting this information will generally be your first step. Having the information up front can make it much easier to make such decisions as selecting switches and repeaters in the later steps.

One of the most important, and often overlooked, advantages of performing a good requirement analysis is developing the business case for spending big money on new networking equipment and infrastructure. Often, everyone in an organization knows something needs to be done to the network to make it better or faster. Even the CEO may intuitively know this. At some point in time, a network manager will be commanded, Go forth and bring the blessings of Speed and Reliability to our network! And by the way, spend only a tiny amount of money, since we don't have any network equipment in the budget this year. The usual scenario goes something like this:

- The network manager goes off and works furiously in his office for some time, then emerges with a plan that will probably work.
- Many users see the plan and say, Wow! When will it be up and running? Next week? The network manager becomes enthused with confidence.
- At a meeting with the CEO and CFO, the network manager gives a detailed description of all the new leading edge widgets he wants to buy, and all the new Cat-5 cable that will be

installed. He describes the bandwidth everyone will have and how desktop video and Internet access could easily be supported.
- CEO and CFO ask, How much is all this going to cost?
- The network manager shows a bunch of cost estimates and vendor quotes that add up to the proverbial really big number.
- The CEO and CFO then say, You can spend only a really smaller number of dollars. Go redo your plan. See you at the staff meeting on Monday, and have a nice weekend. We'll be at the golf course spending our bonuses for cost cutting. Sometimes they even do a high five and that funny executive handshake.

This story could further detail the painful life that many network managers have. However, the whole scenario could have been avoided if the network manager had justified his numbers and requirements. Most executives want to know how much things will cost and what the benefit is, not what kind of widgets and gadgets will be used to get the job done. Costs, benefits, and ROI are the pieces of information you need to give them.

Planning the Network

The requirements for a network will determine its size, cost, and complexity. Larger and more complex LANs will take more up-front planning than a more simple LAN. Planning your network can be divided into six steps:

1. Sizing your network
2. Partitioning: identifying workgroups and/or departments
3. Identifying enterprise needs
4. Estimating network growth
5. Developing a network management plan
6. Addressing security and reliability

Of course, these steps are good guidelines but they are not the definitive answers to network planning. This is just one approach. Consultants, other books, your coworkers and colleagues may have other input for you, much of which can be very valuable. There is no one, right path to networking nirvana. This is true not only for the processes described in this book, but for most other topics regarding networking as well. The best method will be one that leads you to a network that meets the users' needs at a reasonable cost, and can be expanded without too much reengineering.

On the other hand, all of these steps are important for setting up *any* network. Tiny LANs may not have enterprise needs or need any network management, but the questions still need to be asked. After a careful analysis of the users' needs you may be surprised at the answer. In any case, the following steps can provide a good foundation for analyzing what is required.

Sizing Your Network

Basically, this is a matter of figuring out how big your network is or will be. *Size* in this context is primarily defined by how many users a given network will be servicing. However, other factors come into play as well, such as the number and location of servers, what kind of applications are being run, and how critical the network is to the running of the business. In short, the size of a network is determined by the amount and type of network resource that needs to be provided to users.

If you have an existing network, you probably have a good idea of this already. However, doing a detailed analysis of the existing system, and what your users' expectations are for a new system, may give you some surprising information. Users who a year ago were using only a word processor and a spreadsheet may have graduated to developing their own databases or using lots of graphics. Their requirements for network resources may be much greater than you realize.

Another good way to size your network is to baseline it and measure a few key metrics, such as maximum utilization and throughput. This will also give a clearer picture of how the network is really used.

Partitioning and Identifying Workgroups and/or Departments

This is another task that may seem straightforward. Again, doing this analysis can be very useful. In addition to helping you better understand users' needs, it will also be extremely beneficial when it comes time to pick equipment. Vendors will often try to sell you more expensive equipment than is really needed. Knowing exactly what problems you need to solve will allow you to select equipment that meets your requirements, instead of equipment that makes the salesperson the biggest commission. There are many ways to categorize network configurations. These are generally discussed in terms of their size and complexity. For our purposes, we use the following categories:

- Workgroup and small office LANs
- Departmental LANs

- Backbone networks
- Enterprise networks

Note that we have used the terms LAN and Network in the preceding list. A LAN is typically a network covering a relatively small geographic area, such as a suite of offices or a wing or floor of a building. For our purposes, a LAN is made up of Fast Ethernet and Ethernet components consisting of one or more collision domains, but usually a single broadcast domain. In other words, we use the term LAN to mean a single, switched Fast Ethernet and Ethernet system. Networks are distinguished from LANs, as they usually consist of multiple broadcast domains tied together with routers. Networks also often consist of multiple networking technologies, such as Token Ring, FDDI, and WAN links. Another way to look at the term *network* is as a system of interconnected LANs.

There is a lot of gray area in the terms *workgroup, department, backbone,* and *enterprise*. Many vendors define these terms in different ways, usually so that their equipment is obviously suitable for one or more market segments. The network examples in the following sections are by no means the only ways to configure these types of networks or to define these terms.

Manufacturers are extremely inventive when it comes to devising product features to solve networking problems, and many of these products don't fit into a single category. For example, many products are suitable for both workgroup and departmental applications. As time progresses, expensive features and capabilities that are considered high-end and optional today will be considered as essential tomorrow, becoming commonplace in low-end, inexpensive devices. Network management is an excellent example of this. In the early 1990s, only expensive, high-end equipment was managed. In late 1996, a fully managed 24-port Fast Ethernet stackable repeater cost about $25 per port. This included support for MIB-II and even basic RMON. High-quality network management software also came with it free.

Later in this chapter are some examples of straightforward network configurations that clearly fit into a given category. By no means are these the only kinds of configurations that are effective. Use these as guidelines or starting points for judging how your Fast Ethernet network should be put together.

Identifying Enterprise Needs

This is another area that requires special attention. Upgrading an existing network to use Fast Ethernet in some or all of your workgroups or departments can cause unforeseen problems in your existing enterprise-level network. This almost always revolves around the vast bandwidth that users will get when you move them to Fast Ethernet. For example, you may have a router that connects buildings or sites. It may be performing well with Ethernet connections. However, when you add a Fast Ethernet interface to it you may find that it is now overwhelmed.

Upgrading to Fast Ethernet to support new, more powerful applications may give you enterprise needs you don't already have. For example, many companies that are moving to highly integrated business automation software, such as SAP, use databases extensively. They often find that workgroups or departments that have their own isolated LANs and servers now need to be connected to a central database system. Older Ethernet backbones or slow WAN links are often completely inadequate to support such applications. In general, increasing bandwidth at the workgroup and departmental level often requires a corresponding increase at the backbone and/or enterprise levels.

Of course, connecting to the Internet is something that every company will at least consider and many will implement. Connecting a Fast Ethernet system to the Internet is straightforward but can have some unexpected land mines—for example, not all router equipment supports Fast Ethernet. Other enterprisewide impacts of connecting to the Internet include security and bandwidth needs.

Estimating Network Growth

This requires some crystal-ball thinking. Where new people might physically be located is a good place to start. You will want to ensure that you have some spare ports on your repeaters (10 to 20 percent spares is a good rule of thumb). You might want to pull extra cable to unused office space or to offices where people might double up. Using stackable repeaters is also a great way to keep your Fast Ethernet LANs easily expandable. They are only a few percentage points more expensive than nonstackable units and are almost always managed.

Estimating future bandwidth needs is a little more difficult. Fast Ethernet is extremely fast, but even 100Mbps can be used up in a hurry—especially if you plan on implementing desktop video teleconferencing or heavy client/server-based applications. If this is the case, you might want to invest in repeaters that support RMON or a good network analysis tool from Shomiti, Network General, or Wandel and Golterman. It would be hard to justify to company executive management why the fancy, new Fast Ethernet system recently installed apparently slowed to a crawl when the new client/server system was rolled out.

Both the workgroup/department and backbone models are good ways to segment your network to give users lots of bandwidth. However, if you need to segment for bandwidth reasons at a later date, the workgroup/department model offers a little more flexibility. This will usually happen as workgroups get bigger and more people are trying to access the same server. Splitting up a workgroup into two (or more) workgroups can be an effective way to solve this problem.

Purchasing switches with more ports than you need at first can also pay off at a later date. This will postpone the time when you need to purchase new equipment. If you believe that network growth is going to be rapid, then having 30 to 50 percent spare ports on your switches can make network expansion a snap.

One area of growth that really doesn't have anything to do with Fast Ethernet is network disk space. One of the most frustrating messages a user can get is the Disk Full on a network server. If one user gets it, all users will get it. The situation is even worse if the network administrator has instituted disk quotas, limiting each user to a fixed amount of disk space. Buy lots and lots of disk space; 200 megabytes per user is not unreasonable. Some networks have 800 to 1,000 megabytes per user for a workgroup or department. Of course, this is average. Each user will not have 200 megs of server disk space all to himself or herself. Much of this will be taken up with today's huge office applications, databases, user's intranet web pages, and large graphics files.

You will probably have a SCSI, or possibly a Fire Wire disk subsystem on your servers. This is highly recommended, as these work well with today's multitasking network operating systems, such as Windows NT Server, Novell NetWare, and UNIX. If you are thinking about an EIDE or some lower-cost disk subsystem, you may want to reconsider. Adding drives to a SCSI or Fire Wire interface is straightforward. EIDE supports a maximum of four drives and does not support interfaces external to the box.

Another good idea is to create a partition on your server that is as large as the largest disk drive you have on your workstations, which will usually be in the 1.2- to 2-gigabyte range. This will give you enough space to completely copy a user's hard disk to a server. You can then back it up or copy it to a new machine.

Developing a Network Management Plan

This is something that can have concrete benefits at the time of network installation and in the future. For small networks it is enough just to purchase managed components and leave it at that. Many modern managed repeaters and switches come with free NMS software. A system consisting of only two or three Fast Ethernet segments is not difficult to babysit. However, if your network is much more complex, you will need to think carefully about how you manage your network. Here are some good questions to ask yourself.

- Will I need to manage my network remotely? If so, will it be over dialup links or WAN links? How secure do the managed devices need to be? Remember, keeping your security tight and effective can be a complex task itself.
- Do we need RMON? If so where? What about RMON-II?
- How good is the management software from the vendors being considered? How much is available free? If it is not free, how much does it cost?
- How many people will be managing the network? How experienced are they?
- How much network management responsibility needs to be centralized? How much can be distributed to network managers at the department or site level?
- Is being able to manage the network over the Internet necessary? If so, how will security be implemented?
- How much training will be needed for those people with network management responsibility?
- How will information gathered by the network management system be tracked and analyzed? How will this information be passed to upper management to help them make decisions regarding network growth and operation policies?

Addressing Security and Reliability

These are also important issues. Security at the LAN level is still an immature area. Some vendors have developed hubs that help prevent eavesdropping and address aliasing, and allow nodes to operate only on certain ports. Encryption at the LAN level is a very small market. A few vendors have special bridges that can encrypt data between them, allowing for a secure link between buildings or over a WAN. However, most encryption is being done at the protocol and application level, where it is independent of the physical network technology used by the node.

Managed network equipment itself can be made relatively secure by using passwords and community access strings. This is perfectly adequate for keeping out the inquisitive user but does little to deter a malicious hacker.

Reliability can be easily addressed at the LAN level. One of the most basic techniques is to put all networking equipment on uninterruptible power supplies (UPS). Many devices support redundant power supplies, allowing them to be plugged into two power sources.

Many switches support redundant links, automatically switching to a backup link if the primary goes down. Fast Ethernet repeaters from

Compaq support backup ports, allowing two adapter cards to be put in a server. If one link goes down, both the machine and the repeater will switch to the backup link.

For critical equipment, many companies keep spare units. Sometimes duplicate switches or repeaters are kept in the same rack, powered up and ready to go. If a unit fails, the cables are moved from the failed unit to the backup unit, limiting downtime to only a few minutes.

Higher levels of security and reliability don't come free. Repeaters and switches with security features cost more, and spare units can significantly increase the capital costs of a Fast Ethernet network. A good interview with key users and upper management can help the planner evaluate the costs and benefits associated with security and reliability.

In summary, carefully planning an upgrade to Fast Ethernet or an entirely new Fast Ethernet system is crucial for the proper functioning of the new system. In a well-planned upgrade, it can appear to users and management that nothing is happening except that network performance and reliability increase, and both groups will be quite happy when their Fast Ethernet upgrade occurs painlessly and *just works*. Management will be happy that nobody is complaining about downtime, and all the expenses can be easily justified. Planning will also benefit the network managers who have to keep the network running. A well-planned and installed network will mean fewer unplanned outages, less overtime, and less nastygram e-mail from unhappy users. If all this happens, the network manager may even get to go play golf with the executives, without a beeper or cell phone.

Workgroup LANs

The workgroup LAN is one of the most commonly used networking configurations. In a workgroup, a single LAN is generally shared by a small number of people all working on a common task or for a common purpose. The group members frequently need access to the same information and also need to regularly share data with other group members. The key feature is that the people who use the workgroup work together on a daily basis. Another important feature of many (but not all) workgroups is that they communicate and share data among the group much more frequently than with people outside the workgroup. Workgroup LANs also share another characteristic, they almost always provide connectivity to other networks. The exception to this is the small office LAN.

There are *many* examples of workgroups; the following sections detail three:

- Accounts Payable group in an Accounting Department
- Engineering group
- Marketing group for a small company

All three of these workgroups have similar characteristics—the people in them work closely together and need frequent access to the same data and network resources. Each workgroup is designed for expansion by using stackable Fast Ethernet repeaters. Each workgroup also needs access to resources outside the workgroup, which is provided by a link to the corporate network.

Another topic that is workgroup related is Fast Ethernet and the small office. Chapter 4 has some information on this topic.

Accounts Payable (AP) Group in an Accounting Department

These people work closely together to pay the invoices for a large company. Some Accounts Payable groups have 20 or 30 people in them. Some have more. A typical AP group needs access to the same accounting databases and e-mail that works quickly between members of the group. They may also need frequent access to policies and procedures documents, or other information regarding how the group runs. A large AP group could have a Fast Ethernet network that looks like the one shown in Figure 8.1.

This workgroup has 30 or so nodes connected to a stack of 12-port repeaters. Each person in the workgroup has direct access to a workgroup server. This server provides file services, e-mail, print services for a workgroup printer, and an accounts-payable database.

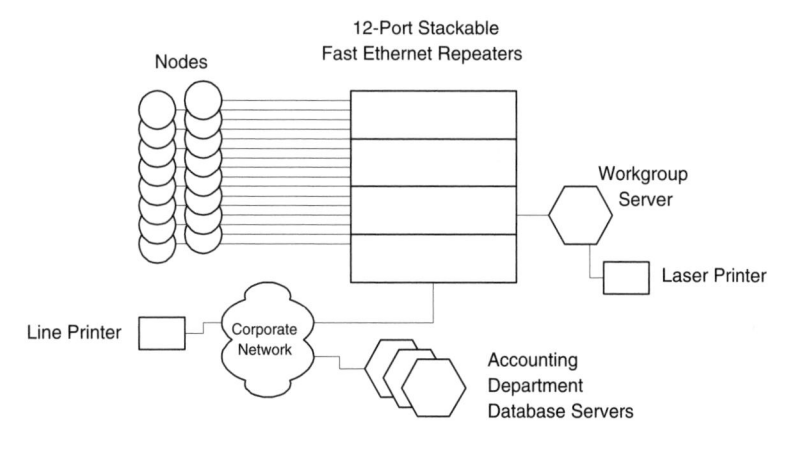

Figure 8.1
Accounts Payable workgroup.

There is also a connection to the larger corporate network, which provides corporate e-mail, Internet connectivity, and connections to other accounting databases and to a large line printer used for printing such forms as checks.

Engineering Group

Engineering teams are often ideal examples of workgroups. Many engineering applications are extremely demanding and require as much performance as possible. An engineering group that designs Fast Ethernet equipment might have three teams—the software team, the hardware team, and the test team. Each one of these teams needs its own high-speed, high-capacity server, but also needs frequent access to the other teams' data. Their Workgroup LAN might look like the one shown in Figure 8.2.

This engineering workgroup is split into three teams, each with their own 12-port repeater. Each repeater is also connected to one port on a 6-port Fast Ethernet switch. Note that the three repeaters are stackable but can be segmented from each other. This means they can be managed and controlled as a single unit but still provide three separate Fast Ethernet LANs (collision domains). These three LANs are connected to each other and to the teams' servers using a 6-port Fast Ethernet switch. The switch supports full-duplex links to the servers, and provides connectivity between the teams at full Fast Ethernet speeds. Each team has direct high-speed access to its server. The software team could be doing some serious compilation work while the hardware team is performing some complex simulations. Since the switch provides the connectivity, both

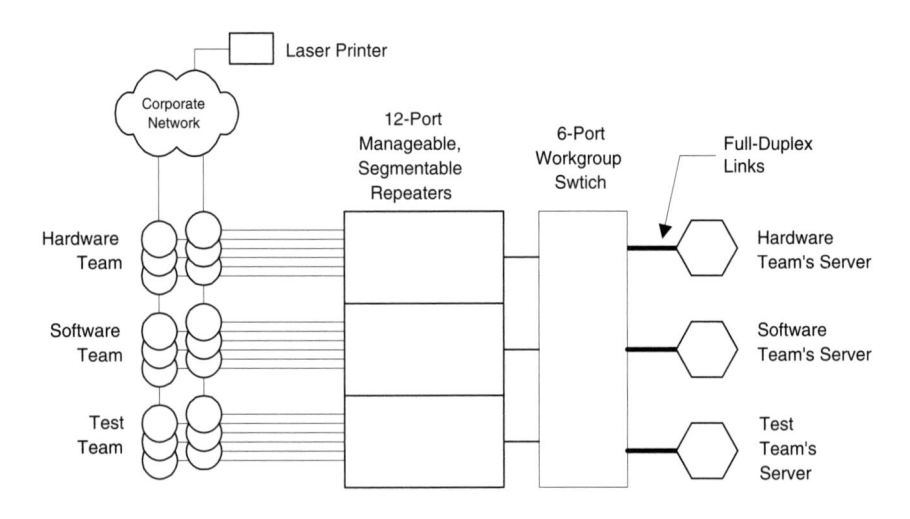

Figure 8.2
Engineering workgroup.

these activities plus the activities of the test team could all happen in parallel without affecting each other from a performance standpoint. However, each team will often need access to the other teams' servers to get the latest software or read the most recent hardware specs. Since this is a switched network, all the teams have high-speed access to all three servers.

One of the most important features of the network in Figure 8.2 is that the servers are on *full-duplex* links to the switch. This gives them 200Mbps of bandwidth to the switch and allows the servers to simultaneously send and receive over 24 megabytes of data per second.

There is another interesting feature of this network: The members of the team do not depend on the workgroup LAN for connectivity to other network resources. Each of the nodes has *two* network adapters installed—one to connect to the engineering workgroup LAN, and another to connect to the corporate network. Modern workstation operating systems, such as Microsoft Windows 95 and Windows NT Workstation, support this extremely well.

This configuration has three strong points:

- It completely isolates the development activity from the corporate network. This type of activity can use lots of network bandwidth, and if it were on the same network as another group, there wouldn't be enough for everyone. The configuration also gives the development group a private, high-performance network.
- It keeps development secure, as source code, design documents, and other potentially sensitive information cannot be reached by other people in the company.
- It keeps potentially dangerous traffic off the corporate network. During the development of a network device, such as a switch, erroneous network traffic is often generated. This can actually be damaging to a functional network. Keeping this traffic only on the development network prevents it from disrupting other parts of the company.

Of course, the members of the development workgroup still have full access to resources on the corporate network; this is completely transparent. People in the development group do not have to make a conscious decision about which link to use; the operating system takes care of that. This type of **dual connectivity** can be very useful in other situations as well: For example, the executive group in a very large company may want to have a separate network and server on which to keep extremely sensitive corporate data, such as contracts and financial data.

Marketing Group for a Small Company

A small company may have a marketing group consisting of four people: the VP of marketing, a secretary, and two marketing people. These people need to work closely together on many different projects. The things they work on—presentations, product literature, and flyers—can change on a rapid basis. A small Fast Ethernet LAN is perfect for such a group, which, though small, still needs a high level of network performance, as time is critical and they work with large graphics files and complex applications, such as page-layout programs and graphics design software. The marketing workgroup could be set up like the one shown in Figure 8.3.

This is a basic workgroup with one repeater, six users, and a single file server with one interesting feature: The link to the corporate network is via a fiberoptic cable. This allows the link to be a little longer than a copper link, and provides electrical isolation from the corporate network equipment. Typically, this fiber link would connect to a switch or a router, giving the marketing group access to e-mail, the Internet, a printer or two, and other corporate network resources. Another important feature of this small workgroup is that the repeater is stackable, which allows the workgroup to grow easily. This can be more important in a small company than a large one. Most small companies can really suffer when growth is fast. Having a network that can cope can be a strategic advantage.

Fast Ethernet and the Small Office

Many industry pundits do not believe that Fast Ethernet is appropriate for the small office or home office network (often called the SOHO market). They argue that the cost is too high to justify Fast Ethernet. After all, the small office may have only a few people, and the home office usually serves just one person and a couple of computers.

In 1995 this was certainly a valid argument. Fast Ethernet equipment was still four to five times the cost of Ethernet equipment. However, by

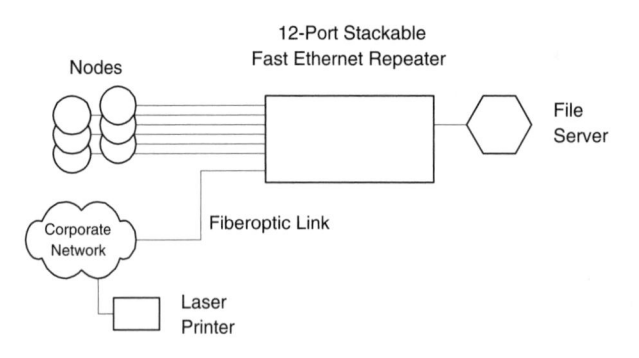

Figure 8.3
Marketing workgroup.

early 1997 the prices for Fast Ethernet network adapter cards and repeaters had fallen dramatically. Fast Ethernet adapters could be purchased for less than $100, and repeaters could be purchased for $30 per port.

For a small office today, this certainly means that Fast Ethernet is a credible choice, especially given the network-intensive applications in use today. A small office of 30 to 40 people could easily be supported by a single Fast Ethernet segment. Fast Ethernet coupled with modern workstations and a powerful server would give a small office a high-performance network for a relatively low cost per user. This would allow them to run today's sophisticated applications, allowing them to be more competitive with a smaller number of people. For example, a 30-person real-estate office could be set up like the one shown in Figure 8.4.

Of course, even a small office would initially be set up with stackable repeaters. As in the other examples, this provides an easy upgrade path as the organization grows or changes. Switches or routers can easily be added as needed to segment the system into multiple LANs.

In Figure 8.4, connectivity to the Internet is provided by the server, which routes traffic from the LAN to the Internet. All modern network operating systems, such as Windows NT Server, Novell NetWare, and UNIX, can act as a router. This is an ideal situation for a small office. Modern servers can easily handle routing for an ISDN line or frame relay link, an attractive alternative to purchasing a separate router.

As mentioned before, most businesses considering Fast Ethernet will be upgrading or expanding an existing network. However, the small office is a market segment in which a significant percentage of LAN installations are new, and Fast Ethernet is particularly well suited for the first-time, small-office installation. It may be tempting to initially set up a small office with 10Mbps Ethernet, as it is very inexpensive. However, chances are that as the organization grows and as people become more

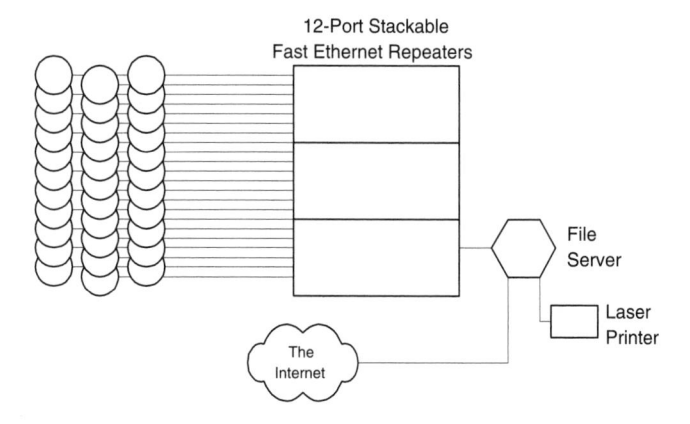

Figure 8.4
Real-estate office.

familiar with using computers as productivity tools, 10Mbps Ethernet will quickly run out of steam.

The tiny, remote office and home office are probably the only workgroup-level networking situations for which Fast Ethernet is not well suited. Most home offices have only one computer, so networking isn't even an issue. The Internet is the only network used, and that is accessed by a connection via a modem or an ISDN or xDSL line.

Some home offices have multiple computers. This often comes about because someone has purchased a new, more powerful computer and still has a use for the older machine. In these cases, networking can be quite useful, as it can allow the computers to share disk space resources, a printer, and a fax modem. For this type of networking, plain, old Ethernet is still the best choice. It's much cheaper and provides great performance, especially for just two or three machines and a printer.

Another problem is that many home offices are connecting to the Internet with small ISDN remote-access routers, cable modems, or XDSL links. Many of these products connect to one or more computers using a 10Base-T (twisted-pair) or 10Base-2 link. The network shown in Figure 8.5 is a case in point. In this case, it is impractical to use Fast Ethernet to connect the computers, because there would have to be some kind of bridge to connect to the ISDN remote-access router. Using 10Base-2 allows this small LAN to be built using coaxial cable instead of a repeater, which helps to keep down costs. Networking more than two devices with Fast Ethernet or 10Base-T would require a repeater.

Departmental Networks

Departmental networks are generally bigger than workgroup LANs and are often made up of multiple workgroups. A workgroup LAN's primary

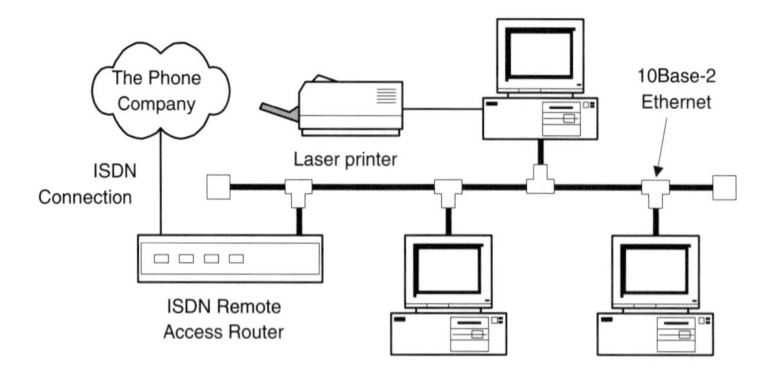

Figure 8.5
A home office network.

purpose is to provide connectivity between users and the network resources they need, but a departmental network's purpose is generally to tie workgroups together and provide connectivity to more centralized resources. In short, the distinguishing feature of departmental networks is that they provide more connectivity than workgroup LANs. Departmental LANs can provide:

- Support for two (or more) network technologies, such as Fast Ethernet, Ethernet, and FDDI
- Connectivity that ties workgroups together
- Connectivity that ties the department to the enterprise

For example, the Accounts Payable workgroup in Figure 8.1 is part of the Accounting Department, which could be structured like the one shown in Figure 8.6. In contrast to the workgroup switch in Figure 8.2, this switch has 6 more ports for a total of 12, supports 10 or 100 megabits per second (Ethernet or Fast Ethernet) on each port, and has an FDDI uplink port. This switch ties the accounting workgroups together and provides them connectivity to the department servers, the rest of the corporate network, and other devices. Like the example in Figure 8.2, the department servers are tied to the switch using full-duplex links.

An interesting feature of this configuration is the line printer and EDI, or Electronic Data Interchange, interfaces. EDI is a standard used to trans-

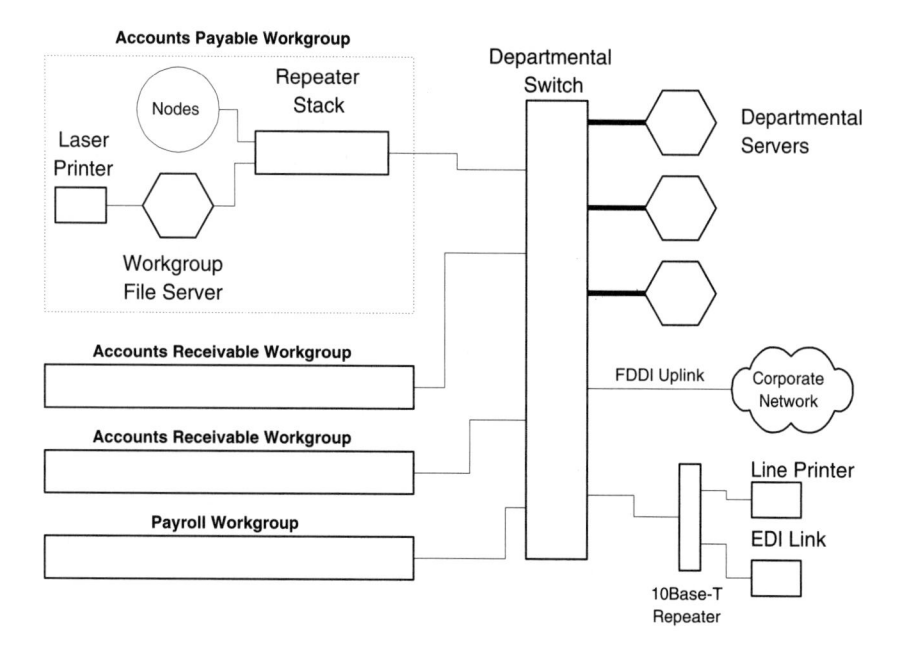

Figure 8.6
Accounting Department.

mit electronic accounting information, such as purchase orders and invoices between companies. Many large companies rely extensively on EDI, prefer suppliers that use it, and encourage the customers to use it as well. A lot of equipment that has been around for awhile supports Ethernet and cannot be upgraded to Fast Ethernet. Even new devices such as printers still support only 10Mbps Ethernet. This departmental network gives all the users access to these legacy and other Ethernet devices in a completely transparent manner. The department switch handles the speed difference between Fast Ethernet and Ethernet by buffering packets in its memory.

In this case, the connection to the rest of the company is via FDDI and not Fast Ethernet. FDDI is well suited for these types of connections. It inherently supports redundant links, also runs at 100Mbps, and can span much larger distances than Fast Ethernet.

This configuration gives the users in each workgroup access to the servers in the other workgroups, the departmental servers attached to the department's switch, the old printers and EDI interface, and the enterprise. As you can see, this is much more connectivity than that provided at the workgroup level.

Backbone Networks

The word **backbone** has been used in many different ways, and has been applied to several networking technologies. Originally, a backbone was a thick Ethernet cable that snaked through a building and was tapped into at various points to provide service in a particular area. When FDDI came along the term *backbone* was used to mean a central FDDI ring to which smaller LANs were attached. In general, a backbone is a network system that provides a central mechanism for connectivity between different workgroup and department LANs. The definition of a backbone cannot get much more detailed than that without a discussion of specific technologies.

Fast Ethernet backbones are very similar to the departmental/workgroup network model, but a backbone design is a more centralized way to build a LAN system. A Fast Ethernet backbone is usually built with a very high-performance switch, which is the backbone itself. A Fast Ethernet backbone network provides the same type of connectivity as a departmental network but generally does so without workgroups. Sometimes this is called a **flat network**, as there is little or no hierarchy to the LAN components.

If we take the configuration in Figure 8.6, and build it using the backbone approach, we could end up with something like the one shown in Figure 8.7. This backbone network is built using a high-performance, 12-

port Fast Ethernet switch that supports both 10- and 100-megabit speeds on each port. Six of the ports support 100Base-FX fiberoptic connections. These are used to connect to the repeater stacks. A router is used to connect the backbone to the corporate site network and WAN. An example of this is shown in Figure 8.7.

A distinction between the Fast Ethernet department/workgroup model and the backbone model is that a Fast Ethernet backbone switch requires much more total bandwidth. The switch in Figure 8.7 has 12 100Mbps ports, six of which are running in full-duplex mode. This requires an internal aggregate bandwidth of *219.6 megabytes per second*. Each port running in normal CSMA/CD mode requires 12.2 Mbps, and each full-duplex port requires 24.4 Mbps. Not only is more bandwidth required, but backbone switches must also handle congestion better. This usually requires more buffer memory and smarter hardware than a workgroup- or department-level switch.

Another interesting feature of the LAN in Figure 8.7 is how 10Base-T Ethernet devices are connected. This is done by a minibridge installed as a plug-in module in a Fast Ethernet stackable repeater. The minibridge is a small, two-port learning bridge with no spanning-tree support. Its purpose

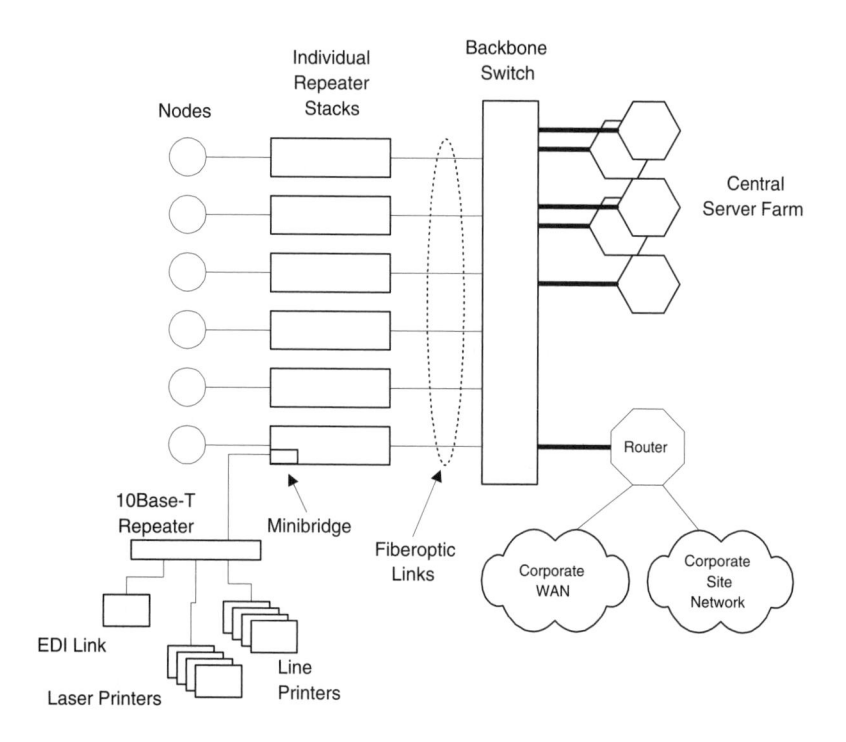

Figure 8.7
A backbone switch.

is to provide Fast Ethernet to Ethernet connectivity. For more information on such devices, see Chapter 4.

Enterprise Networking

Enterprise networking comes into play when multiple workgroups, departments, and backbones must be tied together to form a single, large, networked system. These types of systems used to be called **internetworks.** This exactly defines the Internet; a system that ties together many, many networks. The Internet has become so prevalent and important that the term *internet* now really applies only to it. Today, we use the term **enterprise network** to describe the systems, components, and techniques used to connect together the individual LANs in a company into an integrated networked system that is used by an entire organization. Enterprise networks are usually designed to support a large number of users, such as an entire corporation, or mission-critical functions that require extremely high network up time.

Enterprise networking usually revolves around routers and WAN links. It can also center around equipment that is suited for connecting large numbers of users at a central point. Large chassis-based hubs are generally considered enterprise-level products. Fast Ethernet is a technology that is well suited for local area networking at the workgroup, department, or backbone level. For these applications, it provides excellent performance at a relatively low price.

However, at the enterprise level, routing takes over as the technology of choice (for more information on routing see Chapter 13. All of the examples in the previous sections on workgroups, departments, and Fast Ethernet backbones are LANs. They are all made up of multiple collision domains in different configurations, but they all have one thing in common: Each one is a single broadcast domain. This means that a broadcast transmitted by *any* node on any particular segment is received by *all* nodes. All protocols use broadcasts on a regular basis, and broadcasts can be a significant percentage of network traffic. As the number of nodes on a network increases, the percentage of broadcasts as a proportion to total network traffic increases. This is especially true in such configurations as backbone networks that use switching heavily.

Routers solve this problem and are generally used in four situations:

- Connect together several workgroups, departments, or backbones
- Partition different collision or broadcast domains

- Connect sites over a wide area network
- Connect to the Internet

Figure 8.8 is an example of an enterprise network that shows three of the four situations in which routers are usually used. Enterprise routers are often chassis-based devices that have one or more ports on a plug-in card, which allows the router to support multiple LAN technologies. Most modern routers support Ethernet, Fast Ethernet, Token Ring, and FDDI. A few also support 100VG AnyLAN. The router is used to tie together the various workgroups, departments, and backbones in a large organization.

Most routers also support WAN connections. Typical WAN links are Frame Relay, T1, T3, ATM, and ISDN. In Figure 8.8 the enterprise router directly supports a T1 link to the Internet. This gives the organization a direct high-speed Internet link. On the other end of the T1 will be another router, probably a very large, powerful router maintained by a primary

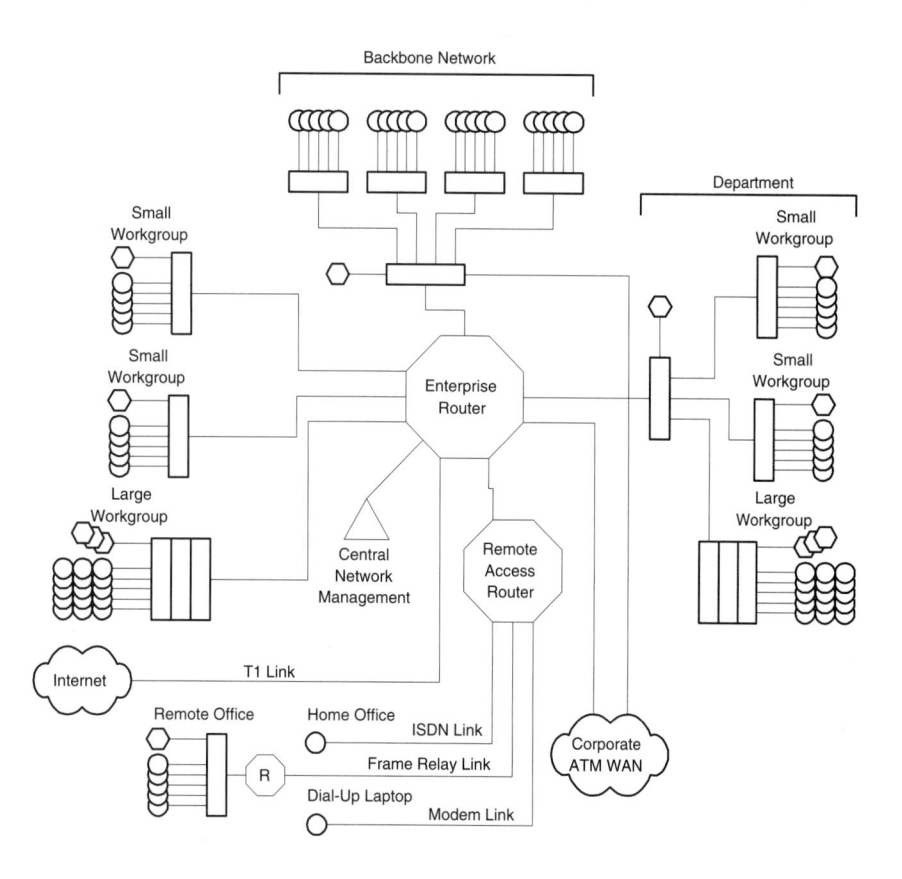

Figure 8.8
An enterprise network.

Internet service provider such as MCI, Sprint, or UUNET. This router will link directly to a high-speed Internet backbone.

The remote-access router provides connectivity to remote offices, home offices, and people traveling with laptops. Remote-access routers are often small chassis-based products, in which each card supports one interface. This allows them to support a wide variety of connections at a lower cost per connection than a large enterprise router. (Remote-access routers can cost one-quarter to one-half as much per port as a large enterprise router.)

Some routers are placed in devices called **collapsed backbones**. A backbone can be *collapsed* by plugging repeaters, switches, and router cards into a single, large chassis. Users simply connect directly to the repeaters and/or switches in this chassis, which provides all the necessary connectivity. A collapsed backbone system can be a powerful tool when a large number of users and devices in a single location such as a building, need to be tied together. However, this technique does have problems. Once all the chassis' slots are full, no more expansion can occur. Another problem, especially for Fast Ethernet, is cable distance limit, which can be hard to overcome, since everyone needs to connect to the chassis via no more than 100 meters of cable.

An enterprise network can be configured in an almost infinite number of ways. Enterprise networking is the topic of entire books. Fast Ethernet should be used in the enterprise to provide high-performance LAN connectivity, and fits into most enterprise models at the workgroup, department, and backbone level.

Enterprise-Level Network Management

Another component critical to enterprise networking is network management. When a company's network gets big enough, it becomes difficult and expensive to manage in a decentralized way. Individual sites or departments may manage their own networks, but a centralized system for managing the enterprise network as a whole is an essential requirement for most enterprise-level systems.

In an enterprise network, most components at all levels are managed. Any management console connected anywhere in the network can communicate to any managed device, thereby allowing a central service group to maintain the network as a whole. This group can monitor network performance, look for potential problems, and help site, department, or workgroup network managers diagnose problems. For example, a workgroup may be having problems accessing the Internet. The central enterprise network management group can help determine if it is a local problem or a problem somewhere else in the enterprise.

Without centralized network management, keeping an enterprise-level network running at peak efficiency is practically impossible. Some devices don't fit well into an enterprise management system, because they don't have support for security or for common enterprise network management software such as HP's OpenView. Selecting products that fit into an enterprise network management scheme is key to implementing such a system.

CHAPTER 9

Fast Ethernet Network Interface Controllers

The **Network Interface Controller** or **Network Interface Card** (NIC) is a basic building block in any LAN. A NIC will be installed in one or more bus slots on all nodes attached to a LAN. Alternatively, it may be an embedded LAN interface on the PC motherboard. The NIC is categorized by its LAN technology and the bus interface, each targeted toward a particular installation or environment. Picking a Fast Ethernet NIC is based on a number of factors:

- Performance and the ubiquitous price/performance parameter
- Driver support
- Hardware features
- Technical support
- Ease of installation
- Warranty
- Network management

The platform in which the NIC will be used is an important consideration, because server platforms place different requirements on a NIC than client or workstation platforms do. The server often supports many clients, and the requirements for a server NIC are very different from those for a workstation NIC. A large percentage of the traffic on a Fast Ethernet LAN is destined to or from a server, which can place an extremely high burden on the server NIC and server host bus, a burden that can be even more pronounced when the server is attached to a Fast Ethernet directly via a full-duplex link segment to a department or backbone switch. A full-duplex link can only exist between a single node and a switch port. Full-duplex allows bidirectional data transmission thereby doubling the transmission bandwidth (200Mbps for Fast Ethernet).

A server typically has multiple PCI slots and multiple ISA or EISA slots, each capable of supporting a NIC of a different LAN technology. Often the LAN workhorses, servers are frequently used for multiple functions, such as print and file services, database servers, e-mail servers, Web servers, groupware applications, communications servers, and many other applications. One of the main criteria to consider when selecting a NIC is its CPU utilization and throughput capability. The ideal NIC will support a very high throughput with very low CPU utilization. The less CPU time the NIC consumes transmitting and receiving frames, the more time the server CPU has for other tasks.

In contrast, a workstation NIC is dedicated to providing connectivity for that node to the server via a switch or repeater. The requirements for a client NIC are often very different from those for a server NIC in terms of the bus architecture, buffer memory size, and data rate to the department network. The operating system typically run on a client is either DOS/NFN or Windows 3.1, although more recently the predominant client workstation operating system has been Windows 95. A client usually has multiple ISA slots and a couple of PCI slots. Older client workstations may have a mix of EISA and MC slots, or EISA and one or two PCI slots (see Figure 9.1).

Price and Performance

One of the parameters used in the purchase of a NIC is the price/performance ratio. The objective is to get the best performing NIC at the most competitive price. The price of the NIC is an easy identifier, but the performance of a NIC is more abstract and difficult to ascertain. The performance of a NIC cannot really be discussed in isolation, since it really consists of three components: the NIC bandwidth, throughput, and the CPU utilization. The bandwidth relates to how fast the NIC can move data across the host bus, while the NIC throughput is the amount of data the NIC is capable of putting out on the network medium. The CPU utilization is the percentage of total host CPU time required by the NIC. The lower the CPU utilization of the NIC the better. A lower NIC–CPU utilization ratio as a percentage of the total system CPU bandwidth is desired.

Figure 9.1
PCI NIC adapter.

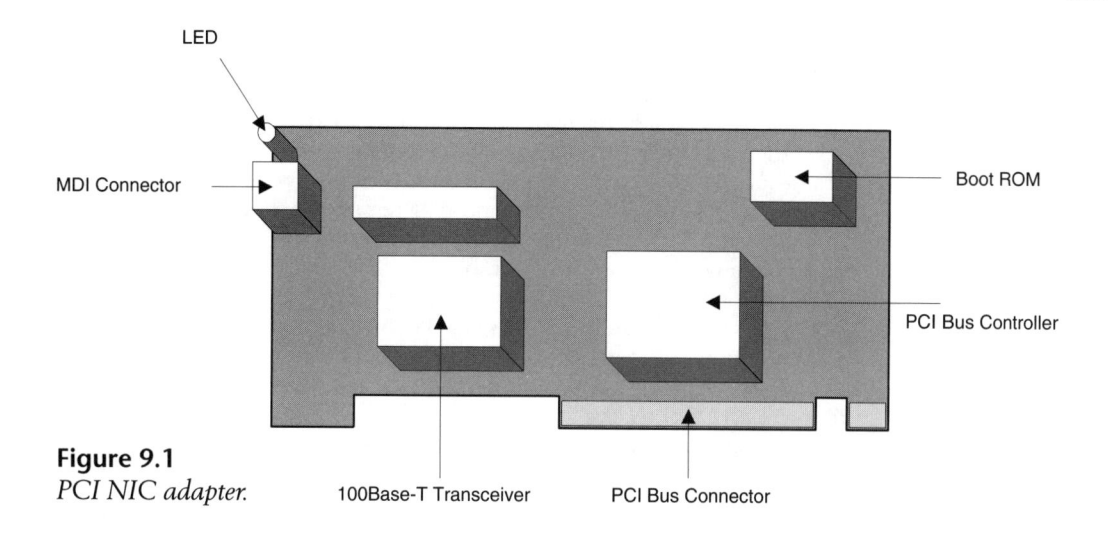

> The methods used to measure server NIC performance and CPU utilization differ from those used for client-based NICs. For server NICs, the performance benchmarks use a single server supporting at least six clients. Often, up to 16 are used. The objective in benchmark testing server NICs is to determine the amount of CPU utilization and the maximum data throughput of the NIC.

A number of different benchmark test suites are available that are used to determine the performance of a server NIC. The two most common are Novell's Perform3 and Ziff-Davis's Netbench 3.0 test suites. Both are used to determine a NIC's CPU utilization and the maximum throughput a NIC can achieve. These benchmark tests sometimes do not reflect real-world situations, but give a good relative-performance measurement of each NIC tested in the same configuration of high-speed server platform and multiple workstation clients.

> The parameters used to measure client NIC performance differ from those used for server-based NICs. For client NICs the performance benchmarks use a single client/one server configuration. The server usually is a very high-speed system that features a very fast CPU with large DRAM memory attached in a peer-to-peer configuration with a single client running benchmark tests, and this same configuration is used against each client NIC being tested with

> the server setup remaining constant. The typical benchmark tests performed are Perform3 and Netbench 3.0. Periodically NIC performance tests and results are published in many of the networking magazines. The amount of packet memory buffering on a client NIC is different from that of server NICs because of the host platform performance. For slower client systems NIC buffering is required to store incoming data temporarily until the host client can transfer the data to memory. This is especially the case for ISA client NICs installed in a workstation with a combination of ISA and PCI slots running a multitasking operating system. The arbitration scheme used in these systems is not always favorable to the ISA bus, and ISA bus transfers can be preempted by PCI bus requests, thereby reducing the bus bandwidth available to the ISA bus NIC, and increasing the amount of on-board buffering required to avoid dropped packets or receive underruns.

Price is the other variable to consider in selecting a NIC. The pricing on dual-speed adapters, such as the 10/100Mbps NIC, is fast approaching that of 10Mbps NICs of a year ago. This helps to accelerate the deployment of Fast Ethernet NICs in traditional 10Mbps accounts. The pricing on 10Base-T adapters has reached commodity level largely because of the integration of the logic into single-chip devices, and also because of competition in the marketplace. For new purchases or upgrades it is recommended that you purchase 10/100Mbps NICs, and at the best price for the level of performance that best suits your application. In this way you are buying a NIC for your current requirements, and investing in a future high-speed migration strategy.

Some NICs may be higher in price than others on the shelf, but the reason may be better performance. Several independent benchmarking lab tests are done each year on top-selling NICs, and these provide valuable data to use when purchasing one NIC or several thousand NICs. You should also understand the test configuration used in the performance benchmark tests, the type of operating system, the number of clients in the testbed, and the drivers used on the server and client. Sometimes you pay a higher price for a NIC that has a better performance relative to the competition. Companies that work hard on their drivers in order to squeeze more performance out of the silicon feel justified in setting the NIC at a higher price point.

Drivers

One of the most important factors to consider when purchasing or installing a NIC in a system is the driver—a piece of code that allows the network operating system to work with the network interface controller hardware in order to transmit and receive data to and from a LAN network. The drivers for the NIC you purchase may already be bundled with the network operating system, but in most cases the NIC may come with a dozen or more different drivers that allow the customer to install and run the NIC in any one of several different network operating systems. Most of the larger NIC vendors offer a full suite of drivers for the major operating systems, while smaller companies typically provide a limited set of drivers.

The development and certification cost for a full suite of drivers is the inhibiting factor for smaller companies, and they generally offer drivers for one or two of the network operating systems (NOS). The development cycle and internal testing of the driver suite is always the critical path in the release of a NIC to the marketplace. A number of the major silicon vendors, whose chips form the basis of NIC designs, provide a full suite of drivers to NIC developers. This ease of development effort and time to market is significant, and having the drivers already provided makes for early market delivery and presence, which reduces the development time, especially if the drivers are already certified. However, this approach does not allow for market differentiation between NICs developed by different vendors based on a common piece of silicon.

The area for differentiation may be in the cost of the card, or hardware features such as connector type or LEDs, but the real prize is in the drivers, where the goal is high throughput and low CPU utilization. It is important to understand whether the NIC vendor developed the drivers internally, or they are based on a common set of drivers distributed by the chipset silicon vendor. On the other hand, the drivers may have been developed by a third party, in which case the issues of driver support and maintenance must be considered. If there is a problem with the driver or installation of the NIC, then the users or IS manager most likely will get caught in the middle between the NIC vendor and the silicon vendor when trying to get driver changes implemented.

The drivers may be written either in assembly language or in the C programming language. Drivers written in assembly language tend to be better optimized and use a smaller memory footprint when installed. Those written in the C programming language are less efficient and are not as optimized to the underlying NIC hardware. If all other aspects of a NIC are equal, it is best to choose drivers that have been developed using the assembly programming language by the NIC vendor.

Drivers must be written for the full-duplex environment, since the architecture of the code flow is a lot different from that in drivers written for the traditional half-duplex Ethernet or Fast Ethernet protocol. Driver support is an area in which the similarities of adapter hardware outweigh the differences. The drivers on full-duplex ready NICs should be developed and architected to exploit the features of full-duplex rather than reworked from existing half-duplex drivers. Built-in features mean an understanding of the technology.

Driver Certification

All drivers shipped with a NIC should be certified to work with the particular operating system under which they run. The certification may be completed by the NOS vendor, such as Novell, Microsoft, or SCO, or it may be done by self-certification groups within the company. There are a number of different drivers for each operating system. Without a certified NIC and driver, the customer has no way of knowing if the driver was tested or certified by the vendor. When choosing a NIC, make sure all drivers that are shipped with it have been certified. This helps to confirm that the NIC vendor has tested the NIC and drivers in a range of platforms. While NIC vendors make every effort to have the latest certified drivers shipped with the NICs, it is suggested that you check their Web page or BBS for updated revisions. Some companies post an advisory, or release an interim CD with the latest suite of drivers.

Technical Support

The technical support group or department of a NIC vendor provides the technical help and assistance if there are problems with the NIC hardware or software. The technical support groups typically provide 7-day, 24-hour phone support. Larger companies tend to have better technical support because they can provide more resources, more training of their staff, and better equipment labs where customer problems can be duplicated. There are normally several levels of support, with problems escalated to different levels based on the degree of complexity. A review of the technical support provided by a NIC vendor should be carefully undertaken before making a decision to purchase a NIC. For large customers, placing an order for several hundred or thousands of NICs, knowing there is a strong technical group in place to support the hardware and software is a big factor in making the final decision. The comfort of knowing that technical help is a phone call or online visit away, regardless of the time of day or night, is very important to the customer:

- **Bulletin Boards.** The Company BBS system has been a mainstay for posting technical documents and new drivers. With the expanded use of the Internet, companies are migrating away from the BBS system.

- **Web Sites.** This is fast becoming the forum of choice for customers looking for information and technical updates on a vendor's product. Most people with a PC have access to the Internet, and any company without a Web page is guilty of committing economic suicide. For networking customers, the important issues are a listing of the product line, technical features, technical support errata information, and the latest posting of drivers—especially for NIC adapters.
- **Multilevel Support.** To better service the customer and improve on response time, companies usually implement a multilevel support structure. The first line of support is a filtering mechanism in which 90 percent of calls can be satisfactorily resolved. These types of calls deal with cabling, plug-n-play setting, default configuration, and basic problems that the customer might encounter during the installation of a NIC card. Second-level support consists of those calls that the first-level support team cannot resolve, and is of a more technical nature, such as hardware and software integration problems. The third-level support team works on complex customer problems, which are often very specific to the networking opening system protocol, or subtle driver and timing issues. The third-level support groups are highly technical in nature and frequently work with chip and board-level designers within the company, as well as designers from other companies if their product is part of the customer configuration. Third-level support groups frequently prepare and deliver technical courses in network architecture and complex network problem solving methods.

Ease of Installation

This is one of the most important and most notable features of a NIC product once it gets into the hands of a customer. For many users the idea of opening up a PC and installing a new NIC is quite a challenging and often daunting task. Nothing is worse than going through the exercise of installing a card and following the often terse installation manual instructions only to hit an impasse. What options are left to the user? Reinstall the card again, carefully follow the instructions as you had done previously and reading the online screen help messages where available. If the card does not configure correctly or the driver does not load, or the driver loads but the workstation does not log into the server, you really are confused and frustrated. You can call the tech support number if it is listed, or you can call in a specialist, which can be expensive.

The ease, or lack of it, with which a NIC is installed really comes down to the amount of effort the NIC vendor has put into the total product delivered to the market. During the NIC development cycle, the primary effort is focused on hardware design, driver-suite development, and the exhaustive testing required of hardware with the drivers in a variety of platforms. Before a NIC can be released to production, all drivers must be certified, which is quite a challenge.

The installation routine or install program is a unique piece of code usually developed and tested independently of, and in parallel with, the driver development phase. The on-screen help files for the install program are developed by the technical writers working with the software engineer. Once the install program and the help screens are complete, they are released to the QA group and then to the product test and certification groups. The personnel doing the testing and certification are all comfortable with the terms, and are knowledgeable with installing NICs—that's what they do thousands of times each year. This is one of the primary reasons why the installation instructions for NICs are often inadequate, terse, confusing, and sometimes misleading. Seldom is an out-of-box exercise performed on NICs once they are ready for shipping. An out-of-box exercise is an evaluation of the product by the vendor as if they were a customer. This exercise provides valuable feedback to the vendor on changes required to make the product more user friendly and easier to install. (In an out-of-box exercise, a production NIC is purchased from finished goods, and a group, independent of engineers and developers, is asked to install and configure the NIC.) It is surprising how many obvious problems are identified during this exercise, such as incorrect pathnames to the driver on the diskette, unexpected results when the wrong mouse button is selected, lack of on-screen help in particular situations, inability to load or detect when the driver is loaded, how to run diagnostics, reference to a nonexistent loopback plug, and so on. Companies, such as Compaq, that have a dedicated human-factors group, in which such products as NICs and other networking products are tested, benefit tremendously from this exercise. The results of these out-of-box exercises are reflected by better help screens, better installation manuals, and better install programs, which result in better *ease of installation* for the customer.

Warranty

One measure of the quality and reliability of a NIC is the type of warranty offered by the vendor. Adapters such as 10Base-T and 10/100Base-T have become so integrated and simple in their design that the level of fallout is small. The cost of these adapters is such that it is easier for a vendor to cross-ship a new replacement adapter to a customer than repair a failed unit. For some customers in mission-critical applications, reliability of the NIC is paramount and is often measured in the mean time between failure (MBTF) of the components used on these adapters. For high-quality, high-performance, and well-designed NICs, the MBTF approaches 250,000 hours, which means a hardware failure may occur, on average, every 250,000 hours or 25 years. This level of reliability helps to explain the warranties for three to five years, or even for life, offered by some vendors.

NIC Network Management

The ability to better manage a network and its component devices is a feature for which all network managers are looking when installing or upgrading a network. The two primary requirements for network management are SNMP and DMI.

Simple Network Management Protocol (SNMP) is a well-understood network management protocol that has been around in various versions for a number of years. There are several levels of SNMP agents, not all of which are implemented in an SNMP managed entity. These agents can reside within a switch, a managed hub, or a NIC in a workstation or server. Few NIC vendors supply SNMP agents with their NICs, which has led to the establishment of the Desktop Management Interface (DMI) by the Desktop Management Task Force (DMTF).

The Desktop Management Interface (DMI) requires all DMI-compliant NICs to gather information and statistics about network traffic and the network. Through network management software, NICs from various vendors can be interrogated to gather data that will help you provide more effective management of the network down to the node level. Network operating systems, such as Windows 95 and Windows NT 3.5 and NT 4.0, have built-in SNMP management applications support, and many of the NICs from the major vendors will support these bundled agents or work with a software SNMP agent. When purchasing a NIC, make sure it has SNMP and/or RMON (remote monitor) software support. DMI is not widely used, but it is gaining acceptance within the industry. NICs with both SNMP and DMI support would be the ideal choice.

Types of NICs

RMON allows statistical analysis of the traffic patterns. RMON agents located on the client NICs communicate with RMON agents on the switch. This provides improved traffic flow and congestion control in the LAN infrastructure.

Server-Based NICs

Modern servers are specialized high-end, high-speed, highly reliable, and expandable systems that require a NIC with equal attributes. Vendors, hardware reviewers, and users often focus on a NICs performance. Although this is very important, the server NIC's CPU utilization is often even more important. In choosing a server NIC, the primary considerations are low CPU utilization, high bus throughput, and a modern NOS driver. Other server-specific features built into some NICs can be valuable, such as multiple interfaces, full-duplex support, and NWAY Autonegotiation.

The measure of the efficiency of a NIC is its CPU utilization, which is a measure of how hard the server's CPU (or CPUs) have to work to support transmitting and receiving frames using the NIC. A low value of CPU utilization, measured as a percentage of the total CPU processing available, indicates a well-designed NIC adapter. If a NIC has a high CPU utilization, this can affect the performance of the server system as a whole. The more demand there is by the NIC on the CPU, the less time the CPU has to spend on doing other tasks, such as file reads and writes to disk memory. Not only can this leave less CPU horsepower available to run the server itself, but it can also limit the number of NICs that can be placed in the server.

Unlike a workstation, which is usually connected to only one LAN via a single NIC, it is common practice to connect a single server to multiple LANs. This has many advantages, the biggest of which is that users on multiple LANs can access a high-capacity server directly, instead of via a switch or router. In installing multiple NICs in a server, low CPU utilization is even more important. Using multiple NICs with a high CPU utilization can completely offset the purchase of a high-end server, as most of its horsepower will be used up in serving the NICs.

Other interesting server-specific features are **multiheaded** or **multiport NICs**. Most of the early PCI servers shipped, and many of those currently shipping, have only three or four PCI slots. Usually two of these are taken up with SCSI disk adapters, video adapters, and other peripherals. This often leaves only one or two PCI slots free for NICs. To overcome this limitation, some vendors are shipping PCI NICs with two or more network interfaces—MAC, PHYs, and all—each sharing a single bus interface implemented with a PCI-to-PCI bridge. This allows multiple segments or shared network connections to a single adapter, optimizing the limited number of available PCI slots.

Other factors that should be considered when selecting a server NIC specific to the physical environment and the software operating platform in which the NIC will be installed include:

- What is the bus type of the server, and does the vendor have a server NIC for the bus type?

- What type of network operating system is installed on the server, and does the NIC vendor have drivers and other software utilities for this environment?
- What is the NIC performance relative to the competition and the CPU utilization?
- What is the bus throughput of the NIC?
- What size buffer memory does the server NIC support, and is it field upgradable?
- What is the physical media type supported by the server NIC (Category 3, 4, 5, STP, or Fiber)?

One of the fundamental rules in designing an optimized network is a high bandwidth link to the server, since all application and shared data are stored at the server. One of the more recent paradigm changes in the client/server model is having a dedicated, full-duplex, switched connection between the server and the switch. A PCI 100Base-TX/FX full-duplex NIC located in a server will deliver a theoretical throughput of 200Mbps when connected to a switch.

The actual increase is dependent on what other tasks the server CPU is doing and the type of network protocol being run over the link segment. If you are considering a full-duplex NIC for the server, it should be a PCI 100Base-TX or 100Base-FX. A 10Mbps full-duplex NIC should not be considered for server applications. Other features specific to server NICs that support full-duplex are the drivers, and whether they are optimized for the full-duplex support. A well-written driver will be written from the start to support full-duplex mode of operation. Some drivers were not originally written to support full-duplex operation, and have been patched to add this support. These patched drivers are not as efficient or robust as those specifically written for full-duplex operation.

The media type used to connect to the server is also an important element in choosing a server-based NIC. Sometimes a server NIC is chosen because of the wiring infrastructure already in place. If the cable plant is wired with Category-3 or Category-4 UTP cable, then the only choice is a 100Base-T4 NIC, and in this case full-duplex support is not an option. If the cable plant is Category-5 UTP cable, then either 100Base-TX/FX or 100Base-T4 NICs may be selected. For server-based NICs every effort should be made to install 100Base-TX or 100Base-FX NICs with full-duplex support enabled.

To automatically determine the data rate support by a NIC installed in a server or workstation, the NWAY Autonegotiation scheme was developed and standardized by the IEEE 802.3 committee. The NWAY scheme is designed into the transceiver, and allows a NIC and a hub port to exchange a series of signal pulses that communicate the speeds each entity is capable of supporting. The NIC and hub port will autoconfigure to the highest common speed, whether this is 10 or 100Mbps. It is important that the server NIC you choose supports the NWAY Autonegotiation scheme.

Workstation NICs

The requirements and features of a workstation NIC can differ greatly from those for server NICs. Both the hardware and software for these types of NICs can also differ. A server NIC can be used in place of a workstation NIC, as long as the right OS driver is available, but you may be paying more money than is necessary.

Traditionally, client workstations have run single-tasking operating systems, such as DOS and Windows 3.1, which placed less stress on the drivers and hardware. Workstation NICs for these systems are commonly 10Mbps ISA or PCI adapters. Unlike a server NIC, in which performance is the key factor, low cost, ease of installation, and full driver suites are usually the deciding factors when looking for a low-end workstation NIC.

The majority of workstations shipped today are bundled with Windows 95 or Windows NT and sometimes a UNIX-derived OS. All of these are multitasking operating systems, and like a server, work best with NICs that have a low CPU utilization. Like a server, these modern OSs can perform multiple tasks simultaneously. A poorly designed NIC can cause performance to suffer here as well as in a server, and for the very same reasons. It is easy to make the mistake of purchasing an expensive, high-performance workstation only to waste its benefits by installing a poorly designed NIC or a NIC with an inefficient driver.

The media requirements of a client NIC also often differ from those for server NICs. When using Fast Ethernet, a server will almost always be on a Cat-5 or fiber connection to a repeater or switch. However, a large percentage of the existing wiring infrastructure for workstations uses either Cat-3 UTP or coaxial cable.

Workstations with Cat-3 connections can be upgraded to Fast Ethernet by using adapters that have 100Base-T4 interfaces. However, this is less than ideal, as few, if any, 10/100 adapters support 100Base-T4 connections (as of late 1996, there were no 10/100 adapters that supported 100Base-T4 as the 100Mbps interface). This forces workstations with access to only a Cat-3 cable drop to be upgraded to Fast Ethernet in a single step, which is often inconvenient. Workstations with 10Base-2 Ethernet connections simply must be moved to a Cat-3 or preferably a Cat-5 connection in order to be upgraded to Fast Ethernet, which requires NICs with combination ports to support these media types.

Client NICs usually feature combination ports to support 10Base-T, 10Base-2, and (for that 5 percent of the market) an AUI port. When selecting a client NIC, you should be aware of the type of wiring used in the workgroup environment, and plan accordingly. The cost of PCI-based 10Mbps Ethernet adapters over ISA 10Mbps Ethernet adapters is decreasing to the point that new client workstation installations should consider using PCI 10Mbps for their client NIC solution. So, the question of whether to use 10Mbps PCI client NICs or 10/100Base-T client NICs, and if full-duplex support is required for client workstations, must be addressed. The type of workgroup and the end applications being run by the client workstations are important parameters when choosing a NIC. For data entry and general administration, a 10Mbps ISA client NIC should be considered.

The media type deployed in the workgroup determines the connector type required on the NIC. Most of the major vendors provide 10Mbps NICs with combination ports for different media systems. Some vendors have narrowed the choice even further by offering a range of client NICs, each with a particular media port. This eliminates the burden of paying for a port type that you will not use. If the client workstation is running Windows 95 or some other multitasking operating system, in which other peripherals compete for the host client CPU, you should use 10Mbps PCI NICs. Workgroups running CAD design packages, as well as office applications under Windows 3.1 or 4.0, should use 10/100Base-T NICs. Again, choosing between 100Base-TX or 100Base-T4 client NICs depends on the type of wiring found in that workgroup. For those workgroups that have Category-3 UTP cable, the choice is 100Base-T4; while those workgroups with Category-5 UTP can support either 100Base-TX or 100Base-T4 client NICs. It is best to determine the end application, the type of client user, and the client platform where the client NIC will be installed. Full-duplex does not translate into twice the performance for client NICs, and it accounts for up to 15 percent over 10 or 100Mbps data rates. If you use dual-speed 10/100Mbps or 10Mbps client NICs, make sure they have NWAY or Autonegotiation support.

Embedded NICs

Given the high degree of integration of the MAC and other functions of the NIC into a single piece of silicon, a number of PC vendors, such as Compaq have placed the NIC silicon directly onto the motherboard. Embedded NICs may be found in laptops, workstations, or servers, and eliminate the need for add-in NICs or PC Card/CardBus NICs. This approach frees up a bus slot, which may be used for other controllers, and it also ensures the PC is network ready with the correct drivers integrated into the OS—an important feature in certain classes of PCs, such as educational or small office environments, where the customer is on a limited budget and cannot afford the additional expense of installation and maintenance fees.

Embedded NICs are very cost effective, since the price of the NIC PCB is eliminated and the users or IS manager do not have to open the box to install the NIC card when connecting to the network. Of course, if there is a problem with the embedded NIC, the whole system must be returned for repair (or replacement if there is a problem with the network connection). One way around this is to use an MII interface on the host motherboard, and external PHYs for the media type. This approach eliminates being locked into a particular media interface, and provides the opportunity to use future external PHYs as they become available. Embedded NICs have not been widely deployed in desktop PCs, with the exception of the Compaq DeskPro, primarily because of the wide range of protocols available on the market. With Ethernet and Fast Ethernet gaining more of the networking market, embedded 10/100Base-T NICs are showing up in the newer product lines.

Mobile NICs

With the increase in travel by corporate America, the laptop computer has become an indispensable tool, allowing instant access to the corporate LAN and WAN system. In addition, these mobile laptops allow the user to connect via modems to public databases, the Internet, and other database systems, such as AOL and CompUSA. Mobile customers on the road have a regular need to access e-mail, the corporate LAN, and the Internet. Connecting a laptop to the LAN is easier today because of the laptop NIC or laptop NIC/modem. These PCMCIA NICs have an 8/16-bit slave interface and are not suited for high-speed LAN connectivity. The PCMCIA interface is used to support legacy LAN connections such as 10Mbps Ethernet and 4/16Mbps Token Ring. The newer PC Card and CardBus standards are better suited to high-speed connectivity for laptops, so make sure your laptop or notebook computer comes with a CardBus slot or connection. The NICs for the PC Card slots are usually dual speed, with some versions featuring a combination of 10/100Base-T and a 33.6Kbps modem port. The PC Card slots should be used for combination 10Mbps LAN connectivity and 33.6Kbps modem ports, and the 10/100Mbps dual-speed NICs with modem ports should be used in CardBus slots in order to gain the optimum performance from the LAN connection. CardBus is a 32-bit bus mastering architecture that operates at 33MHz, similar to the PCI bus architecture.

CompactPCI NICs

CompactPCI is a standard for PCI-based industrial computers, formed under the auspices of the PCI Industrial Computers Manufacturer's

Group (PICMG). It has the support of over 125 companies, with the charter of developing specifications for PCI-based systems and boards for use in industrial computing applications. CompactPCI is essentially the PCI local bus specification adopted to the Eurocard 3U or 6U standard. These cards plug into an 8-slot PCI passive backplane using high-density 2mm press-fit pin-and-socket connectors. These connectors feature staged pin lengths, which are for future hot-swap capability. The basis of CompactPCI is a gas-tight, high-density pin-and-socket connector, which was originally developed for the telecommunications industry. This is a keyed connector allowing for 3.3V, 5V, or a universal card application. The connector has 45 rows with 5 pins per row, for a total of 220 pins for signaling (15 pins are lost due to the connector key), and features an additional external metal shield and a large number of grounding pins to minimize signal reflections.

These features enable CompactPCI systems to have up to eight slots for add-in cards, compared to four on a typical PC desktop system. The number of slots can be expanded using PCI bridge chips. All CompactPCI cards have the standard 220-pin connector located at the bottom half of the module, with the add-in card using a male connector. The backplane also features two additional connectors for I/O connectivity to other add-in cards—a center connector with 95 pins, and a 220-pin connector located in the upper half of the backplane. These two connectors feature pass-through pins, allowing the user to plug in I/O cards from the front or rear of the chassis. The add-in vendor is free to pin out these two connectors, but must supply the add-in card to mate with this pin-out. Typically these connectors may be used to provide access to I/O peripherals, such as SCSI controllers, LAN adapters, memory expansion units, graphics controllers, and so on. The primary applications for CompactPCI today are the telecommunications industry, computer telephony, industrial automation, and future hot-swap environments, such as superservers, in which the user does not have to open up the box and shut down the system in order to replace or change an add-in module.

NIC Architectures

The transfer of data between the PC and the NIC adapter may be implemented using any one of four different methods. A basic understanding of these four techniques is a prerequisite to making a balanced decision regarding the performance, complexity, and cost of the adapter. The four methods of data transfer across the PC bus are Programmed Input/Output (PIO), Direct Memory Access (DMA), shared memory, and bus-mastering DMA.

NIC Chipsets

All 10Base-T and 10/100Base-T adapters shipped today are designed using **chipsets**. A chipset combines the multiple functions required by a NIC into a single chip or device. Most modern chipsets combine many of the following:

- Bus interface
- MAC
- Buffer memory controllers
- Arbitration logic
- Device and vendor IDs for configuration
- Plug-n-play capability
- Integrated 10Base-T PHY
- LED controls
- Diagnostics

Some Fast Ethernet PCI adapters support both 10Base-T and 100Base-T operation by supporting a 10Base-T PHY and a 100Base-T PHY. The 10Base-T PHY is so simple that it is often integrated directly on the chip. The 100Base-T transceiver is implemented using an external PHY, but it is expected that silicon vendors will soon integrate even this component into Fast Ethernet NIC chips. This will further lower the cost of manufacture and end-user costs, allowing Fast Ethernet technology to be used for more cost-sensitive applications. A similar approach is used for ISA and EISA-based 10/100Base-T NICs, although the majority of Fast Ethernet NICs shipped today are based on the PCI local bus.

Physical Interface (PHY)

The other main functional block in the NIC architecture is the PHY or, as it is sometime called, the transceiver. The PHY is the interface between the MAC and the external network medium. It is responsible for signal conditioning and translating the MAC data into a format that can be transmitted to the network medium. The PHY is usually implemented as a single chip and connects directly to the MAC on one side without external logic required, and to the MDI connector through a filtered transformer on the media side. Some external components are required to filter out noise and provide signal equalization and voltage reference levels. The transmit and receive signals between the PHY and the MDI are passed through a filtered transformer, which provides isolation from the network medium as well as signal and impedance matching the particular media. In dual-speed NICs the 10Mbps PHY is normally integrated into the MAC, and the 100Mbps PHY is the external one (see Figure 9.2). You can expect to see NICs in 1997 with fully integrated 10/100Mbps PHYs in the MAC, which will allow the development of single-chip NICs. This will result in cheaper pricing for dual-speed NICs, managed hubs, and switches.

Boot ROM

An optional component on some classes of NICs is a **boot ROM**, a hardware memory device containing software code that allows a diskless workstation to boot up and log in to the server over the network. (A diskless workstation is a node on the network, without any disk drive or floppy drive. It cannot access the server until it is powered up, and then it boots up by virtue of the NIC boot ROM, and loads all the required files over the network from the server.) A boot ROM is required in NICs intended for diskless workstations. These workstations minimize security risks by eliminating the risk of software theft or proprietary files stored on a local disk drive. They also prevent an intruder from booting off a floppy drive and running *cracking* software or other undesirable programs. Believe it or not, this is a *very* common way of bypassing many security schemes.

Buffer Memory

Some NIC architectures provide interface pins in the MAC to support the addition of external buffer memory. Client NICs tend to require more buffer memory capacity than server NICs, especially if they are installed in platforms with an ISA bus and 486-class processor. Server NICs are typi-

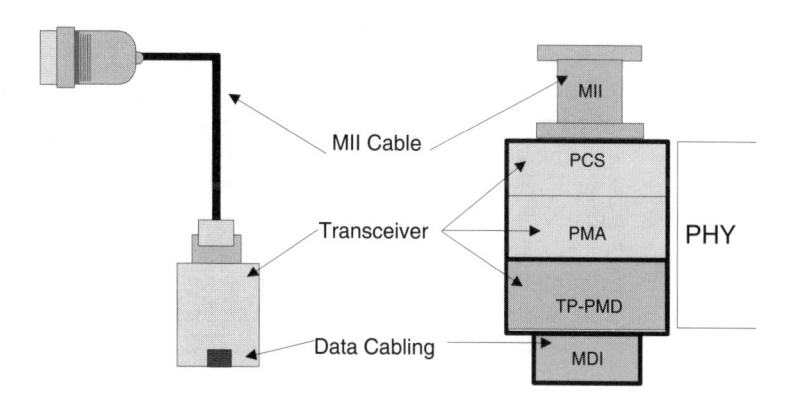

Figure 9.2
EXT MII PHY.

cally installed in high-speed PCI bus platforms capable of supporting Fast Ethernet data rates.

Adapter Bus Architectures

The most logical bus type for Fast Ethernet adapters is the PCI bus, which is better suited for high-speed LAN traffic than EISA or the ISA bus. It has been accepted that the PCI bus signaled the demise of the EISA bus, and in fact most if not all servers and desktop PCs shipped today feature the PCI bus with ISA bus slots. A number of vendors ship ISA-based Fast Ethernet adapters, probably for those customers with legacy ISA-based workstations, who want to upgrade to a higher-speed bus. With the limited bandwidth of the ISA bus, moving to 100Mbps NICs doesn't always provide a linear performance increase. It makes no sense to install ISA Fast Ethernet adapters in servers for performance and CPU utilization.

PCI Bus

The **Peripheral Component Interconnect** bus is an open, nonproprietary, high-performance local bus standard developed by Intel and supported by all the major PC vendors and add-in peripheral controller developers. The PCI bus provides a processor-independent data path between the CPU and high-speed peripherals. It is a well-defined, robust interconnect mechanism designed specifically to accommodate multiple high-performance peripherals, such as high-speed LAN controllers, graphics controllers, full-motion video, SCSI controllers, and so on. The architecture of the PCI local bus ensures interoperability and reliability of the PCI add-in cards in any PCI system, regardless of the CPU architecture or CPU speed. It isolates peripheral components and add-in cards from changes in processor technology and architecture by presenting an interface that stays constant over successive generations of processors.

The bus isolation feature of the PCI Local bus allows developers to design in embedded peripherals directly on the motherboards, and supports a market for cost-competitive add-in peripherals. This has resulted in the PCI bus fast becoming the *de facto* standard for all PCs, including mobile computers, industrial computers, desktop PCs, low- and high-end workstations, and multiprocessor servers. The PCI local bus has a maximum speed of 33MHz, with bus configurations of 32 or 64 bits, for a theoretical throughput of 132MB/s (Megabytes per second) and 264MB/s, respectively. It provides increased performance for high-speed peripherals, such as network controllers, disk controllers, graphics, and video controllers, while maintaining compatibility with the existing ISA/EISA/MicroChannel expansion bus architectures. Its throughput is 20 times faster than the ISA bus and four times faster than the EISA bus. Because of its low CPU utilization, it is an attractive solution for lower-bandwidth LAN protocols such as Ethernet and Token Ring. It is an ideal choice for high-speed LAN protocols such as Fast Ethernet and FDDI. With the increased use of multitasking operating systems, such as Microsoft's Windows NT, Windows for Workgroups, Windows 95, IBM's OS/2, and the different versions of UNIX, these support an application-server environment. The low CPU utilization and bus master feature of the PCI bus make it an ideal bus to offload the host CPU and allow for true multitasking. The future of NIC adapters is the PCI bus.

When Intel initially developed the PCI bus, its idea was to develop a local bus for the Pentium and X86 family of high-performance processors. Due to the large support for the architecture by third-party vendors, and the proliferation of material and understanding of the standard through the PCI SIG (Special Interest Group) forum, this bus has now become a standard for DOS/Windows, Macintosh, OS/2, and UNIX platforms. The early availability of PCI silicon controllers made it relatively easy for NIC developers to bring products to market early. The PCI SIG was set up to promote the PCI local bus standard by organizing regular meetings and training workshops to share technical information, present papers, and discuss changes to the specifications. These meetings are highly organized, and member companies receive up-to-date technical information and technical support in order to deliver compliant product to the market.

Initially Intel targeted the PCI bus toward the video and graphics markets. The early involvement of LAN chip developers, such as AMD, DEC, NCR Microelectronics, and TI, together with the marketing they provided to the LAN companies, accelerated the delivery of LAN NICs to the marketplace. The low cost of PCI silicon for the LAN market ensured the overwhelming acceptance of PCI as the bus of the future. The electrical characteristics of the PCI local bus specification limit the number of PCI slots to two or three, depending on the system architecture. Given that one of these slots would be used for a high-speed graphics controller and one for a SCSI controller, this left at most one for the LAN controller. In a server platform in which a user may have multiple LAN protocols, this was a dilemma. The development of the PCI-PCI bridge controllers by DEC, PLX, and other companies allowed PC developers to increase the number of slots available for add-in modules. High-end servers now feature up to eight PCI slots and an equal number of ISA slots.

Linear Bursts

The PCI local bus architecture supports **linear burst transfers**, whereby large amounts of data are read from or written to a single address, which is then automatically incremented for the next byte in the transfer. This ensures that the bus is continuously filled with data during a burst transfer, resulting in higher bandwidth utilization.

Low Access Latency

PCI peripheral controllers have **low access latencies** which reduce the time required to gain control of the bus after it has posted a request for a data transfer. This allows for faster access to the bus, and reduces the amount of buffer memory required on the peripheral controllers, reducing the overall cost of the add-in cards.

Bus Mastering and Concurrency

The PCI local bus architecture supports bus mastering and concurrency. Bus mastering is where an intelligent peripheral, such as a network controller, takes control of the bus and accelerates high-throughput, high-priority tasks without the need for processor intervention. Concurrency allows the processor to operate simultaneously with the bus mastering devices, and work on other tasks.

Compatibility

The PCI local bus was designed and developed as a supplement to the standard expansion buses, and not as a replacement. It is compatible with the ISA, EISA, and MicroChannel buses, and most systems shipped today feature a shared slot that can accommodate both a PCI and an ISA connector. All PCI add-in boards will function in any PCI platform, independent of the processor or type of expansion bus. This protects user investment in existing add-in cards, provides new bus slots, and eases the integration and selection of newer high-speed peripheral devices.

Almost all Pentium processor class systems shipping today feature PCI slots with either ISA or EISA slots. The logical slot for the high-speed network adapter is the PCI slot, given its true plug-and-play support, and high bus bandwidth. The dramatic advances in processor technology over the last few years, and the widespread use of complex application software have enabled users to demand more from PCs than previously available. Compute-intensive applications, such as sophisticated graphics, high-speed networks, and real-time video controllers, require that large amounts of data be moved between the host processing unit and the peripheral controllers; and clearly the ISA and EISA bus architectures were not capable of supporting these bandwidth requirements.

The PCI local bus was developed to overcome these limitations by moving high-performance peripherals, such as video controllers, network controllers, and disk controllers, closer to the processor; and moving the lower bandwidth peripherals, such as FAX/Modem, tape drives, and printers, onto the standard expansion bus. The ISA and EISA expansion bus interfaces to the PCI local bus similar to another peripheral through a PCI to expansion bus controller. All PCI-based systems now come standard with PCI slots along with either ISA or EISA slots. The majority of the PCI-based systems come standard with ISA slots.

PCI Bus Width

The PCI bus specification specifies a 64-bit data bus extension to the current 32-bit bus. At 33 MHz this will provide a maximum sustained throughput of 264 Mbps. For higher-speed network protocols and increased performance, the emergence of NICs for the 64-bit PCI bus will open new opportunities. There are really no 64-bit PCI NICs available at the time of this writing, but you can expect to see them late in 1997, especially with the development of Gigabit Ethernet and other high-speed network protocols like fiber channel. The PCI bus architecture preserves forward and backward compatibility between the 32-bit bus and the 64-bit bus, with the transparency provided by the PCI connector. This connector accepts both 32-bit and 64-bit PCI NICs, and will automatically adjust to the correct data bus width. The NIC drivers must also be aware of the bus width so that it can automatically configure to the correct bus width in order to maximize the bus transfer rate.

EISA Bus

The EISA bus architecture was developed as an extension of the ISA bus architecture. It was developed by a consortium of companies led by Compaq. It is identical to the ISA-compatible bus architecture with enhancements that support all PC, XT, and AT hardware and software. Additionally, it supports a 32-bit data bus in a 32-bit address space. The primary difference between the EISA and ISA architecture is that some slots have a special EISA connector that allow add-on modules compatible with ISA to use the slot without touching the EISA-specific signal lines. This special connector supports the additional address, data, and control signals needed to support EISA-compatible modules. The 32-bit address and data bus lines provide 32 data bits over a four-gigabyte address space.

While the ISA bus is asynchronous to the BCLK, the EISA bus is synchronous, providing increased functionality and performance. The EISA bus architecture supports the asynchronous nature of the 8- and 8/16-bit slots, but additional bus cycles unique to the EISA bus are executed using only the synchronous control signals of the EISA connector. This support of both asynchronous and synchronous bus cycles allows EISA-compatible platforms to be compatible with ISA-compatible add-on modules.

ISA Bus

The Industry Standard Architecture bus was developed and introduced by IBM in the early 1980s. The ISA standard is the generic name for the 8-bit and 8/16-bit PC-, XT-, and AT-compatible bus. Two types of connectors can be used in an ISA slot: 8-bit and 8/16-bit. The 8-bit slot is a single, 62-pin connector and supports only 8-bit add-on slave devices. The 8/16-bit slot contains both the 8-bit slot 62-pin connector, and an additional 36-pin connector. This second connector supports additional address space, more DMA channels, more interrupt lines, and additional data lines.

The ISA bus can execute bus cycles at 8.33MHz, and on AT platforms the ISA add-on adapters must execute cycles at 8MHz. The ISA bus architecture is not well suited to multiple adapters, and this is particularly noticeable in PCI/ISA platforms. The arbitration used between the ISA bus and the PCI bus gives a higher priority to the ISA bus than the PCI bus, because the PCI bus is much faster than the ISA bus at getting on and off the bus. The ISA plug-and-play bus specification was a welcome addition to the ISA bus architecture, and is meant to make ISA-based add-in cards easier to install.

ISA and EISA Bus Compatibility

The ISA and EISA bus specifications support two address spaces: memory and I/O. To maintain backward software compatibility, a number of restrictions are placed on the memory and I/O address spaces. The memory address space is divided into three groups: platforms memory, EPROM memory, and slot memory resources. The first 640Kb are reserved for DOS, the next 256Kb for bus memory resources such as video and hard disk, and the next 128Kb for the ROM devices, which include the BIOS. For the PC- and XT-compatible platforms, 20 address signal lines are supported for a memory address space of 1Mb. AT-compatible platforms support 24 address signal lines for a memory space of 16Mb. The EISA-compatible platforms support 32 address signal lines for a total memory address space of 4Gb. The first 1Mb of memory address space on the AT- and EISA-compatible platforms is defined in the same way as in the PC- and XT-compatible platforms.

> The size of the I/O address space on the ISA- and EISA-compatible CPU platforms is 64Kb, and this varies from system to system. On ISA-compatible platforms, typically only 1Kb of the 64Kb I/O address space is used. The first 256 bytes are reserved for the I/O platform resources, such as interrupts and DMA controllers. The remaining 768 bytes are available for general add-on I/O slave modules. Since the ISA bus supports only 1Kb of I/O address space, only the first 10 address signal lines are decoded, resulting in the 256 platform address locations and the 768 bus address locations being repeated 64 times in the address space. On EISA-compatible platforms this feature is used to assign 63 of the 64 repeated blocks of 256 address locations to specific add-on card slots. This partition results in four groups of 256 address locations being assigned to each slot for a total of 1,024 specific address locations per slot.

PC Card

The continuing evolution of notebook computers into fully functional workstations has become strategically important to the mobile business traveler. No longer is it the second PC that is taken out of the office at the start of a business trip. With the introduction of powerful Pentium-class processors, PC Cards, which benefit from their flexibility and lightweight design, are becoming the most popular way to connect the laptop to the corporate network. One of the primary reasons for the increased use of the laptop is the availability of PC Card adapters, and the applications and networking protocols they support, such as 10Mbps combo cards and 10/100Base-T combo cards. The PC Card standard was developed by PCMCIA and JEIDA. PCMCIA stands for Personal Computer Memory Card International Association—an association of over 500 member companies representing computer manufacturers, silicon companies, peripheral vendors, software developers, mechanical and connector developers, and many others dedicated to the development and promotion of credit-card-size adapters for notebook, laptop, and portable computers. JEIDA stands for the Japanese Electronic Industry Development Association, which was established in 1958 as a nonprofit organization to promote growth in the Japanese economy by stimulating development in the electronics industry. Both PCMCIA and JEIDA developed the standard for a credit-card-size adapter for portable computers. The PC Card standard defines a 68-pin interface between the peripheral card and the PC Card socket in the portable computer. There are three standard PC Card sizes, called Type I, Type II, and Type III. All PC Cards have the same dimensions for width and length, but the thickness of the card depends on the PC Card type:

- **Type I** has the smallest thickness, measuring 3.3mm. It is primarily used for memory cards.
- **Type II** measures 5mm in thickness and is used for applications in which the internal components are taller, such as LAN adapters and modem cards. Most silicon vendors offer a wide range of packaging for their LAN controllers, so it may be possible to fit these into a Type-I PC Card. Add-in cards are now capable of supporting 10/100 Fast Ethernet with additional modem support.
- **Type III** measures 10.5mm in thickness and is the tallest form factor of the three types. Type-III PC Cards can be used in applications in which there are tall components such as motors and disk drives. The smaller-size PC Cards can fit into the thicker host sockets, but this is not always the case for Type-III PC Cards.

The PC Card standard specifies the electrical and mechanical requirements, as well as a defined software architecture to provide plug-and-play capability across the widest range of platforms. These sockets services are BIOS-level interfaces that mask the hardware implementation of the add-in card from the PC Card vendor's driver. They identify the number of sockets in the system, and detect when a PC Card is inserted or removed from a socket. The socket service interface isolates the driver from specific hardware implementation features in PC Card. Card services interface to socket services, and automatically provide management capabilities of system resources, such as interrupts, DMA channels, and memory space for PC Cards as they become active in the system. With card and socket services installed in the host system, PC Cards can be inserted and removed from a socket without powering off the host or rebooting the system. The new PC Card standard set in early 1995 improved compatibility and added three new improvements to the standard:

- PC Card will run at 3.3V instead of 5V, thereby extending battery life.
- The new standard incorporated CardBus bus mastering support.
- Support is provided for Direct Memory Access (DMA). This allows PC Card adapters on the bus to exchange data with each other directly without the host CPU.

The CardBus standard is backward compatible, but not forward compatible. Legacy 5V cards will fit into the new standard slot, which will interrogate the PC Card and switch to the appropriate voltage to support the installed PC Card. New 3.3V PC Cards will not fit into legacy 5V slots. The initial migration of LAN technology to the PC Card Standard was 10Mbps Ethernet and the ever-present Token Ring adapters. To provide remote access to the corporate network, PC Card combo versions quickly hit the market with the addition of a modem port along with the LAN port. This same trend is happening with the Fast Ethernet protocol, with some of the leading PC Card vendors shipping PC Cards with 10/100Mbps ports and 33.6Kbps modem ports. When selecting NICs for laptops and portables, make sure the vendor supplies cards for the CardBus standard, or at least has plans to develop CardBus cards. The PC Card bus interface is analogous to the ISA bus specification, while the CardBus interface is analogous to the PCI local bus specification.

CardBus

This is the 32-bit version of the PC Card and is based on the PCI bus architecture. It supports 3.3V operation, making it ideal for mobile computing. The CardBus interface is modeled after the PCI local bus specification, but mapped to the PCMCIA 68-pin connector. There are some modifications to allow for hot-swapping, dynamic resource configuration, and the electrical pin assignments, because of the reduced pin count. CardBus supports:

- 32-bit bus mastering
- 32-bit memory slave
- 32-bit I/O slave
- Memory read and write cycles
- I/O space read and write cycles
- Configuration space read and write cycles
- Memory read multiple
- Memory read line
- Memory write and invalidate

The CardBus standard is better suited to high-speed LAN connectivity such as 100Base-T. When choosing CardBus NICs, make sure you understand the different options offered by the vendor, such as 10/100Base-TX NICs, 10/100Base-T4, and combo cards with these media interface and modem ports. Fast Ethernet deployment for laptops should really be targeted to CardBus NICs.

Bus Transfer Modes

There are a number of different methods for transferring data across the bus interface between the host platform and an add-in peripheral module.

Direct Memory Access (DMA)

In this technique the add-in card or NIC signals the host CPU that a data transfer request is pending. When the host CPU receives the DMA request from the NIC, it halts all other operations to handle the data transfer. Newer NIC designs replace DMA with Bus Mastering DMA.

Bus Mastering DMA

This is a bus mastering method in which the add-in peripheral module has an on-board DMA controller, which is usually integrated inside the bus controller device. The DMA controller uses the system memory to store, transmit, and receive packets directly without intervention by the host CPU. The DMA controller has direct access and control of the system memory for read/write cycle and data transfers. It relieves the host CPU from the overhead associated with read/write cycles and block data transfer across the bus.

Fast Ethernet controllers are primarily bus mastering and feature local on-board memory called FIFO (first-in/first-out). The FIFO memory may be external to the controller, which drives up the cost of the module, or it may be integrated inside the bus controller device. For network devices, FIFO memory is required to buffer data being received from the LAN before being transferred across the system bus, to system memory. For a highly optimized bus architecture and efficient packet transfer, the DMA controller needs guaranteed access to system memory.

The size of the FIFO should be capable of sustaining packets being received at full wire speed, without dropping packets, while the DMA controller arbitrates and gains access to the bus. If the FIFO memory is too small, receive overflows occur and the incoming packets are lost and must be transmitted by the sending node. This leads to dropped packets and poor performance of the overall network.

Some PCI Fast Ethernet controllers feature programmable FIFO threshold levels. This feature allows the driver to dynamically adjust the FIFO depth to meet the system bus I/O availability in order to provide maximum throughput. The PCI bus architecture supports guaranteed bus access, whereas the ISA bus does not. Running Fast Ethernet in an ISA bus is not recommended.

Shared Memory

The shared memory architecture does not have a DMA engine and depends on the host CPU to handle the data transfer between system memory and on-board shared or local memory. This technique is also known as store-and-forward. While the system CPU is controlling the transfer of data between the host memory and the local on-board memory, it is not performing any other tasks. This leads to high CPU utilization and lower throughput, which is not what is required on a network adapter. Network adapters based on the store-and-forward architecture are less expensive than DMA-based adapters, but their ability to handle system latencies and bursty traffic patterns without dropping packets is suspect. Shared memory adapters are not easy to install and can lead to memory conflicts, especially with NICs that try to use the same shared memory location at the same time as other installed devices.

Programmed Input/Output

Programmed I/O transfers between system memory and the adapter buffer memory are controlled by the host CPU on the host side, and an on-board special processor on the NIC. Each transfer is done through register reads and writes to the same block of memory. The two processors communicate with each other through an I/O interrupt scheme to signal when data is ready to be read or written by the other entity. Programmed I/O uses less memory than other transfer techniques, but it is also less efficient in data throughput.

Other Hardware Features

The Fast Ethernet NICs available from various vendors are distinguished from each other by how vendors use these chipsets. Not all NICs that use the same chipsets are created equal. Some are definitely more equal than others. Many vendors add unique features to NICs implemented around common chipsets. For example, many NICs support boot ROMs.

One of the most critical areas of a NIC design is the physical interface between the NIC chipset and the MDI connector. This is, of course, the PHY. A critical part of the PHY is the PMD, which is where signal wave shaping and filtering takes place, usually with integrated filter and magnetic transformers. Several well-known companies manufacture these devices, and a high-quality NIC design will have second or third sources for suppliers. The lead times, quality, and reliability of the magnetic components used on NIC designs can be the difference between success and failure for a company regardless of the chipset used or the robustness of the drivers. When choosing a NIC vendor, understanding the chipset and magnetic components used on the design can be important. NIC vendors should have support documentation showing that each of the PMDs used on their NICs were tested and qualified for FCC emissions, and compliance with the electrical signaling, physical connections, and media-specific protocols of the IEEE 802.3u specifications.

If you are just purchasing a few Fast Ethernet NICs, you many not need to request this information from the vendor. Most first tier vendors of Fast Ethernet NICs, such as Compaq, test all their NICs in this manner.

However, if you are purchasing hundreds or thousands of NICs for an entire enterprise, then doing this kind of research can really pay off. Even major manufacturers will take the time to work with you if you are making a large purchase. If a vendor is reluctant to provide you with this information, then you may want to look elsewhere.

Other hardware features added to a NIC are LEDs visible from the outside of the PC through the bracket. These LEDs may be used to indicate the line data rates and link activity, or transmit and receive activity on the LAN media. They are extremely useful during installations, or if the network is down and you are troubleshooting a physical network component problem. The LEDs will give a quick, at-a-glance indication of the status and activity of the NIC without having to remove the PC cover. External LEDs are often required by large NIC purchasers for this very reason.

Dual-Speed NICs

Many Fast Ethernet NICs support both 10Base-T Ethernet operation and 100Base-TX operation on one card. As mentioned before, these NICs actually have two PHYs, one for Ethernet and one for Fast Ethernet. These NICs are often called 10/100 adapters and can automatically detect configuration themselves, according to the type of repeater they are plugged into, either 10Base-T or 100Base-TX.

The deployment of 10/100 Fast Ethernet adapters in your organization can make it much easier to upgrade users from Ethernet to Fast Ethernet. Often installing 10/100 adapters is the first step when upgrading users from Ethernet to Fast Ethernet. These adapters will work fine with existing 10Base-T LANs. This approach allows the new Fast Ethernet infrastructure to be installed without interrupting network services to users while the new Fast Ethernet repeaters and switches are installed and new Cat-5 cable is pulled. After the new Fast Ethernet infrastructure is in place, tested, and operational, users can easily be moved from the 10Base-T equipment to the new Fast Ethernet system without interrupting their network service. 10/100 NICs are priced low enough, often only a few dollars more than a 100Mbps only NIC. Often, the cost saved by the easy upgrade of users more than offsets the extra costs of the dual-speed NICs, which makes it very easy to justify purchasing them.

A dual-speed NIC requires an on-board PCI-PCI bridge. The PCI bridge provides a primary PCI bus interface for the host platform and a secondary PCI bus interface, behind which cascaded design can be placed.

Autosensing

Most of the Fast Ethernet adapters being designed and shipped today are 10/100Mbps. This is ideal for those users who are installing new adapters in a 10Mbps environment, but want the flexibility to upgrade to the faster 100Mbps rate when budget and schedules allow. A required feature for customers purchasing 10/100Mbps adapters is the autosense driver and Autonegotiation support in the NIC, which will make such higher-speed upgrades easier.

Autonegotiation support in NICs, hubs, and switches makes it possible for these devices to exchange information about their ability to support different media data rates. Each end node autonegotiates with the hub or switch port to determine the highest data rate each can support, and then automatically configures to that speed. This capability provides for automatic speed matching of dual-speed NICs with dual-speed hubs and switches. Using dual-speed devices in the network ensures that the network will be configured to run at the highest speed autonegotiated between end nodes and hubs or switch ports. A more detailed discussion of Autonegotiation is found in Appendix D.

The Autonegotiation protocol is also used by hubs and switches to signal to end nodes whether they support full-duplex operation on some or all of its ports. If the NICs connected to these ports also support full-duplex operation, then they configure themselves to use full-duplex mode when connected to these ports. The Autonegotiation protocol is defined to support future high-speed data rates for Ethernet, thereby maintaining forward and backward speed compatibility with future products such as Gigabit Ethernet.

PCI Bus Voltages

The architecture of the PCI bus specifies three voltage interfaces: 5V, 3.3V and universal. Almost all NICs shipped are based on the standard 5V electrical bus interface. The PCI bus architecture provides support for a 3.3V, a 5V, and a universal electrical interface, the goal being that eventually all PCs will use 3.3V as the standard. The reasons for this are power saving and low-power operation, especially for mobile computing needs with extended battery life and smaller and lighter batteries.

The PCI bus specification also provides support for a universal electrical interface. The universal bus interface connects the add-in card to both the 3.3V and 5V power systems of the host. The mechanical design of the NIC bus connector must support this feature through mechanical keys in the bus interface. The mechanical keying used on the PCI bus connector is such that a 5V-only card can be plugged into a 5V-only host PCI slot. A NIC with a universal bus interface can be inserted into a 5V-only PCI slot, a 3.3V-only PCI slot, or a PCI slot that supports both 3.3V and 5V bus interfaces. The electrical design of the NIC PCI bus interface must also support the type of PCI slot in which the module can be used (see Figure 9.3).

3.3v   5.0v

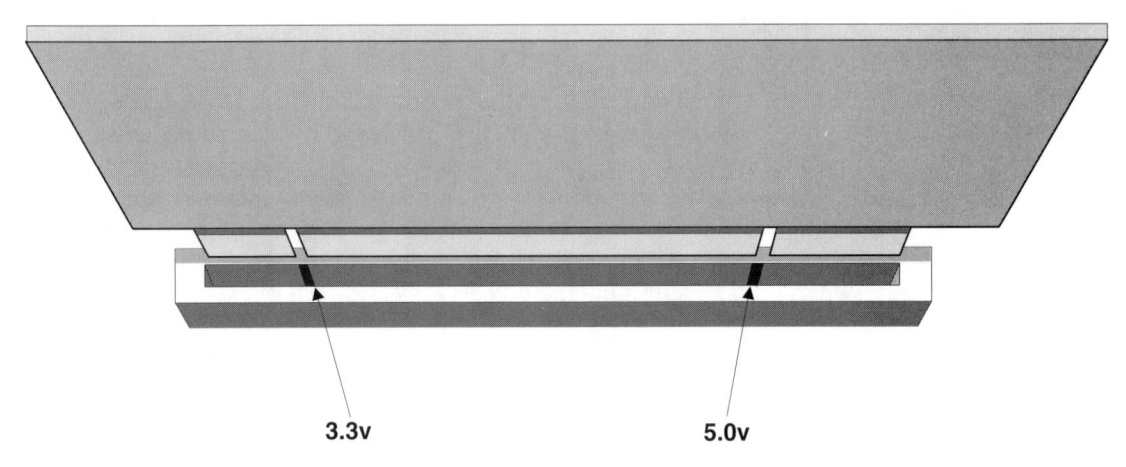

Figure 9.3
PCI bus universal connector.

NIC Power Management

The millions of computers used throughout industry and in the home have a big impact on the amount of power used each day. The heat generated by banks of computers in the lab and office environment also puts a demand on the cooling system. If you are like most users, you leave your computer switched on all the time. Chip developers and PC manufacturers have addressed this problem by introducing the concept of low power down modes. This causes the computer to enter a lower power state when it is not being used for a period of time. This had had a big impact on power consumption by the devices themselves, and also on the cooling systems where computers are used.

A new hardware requirement specified by Microsoft in their PC '97 Hardware Design Guide describes the "Wake on LAN" hardware feature required in all NIC adapters after January '98. A new concept called the **magic packet** has been developed and has the support of the PC and networking industry. The idea of the magic packet is that the PC is turned on whenever it receives a magic pattern over the LAN. This requires that the NIC and the host platform have this feature incorporated into their design. Hardware on the NIC card provides an external physical connection to the host motherboard, which enables it to power up the host once it receives the magic packet over the network.

This feature will allow IS and system managers to remotely power up and down remote clients during off-peak times to upgrade software, gather statistics, and general platform maintenance. The PCI bus interface provides support for power management. Computers with embedded NICs on the motherboard with support for magic packet do not require an external electrical connection between the embedded NIC and the host motherboard. The connection is part of the layout of the whole motherboard.

NIC Media Flexibility

The three media specifications in the Fast Ethernet standard provides great flexibility in choosing the proper NIC for your application. The location of the client and the server impacts on the media interface required on the NIC. The servers are typically located in the wiring closet or in a local workgroup, while the client workstations are distributed throughout the horizontal floor offices. For server NICs at the workgroup level the choice is usually between 100Base-TX and 100Base-T4. The fact that the server connects to a hub or switch in the wiring closet makes the choice of using 100Base-TX or 100Base-T4 less critical, because cable changes can be made quite easily given the structured wiring infrastructure.

At the workgroup level, the cabling in the walls and ceiling may be a mix of Categories 3 and 5. If the cabling is Category 3, then 100Base-T4 NICs and hubs will be required for the server connections. If all of the cable is Category 5, then 100Base-TX NICs and hubs may be used for the server connections. The choice of NIC media interfaces for the client workstations depends entirely on the cabling used to the offices—100Base-T4 NICs for Category-3 UTP cable, and 100Base-TX NICs for Category-5 UTP cabling. If there is any uncertainty about the actual mix of cables throughout the office space, the safest choice is 100Base-T4 NICs. Most of the larger NIC companies carry a range of NICs based on bus type, media, and end-node application.

Media-Independent Interface

The 802.3u specification provides for media-independent interfaces (MIIs) external to the NIC or hub or switch ports. The MII is a well-defined electrical and mechanical interface between the 100Base-T MAC and various PHYs that may be internal or external to the NIC, hub, or switch port; and allows designers of NICs, hubs, and switches to design and develop products independent of the PHY. The MII may be embedded in the design, in which case the component of the PHY will be located on the NIC or in the hub and switch ports. If the NIC design supports an external MII, the layout of the module will be different from the standard NIC, to allow an external MII to plug into the on-board MII electrical connector. The MII specifies a logical interface capable of driving signal a maximum of 0.5m, over a 40-pin mechanical connector similar in style to the SCSI connector. If your design uses a NIC, hub, or switch with external PHYs, the MII cable length of 0.5m should be factored into the calculations for determining and validating the worst-case delays for that link segment (see Figure 9.4).

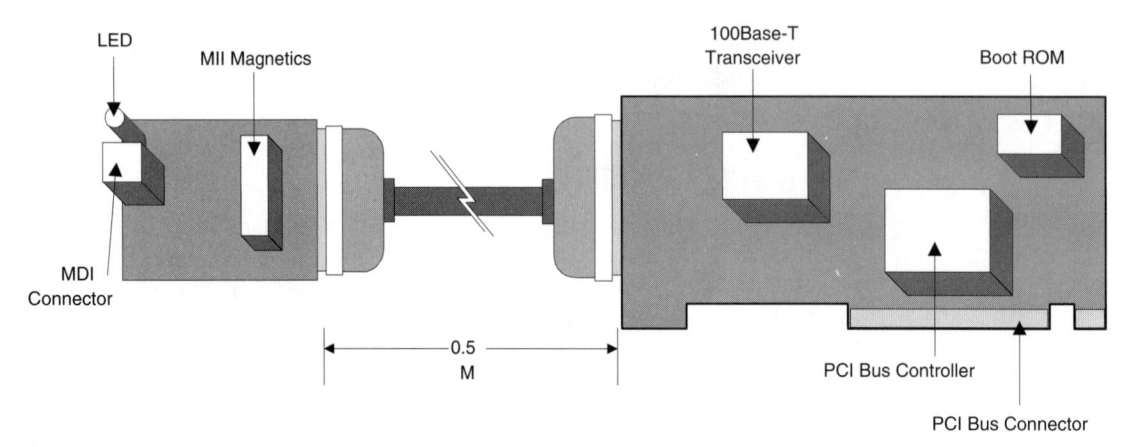

Figure 9.4
NIC with external MII PHY and MII cable.

By using external PHYs, a systems integrator can structure the NIC, hub, or switch with different PHYs to support his cable media infrastructure. The MII is an open standard that guarantees interoperability between hardware from different companies. For PC developers and manufacturers, the MII allows them to build servers and clients with the NIC installed during the build process, and then customize the platform to the end-user media specification. The external MII PHYs are also used in platforms other than servers and clients, such as routers, switches, and wide area network products. Because of the size of the PCB and the mechanical connectors used in the interface, NICs designed with external PHYs are more expensive than integrated NICs (see Figure 9.5).

NIC Feature Set

The list below indicates the features of a client NIC and server NIC.

Feature Set	ISA Bus	Embedded NICs	PCI Bus	PC Card	CardBus
UTP Media	C	C/S	C/S	C	C
STP Media	C	C/S	C/S	N/A	N/A
Fiber Media	N/A	C/S	C/S	N/A	N/A
Single Port	C	C/S	C/S	C	C
Dual Port	N/A	N/A	S	N/A	N/A
Boot ROM	C	N/A	C	N/A	N/A
Power Mgr.	N/A	C/S	C/S	N/A	C

Note that, in the table, C = client and S = server.

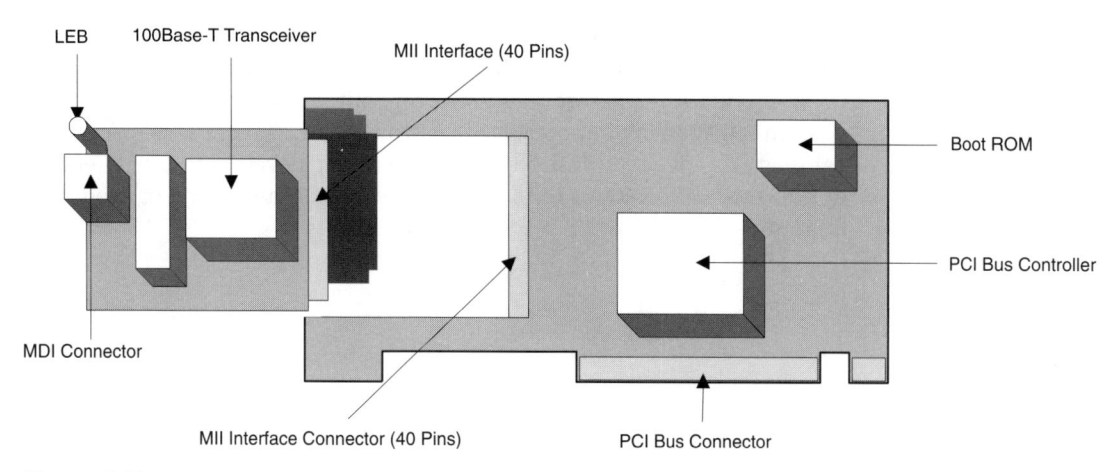

Figure 9.5
PCI NIC with external MII PHY.

Hardware Certification

All NIC adapters must have FCC Class A certification at a minimum. This certifies that the product meets Part 15 of the FCC emissions standard, and is safe for use in a business environment without causing electrical interference to other equipment, such as heart monitors, televisions, and telephones. To address the growing small-office/home-office industry, NIC vendors are now certifying NICs for FCC Class-B compliance. This standard states that the product complies with the safety regulations for domestic use.

Another certification that has become a check item in the features list is CE compliance, the European certification requirement for electronic products shipped for sale in the European market. Each NIC certified for FCC Class-B compliance will have an FCC assigned identification number. The certification type and unique number will be displayed in a prominent place on the NIC board either etched or in silkscreen. The FCC does not consider fiber-based NICs or fiber-based media modules such as 100Base-FX to be computer peripherals, especially since fiber, unlike UTP- or STP-based modules, does not radiate or absorb electrical interference. For this reason the NIC cannot display an FCC number.

For NICs with fiber PMDs, the FCC has suggested using the term "FCC Class type compliant," where "type" will be either A or B to designate the class of certification, on the NIC PCB (etched or silkscreened). A number of other compliance and regulatory certifications are required by the FCC. The European certification or the CE mark is required for products shipped to Europe.

Additional certification standards are required for Germany, Japan, and Canada, so if you are purchasing NICs or networking products for those countries, make sure they are compliant. For full details of the certification required in your area, it is best to check with your local or national FCC agency. Most NIC and networking developers specify details of the certification status of their products in their marketing or product literature.

CHAPTER 10

Designing the Cable Plant

The cable plant is that part of the network that encompasses the cable media selection, the physical placement and installation of the cable media, and the termination of the cable media at the end node and in the wiring closet. The design and installation of the cable plant have a big impact on the quality, reliability, and flexibility of your current and future networks.

A primary requirement in a structured cable layout is that the layout should accommodate equipment relocation and network growth. The diversity of the workforce and areas of responsibility within a company cause over 50 percent of users and equipment to move each year. The increase in the number of computers used within groups and the growth of the workforce require that networks should have the flexibility to support growth without recabling.

Networks are created physically when active and passive devices are connected together by a structured cabling system. The active devices are end nodes, switches, and routers; the passive devices include connectors, terminators, patch panels, and passive repeaters. A well-defined, structured cabling infrastructure is independent of the equipment it services and the applications being run on the network.

A structured network is analogous to the infrastructure of highway roads that carry various types of traffic between different cities. The quality, dependability, and ease of use of these roads make the transportation of traffic more efficient and reliable. The access method and rate of speed are determined by other factors, not the road. Likewise, good design and structure are the bases for a dependable and flexible network, one that allows network managers to make changes easily and with minimal disruption to the users.

Planning a Structured Network

A structured network makes an ideal platform for migration from legacy networks to high-speed networking, such as Fast Ethernet, FDDI, ATM, or Gigabit Ethernet. Once a network infrastructure is in place, any major changes to network architecture or media type will be very expensive and will result in major disruption in productivity, so when you are designing a network cable plant, it is important to conduct a thorough analysis of the site requirements, plan for growth and user changes, and provide the capability to handle increased bandwidth-intensive applications. To achieve these objectives, a three-step process for planning, designing, and implementing a structured wiring system is recommended.

The first step is a site survey of the location where the network will be installed. This should include the types of users, the applications being run on the network, planned and unplanned growth requirements, and the frequency of moves, additions, and deletions. A site survey should be conducted to determine the space, size, safety, environmental, and grounding requirements.

The planning and design phases should include detailed diagrams of the site for cable runs, number of drops per office, termination requirements, and the physical location of wiring closets and equipment rooms. The planning phase should also include provisions for fire and safety compliance, local restrictions on building changes, environmental impacts to the building, and structural changes and modifications that may be necessary. The cable and equipment used in the cable plant design should comply with local, national, and regulatory guidelines.

During the cable installation and certification phase, procedures should be in place to make sure that the cable plant meets the designed standards, cable specifications, and quality. The cable plant installation should meet with the Electronic Industries Association/Telecommunications Industries Association (EIA/TIA) 568 wiring standard for commercial buildings. This standard defines the requirements and guidelines for the following installations:

- Campus backbone subsystem with its main cross-connects
- Intermediate backbone subsystem with its intermediate cross-connects
- Horizontal subsystem with its telecommunications closet
- Topology of the media
- Termination and connections
- The network media type (fiberoptic cable, copper cable)
- Cable plant maintenance and administration

Site Survey

A site survey is required to understand the physical layout of the building and its location relative to other buildings, and to identify the location of the equipment and equipment rooms that are to be connected to the network. It is important at the start of network planning to determine if there is sufficient room in the cable distribution system to accommodate more wire for the new network, or in the case of a new installation, if there is sufficient room for the new network or any physical limitations on it.

The purpose of the site survey is to document the requirements and limitations of the site, factors that will directly influence the planning of the proposed network. The site survey is conducted by the contractor selected to install the network, and is not necessarily technical in nature; rather, it deals with administrative, legal, and often political issues. For example, whether the building is owned or leased often determines the type of cable that can be used as well as the contractors who can install the cable and equipment, and who can or cannot approve the work.

The survey also investigates the environment where the cable will be run, such as duct locations, riser locations, wiring closet locations, high temperature areas, high humidity conditions, and requirements for fire-retardant cabling. These are all marked and recorded on the site building plans.

Another consideration are the power and grounding requirements for the equipment to be installed. If multiple buildings are part of the campuswide network, the grounding of different buildings is not usually the same due to different power grids, power surges, and load balancing, which often leads to unexpected network behavior. One way to overcome this is to use fiberoptic cable links between buildings.

Planning and Design Phase

The planning phase is where the data collected during the site survey is combined with the guidelines specified in the EIA/TIA 568 structured cabling rules, and the guidelines of the Fast Ethernet media specifications. This phase of the process results in the generation of a Network Plan, which is the blueprint of the project, combining the data collected during the site survey with standard specifications for network installation and the type of network to be installed. The Network Plan should have sufficient detail and guidelines that the contractors hired to install the network have enough data to successfully install the network at the specified site with minimal supervision.

Cable Installation and Certification

For a new cable plant design, there is a greater flexibility in the type of cable that can be used in the horizontal and vertical plant. All new cable plant installations should use only Category-5 UTP cable for the horizontal cable runs to the work area, and at least one strand of two-pair fiberoptic cable if the budget allows. Running fiber cable in the horizontal cable plant provides the bandwidth for future bandwidth-intensive applications that migrate to the desktop environment, such as desktop video-on-demand, clip art, videoconferencing, graphic images for medical applications, and other high-speed network applications that have not yet been developed.

Using Category-5 cable should be a required minimum for the desktop. All cable installations should be installed by a qualified professional and should meet the guidelines set forth by the EIA/TIA 568 wiring standard. Cables should not be pulled or stressed during installation, and should not have acute bends or kinks, as these can cause characteristic changes in the physical cable and may also change its characteristic impedance, which can lead to an unreliable cable plant once it is in production.

Cable Plant Certification

After the cable wiring plant has been installed, it must be tested and certified before the installation contract can be completed. The cable plant certification is a way of testing the performance of the network, and also serves as a measure of the quality of the installation work of the cable wiring and the networking equipment. The cable plant certification is not limited or confined to the wiring closet; it covers all elements and wiring for the whole network. With the older, Category-3 UTP cable, the certification of a cable plant was easier because of that cable's relaxed parameters. For Category-5 UTP cable and fiberoptic cable, the rules and guidelines are clear and specific. Therefore, the quality of the workmanship, the equipment used, and the way cables are terminated can be major factors in getting certification for Category-5 or fiberoptic cable plant installation.

To help with this, a number of high-caliber, hand-held cable testers are available on the market. These devices are quite sophisticated and can measure the cable length; cable attenuation; near- and far-end crosstalk; basic wiring faults, such as crossed pairs, split pairs, reversed wires, opens, and shorts; and the resistance and characteristic impedance of the line. In buildings where STP has been run to the work area, as in the case of a Token Ring environment, these cables must be reterminated with Category-5 RJ45 connectors at either end, since there are very few adapters or other Fast Ethernet components with a DB9 connector.

Cable Plant Topology

The EIA/TIA Commercial Building Wiring Standard recommends a **cable plant wiring topology**. This is basically a three-level star wiring topology designed to cover all aspects of network configuration, such as Ring, Star, and Bus type networks. In well-design structured cable wiring plants, these three wiring structures can easily be identified. The design of the cable plant wiring topology provides the flexibility to configure the cable plant in either a Star, Bus, or Ring simply by using the patch panels located in the wiring closet.

Three levels of cable plant configuration schemes are used to interconnect the network equipment, such as repeaters, hubs, switches, routers, servers, and workstations, to form a functional network. The three levels of wiring hierarchy are not necessary in every network installation, but their presence signifies a well-designed structured network. The three levels are:

- Horizontal wiring
- Vertical backbone wiring
- Campus wiring

Elements of a Structured Cabling System Design

The EIA/TIA Commercial Building Wiring Standard recommends a cable plant wiring topology to provide the maximum flexibility for network configuration and changes. The cable plant wiring topology encompasses the horizontal, vertical, and campus backbone wiring cable plant, which forms the structure on which the network design, performance, and reliability are based. In addition to the cable wiring topology, a number of basic elements are identifiable in well-designed structured cable plants (see Figure 10.1). The six main elements of a well-designed structured cabling plant are:

- Building entrance
- Equipment room
- Wiring closet
- Backbone cabling
- Horizontal cabling
- Work area

Building Entrance

This is where the outside cabling from another building or facility interfaces with the intrabuilding backbone cabling. This interface is usually

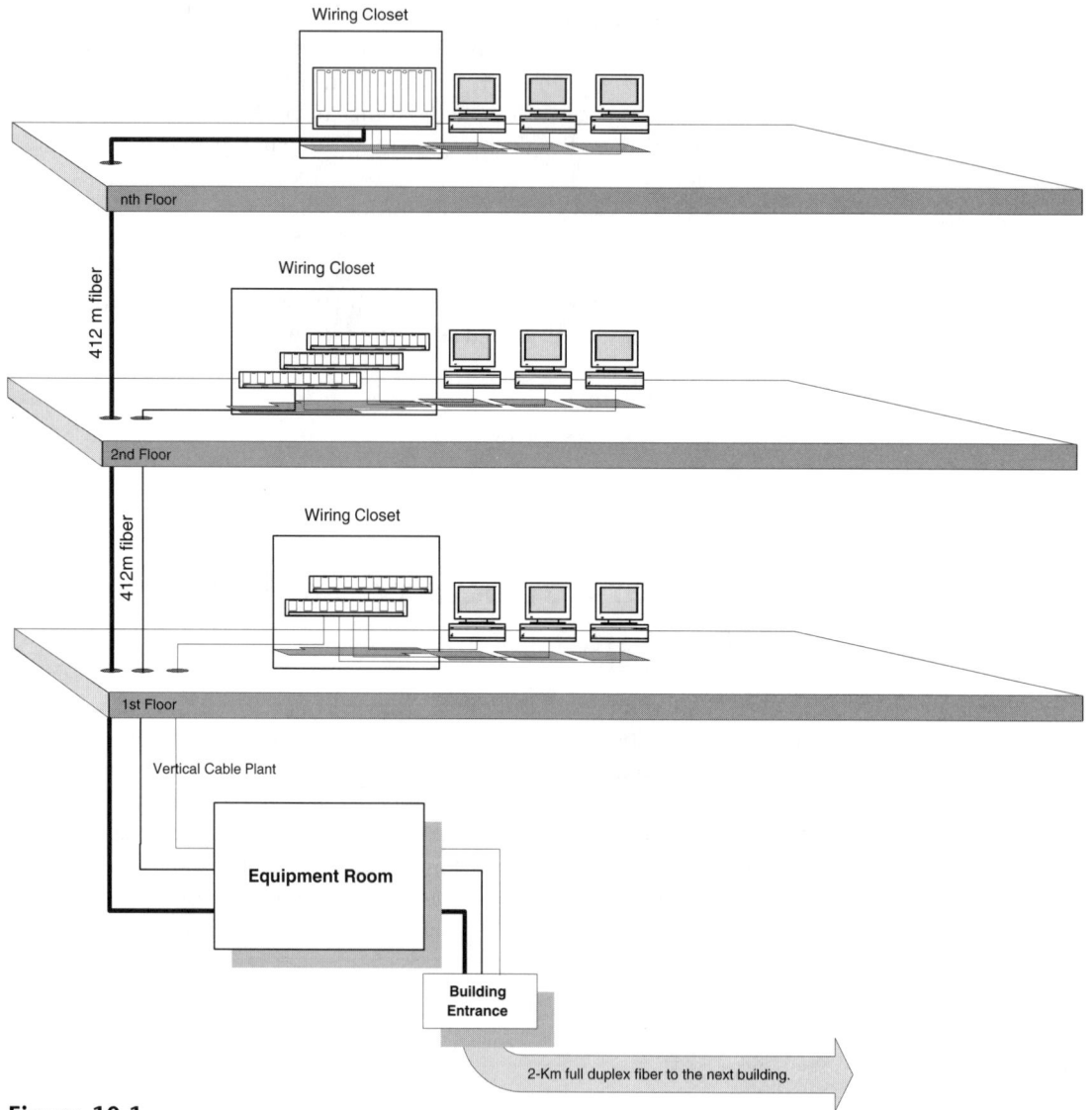

Figure 10.1
Structured cabling system.

located within the equipment room in the form of a punch-down block for cable, or a router that is one of the interfaces between WAN and LAN environments. The type of cable used in the building is often specific to the site, and a connection between buildings almost always dictates that the type of cable used be multimode fiber. The primary reasons for using multimode fiber are its immunity to electromagnetic interference (EMI), and its capacity to operate over extended distances.

Other cables typically identified at the building entrance connect to WANs. The WAN network may be private or it may be across the public telephone network or another communication medium, such as satellite links, microwave links, or leased lines from long-distance telephone carriers. Companies and businesses with offices in different cities across the country or overseas have to connect all the sites together in order to share and access data that is essential to running the business. The connection outside of the office or building environment to these other sites is through a WAN network. That part of the WAN at the building entrance requires special equipment to interface between the LAN and the WAN, depending on the medium used at the WAN point of access.

Equipment Room

The equipment room is a secured area, with limited access provided to key personnel such as the network manager and the IS department members responsible for network support and maintenance. The design and layout of the equipment room is specified by the EIA/TIA 568 standard, which contains guidelines for placement and mounting of equipment racks, overhead cable trays, power supplies, and lighting, as well as cable types and specifications. The equipment located in the equipment room includes servers, uninterruptible power supplies (UPSs), and equipment that is more complex than that found in the telecommunications closet. Some or all of the functions of the wiring closet and telecommunications closet may be located within the equipment room.

Wiring Closet/Telecommunications Room

The wiring closet or telecommunications closet is the area within the building that contains the network cabling system equipment, and is where all the cable runs from each office in the work area of a floor are concentrated. Cable connections from other floors or buildings are also brought into the wiring closet. The cables brought into the wiring closet are terminated and connected to the repeaters, hubs, switches, and routers to form a network. The wiring closet is the central cross-connect access location for the horizontal building wiring and the vertical backbone wiring, which interconnects the equipment rooms on each floor.

Punch-down blocks are used to terminate the cable plant entering the wiring closet. A punch-down block is so named because a special spring-loaded hand tool is used to punch or push down a shielded wire between the jaws of a retaining clip. As the wire is forced between the jaws of the retaining clip, it slices the outer PVC covering of the wire, thereby making electrical contact with the wire. These punch-down blocks have been used for years by the telephone companies, and have migrated to the LAN wiring closet. Older punch-down blocks used to terminate 25-pair wire bundles were Category 3, and are not suitable for 100Base-TX cable systems. It is important that you know the type of punch-down blocks used in your cable plant, and you should always specify Category-5 punch-down blocks for new installations or upgrades.

The wiring closet uses cross-connect devices or patch panels, which allow easy reconfiguration of the network without tearing out cable and equipment. Patch panel cables are terminated in RJ45 connectors and provide easy reconfiguration between different ports in the network. All RJ45 connectors should be Category 5 for new installation, or whenever there are upgrades to existing wiring or equipment throughout the network (see Figure 10.2).

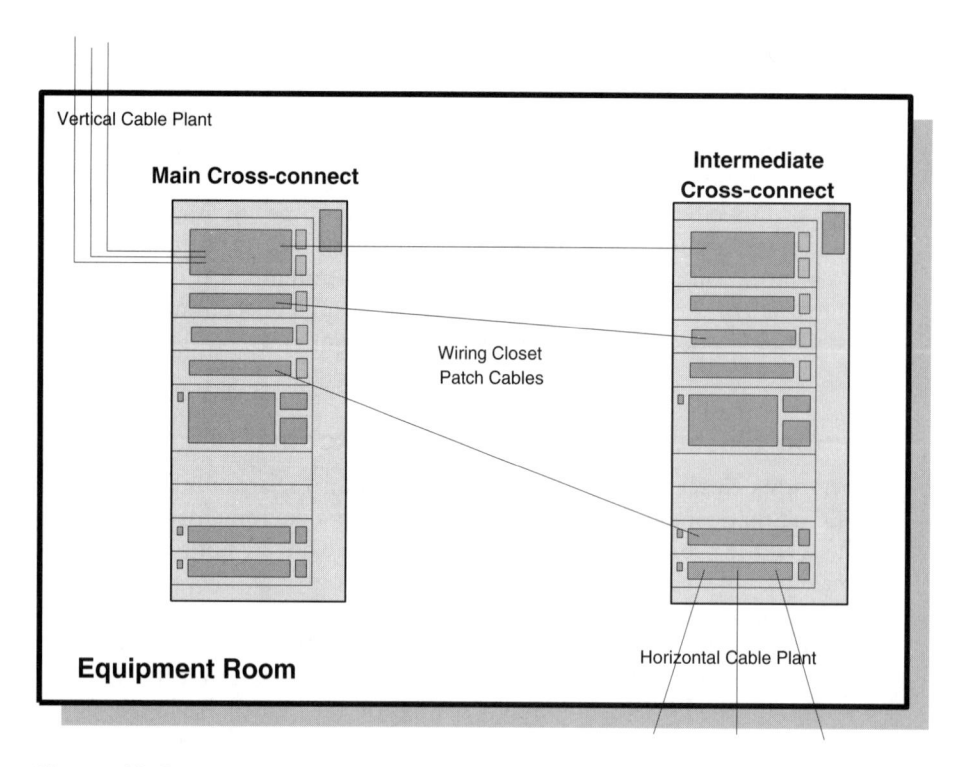

Figure 10.2
Network equipment room.

Elements of the Wiring Closet

The vertical and horizontal cabling always intersect at the wiring closet provided on each floor of the building. A wide range of complex equipment is used to connect all these wires and hence the attached end node into a network topology. The primary elements are network repeaters, hubs, switches, and routers. In addition there may be phone equipment or a PBX located in the wiring closet. In order to maintain a high degree of reliability and protect against network failures due to environmental factors such as lightning and power loss, most wiring closet equipment is powered off a UPS supply.

Cable Distribution Systems

In large networks, the wiring closet is located within the equipment room along with all the servers, UPS equipment, and LAN and WAN equipment. The increased number of cables entering the equipment room, and the associated number of patch panel cables, must be supported and managed by using specialized support equipment and structures. The support structures for cable management and distribution within the wiring closet and in parts of the horizontal and vertical cable plant include cable trays, conduits, and other routing mechanisms that will guide and protect the cable. The main types of cabling support and management systems used in a structured cable plant are:

- Suspended cable trays
- Conduits
- Raised floors

The most convenient and accessible method to manage and route cables into and out of the wiring closet is to use cable trays. These are usually suspended from the ceiling or located in the area above the ceiling. Cables are easily added or removed from these flat ladder-type structures, which are very effective in keeping cables organized, structured, and out of the work area and off the floor.

Conduits are generally used underneath floors or in risers between floors to contain and protect cables. They are not as accessible as cable trays and are limited to specialized applications, such as building the entrance to the wiring closet or as risers to other wiring closets on adjacent floors.

Raised floors, which consist of removable panels set on small metal grids above the building floor, are the most expensive method used for cable installation and are used mainly in computer or test labs, where there is a large concentration of computers and equipment, and miles of cable interconnecting these devices together. Raised floors are practical and flexible, but they are very expensive to install. Panels are easily removed by using a suction grip to expose cables for maintenance or to install new cables between equipment. A raised floor in a lab or computer room requires that ramps be placed inside each door leading to outside hallways.

Cable Labeling

All LAN circuits should be clearly identified by labels at the jacks, closet, and panel. These labels should be generated using a computerized label and cable management system. They are typically installed by the Telecommunications Department or the cabling subcontractor, and will be placed on each jack, panel, or block on all LAN circuits. The labels should clearly identify each RJ45 data connector relative to its closet termination, and panel designation within the wiring closet. Each local circuit (patch panel to jack) within the wiring closet is identified by three numbers, which are assigned by Telecommunications:

- Closet ID
- Patch ID
- Jack ID

Each RJ45 jack is marked as shown in the following example. The labels are provided by Telecommunications, who also assign and record each label ID:

Closet ID	Panel ID	Jack	Label
1924L	03	025	1924L:03:025

The number 1924L designates the closet ID; 03 designates the particular panel or block within the closet; and 025 designates the unique RJ45 jack ID on a particular panel. The ordering of the numbers on the RJ45 jack is not important, but they should be marked in ascending, sequential order when first labeled. All fire and safety standards and rules should be observed during the installation and commissioning of the wiring closet and the structured wiring plant.

Wiring Closet Layout

In keeping with the structured wiring cable standard, the organization and layout of the wiring closet should be well designed and planned. Almost all equipment found in a wiring closet should adhere to a standard form factor to fit into a standard 19-inch RETMA or NEMA style rack. The wiring closets should include only equipment required for information services, such as hubs, routers, switches, and other IS equipment; and should not include computer equipment such as servers or workstations. (Besides, most wiring closets are not fitted with the necessary air conditioning and power required for computer equipment.) All equipment should be mounted in racks or secured to the walls on standard backboard. In designing the structured wiring plant for a new building or upgrading an existing work environment, the location of the wiring closets and location of the server rooms should be defined.

Wiring Closet Organization

Wiring closets should be kept clean and organized, and should not be used for storage of unused equipment, excess cable, cleaning supplies, or other noncommunications type equipment. Cable routing should be clean and orderly, without any dangling wires that may pose a safety hazard. Cable ties should be used to cleanly route cable to the patch-panel punch-down blocks. LAN cabling should be clearly identified and separated from voice and other cabling when routed in the same areas.

UPS

A network can be only as strong as its weakest link, and one of the most volatile issues for the network in general is power outages due to storms or lightning. It's inconvenient when there is a power spike or power loss if you are a workstation user, but you can always reboot the system. If the server goes out as well, then rebooting the system will not get you back on the network. The server may have to be reconfigured, data must be backed up or reinstalled, and meanwhile all the users who need access to the server are standing around idle.

Among the more important pieces of equipment in the wiring closet and the equipment room are uninterruptible power supplies (UPSs). These are capable of keeping power supplied to equipment during periods of power spikes, lightning strikes, or other causes of power loss. As long as the servers remain powered up, it is easy for workstation users to reboot their systems and connect back into the server and continue work. A system power loss is serious and expensive because of equipment damage, but more important is the loss of productivity, especially when hundreds or thousands of workers can be idle for hours.

Backbone Cabling

The portion of the cable wiring from the wiring closet to the cross-connect or between cross-connects is known as the vertical backbone or campus backbone wiring. The cable used for the backbone is usually Category-5 UTP or multimode fiber cable. Fiber cable should be used when connecting wiring closets between floors, and especially when connecting buildings in a campus environment. The primary reason for using fiber cable between buildings and between floors, if the main wiring closet with routers is located in the basement, is the extended distance capability and immunity to electromagnetic interference.

Horizontal Cabling

The portion of the cable wiring from the wall outlet to the wiring plant is called the horizontal wiring plant since most of the wiring on a floor to the wiring closet will be on the same horizontal level. The horizontal wiring length is limited to 90 meters between the punch-down block in the wiring closet and the office wall plate, and is independent of media type. A maximum of three meters is allowed between the office wall plate and the end-node connection point. This leaves seven meters for the wiring closet patch panels and patch panel jumper cables. The 100-meter, maximum-length limitation for any horizontal cable run between the wiring closet and a workstation on the same floor should not be exceeded. In addition three media types are recommended for the horizontal cabling in a structured cabling system, with each one limited to a maximum of 90 meters:

- 4-pair 100 ohm UTP cable (24 AWG solid conductors)
- 2-pair 150 ohm STP cable
- Fiber 62.5/125 µm optical fiber cable

The horizontal wiring system consists of the following elements. The actual implementation of the horizontal cabling is site-dependent and often determined by the type of cable already installed in a building. Each element outlines the type of cable, termination, or connector that may be used in the horizontal cabling.

Horizontal Cabling Type
- Category-3 UTP cable and connecting hardware with transmission parameters characterized up to 16 MHz
- Category-4 UTP cable and connecting hardware with transmission parameters characterized up to 20 MHz
- Category-5 UTP cable and connecting hardware with transmission parameters characterized up to 100 MHz
- IBM Type 1A 150 ohm 22 AWG two-pair shielded twisted-pair cable characterized up to 100 MHz
- 62.5/125 µm multimode fiberoptic cable, two fibers per cable

The characteristic impedance of the Category-3, -4, and -5 UTP cable is 100 ohms ±15 percent.

Wall Plate Outlet

The hardware used for cable termination at the wall plate or the wiring closet should be of the same category or higher. The amount of exposed cable at the back of the wall-plate connections should be less than 0.25 inches.

Patch Cables

The patch cables used in the work area and in the wiring closet should be of the same performance category or higher than that used in the horizontal cable run. Jumper and patch cable maximum length limitations are

- 6 meters (20 feet) in the wiring closet
- 3 meters (10 feet) in the work area

Cable Termination

UTP cables are not Category-3, -4, or -5 compliant unless all components of the system used throughout the horizontal cable wiring run are terminated in the same respective category requirements.

Cross-Connection

The cross-connect cables used inside the wiring closet should be of the same category or type as that used in the horizontal cable plant, or higher.

- The length limitation of the main cross-connect cable is 20 meters (66 feet).
- The length limitation of the intermediate cross-connect cable is 20 meters (66 feet).
- The horizontal and vertical distribution cables and patch panels in the wiring closet should always be wired straight through, end to end, without any crossover cabling. This means than pin 1 at one end should be connected to pin 1 at the other end of the cable (see Figure 10.3).

Work Area

The work area is defined as that area that extends from the wall plate outlet to the end node. This is the office cubicle or walled office. The patch cable used in the work area must not exceed a maximum of three meters. This work-area wiring scheme is designed to be simple so that moves, additions, or changes are easily managed. The components of the work area are:

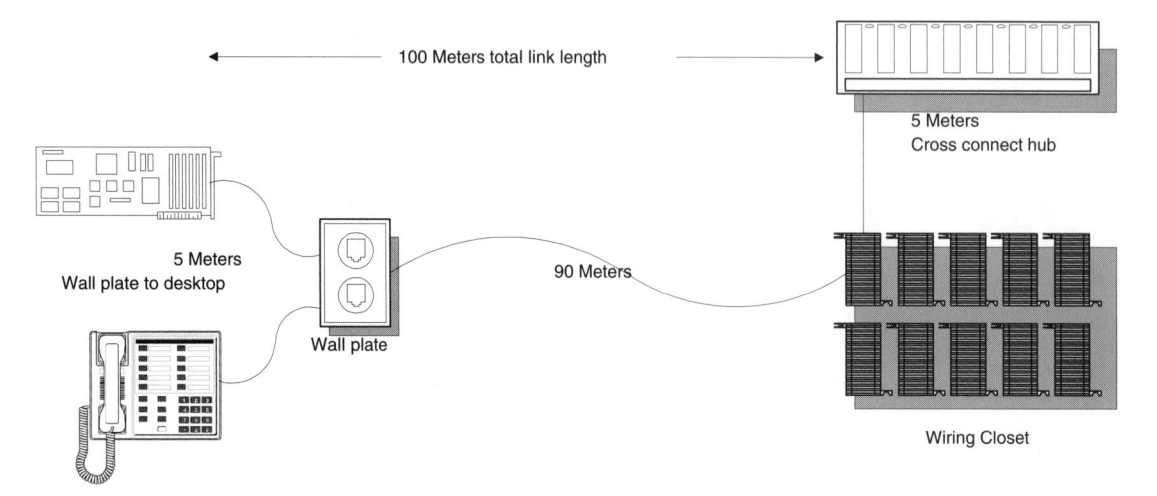

Figure 10.3
Horizontal cable distribution plant.

- End-node equipment
- Work-area patch cable
- NIC adapter located inside the end station

System-Level Design and the Cable Plant

The network topology is the physical arrangement of the structured cabling and components that connect a customer's building and floors. A number of factors and considerations must be determined before designing a network topology, and these are often independent of the building environment and the equipment used in the design of the network. They can be implemented in parallel to the site survey phase of a network design.

Security

Information is power, and there are people, companies, and even countries willing to take information and use it for their own benefit. Most of the information carried in a company LAN is specific to that company and the goods and services they provide to their customers. A lot of the data is unclassified and would not benefit or be of interest to people outside of the company or organization. Within each company there is also restricted data, such as financial or payroll data, that is not available on the corporatewide LAN but is localized to a specific group of users. In government or military environments the data carried on the LAN is usually top-secret and classified. This is where security of the LAN data becomes extremely important. With copper-based media, the energy radiated can be picked up using highly sensitive antennas or by tapping the wire. To provide secure LAN networks, companies and certain businesses and organizations use fiberoptic cable, because it does not radiate electromagnetic energy and is virtually impossible to tap without being detected. Fiberoptic cable is considered a secure medium.

Services

The primary functions performed by a network, those that are most visible to the users, are known as network services. One of the primary considerations in designing a network and providing reliable network services to the users is the physical aspect of the network environment. Will the network be located in one building, or spread out between several buildings or between multiple floors in a multistory building? The location of the equipment room and the wiring closets within the building must also be considered. The physical location and placement of the cables, whether in the ceiling, raised floors, or buried conduits, are also factors in the cable plant design. Security and privacy of data must also be considered when designing a cable plant.

Traffic

The design of the network must be able to meet the expected traffic load and also the growth potential for future traffic loads. The network throughput, response time, and peak load requirements must be understood. A general rule of thumb is to estimate the current load requirements for the network, and then design and install a network with at least 10 times the calculated capacity to allow for expected growth.

Reliability and Quality of Service

The most important issue for network users is the reliability and quality of service of the network. Users expect the network to always work when they come to work in the morning, and throughout the day. The downtime of a network must be minimal, if there is any at all, and any maintenance of the network or network services should be done outside of business hours. Computer network users expect the same level of service and reliability as the phone company—it should always work.

Growth

It is difficult to predict the growth of a network or an organization when the network is being installed. As mentioned previously, it is best to plan for a tenfold increase over the current requirements. This will allow for the increase in traffic due to new types of applications, new hirees, or workstations being added to or deleted from the network. A well-designed and structured wiring plant makes it a lot easier to support network growth requirements.

Selecting the Cable Plant Media

The design, performance, and reliability of a network depend on the quality of the network installation and the type of cable media used. It is easier to design a network in a new building than to upgrade or change an existing network. To take advantage of Fast Ethernet in an existing network installation, a number of issues should be considered, as deciding on the best use of an existing cable infrastructure can be critical to the success of the network. The next section discusses how to use an existing installed cable plant to migrate Fast Ethernet or the type of cable best suited to your needs if you are cabling for Fast Ethernet.

Upgrading to 100Base-T Fast Ethernet

100Base-T Fast Ethernet provides a well-defined, high-speed LAN alternative to legacy LAN installations such as 10Base-T Ethernet. The availability of dual-speed NICs has made the migration easier for customers deciding between their current bandwidth requirement and their expectations for future expansion. The migration is also made easier and more affordable because Fast Ethernet is the same as Ethernet but runs at a higher bit rate, so an experience dimension and a comfort factor are involved in the migration path. The questions of why and to what physical layer media technology should be used are addressed in the next section.

When to Use 100Base-FX

Fiberoptic cable has a number of major advantages over UTP and STP cable. Until recently it has been a lot more expensive than copper cable, but with the decrease in price of the fiber cable and the fiber transceivers used on the NICs and repeaters and switches to within 10 percent of UTP, more and more fiber cable is being pulled as dark fiber. (The term *dark fiber* refers to fiber cable that is deployed in new installations and left unterminated for future use.) Fiberoptic cable deployment is used in backbone applications, between wiring closets in buildings, and in large campus environments to interconnect LANs between buildings.

In many cases buildings in a campus environment may not be physically located adjacent to each other, or may be separated by roads, lakes, streets, railroad tracks, or any number of natural or manmade structures. The distance between buildings most often violates the 100m link segment rule for node to repeater or switch distance. For new-building, cable-plant installations and wherever major rewiring is planned, fiberoptic cable should be pulled in equal quantity to Category-5 UTP cable when the budget will allow. This dark fiber can sit idle in the walls and wiring closets until the cost of the remainder of the 100Base-FX components decreases to those of the 100Base-TX components.

The major cost component of 100Base-FX is the per-port cost of the adapters and the hubs. The fiberoptic transceiver used in each port is much more expensive than any other component on the module or hub card, and is the sole cause of the high price of fiber adapters and hubs. The high bandwidth capacity of fiber makes it a natural fit for Fast Ethernet, and provides an upgradable migration path for future, higher-speed LANs and multimedia applications. The migration to 100Base-FX should be based on bandwidth requirements, the types of applications being run on the network, security, reliability, and the physical location of workgroups within the network enterprise.

When to Use 100Base-TX or 100Base-T4

The type of Fast Ethernet NIC to use in a particular application is determined primarily by the type of cable already installed for a particular LAN. For new cable-plant installations or building upgrades, the choice is easy: Install Category-5 cable as a minimum requirement. If the building cable plant is Category-3 UTP, then the only choice for Fast Ethernet is 100Base-T4. This should make 100Base-T4 the predominant 100Base-T media type, but so far the overwhelming demand for 100Base-TX means that most of the deployment of Fast Ethernet is in buildings that have Category-5 UTP cable installed. If the building or premises are wired with Category-5 UTP cable, either 100Base-T4 or 100Base-TX may be used.

In applications where there is a mix of Category-3 and Category-5 cable, the best and safest option is to choose 100Base-T4. It is also recommended by the IEEE 802.3u standard that Category-5 UTP cable should be used instead of 100Base-T4 wherever possible, such as from equipment to the wall plate, or in the equipment room from the patch panel to the repeater, hubs, or switches. The cable in the wall is often unknown, and for these situations 100Base-T4 is best deployed. 100Base-T4 operates at a lower frequency than 100Base-TX and is more suited to applications with legacy wiring plants or inferior cabling installations. 100Base-T4 requires all four pairs of the UTP cable, and it does not support full-duplex operation, while 100Base-TX uses two pairs of Category-5 UTP cable and supports full-duplex operation when used with a recommended switch. The widespread deployment of Category-5 wiring over the past few years ensures that 100Base-TX is the dominant choice over 100Base-T4.

When to Use 100Base-TX with STP

Many buildings and businesses are wired with Type-1 STP cable, which is normally used for Token Ring LANs. One way to exploit the cable in the wall is to reterminate the STP cable with Category-5 RJ45 connectors at both ends. Few NIC vendors supply 100Base-TX adapters with DB9 STP connectors, but these exist in applications where the STP cable is already installed. Reterminating the installed cable plant avoids the need to pull new cable. It you reterminate the STP cable for use with 100Base-TX NIC and cross-connect equipment, it is important that Category-5 RJ45 connectors be used throughout the STP cable plant installation. A detailed pin-out of the RJ45 connector and the color code for the STP cable is given in Appendix B. The following list shows the recommended structured cable plant media:

Media Type	Used
100-ohm unshielded twisted-pair	Data grade; may be used for 10/100Base-TX/T4
150-ohm shielded twisted-pair	Used for 100Base-TX/T4, 4/16Mbps Token Ring
62.5/125 µm multimode fiber	Ethernet, Fast Ethernet 100Base-FX, FDDI

CHAPTER 11

Selecting Repeaters

Repeaters are the heart and soul of a Fast Ethernet system, as most devices connected to a Fast Ethernet system will be plugged into a repeater. Repeaters come in a wide variety of port counts with many innovative features and, unlike switches or routers, are most often differentiated by their price per port and entry price—after all, Fast Ethernet repeaters all do the same basic thing, repeat. Usually you will want to pick the repeater that has the lowest price with the features you need, without purchasing too many extra ports.

Stackables

Most Fast Ethernet systems will use stackable Class-I repeaters. **Stackables** allow a single, Fast Ethernet collision domain to start out small and grow as needed, without spending a lot of money up front for ports that are initially unused. In other words, using stackable repeaters allows you to keep your entry costs and cost per port relatively low while still providing for expansion.

Almost all stackable Fast Ethernet repeaters are Class-I devices. In the early days of Fast Ethernet, the internal bit budgets in a Class-II repeater made it impractical to build a stackable Class-II device. Later on, this became feasible, but stackable Class-I devices had already become the prevalent technology, so not many companies produced stackable Class-II devices. This is really not a drawback, because a stackable Class-I repeater is much more flexible than a Class-II device.

Stackable devices are called stackable because they are literally stacked on top of each other to form a single, Fast Ethernet repeater.

The individual hubs in a stack can be connected together in a surprisingly varied number of ways. Each manufacturer of stackable hubs implements the intrahub connection and the control bus differently. As you can imagine, this allows for a great deal of engineering creativity, and has resulted in some very sophisticated and useful products. Typically, there are two connectors on the back of each hub. A cable connects a hub to its neighbor above or below. Usually these cables are very short and require that the repeaters literally be stacked one on top of the other. Other hubs have integrated connectors that mate when the units are stacked (see Figure 11.1). The connections between stacked repeaters carry the network data and usually some control information.

Individual repeater units in a stack are often just called hubs. Stackable Fast Ethernet hubs come in many port densities. Port counts of 8, 12, 16, and 24 are common. Many stack architectures allow hubs of different port densities to be stacked together. For example, you might start out with a 24-port hub and then need to add just a few users. To keep costs down you might be able to add another 12-port hub. Of course, there are usually limits to stacking, typically 3 to 8 repeaters per stack.

High-density stackable hubs can allow very large Fast Ethernet repeaters to be built. Using 24-port units that can stack eight high, a single Class-I repeater can be built with 192 ports. There is no doubt that higher port densities will be available. Since there are a wide variety of port densities and maximum stack heights, chances are that you will be able to build exactly the size of Class-I repeater needed at a very low cost per port and still maintain a low entry cost.

Stackable hubs also have an advantage from a network management standpoint. Many vendors build two versions of a stackable hub—one that has management built in and one that doesn't. For example, Compaq's

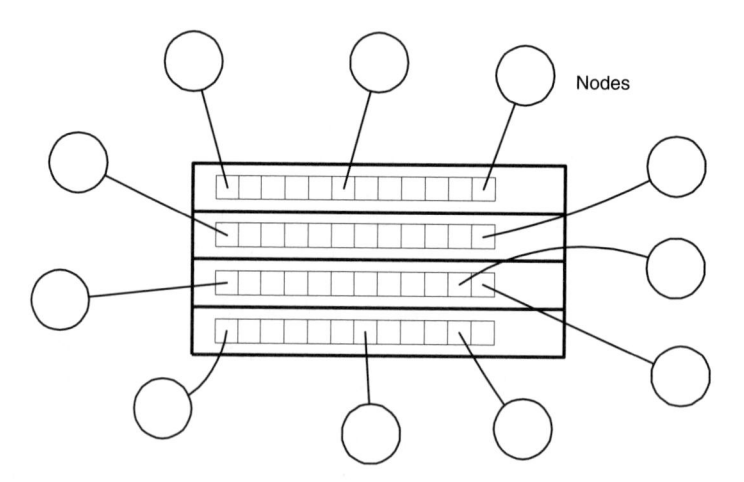

Figure 11.1
Stackable hubs.

stackable Fast Ethernet hubs come in two flavors, a managed and a manageable version. The managed hub costs a little more than the manageable hub and contains an Intel 25MHz 386 processor and 512K of RAM. The manageable hub is essentially the same with no processor or RAM. The advantage is that a single managed unit can both manage and control an entire stack of units. This design really pays off when a stack gets large, as the cost of the network management is spread over many ports.

The greatest advantage of stackables is that they help keep the cost per port down. A 12-port stackable is very economical, especially when three or more units are stacked together. For example, if a 12-port stackable hub cost $2,500, then the cost per port chart looks like the one shown in Figure 11.2.

Stackable repeaters generally offer greater flexibility for a lower price per port than Class-II repeaters and chassis-based repeaters, which should remain true over time as designers find more ways to make stackable repeaters less expensive and give them more features.

How Stackables Work

When stackable hubs are connected together, by connecting the repeater units in each hub together using a digital intrahub connection, they form a single Class-I repeater, as shown in Figure 11.3.

Figure 11.3 shows a stack with four hubs. While there are four individual hubs, each port is still on the same Fast Ethernet collision domain. This is very different from how Class-II hubs are connected. A big advantage to this method is that the intra-hub connections do not depend on the types of PHYs used in the devices. Packets moving between hubs are kept in digital form and do not have to be translated by two PHYs. This is what allows designers to build stackable Class-I devices.

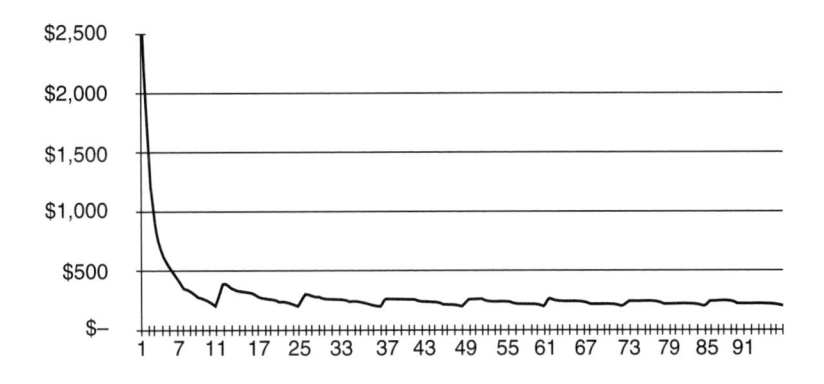

Figure 11.2
Cost per port.

Figure 11.3
Stackable connections.

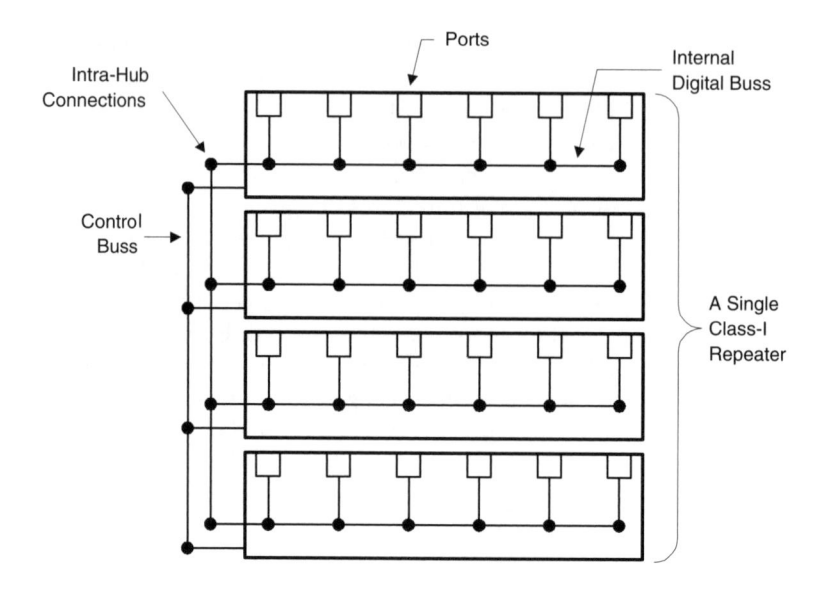

Stackable hubs have only one drawback. Class-II repeaters from different manufacturers can easily be connected together because Class-II repeaters are standard devices: They all have to work the same way no matter who builds them. In contrast, there is no standard for connecting stackable hubs to form Class-I repeaters. Thus, all hubs in a stack must be purchased from the same manufacturer. This does not mean that stackable hubs (or chassis-based hubs) do not meet the IEEE 802.3 Fast Ethernet standard; they certainly do. A set of stackable hubs operates as a single, Class-I repeater with lots of ports. The intrahub connections are not standard, but how the stack operates as a whole is.

Some more sophisticated Fast Ethernet stackable repeaters can be stacked and **partitioned** or **segmented** into more than one segment or collision domain like the chassis-based hubs discussed in Chapter 4. For example, a Fast Ethernet from Compaq has three Fast Ethernet segments on its intrahub bus. This product has a medium port density of 12 ports per hub, can stack five high, and is ideal for use in combination with a switch in a workgroup/department or backbone model network.

Chassis-Based Hubs

Stackable hubs are really a new variation on chassis-based hubs. A **chassis** is a box with a backplane and usually 4 to 12 slots. Hub cards slide into the slots and plug into the backplane. Chassis-based hubs have been around a long time and tend to be more expensive devices. They also tend to support more features than other types of equipment. Often chassis-based devices support multiple network types in one chassis—for example, Ethernet and FDDI—and they also often support other types of plug-in cards, such as switches and routers.

Like a stackable hub, two or more Fast Ethernet hub cards plugged into a chassis can act as a single, Fast Ethernet repeater. Chassis-based devices almost always support partitioning or segmenting, allowing individual hub cards to be attached to one of several Fast Ethernet segments.

This is where the chassis backplane comes into play. The backplane connects hub cards together, such as the intrahub connections and control busses used by stackable hubs. A chassis backplane will have several (often four or more) separate communications paths to which individual hub cards can be assigned, often called **backplane segments**. Thus chassis-based hubs can support multiple collision domains in one box, as each backplane segment is a separate network.

Chassis-based hubs can be very flexible: A 12-slot chassis with 12 Fast Ethernet hub cards and a backplane that supports four segments can be configured many different ways. One example is shown in Figure 11.4. Hub cards 1, 2, and 12 are connected to segment 1 of the backplane; cards 3, 4, and 7 are connected to segment 3; cards 9, 10, and 11 are connected to segment 2; and cards 5 and 8 are connected to segment 4. Note that hub 6 is not connected to any backplane segment, and operates as a stand-alone Fast Ethernet collision domain.

The flexibility and high port density of chassis-based hubs make them particularly well suited to enterprise environments. Since chassis-based products are very flexible and can be configured while in operation, they are often well suited for these applications. Here are some of the advantages of chassis based devices:

- They are very **configurable**. In general, chassis-based products can be configured in an almost infinite number of ways. Changes in configuration can usually take place while the unit is operational. Most

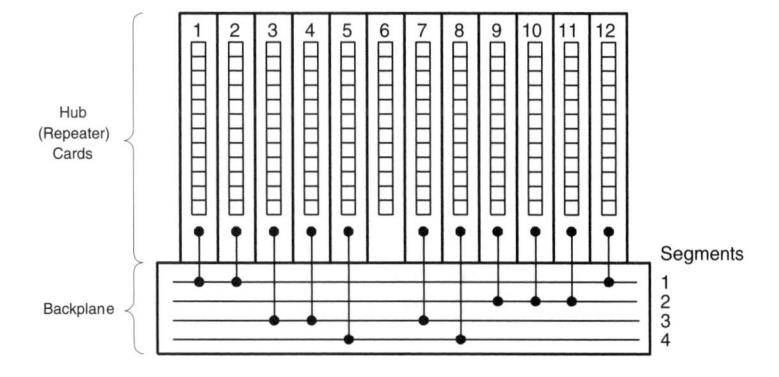

Figure 11.4
A chassis configuration.

chassis-based products allow cards to be added and removed with the power on.

- They can have **high port density**. Hub cards with 12, 16, and even 24 ports are common. Some chassis can support up to 288 ports in one box. When used in this way, chassis-based products can offer a very low cost per port.
- They are very **manageable**. Usually these products support very sophisticated management features, such as RMON and proprietary features, which are essential when large networks are built.
- They support **heterogeneous** technologies. Often, chassis-based products support multiple technologies in one box. Some products allow Ethernet, Token Ring FDDI, and recently ATM cards all in one chassis, and often support routing and switching.
- They are **upgradable**. Most manufacturers design their chassis-based products to support future technologies. Often an upgrade to a new technology like Fast Ethernet can be accomplished just by plugging in a new card.

There is a drawback to chassis-based products: They are almost always the most expensive alternative. Stackable units have become so popular because they have many of the advantages of chassis-based units but cost less per port (see Figure 11.5).

As you can see in Figure 11.5 the cost of entry for a chassis-based product is usually much higher than for a stackable hub. Because of this initial cost, chassis-based hubs do not become cost competitive with stackable products until port density starts to really climb. The chassis used in the example costs $4,500, which does not include any hub cards. This price includes only a box, backplane, and power supply. Sometimes power supplies are modular and must be purchased separately. The real cost advantage of a chassis-based product are the hub cards. A hub card can be very dense (the example hub cards have 24 ports) and is much cheaper than a single stackable hub. Repeater cards do not need their own power supplies or enclosures, which are provided by the chassis box itself.

The big cost advantage of a chassis-based hub is at higher port densities. Using the preceding examples, the chassis starts to beat the stackable hubs at a port count of 36. The cheapest cost per port using stackables is $208/port, which occurs when all the ports on each stackable hub are used. The cost/port for our chassis hub hits $208/port when 36 ports are used, and goes *down* to about half the cost of the stackable (per port) at a count of 96 ports to a fantastic low of $78/port at the maximum port density of 288 ports.

Many networks never get big enough to warrant purchasing a chassis-based hub, and even if a network starts out small and is planned to grow

Figure 11.5
Chassis costs vs. stackable costs.

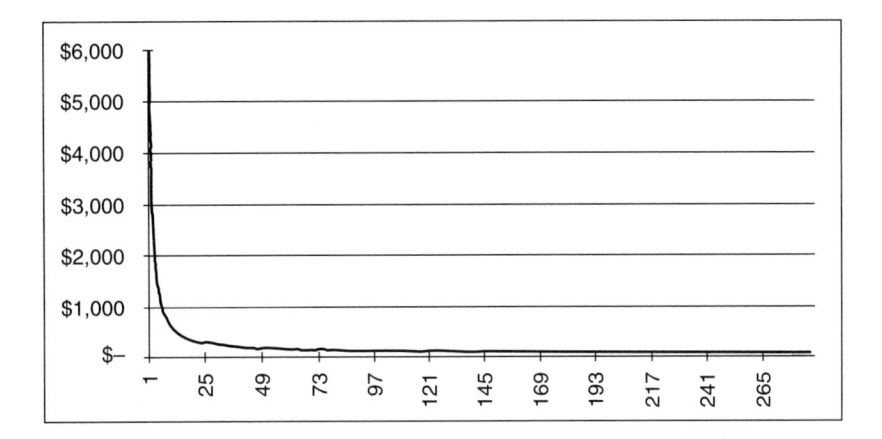

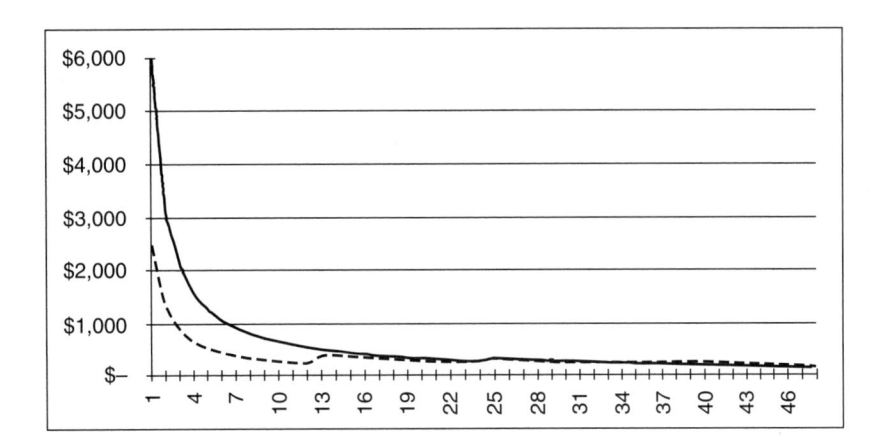

very big, the initial high cost of a chassis product often precludes its use. However, if you know your network is going to be large, it really can pay to examine purchasing a chassis-based product.

The use of chassis-based hubs is being challenged by stackable hubs, and the more cost sensitive segments of the networking market have adopted the use of stackables. While chassis-based hubs are still used, they are placed only in a network where their flexibility and higher-end features justify their higher cost.

Newer stackable hubs approach chassis-based products in sophistication, flexibility, and the availability of high-end features. These devices will continue to displace chassis-based products in the middle range of the Fast Ethernet market. However, we can expect that chassis-based products will continue to be developed as network needs, especially at the enterprise level, continue to become more complex. These high-end needs will be met only by sophisticated, chassis-based products.

Class-II Repeaters

Class-II repeaters are not as useful as either Class-I stackable or chassis-based devices. Only two of them can be used together, which limits the port count of a single segment that uses them. If you need management on a LAN with two of them, you must pay for management in both.

Class-II repeaters also cannot mix media type. A Class-II repeater cannot mix 100Base-TX or -FX ports with 100Base-T4 ports. This means that a Class-II repeater with 100Base-TX or -FX ports cannot be linked to another Class-II repeater with 100Base-T4 ports. It also means that a Class-II repeater with 100Base-T4 ports cannot support fiberoptic cable.

In general Class-II repeaters are not nearly as flexible as stackable Class-I devices. The ability to uplink one repeater to another is functionally similar to 10Base-T hubs, but the limitation of only having two Class-II devices five meters apart negates any value this feature may have.

Class-II repeaters have only one real advantage: Since their propagation delay is much lower than that of a Class-I repeater, longer fiberoptic runs can be used with a single Class-II repeater. This ability could be used to reach some devices that might otherwise require the purchase of a switch to overcome this topology limitation. While this is certainly possible, the circumstances that would require it will seldom happen.

In short, it is almost always a better decision to use stackable Class-I hubs instead of Class-II repeaters. They are no more expensive and are much more flexible.

Common Repeater Features

Since repeaters tend to be commodity items and are mostly selected by price, vendors have been very creative in designing features to differentiate them from competitors' products. As with switches, they often design in features that solve specific customer problems. Here are some of the more innovative or interesting features available.

Backup Ports

Some repeaters allow a port to be backed up with another port. This is usually for server connections and works by installing two network cards in the server, and attaching them to the repeater. One NIC and repeater port pair are designated the back path. If the primary path is lost, the backup path is enabled. Note that this takes support in the network operating system.

Out-of-Band Management

Most managed repeaters are designed to be managed over the network of which they are a part. This is usually called **in-band** management. Most managed repeaters also have serial port connections that allow them to be configured with a terminal or a PC running a terminal emulation program. Many repeaters support PPP and/or SLIP over their serial port, allowing conventional network management software to dial into the hub. (This is called **out-of-band** management and is very handy for remote office sites.)

RMON Support

Many modern managed repeaters support RMON, which is extremely useful for diagnosing network problems and discovering bandwidth problems. Note that RMON console software must often be purchased to take advantage of this feature.

Port Control

Almost all managed repeaters allow ports to be enabled or disabled using network management. This can be extremely handy when troubleshooting a LAN. A port with a suspected problem can be turned off. If the problem goes away, then the problem is on that port.

Full Screen Interfaces

Many hubs support full-screen, menu-based interfaces via Telnet and directly over a serial port (in contrast to terse, hard-to-use command-line interfaces). Full-screen interfaces are usually very easy to use and can often display basic port and network statistics. Often, these statistics screens are updated automatically, giving a network manager *live* readings on network operation.

Downloadable Code

Most modern managed repeaters store their software in FLASH memory, allowing new software to be downloaded to the repeater. Often a vendor will release software with bug fixes or new features. Be very wary of a managed repeater that does not allow this. Code can usually be downloaded over the serial port using Xmodem or Zmodem. Many repeaters also support TFTP.

BOOTP and DHCP Support

All managed hubs can be assigned an IP address manually, usually through a command-line or full-screen interface over the serial port. Many hubs also support BOOTP and/or DHCP, which allow an IP address to be assigned dynamically when the device starts up.

SNMP over IPX

It is surprising, but many managed devices (repeaters and switches) don't support SNMP over IPX. This is very easy to do in software, but some vendors do not think it is a valuable enough user feature to implement—a strange idea, considering that IPX is the default protocol for *all* Microsoft network-aware operating system products (Windows for Workgroups 3.11, Windows 95, Windows NT Workstation, and Windows NT Server) and, of course, for Novell NetWare.

Telnet Support

Some managed repeaters have command-line or full-screen interfaces but support them only over the serial port. Many support the same interface over Telnet. This can be extremely handy for making quick checks or configuration changes to a repeater remotely.

Two very useful features deserve more explanation, **Smart Uplink Modules** and **security features.**

Security Features

Some repeaters have built-in security features that help prevent tampering, intrusion, and other security attacks on a Fast Ethernet LAN. Usually, repeaters are only layer-1 devices and operate only on packets. However, many repeaters can process layer-2, or frame-level, information as well. This allows them to gather frame-level statistics such as octet counters, broadcast counters, and so on. Being frame aware allows them to implement some interesting security features too.

There are many, many different types of network security. At the layer-2 level, three types of security can be implemented on a Fast Ethernet repeater, and these features are often available in 10Base-T Ethernet repeaters:

- Eavesdropping Prevention
- Identity Enforcement
- Alias Prevention

It is important to note that these security features are specific to the chipset (a set of highly integrated electronic components) used to build the repeater. Most of these security features are patented and not available in all repeaters. These security features are also *not* part of the 802.3u Fast Ethernet standard, which does not cover security at all. However, a repeater that implements them is still 802.3u-compliant if it meets all the requirements of repeater operation. This type of security is often called **Data Link-Level Security**, and operates at the layer-2 level.

What Is Eavesdropping Prevention?

One type of security violation is called **eavesdropping**. Normally, a node on a network ignores packets that are not addressed to it. Eavesdropping occurs when a node goes into a mode in which it receives all packets, usually called promiscuous mode and sometimes monitor mode. Normally this is a good thing: Bridges and network analyzers must operate in promiscuous mode to do their jobs. However, on a secure network you don't want just anybody to eavesdrop on the network.

Eavesdropping is most commonly exploited by password capture programs. These programs watch for packets on a network containing passwords and record them. These passwords can then be used to completely compromise the security on an organization's servers. Don't think that these programs are hard to write or hard to find. They are easy to write and easy to find, and they come in many different flavors. Believe it or not, many PC network systems send passwords unencrypted over the network. Even if passwords are encoded, they can still be sent to the server to log in a session. Only using hardware keys and new password handling techniques, such as challenging, can block this attack.

Lots of other traffic can be snooped as well. Eavesdropping can be used to capture all kinds of data from a LAN. For example, any file transfer can be captured. A spreadsheet file containing all the salary information for your company could be captured when the CEO opens it. To accomplish this, the criminal does not need access to the servers or workstations being used, which will usually be quite secure. All he or she needs is access to the same segment the CEO is on, and a laptop with a snooping program.

SQL database queries and e-mail transfers can also be easily eavesdropped. This is especially true for e-mail that runs over well-known application-level protocols. Don't think this hasn't been done. It has, and snooping programs are becoming more sophisticated all the time.

On Ethernet and Fast Ethernet, a node can enable promiscuous mode on its network interface(s) whenever it wants to, and there is no centralized way to prevent this. Typically this is done with a program called a **network analyzer**. These programs capture all the frames transmitted on a

LAN and display them in decoded format (for more information, see Chapter 14). This is a legitimate reason for running in promiscuous mode.

To prevent eavesdropping, a repeater will learn the MAC addresses of the nodes attached to each port. It does this much as a bridge would, but it needs to learn only one address per port. A network manager can also program into a repeater the MAC addresses of the nodes that are allowed to connect to the repeater and/or to each port. In essence, the repeater knows what nodes are supposed to be connected to it.

Once a repeater knows the MAC addresses of the attached nodes, it prevents eavesdropping by scrambling unicast frames that do not have a destination address for the node on a particular port. Frames that match a port's MAC address are not scrambled. This means that the nodes on a secure repeater receive all frames on the LAN, as they are supposed to, but only unicast frames with their own MAC addresses are not scrambled (see Figure 11.6).

Nodes **A** through **F** are on a secured repeater. The repeater knows the MAC addresses of each node attached to it, and to which port each node is connected. When node **A** transmits a frame to node **D,** the repeater will send scrambled frames to all the nodes except **D**. Only node **D** will get an unscrambled frame. The only similarities between the scrambled frames and the original frame are their lengths. This keeps the CSMA/CD mechanism working properly.

Note that this kind of eavesdropping prevention scrambles only unicast frames. Multicast and broadcast frames are not scrambled, as all nodes need to receive and process them. From a security standpoint, this is not a big issue, as broadcast and multicast frames rarely contain sensitive data.

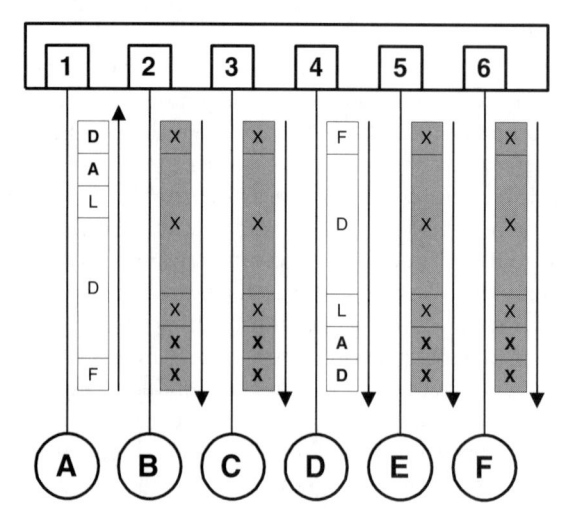

Figure 11.6
Eavesdropping prevention.

What Is Identity Enforcement?

Identity enforcement, often called **intrusion prevention** or **intrusion detection**, is designed to prevent unauthorized computers from connecting to your network. Like eavesdropping prevention, alias prevention requires a repeater to process layer-2 information, specifically MAC addresses. In fact, alias prevention and eavesdropping prevention are usually implemented together, as both are based on the repeater knowing what MAC addresses are allowed to be connected to the LAN, or connected to specific ports.

Intruders will often need to connect their own computers, usually laptops, to the corporate network in order to gain access to servers and other resources on the LAN. Eavesdropping prevention is a good step to thwarting these criminals but it is often not enough. Criminals often gain access to networked resources, such as servers, by stealing account names and passwords. These can often be obtained by bribing people, or simply watching someone log in. With the account information, all a criminal needs is physical access to the LAN in order to connect to a server and compromise security.

For example, receptionists often have networked computers for e-mail and to do light word-processing tasks. Often they are located in a lobby, entranceway, or other area of a building that does not have controlled access. These kinds of stations are prime targets for criminals, as they are often left unattended. These are often easier to break into after hours.

Identity enforcement fights these attacks by controlling which nodes, identified by their MAC addresses, can attach to a repeater. This is done by programming the MAC addresses of trusted stations into the repeater. A repeater can then examine the source MAC addresses of transmitted frames to determine if a node is a trusted node. If a node is found with an unauthorized MAC address, then the port to which that node is connected is disabled, locking that node off the LAN.

For this to be completely successful, secured repeaters are usually installed in a locked wiring closet, and the nodes most subject to attack have locked cases and no floppy disk drive. Often, the entire computer, except for a monitor, keyboard, and mouse, is locked inside a desk. Some installations even run the network cable through steel conduit so it is never exposed.

Usually a port can be restricted to a single MAC address or to a set of MAC addresses. A repeater can also prevent the same MAC address from being used on more than one port. This is also a common attack.

What Is Alias Prevention?

Alias prevention is very similar to identity enforcement, and is really just an extension of the idea with a different twist. They work together hand in hand and are best used together. Like both other security features, alias prevention works by examining the MAC address in frames.

Most adapter cards (or on-board chipsets) for Ethernet or Fast Ethernet allow the node's MAC address to be programmed and/or changed on the fly. It is a relatively simple programming task to write software that can send packets with different source MAC addresses. This is called **MAC address aliasing**.

The common response to this is: So what? How can that be used to compromise a network's security? Well, the answer is not as obvious as how eavesdropping can be improperly used. Attacks using MAC address aliasing are used to trick networking operating systems and other MAC-aware software into doing things they would not ordinarily do.

For example, a few years ago, a couple of guys wrote a program called HACK.EXE, which used exactly this technique. HACK.EXE used eavesdropping and MAC address aliasing to gain supervisor privileges on *any* NetWare 3.11 network file server. (Note that Novell quickly provided a patch to plug this security hole.) While we are not personally familiar with any other publicized instances of complete security breaches using this technique, there are other holes in UNIX, Microsoft Windows NT, and Windows 95 that can be exploited via MAC address aliasing.

This technique can also be used for **denial of service** attacks, which keep a system from operating properly and providing required services. For example, it can be used to kill network sessions between clients and servers, and can even crash some machines.

Alias prevention is used to prevent this kind of attack. On a repeater, this works by preventing a node on a port from transmitting frames with a MAC address other than one specified for that port. The repeater watches each of the frames that the node transmits. Each one must have a source address that matches the one specified. If a frame is sent that does not match, the repeater will permanently shut down that port.

Identity enforcement and alias prevention are sometimes just called something like **MAC address security** (different vendors use different catch phrases), as they really must be used together to be completely effective.

Why Are These Security Features Effective?

Many people point out that these data link-level security features are really not security at all, but just minor impediments to criminals. However, we disagree. The following reasons illustrate why these security features are effective and valuable:

- These features are implemented in the repeater and do not depend on hardware or software that runs on nodes or workstations to be effective. Nothing on a node can be hacked to overcome these features. If a Fast Ethernet network's repeaters are physically secure (pretty easy to do), then it can have a very high degree of data link-level security.

- These features are completely transparent to legitimate network users. They do not interfere in any way with the normal use of the network. Users can turn their machines on and off, log them in and out, or whatever, just as they would on regular Ethernet or Fast Ethernet systems.
- Since all these security features are implemented in the repeater, they can be centrally managed by traditional network management tools already in place in most medium-size and large organizations.
- Security is a complex problem, and good solutions to it will be implemented in layers. There is no one answer or silver bullet that solves all network security problems. Although not 100-percent effective by themselves, these security features provide good data link-level security, which can make it much more difficult for a criminal to compromise network security. Here is a simple example:
    The fictional plot of a criminal plugging a powerful, specially programmed laptop into the corporate net and compromising its security is not far from the truth. On all shared media LANs this actually is pretty easy to do. If the criminal can gain physical access to a network port (and often just a cable), then nothing can be done to keep the criminal from attaching and eavesdropping on the network. If this occurs, especially if it happens on the secure side of a firewall, there is a high degree of probability that security will be severely compromised.

Data link-level security can make this more difficult. First, the criminal must somehow obtain the valid MAC addresses for the port he thinks he can get access to. Without data link-level security any port would do, but with it, the criminal must access a specific port. Even if the criminal gets a valid MAC address for a specific port, he still can't eavesdrop on the network—an almost essential requirement for compromising most security schemes.

The obvious way around this is to get inside information from a dishonest employee who had access to the information. However, this could be difficult and time-consuming; more importantly, it increases the criminal's chance of detection.

In short, data link-level security should be used in conjunction with other well-known security techniques. A layered security approach can make a network extremely secure without being too inconvenient for the people using it.

Smart Uplink Modules

Fast Ethernet Repeaters from Compaq have a feature that allows the topology limitations of Fast Ethernet to be overcome, and allows Fast Ethernet repeaters to be connected together much like 10Base-T Ethernet repeaters. This is accomplished by a device called a **Smart Uplink Module** or SUM (see Figure 11.7). The SUM is a very innovative and useful device that plugs into a slot on Compaq's Fast Ethernet stackable repeaters. The SUM provides an additional uplink port, just like on a Class-II repeater, that can be attached to a regular MDI-X port on *any* other Class-I or Class-II repeater. A node can also be attached to another SUM if a special crossover cable is used. The SUM connects two Fast Ethernet collision domains in a very simple but effective way, essentially allowing them to operate as a single Fast Ethernet LAN.

This apparent contradiction of Fast Ethernet topology rules is possible because a SUM is essentially a basic 2-port, store-and-forward switch.

The SUM is a fairly straightforward device; Figure 11.7 shows its basic architecture. There are two MACs and some buffer memory. MAC 1 is connected directly to the repeater unit by the standard MII interface; there is no PHY between them. MAC 2 is connected to the external RJ45 port using a standard PHY (both 100Base-TX and 100Base-FX modules are available). Between the two MACs is some buffer memory. Both MACs operate in promiscuous mode; that is, they receive *all packets* on the collision domain to which they are connected. When a packet is received by one MAC, the frame contained in the packet is put in the buffer memory for transmission by the other MAC. The buffer memory operates using a first-in-first-out scheme, which ensures that frames are retransmitted in the same order in which they are received.

Note that the SUM is a layer-2 device. It operates on frames, not on packets. This has the same advantage as store-and-forward switches—error

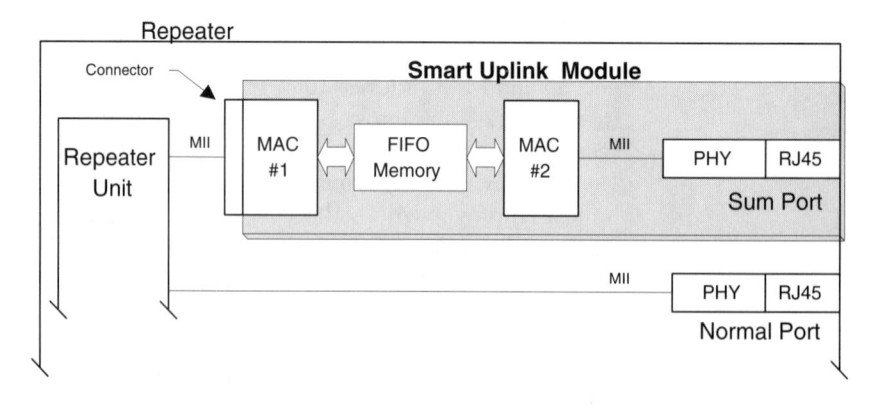

Figure 11.7
Smart Uplink Module.

frames are not propagated from one side of the SUM to the other. This includes runt frames, frames with CRC errors, frames that are too long, frames with framing errors, and jabbers.

A SUM can become congested, just like a switch (see Chapter 7). If a packet is received by a MAC and the SUM's FIFO memory is full, then the packet must be dropped. Fortunately, the SUM handles congestion the same way a switch does, by issuing a jabber on the incoming port, which is one of the reasons a SUM is called *smart*. For example, if packets are being received by a SUM on MAC 2 and the FIFO memory becomes full, then MAC 2 will intentionally transmit a jabber until enough packets have been transmitted out from MAC 1 and there is room in the FIFO memory for more frames.

However, unlike a bridge or switch, a SUM is not a learning device and does not support the spanning-tree protocol. Any packet received on one side is transmitted out the other port, including broadcast, multicast, and unicast frames. This is why a SUM is not a performance-enhancing device but a device that is designed to overcome Fast Ethernet topology limitations and provide connectivity.

When using a SUM, the stackable Class-I repeaters from Compaq are very useful indeed. They have all the advantages of stackable devices, and they can be uplinked to each other or to repeaters from other manufacturers to build networks in a way similar to 10Base-T.

CHAPTER 12

Fast Ethernet Switches

Switching has been promoted as the great cure for all modern networking problems. It has indeed become a technology enjoying widespread use, but a switch used in the wrong situation can cause you more problems than it is worth. Switching is used with Fast Ethernet for one or a combination of three reasons:

- To overcome Fast Ethernet topology limitations
- For performance, by segmenting a Fast Ethernet segment into smaller pieces
- To provide higher network performance for specific nodes

Overcoming Topology Limitations

One of the most often criticized limitations of Fast Ethernet is its 205-meter network diameter (when using the Model-1 topology rules), which makes it difficult to directly replace some Ethernet installations with Fast Ethernet. Vendors of other technologies, such as Token Ring, 100VG AnyLAN, and FDDI, have pointed out that these technologies can support much greater network diameters than Fast Ethernet does. This is quite true and is what primarily keeps the application of Fast Ethernet most suitable for workgroup and departmental LANs. However, these topology limitations can easily be overcome using switches and full-duplex fiberoptic links.

The first way switches can be used to overcome topology limitations is by breaking a single collision domain into multiple pieces. With copper cable, a Fast Ethernet network using a Class-I repeater cannot have a network diameter of more than 200 meters. If we add a single switch to this network and put repeaters on different ports, this maximum network diameter for the entire switched LAN jumps to 400 meters, as illustrated in Figure 12.1.

The important thing to note about Figure 12.1 is that there are *two* collision domains, or segments, but still only one broadcast domain. Even if more segments with Class-I repeaters are added, the maximum network diameter remains at 400 meters.

The real benefit comes when multiple switches are connected using full-duplex fiberoptic links, which can be up to 2,000 meters long. The backbone model works extremely well when using this technique. Take a six-story university building for example, in which multiple floors all need Fast Ethernet connectivity. Connecting the floors in a single Fast Ethernet segment is certainly not possible. Using a single switch on one floor isn't practical either, as there are multiple workgroups on each floor with high bandwidth requirements. Using a router to connect the floors isn't desirable, as there will still be a lot of traffic between floors.

Workgroup switches, like the one in Figure 8.2, are available with full-duplex fiberoptic ports. This type of switch combined with a departmental or backbone switch supporting multiple full-duplex fiberoptic ports is an almost perfect solution to this problem. Figure 12.2 shows how such a network could be configured.

The backbone switch ties all the workgroups together with full-duplex links. Since each can be 2,000 meters in length, reaching any place in the building with a backbone drop is not a problem. Since backbone switches typically support 12 or more ports, expansion of the system will be easy. There is also plenty of room for centralized servers, each directly connected to the backbone switch by full-duplex links. As you may have already noted, this system doesn't exactly fit into either the backbone or

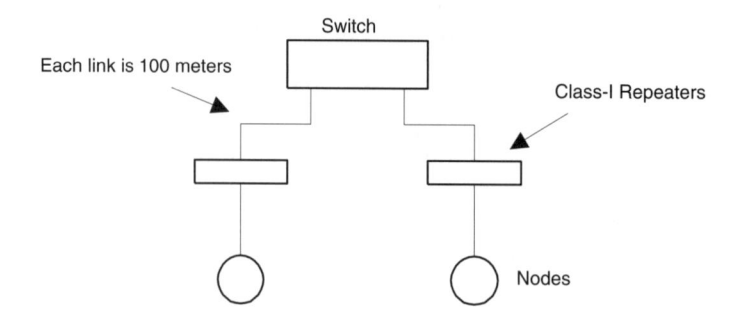

Figure 12.1
400-meter network diameter.

Figure 12.2
Six-story building.

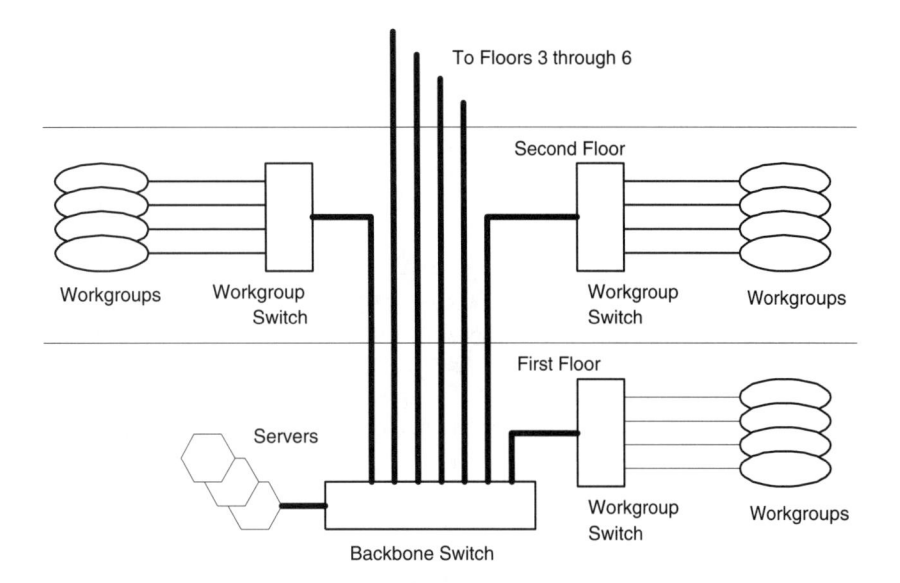

workgroup/department model but is a hybrid of both. It would even be reasonable to have a system on a floor follow the workgroup/department model and tie into the backbone, in the same way as the other floors. Not only does the network in Figure 12.2 span a large area, but it also is an extremely high-performance system.

Using network switches to overcome Fast Ethernet topology limitations can be extremely effective. If planned correctly, this technique will not only allow a Fast Ethernet system to span a large area and service a large number of users, it will also provide extremely high performance.

Performance and Segmentation

Sometimes a single Fast Ethernet segment, or collision domain, will get too busy. Users will start to complain about response times, connections will drop, or access to the Internet will be slow. When this occurs, the first thing to do is figure out why. This is where network management comes into play. Often you will find that these problems are occurring at the workgroup level and not at the department, backbone, or enterprise level due to the CSMA/CD access method used by Fast Ethernet. As the number of users on a segment and/or as their demands on the network grow, network utilization will drop, a problem that can be triggered by the use of a new application or even the addition of a single user. Using an inexpensive workgroup switch to solve this problem is an effective solution.

For example, an accounting group of 30 or so people may switch to a new, high-powered client/server accounting system. Originally the entire group was configured as a single workgroup on a stack of Class-I hubs, but afterward the conversion response time was slow and the servers were not busy; a good indicator of a bandwidth problem.

To solve this problem, this big workgroup could be segmented into three separate Fast Ethernet collision domains using a workgroup switch, as shown in Figure 12.3.

We have taken the three stacked hubs, which are working as a single Fast Ethernet Class-I repeater, separated them, and connected them to a switch. The server has been moved from a normal Fast Ethernet link to the stacked repeaters to a full-duplex link on the switch. This will significantly reduce contention for the network and avoid one of the classic pitfalls of using switches.

Single Node Performance

In several network examples servers have been connected to switches using full-duplex links. Any node can be attached to a switch using a full-duplex link, and both 100Base-TX and 100Base-FX support full-duplex operation. Note that 100Base-T4 does not, due to the inherent half-duplex operation of the T4 PHY. Full-duplex links are most frequently used for performance reasons, although, with fiberoptic cable, FD links allow a node to be up to 2,000 meters from a switch.

When a node is attached directly to a switch with a normal Fast Ethernet link, the regular CSMA/CD rules still apply to both ends of the connection. Only one end (the node or the switch) can transmit a packet at a

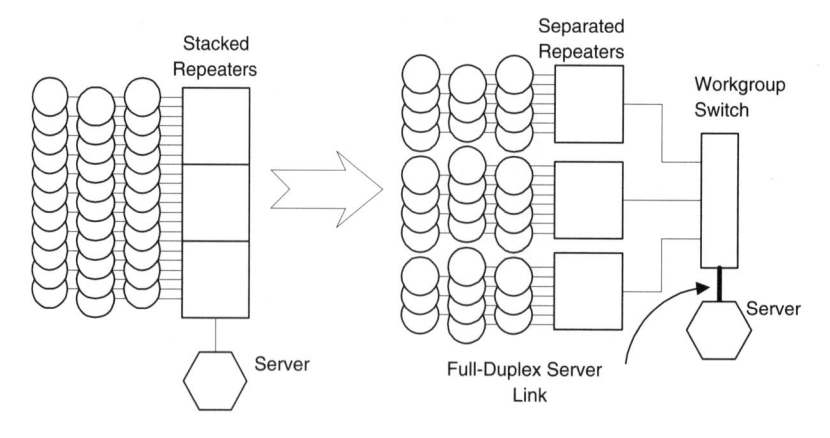

Figure 12.3
Workgroup upgrade.

time. If both attempt to transmit a packet at the same time, then a collision occurs and the normal collision recovery procedures will be executed.

When a node is attached to a switch with a full-duplex link, it will have no collisions when transmitting and the switch will be free to send it data anytime, not merely when the node is idle, because the link between the switch and the node are separate transmit and receive channels. A full-duplex Fast Ethernet link is inherently point to point, and can connect only two devices (see Figure 3.14 for an illustration). One pair of wires is used for data going in one direction, another pair for data going in the other direction. Since there are two physical channels, each end can transmit a packet as soon as one is available, and only the IPG gap time needs to be maintained.

This allows the link to the server to be much more efficient. Instead of a shared 100Mbps link to the node, there is a dedicated 200Mbps link, 100Mbps for transmitting and 100Mbps for receiving. Not only is there more bandwidth, but there also will be no collisions for packets sent by either end. The node does not contend with any other devices on the link, and its average transmit latency time will be *much* lower on a full-duplex link than on a regular link. Another thing that makes the full-duplex link more efficient is that the node can be transmitting a packet and receiving a packet *at the same time.*

A full-duplex Fast Ethernet link to a switch is an ideal connection for a high-performance server. Not only is there 200Mbps of bandwidth available to the server, but this link also can (and will) run at a much higher network utilization than a normal link.

The big caveat to using a full-duplex link is the server, or node, itself. Not just any server can be on such a link. An old 486/66 EISA box on an Ethernet link would probably be completely swamped by the data coming in on a full-duplex Fast Ethernet link. It simply would not be able to keep up with the incoming data stream.

Probably the smallest server you would want to put on a full-duplex Fast Ethernet link is a 166MHz Pentium EISA or PCI server with a high-performance network adapter card. If set up correctly, this class of machine will perform extremely well on a full-duplex link. High-performance workstations that have a similar performance can also be put on a full-duplex link. Workstations that are used for complex graphics or engineering design and simulation are perfect candidates for this.

Categories of Switches

Many different Fast Ethernet switches are available, with a wide variety of powerful and often complex features. Classifying them into workgroup, department, backbone, and enterprise categories can be very useful. These classifications can help you determine the features you need for a specific application, but the real benefit comes into play when comparing prices. The value of networking devices is often measured by price per port. This is a very useful measurement for devices in the same class, but it can be somewhat misleading when comparing devices in different classes.

Workgroup Switches

These switches are usually distinguished by their low cost per port. This makes them attractive for the workgroup, because you may need several of them. Workgroup switches also tend to have a higher number of ports than other switches (12 to 16 ports is typical). Some devices have as many as 24 ports. Having a high port count allows the entire cost of the device to be amortized over several ports. The designers of workgroup switches also often sacrifice such features as full-duplex ports, fiberoptic support, and uplinks to keep down the cost of the device. Some workgroup switches are even unmanaged.

Many workgroup switches also support both Fast Ethernet (100Mbps) and Ethernet (10Mbps) operation on *all* ports. These switches are excellent when upgrading a system from Ethernet to Fast Ethernet, and can make network operation completely transparent regarding differences in speed between segments.

Workgroup switches are also often distinguished by their performance. Early workgroup switches were intentionally designed to be oversubscribed (see Chapter 7). Of course, this was to keep down costs. More importantly, it means that workgroup performance could suffer if the demands for throughput exceed the capabilities of the switch. Today, even the least expensive workgroup switches can handle maximum throughput if all their ports are in normal, half-duplex mode. Some workgroup switches may support full-duplex mode on some or all of their ports, but some may be oversubscribed when one or more full-duplex ports are in use.

Desktop Switches

These switches fit into the low end of the workgroup category. A desktop switch is distinguished from other switches by the number of MAC addresses it supports—usually between one and four MAC addresses per port. This means that only nodes or very small repeaters can be plugged into desktop switches. Their purpose is to provide connectivity directly to the desktop, not a workgroup via repeaters. Some desktop switches only support one MAC address per port, and only nodes can be plugged into these switches. Others support up to four MAC addresses, which allows one switch port to support up to four nodes using a small five-port repeater. This is intended for individuals who need multiple nodes. For example, many upper management people have their own networked printer or require an additional connection for a laptop computer. These small repeaters are often used to provide connectivity for a small area, such as a group of cubes or desks. Using this technique, one cable drop instead of four can be made for a small area, which can really help to cut costs, as a small, five-port repeater and some patch cables can actually cost less than three cable drops.

Of course, a desktop switch must provide more connectivity than just a bunch of ports for nodes. Most of them provide one or two uplink ports designed to connect them to a sever or a department or backbone switch. In other words, since only single nodes (or a few nodes) are attached to each port, frames with unknown unicast addresses can be filtered for all ports by the uplink by simply forwarding any frame with an unknown destination address to the uplink port and not to the other ports. Frames with unknown destination addresses that are received by the uplink port are often filtered in the same way. This is a modification of the basic learning-and-forwarding algorithm, and takes advantage of the fact that only nodes, not other switches or bridges, will be plugged into the switch ports.

The idea behind desktop switches is that they are designed to replace repeaters. Usually, a desktop switch will cost only a few dollars more per port than a repeater. Many vendors believe that as the price of switches comes down, they will actually take the place of many repeaters. Since they are designed to replace repeaters, desktop switches often have no or minimal management, and they often do not support the spanning-tree protocol. This is not a problem, because only nodes and/or tiny repeaters will be plugged into them.

> Workgroup switches are often called **segment switches** because they are designed to switch traffic between segments. In other words, each port on a segment switch is usually connected to a repeater or stack, not a node. Since segments can be connected to multiple switches (and often are), workgroup switches, unlike desktop switches, must support the spanning-tree protocol, multiple MAC addresses per port, and the full learning algorithm.

Many companies never upgrade everyone to Fast Ethernet. Some people don't need the full performance of 100Mbps, cabling costs can be prohibitive, or the equipment may not be physically upgradable. However, even users on 10Mbps links could use more performance. For example, printers are often kept on 10Base-T links, as most of them have built-in Ethernet links that cannot be upgraded to Fast Ethernet. Some low-end users, like receptionists, use their computer only for lightweight tasks, such as e-mail for phone messages and simple word processing.

This is accomplished by using **Ethernet 10+100 workgroup switches**. These are devices with many 10Base-T switched ports, in either a segment switch or desktop switch configuration, and one or two Fast Ethernet uplink ports. These devices are usually extremely cost effective, fit nicely into a Fast Ethernet system, and provide an excellent way to provide connectivity to 10Mbps nodes.

10/100 Workgroup Switches

Segment, or desktop, workgroup switches support both 10Mbps and 100Mbps operation on every port. Each switch port will detect the speed of each connected device and operate appropriately. These kinds of switches are more flexible than a 10+100 switch, but usually significantly more expensive, as they provide 100Mbps operation on every port. They are ideal when a LAN is primarily Fast Ethernet and needs to support only a few 10Mbps devices.

An important thing to note about this feature is that it will become more common as time goes along. By 1998, probably all Fast Ethernet switches, even low-cost ones, will support both 10 and 100Mbps operation on all ports.

Department Switches

Often no more expensive on a per-port basis than workgroup switches, department switches are differentiated from workgroup switches by their port count and performance levels. A department switch usually has 8 to 16 ports, usually supporting full-duplex on all ports. Their performance is almost always higher than a workgroup switch, as they are almost never oversubscribed and have a half-duplex aggregate bandwidth equal to or greater than the bandwidth of all their ports. Many of these switches are designed to support full-duplex links on several ports at wire speed without dropping frames. Departmental switches are almost always managed and offer more management features than their workgroup counterparts, such as RMON. They also often support both half- and full-duplex fiberoptic links. Some departmental-level switches are modular, allowing a given port to support 100Base-TX or -FX and perhaps 100Base-T4. This is often done with a device called a **media module**, which is essentially a PHY on a card. A media module plugs into a slot and attaches to the MAC on a switch port via the MII interface.

Backbone Switches

These switches tend to be full-featured, high-performance devices and therefore are the most expensive. A port count of 12 to 24 is common, and by mid to late 1997, 32-port devices will be available. Backbone switches often support at least one uplink port to FDDI and ATM. Many support two or more, and some have modular uplink ports that allow FDDI, ATM, or other types of uplink modules to be plugged in. Backbone switches are almost always very high performance, usually handling full-duplex links on all ports with ease. Management is another area in which backbone switches often excel. In addition to supporting RMON on all ports, backbone switches often have sophisticated proprietary management features. Some backbone switches have dual redundant power supplies, allowing them to be attached to two power sources for ultimate reliability.

Enterprise Switches

Although very similar to backbone switches, the biggest difference here is that an enterprise switch plugs into a large chassis. These chassis products often support many different kinds of modules, such as Fast Ethernet and Ethernet repeaters, FDDI concentrators, Token Ring MAUs, and routers. Enterprise switches are very useful devices for building enterprise-level networks, especially for companies that must support several networking technologies and legacy systems. Chassis-based devices usually have very powerful management features, again making them well suited for the enterprise network environment. The drawback to chassis-based devices is their cost—they can be *very* expensive. Chassis-based devices are always single-vendor products—everything that goes into a chassis is going to come from one company. This can be a drawback if you need a feature or capability that is not provided by the chassis vendor.

Switch Performance

Switch performance is a complex topic. Some vendors would like people to believe that a switch is a switch is a switch, and features other than performance are why you should buy their switches. The long and the short of it is that switches have one overriding purpose: to provide more performance than can be provided by a single segment. In other words, if switches were not fast, then nobody would buy them and this book would be about routers.

The problem with performance is, there is a lot of misinformation on the topic provided by vendors. Each vendor wants you to believe that its switch is the fastest. Vendors may advertise that their switches have a 1-gigabit internal bandwidth, and brag about something called their GigaBlaster Bus. This may be nifty marketing, but it tells the customer nothing. The real measure of a switch is how well it can keep up with demanding offered loads.

Fortunately, a man named Scott Bradner, at Harvard University, developed an RFC1242 and RFC1944 that describe how a switch and other network devices should be tested (both of these RFCs are contained in Appendix D and are available via our Web site at www.wiley.com/FastEthernet. RFC1242 specifies Benchmarking Terminology for Network Interconnection Devices. This RFC clearly defines such terms as latency and throughput as they apply to device performance. RFC1944 describes a Benchmarking Methodology for Network Interconnect Devices. This RFC describes how devices are tested and results interpreted. In essence, these RFCs are a description of what are now commonly known as the Bradner tests.

When Mr. Bradner started testing switches, vendors were not forced to test their switches in a standard way, but as time progressed, the Bradner tests have become the standard by which all switches are judged. The reason is that Mr. Bradner's testing lab at Harvard obtains switches, tests them, and publishes the results. All of this is done independently of the vendor. Of course, they don't test every switch available, but they do test some of the most popular. These tests are clear, easily understood, unambiguous, and, most important, well accepted. For people purchasing switches, the question asked of salespeople is often, How did your switch do in the Bradner tests? You should ask the same question. Most of the test results obtained at the Harvard labs are published on their ftp site, and are freely available (or see our Web site at www.wiley.com/FastEthernet).

The Tolly Group is a commercial testing lab that performs testing much like the Harvard labs do. They publish many of their results on their Web site. Before purchasing a switch, it's a good idea to check www.tolly.com to see what information is available.

MAX Tests

Many types of tests can be performed on a switch to see how well it performs. The two most common are the **MAX traffic** test and the **MAX throughput** test. To perform both tests a special device called a **traffic generator** is used. A traffic generator is a special node that has a Fast Ethernet MAC and PHY and can accurately transmit frames at specified rates and frame sizes. It can also accurately measure received frame rates and sizes. Most traffic generators can be programmed to violate the CSMA/CD rules to test how such devices as repeaters, switches, and nodes handle error conditions.

In the MAX traffic test, traffic generators are connected to each port of a switch.

> The traffic generator can transmit packets at the fastest rate possible. For Fast Ethernet this is 148,809 packets per second with 64-byte frames, and 8,127 packets per second with 1,518-byte frames. This means that packets are being transmitted back to back with only the IPG time between them. When this occurs it is called **wire-speed** traffic.

The traffic generators on all the odd numbered ports are set to transmit 64-byte frames at wire speed, and those on all the even numbered ports are set to receive traffic. Ports are divided into pairs. The traffic generator on port 1 will transmit packets to the traffic generator on port 2, port 3 will send to 4, and so on. Since there is no overlap between traffic generators, there will be no collisions (see Figure 12.4).

When the test is running, all the packets transmitted on the odd-numbered ports should reach their corresponding receiver on the even-numbered ports. If they don't, the switch is said to have *dropped* the missing packets. The max traffic is usually run over several minutes, so only a small number, much less than 1 percent, of dropped packets is acceptable; after all, no media is perfect and some packets will have random bit errors due to electrical noise.

A 16-port departmental-level switch that passes the max traffic test makes 1,190,427 forwarding decisions every second. Since the decision-making and frame-processing mechanisms in the switch are stressed to the absolute maximum during this test, passing it is an excellent indication that the internal workings of the switch are robust.

The max throughput test is just like the max traffic test except that it uses the maximum frame size of 1,518 bytes. This generates only 8,127 packets per second but puts the network utilization at 100 percent on all ports. For a 16-port switch, this is a data throughput rate of 12,191,160 bytes per second on each port pair, for a whopping total of 97,529,280 bytes per second.

Once again, during the max throughput test the switch should drop only a tiny percentage of the total number of transmitted frames. If the switch can do this, its internal mechanisms are extremely robust and have

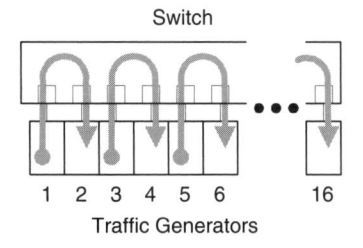

Figure 12.4
Switch testing.

a true bandwidth capable of sustaining the worst possible offered loads that could be placed on it.

The max traffic and max throughput tests are the two most common tests that a switch generally undergoes, and several magazines publish benchmarks using these types of tests. Vendors that make switches that pass these two tests will often describe that product as supporting wire speed on all ports. A high-performance switch will pass both tests. Some switches will have trouble with the max traffic test but pass the max throughput test, and this can often be quite acceptable. The max packet rate of 148,809pps is rarely sustained on a real-world network for more than a few milliseconds, giving the switch time to catch up between bursts.

A switch that does not pass the max throughput test is said to be **oversubscribed**; that is, there are more ports than there is bandwidth in the switch itself. In the early days of switching many switches couldn't pass either test and were very oversubscribed. Switch vendors bragged that their switches were faster than their competitors' switches. It was difficult to pick a switch that could support the desired application without dropping packets. Magazines benchmarked switches and wrote articles detailing their results. Vendors that didn't do well in the test complained that it wasn't fair and didn't mimic real-world networks. This is often the cry of companies that make network products that perform poorly.

In early 1996 the vendors began to ship switches that passed both tests. These switches were often *cheaper* than the older generation of switches. Such is the magic of technological advancement. Switches that couldn't pass these tests were quickly replaced in the market by devices that could. Today, passing these tests should be a requirement for any departmental and higher-level switch. Some workgroup-level switches, newly available in 1997, pass both tests.

Any switch that supports even one full-duplex switched port should easily pass both the max traffic and max throughput tests. If it can't, then there isn't much use in having any full-duplex ports. Testing a switch that supports full-duplex is quite similar to testing a switch when running at half-duplex. The only difference is that each traffic generator is both transmitting and receiving traffic (see Figure 12.5).

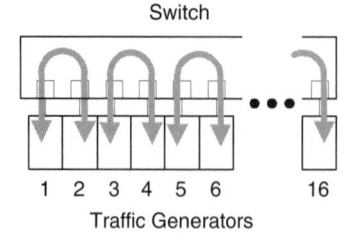

Figure 12.5
Full-duplex switch test.

Testing the full-duplex performance of a switch usually begins by testing one port pair in full-duplex mode, and all the other pairs in half-duplex mode. If the switch passes that test, then a second pair of ports is placed in full-duplex mode, and the test is run again. Many switches, especially those at the workgroup and department level, are designed to support only one or two ports in full-duplex mode. This kind of testing verifies that the switch meets the vendor's performance claims.

The reason for this is that building bandwidth into the switch to support full-duplex operation is expensive. Most applications need only a few ports that run in full-duplex mode, not all of them. Some switches are available that can run all their ports in full-duplex mode and pass these tests. They may be a little more expensive, but you can rest assured that they will always meet your bandwidth needs.

Other Performance Measures

The max traffic and throughput tests are the two basic measures of switch performance, and are the closest there is to a set of standardized performance metrics for switches. Many other tests can be performed on switches, some of which are:

- **Broadcast Test.** This test transmits broadcast packets at wire speed on one port, and tests to see if they all get to the other ports. This is one of the most demanding switch tests.
- **Statistics Accuracy Tests.** Managed switches gather lots of statistics, including the number of frames transmitted, the number of collisions, and the number of errors on each port. These statistics-gathering mechanisms can be tested for accuracy.
- **Latency Tests.** The time it takes for a packet to be received on one port and transmitted out another port is a switch's switching latency. Modern traffic generators can accurately measure this value.
- **Uplink Performance.** The same kinds of tests that are performed on the regular ports can also be performed on switches that have uplink ports. Many switches that pass the basic max traffic and throughput tests on their regular ports do not support that kind of performance on their uplink ports.
- **Asymmetric Performance.** In the max traffic and throughput tests the traffic is generated evenly on all port pairs or all ports. In asymmetric tests, the number of transmitting and receiving ports is varied, so they are uneven. For example, two ports may transmit to one port. An almost endless variety of asymmetric tests can be performed on a switch.

- **Restart Test.** This test measures the time it takes from power-up to full and correct operation. Often, poorly designed devices can take a long time to begin working properly after they power up. Most switches can be up and running in much less than 30 seconds.

Of all of these, the broadcast test is the most useful to someone trying to decide what switch to purchase. A switch's broadcast-handling performance can be very important, as in larger networks broadcast traffic can be a significant percentage of total network traffic. Unfortunately, this measure is rarely available from switch vendors or independent testers.

Switch vendors will often come up with their own measurements that they claim their equipment meets and other vendors' switches don't. Be skeptical of such measurements. This kind of specmanship is rife in other parts of the computer industry. In 1995 and 1996 there was a terrible problem with PC graphic card vendors doing just that.

One of the best ways to find out if a switch has good performance is to talk to other users, read industry magazine articles, and do research on the Web.

Problems with Switching

Switching is not without its problems. Using a switch improperly can cause a network manager huge headaches and make lots of people angry. There are two main problems with switches. The first and easiest to trip over is something we call the **funnel problem**. Fortunately, this is both an easy problem to avoid and also easy to fix if it occurs.

The second problem with switching is **scalability**. Switching simply does not scale well. Switched networks can get only so big before performance problems will require that they be broken up into smaller pieces. Fortunately, most switched LANs don't get big enough for their network managers to worry about this. Only companies that have sites with thousands of users will need to worry about scalability.

Funnel Problem

The most common problem when using switches is the funnel problem. A worst-case example of this is when a switch is added to an existing small Fast Ethernet LAN with only one server. This is illustrated in Figure 12.6. The problem here is that the traffic from the three Fast Ethernet collision domains is all heading toward the server, which is on a half-duplex switch port. This port has only 100Mbps of bandwidth, and is subject to the

Figure 12.6
The funnel effect.

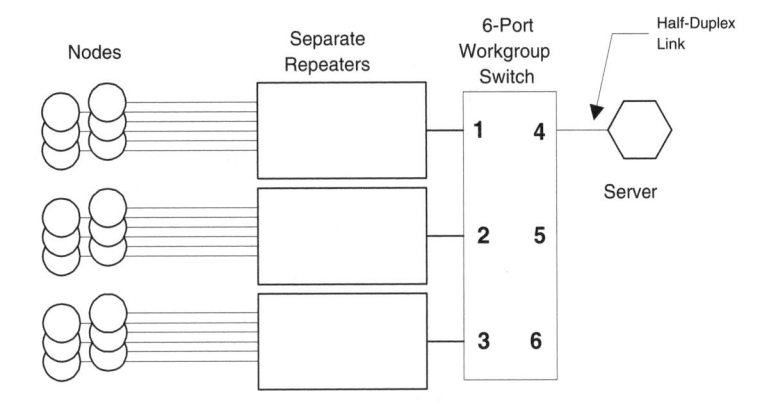

CSMA/CD media access rules. This configuration is trying to squeeze 300Mbps of bandwidth into a 100Mbps connection to the server. It just won't work. This configuration will have poorer performance than a simple network using just a single stack of connected repeaters.

Users on ports 1, 2, and 3 will frequently be making requests to the server. Often packets destined for the server will arrive on ports 1, 2, and 3 at the same time. The problem is that those three packets cannot be sent to the server at the same time. Two of them must wait and are held (buffered) in the switch's memory until the first one has been transmitted. The buffered packets are then sent to the server one at a time. Many packets, several from each port, can be buffered up this way, waiting to be sent to the server.

It gets worse, as the server receives packets, it will need to send responses back to the requesting nodes. To do this, it must contend for the link to the switch with the switch itself. The more traffic is sent to the server, the worse this problem will become. This situation is called **congestion** and can be a self-fulfilling prophecy of doom for a network.

A switch is considered congested if packets have to be dropped due to lack of buffer memory or lack of bandwidth in the switch. A switch that is overly subscribed can easily become congested and drop incoming packets.

Switches are designed to handle distributed loads and full-duplex links. The ideal offered load for a switch is that produced by the max-throughput test, in which the load is equally distributed among all the ports. The worst-case scenario for a switch is when all of the traffic coming in on a switch is destined for one half-duplex port. This destination port could be a server, a router, or a link to another switch. This kind of load will quickly congest a switch.

A switch will handle a certain amount of this kind of traffic perfectly well. Under normal operation, packets will often come in multiple ports destined for the same port. Normally, the switch will just buffer these packets and send them when it can. Disaster strikes when the switch runs out of buffer memory and new incoming packets must be discarded. Sometimes a switch can help avoid this problem by exerting back pressure on the incoming ports. For more information on this topic see the next section.

Another common problem configuration is similar to the preceding one. It consists of putting the server on one of the repeaters connected to a port. In this case, the users on that repeater will have tolerable access to the server, but the users on the other switch ports will have terrible access.

There are three solutions to the funnel problem. The first is to distribute the load over a switch's ports as much as reasonably possible. The second is to keep workgroup servers on the same repeaters as the users that access them most. The third, and by far the most useful, is to put servers on full-duplex switch links, and to link switches using full-duplex connections.

Scalability Problem

Switched LANs, or broadcast domains, don't scale well. There is a practical limit on their size. As a switched LAN gets larger, three problems will start to manifest themselves, and will get worse and worse until the switched LAN just cannot function:

- Broadcasts will become a larger percentage of total network traffic.
- The root switch will become regularly congested.
- End-to-end latency will become a problem.

We've discussed the first problem before. As a broadcast domain gets bigger, in terms of the number of attached nodes, the number of broadcast frames as a percentage of total network traffic will start to climb. The reason this is bad is that it eats up network bandwidth. Usually, a broadcast message transmitted by a station will be handled by just one device; but every broadcast message on a network eats up processing time on *every node* on the broadcast domain.

For example, in Figure 12.7 workstation **A** may need to communicate with the server BILBO. To do this **A** will broadcast a message that says, Hey! Where is server BILBO? The first thing that happens is that the broadcast frame is propagated through all the switches on the broadcast domain. This means every port on every switch. A single broadcast uses up a little bandwidth in each switch and in each attached collision domain.

On a single, isolated collision domain, this isn't a problem. In this case, the number of broadcasts usually scales linearly with the number of nodes attached to the LAN. This means that the percentage of network bandwidth used by broadcasts will not go up, or will go up only a tiny bit. The overall, or aggregate, bandwidth used up by broadcasts is much more

Figure 12.7
Additive broadcasts.

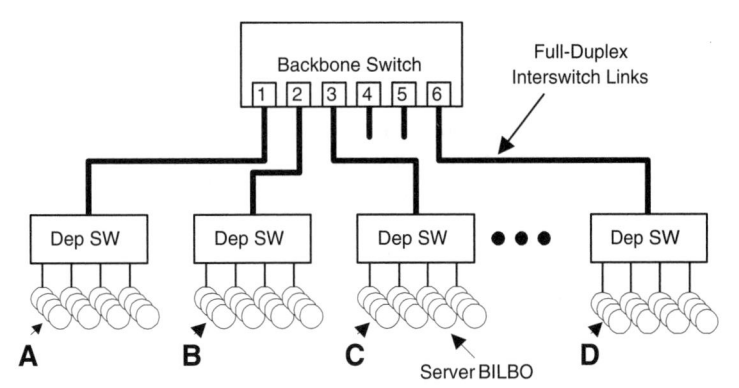

dependent on the types of protocols used by the nodes on the single LAN than it is on the number of nodes. It's generally accepted that about 1 percent of all frames on a LAN will be broadcast frames. (Note that this is only a rule of thumb. Your LANs may have averages that are lower or higher than these numbers. Like any other performance metric, you should baseline this measure.) Periodically, this might climb to as high as 5 percent for short periods of time. This is true even for single segments with a large number of nodes.

This kind of behavior can be seen by comparing the broadcast counter in a managed repeater with the broadcast counters in each node. The repeater will tell you how many broadcast and unicast frames have been transmitted on the segment. This number can be divided by the total number of frames transmitted on the segment to get the broadcast percentage. As nodes are added to the segment, this ratio should not change very much, if at all.

For a switched LAN this isn't the case. As the number of collision domains on a switched LAN increases, the amount of bandwidth used by broadcast frames on each collision domain will increase. Take the backbone network in Figure 12.7, which has six departments connected to a backbone switch. Each department has four collision domains (segments). If nodes A, B, C, and D transmit a broadcast at the same time, all four broadcasts must be propagated to each collision domain in each department. The total number of broadcasts transmitted on a segment is the count transmitted by the nodes on that segment, plus the broadcasts that come from the switch. The number of broadcasts coming from the switch is the sum of the broadcasts generated by *all* the other collision domains.

When using managed switches, it is usually very easy to calculate the broadcast frame percentages. Most switches maintain frame and octet counters for both the transmit and receive side of each port. By directly comparing the transmit and receive broadcast counters on a port, you can measure the percentage of broadcast traffic generated by the segment connected to that port, and the broadcast traffic generated by the rest of the network. Switches also keep counters for unicast frames and octets as well. Using these numbers, it is straightforward to calculate the percentage of frames and bandwidth used by broadcast traffic.

For example, in Figure 12.7 let's assume that each segment generates about 1 percent broadcast traffic. In other words, for every 100 frames transmitted by the nodes on a given segment, one is a broadcast frame. Since all broadcast frames are propagated to each segment, 24 out of every 100 frames on *each* segment will be a broadcast frame.

This may sound like a horrible problem, but it's only a bandwidth problem when network utilization is high. In other words, this problem arises when the network is busy and there is a lot of demand for bandwidth. If the network isn't relatively busy, meaning there is spare or unused bandwidth, the percentage of broadcasts can be high and nobody will care.

There is no magic broadcast percentage number. Some networks may run fine with a broadcast rate of 1 percent, others may find even this value a problem. The only way you can tell if you are having a performance problem is to baseline your network and measure your performance over time. For more information on baselining see Chapter 14.

There is another scalability problem with broadcasts that can be bigger than just eating up network bandwidth. When **A** transmits its find server message for BILBO, the message will be propagated to every segment. More importantly, *every* node on the switched LAN will receive this broadcast and examine its contents. This means that *every* node must spend some processor time and examine every broadcast transmitted from *every other* node on the *entire* switched LAN.

For example, all the workstations will receive this find server request, examine it, and subsequently ignore it; but they *all* still had to spend time examining it. Each server will receive this message and compare the server name in the message with its own name. Only BILBO will respond to the find server broadcast. It will do so by sending a directed frame back to the searching node.

On large, busy, switched LANs this will often get to be a *big* problem long before the bandwidth issue rears its ugly head. A post made to the Internet news group comp.dcom.lans.ethernet in mid-1996 asked why a server was performing poorly on a switched Ethernet LAN. Somebody responded with, "How many broadcasts per second do you get when the network is busy?" The answer was 200 to 300, or about 11 to 16 percent of the network traffic when the network was busy. This was hammering the 486-based server. All it had time for was processing broadcast messages.

This can be a problem for older workstations or servers and small devices, such as printers, when they are directly connected to a Fast Ethernet LAN. Of course, modern Pentium-based servers and workstations with PCI network adapters can handle much higher loads. One of these high-performance machines won't even breathe hard when connected to a plain, old Ethernet LAN no matter what the load, but even high-end workstations and servers have the potential to suffer when connected to a large Fast Ethernet switched LAN serving lots of users.

These two problems with broadcasts are why switching does not scale well. The thing to remember about switched networks is that the percentage of broadcasts on each segment will be in direct proportion to the number of collision domains on the switched system. This puts a practical limit on how big switched networks can get.

There is a limit to the size that a switched network can reach before it is simply too big. Unfortunately there is no magic rule that says, Do not put more than 1,000 users on a single broadcast domain. The good news is that most switched networks do not get big enough to worry about problems associated with broadcasts. Switched LANs with 500 or 1,000 users can operate perfectly well before broadcasts become a problem. Some switched LANs out there have 2,500 users. While this is big, its not big enough for the many corporations who have thousands of users at one or more sites. When networks get this big, they must use routers to link together switched LANs.

Back Pressure

Congestion in a switch is a sticky problem. There is no good way to handle it. A switch can handle this problem in one of two ways: It can throw away (drop) new incoming packets, or it can exert back pressure on the incoming ports to control the flow of incoming packets.

Early switches just threw away incoming packets, often called **dropping packets**. From a performance standpoint, this is about the worst thing that can happen. Dropped packets are detected and handled by the protocol software running in the nodes. When a dropped packet is detected, *one or more* packets must be retransmitted by the node that originally sent the dropped packet. Often this just made the situation worse, since the switch was already busy.

Newer switches have a feature called **back pressure**, which can control the incoming flow of packets on a port. Back pressure prevents the nodes connected to a port from transmitting packets. This can be done two ways: forcing collisions and sending a jabber.

Back pressure can be exerted by forcing a collision when any node on a port attempts to send a packet. If the switch senses an incoming packet, then it transmits a dummy packet, causing a collision. The problem with this arises when congestion lasts long enough for one or more transmitting nodes to have 10 collisions in a row. When this occurs the node will drop the packet. This is just the situation the switch is trying to avoid by exerting back pressure.

The second way that a switch can exert back pressure is by transmitting a jabber, which is an excessively long packet. When a switch detects congestion, it will start to transmit a packet and keep transmitting until the congestion goes away. This is more effective than using a collision. The jabber may initially cause some collisions, but the nodes on the network will then see that a transmission is occurring and defer their transmissions until the transmission stops. The nodes will do this for single 64-byte packet, or for a jabber that lasts hundreds of milliseconds. Most switch vendors will advertise that their switches can exert back pressure when congestion occurs. The best switches will use jabbers to do so.

Unfortunately, there is also a slight problem with using jabbers as back pressure. At the end of the jabber all the nodes with pending transmissions will be in deferring mode, waiting to start their IPG timers. The nodes will start their IPG timers within one-half the collision window time of their collision domain. This guarantees that there will be some collisions when the jabber finishes. However, no frames will have been dropped.

Another problem with both methods is that they exert back pressure on all ports, whether or not the ports need it. This effectively shuts down each segment connected to the switch until the congestion is alleviated.

Back pressure is used by a switch only as a last resort to keep the nodes on the switched LAN from dropping packets. In essence it is the lesser of two evils.

Common Switch Features

Modern switches have an extremely wide array of features. Design teams at switch vendors spend a huge amount of time anguishing over every detail about their switches. They strive to achieve a cost-to-performance and feature ratio that will make their switch more attractive than the other guy's. Often they design in features that solve specific customer problems. Here are some of the more innovative or interesting features available:

- **Smart Back Pressure.** Some switches can exert back pressure on ports in a selective way. For example, if a switch detects congestion on port 4 and knows that all the buffered packets for it are on ports 3, 6, and 7, then it will exert back pressure only on these ports.
- **Spanning Tree.** Often it is desirable to have redundant links between devices. For example, a workgroup could be attached to

two departmental switches in parallel. This would cause a network loop that would be detected by both switches. One of the links would be disabled. If the functional link failed, the other link would automatically be enabled, preventing the users from losing connectivity. Using spanning-tree and redundant links is a very complex topic about which entire books have been written.

- **10/100 Support.** Many switches support Ethernet and Fast Ethernet on each port. This speed of the attached device is usually detected automatically. These kinds of switches are ideal for upgrading an existing Ethernet system to Fast Ethernet.
- **Modular Ports.** As mentioned previously, some switches have one or more modular ports that consist of plug-in slots that support modules for 100Base-TX, 100Base-FX, or 100Base-T4 PHYs.
- **Modular Uplinks.** These are very similar to modular ports and support uplink modules for FDDI, ATM, and even Fast Ethernet.
- **Port Segmentation.** Some new switches allow ports to be grouped so that they behave as a single switch. For example, a 12-port switch could be segmented into three logical switches with ports 1-4, 5-8, and 9-12 each behaving as separate switches (sometimes called **Virtual LANs**). Vendors are very creative in how their switches support port segmentation.
- **Broadcast Rate Limiting.** As a switched network gets large, broadcasts can become a problem. Some switches allow a maximum broadcast rate to be programmed on a per-port basis. For example, on a full-duplex link to another switch port, you could limit the transmitted broadcasts to a fixed number per second. If the broadcast rate exceeded this, then broadcasts to this port would be dropped. Note that, unlike dropping packets, dropping broadcasts is rarely a problem.
- **Gigabit Uplinks.** In 1996, the IEEE started to really work Gigabit Ethernet, which is 10 times faster than Fast Ethernet. Gigabit Ethernet is not expected to be standardized until late 1997 or early 1998. However, that doesn't mean that switch vendors will be sitting on their laurels. In late 1996 switches were available that had support for future gigabit uplinks, allowing a Gigabit Ethernet backbone to be installed when equipment becomes available.
- **WAN Links.** As is the case with modular uplinks, some companies are building switches that allow plug-in links to ISDN and Frame Relay. These sometimes even have routing capability built in. This can be very cost effective for a remote office, as the WAN link installed in the switch eliminates a separate WAN interface.

In summary, unlike Fast Ethernet repeaters, switches are extremely complicated devices. There are many different ways to build a Fast Ethernet switch—or any switch, for that matter—and a wide array of creative features. Most modern switches perform well and pass both the max traffic and max throughput tests. Performance differences between modern switches primarily pertain to congestion and how much internal bandwidth is available to support full-duplex ports.

It's important to remember that *any* switch, even expensive, high-performance ones, can become congested. Under the same circumstances, some switches will behave better than others. Selecting a switch is the area that has the best potential to benefit from planning your network and understanding your performance requirements. When selecting a switch, talk to the vendor and get a good understanding of the switch architecture, then evaluate how it will fit with your network's particular needs.

CHAPTER 13

Routers

Routers are key components in many networks, especially large and/or complex ones. Routers are required in many situations: For example, connecting to the Internet is always done via a router. Connections to WAN links are often made using routers, although bridges can have WAN links too.

Routers are layer-3 devices and work with protocol datagrams and not frames, so they can do things that are either impossible or very difficult to do with bridges. Since routers work at the protocol level, they can also provide all kinds of nifty services, such as being a fire wall and routing voice and video traffic in special ways.

In the early days of switching, many new switching vendors predicted the death of the router. This simply didn't happen and isn't going to happen. In fact, many vendors are working on layer-3 switches. A layer-3 switch is simply a switch that makes the forwarding decision for each frame based on layer-3 protocol information, like a router, and not on layer-2 frame information. A layer-3 switch is a natural evolution from routing, just as switching evolved from bridging.

Routing and bridging are also often combined in the same device. These gizmos are called **brouters** (bridge + router). A brouter can act as both a bridge and a router. When a brouter receives a frame, it will examine it and either bridge it or route it, depending on the frame's type and the protocol datagram in the frame.

In any case, routing is an extremely complex topic, and selecting a router is correspondingly difficult, especially at the enterprise level. Completely covering the topic of routers in this book simply isn't practical, but we will cover some important topics about routing as it applies to Fast Ethernet.

The biggest question about routers is whether *to route or switch*. This chapter will help you decide whether you need to route or switch between different parts of your network.

For example, *connecting to the Internet* is something that is on everyone's mind. This can be easily done with Fast Ethernet, but there are still some pitfalls to watch out for.

To Route or To Switch? That Is the Question

In most Fast Ethernet systems, switching will be the preferred method of connecting together segments to form workgroups, assembling workgroups into departments, connecting departments to backbones, and even connecting backbones to each other. Switches are simpler devices than routers and almost always offer more performance at a lower price. For Fast Ethernet and Ethernet LANs in particular, switching is almost always the preferred method of connectivity.

However, there are many circumstances and applications for which routers are better suited or even the only kind of device that can be used:

- Breaking up existing switched LANs when they get too large
- Connecting switched LANs and/or individual segments that need simple connectivity
- Connecting switched LANs and/or individual segments with WAN links
- Integrating with legacy and other network types
- Connecting to the Internet

As discussed previously, switched LANs don't scale into giant systems very well because there is a practical limit to the size to which a switched LAN can grow. This occurs for several reasons: Broadcasts become a problem, there can be no active redundant paths, there are often single points of failure, and latency and congestion can be big issues. On the other hand, routers and routed protocols are specifically designed to scale well. In fact, routed networks can become really huge. As mentioned before, the Internet is a fully routed network.

When a broadcast domain gets too large, either for performance reasons or from a physical or management standpoint, a router can be used to break up the switched LAN broadcast domain into smaller ones, much the way a switch is used to break up a collision domain that has become too large. For example, four large departments with switched LANs could be moved from a backbone switch to a backbone router (see Figure 13.1).

Routers used like this are usually large, powerful, enterprise-level devices. This is usually for performance reasons. If a large broadcast domain is broken up, the need for a high-performance connection between the new domains will usually be necessary. Inexpensive routers just cannot process data fast enough to connect two or more Fast Ethernet systems. This is especially true if redundant links between the switched LANs is required.

Routers for Connectivity

Routers are often used merely to provide connectivity between switched LANs and/or segments that need to be connected together but do not need high-performance links. For example, a company may have provided a high-performance switched LAN for each department, and given each system its own high-speed servers, local printers, and other network devices. However, everyone still needs to be tied together for e-mail, network management, and an Internet connection. In this case, an inexpensive midrange router may be preferable to using an expensive backbone switch. It provides connectivity between the departments with adequate performance while keeping the switched LANs isolated from each other.

Routers are often also used in campuslike settings in which buildings need to be connected together. It is common to place switched LANs in each building, as in Figure 12.2, and use a routed network to connect them. Often this is done with an FDDI ring that functions as a large routed enterprise backbone for the site. Many modern routers also support

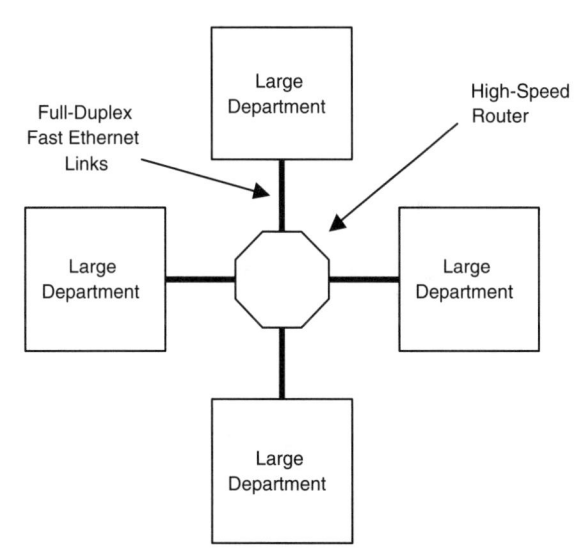

Figure 13.1
Partitioning switched LANs.

full-duplex links, which is ideal for tying them into high-end backbone switches, such as the one in Figure 8.7.

When a router is used like this, it is often called an **edge router,** which connects devices on single segment LANs or switched LANs to a larger, fully routed network. For example, the LAN in Figure 8.7 is attached to a large enterprise FDDI ring, as Figure 13.2 illustrates.

Of course, a routed backbone does not have to be connected to a single FDDI ring or other LAN technology. Routers can be directly connected to each other over both LAN links and WAN links to form a meshed system like the one in Figure 13.3. Often such a system of routers is called a **cloud.** Edge routers connect individual LANs to the routed network, and interior routers provide the backbone-level connectivity. Systems designed like this can be extremely flexible and robust. Many larger companies use routed systems like this to provide connectivity on individual campuses and between cities.

Routers can also be used to shield legacy devices and slower devices from the shear speeds of a Fast Ethernet LAN. Sometimes, printers, old workstations, servers, and low-performance WAN routers can be decoupled from a Fast Ethernet LAN using a router. A typical example is shown in Figure 13.4. This can be very desirable, especially when the Fast Ethernet switched LAN gets very big. If these devices were attached via a 10/100 switch, funneling a lot of broadcasts from the 100Mbps side to the 10Mbps side could swamp the slower devices. Since the router does not propagate broadcasts, the low-performance devices on the repeater will not have to deal with these broadcasts, and will still be able to function normally.

Routers for WAN Links

Connection over WAN links is probably the most common use for routers. LAN technologies such as Fast Ethernet are called *local* because

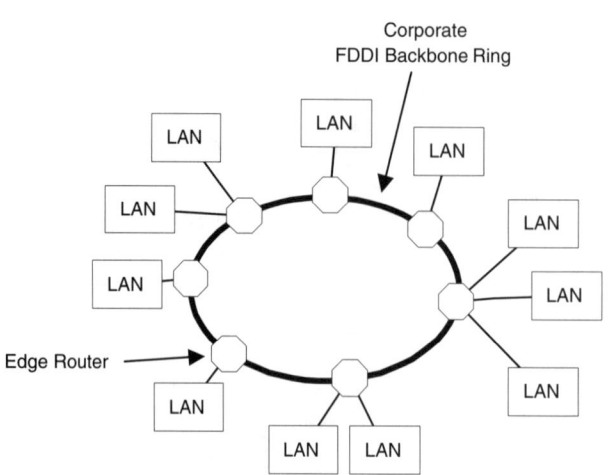

Figure 13.2
A routed FDDI ring.

Figure 13.3
Routed cloud.

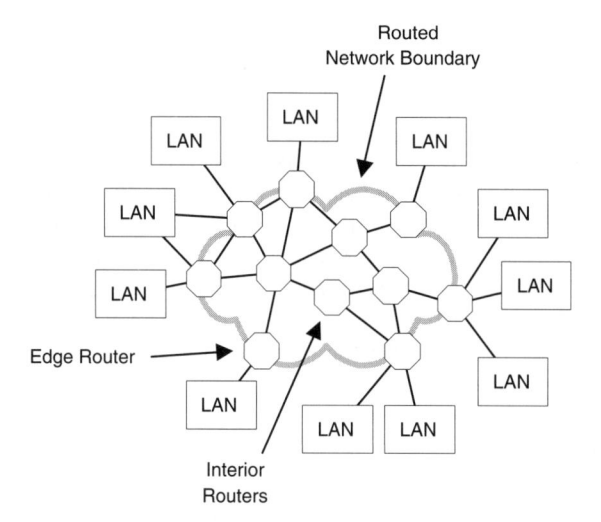

they can physically cover only a relatively small area. A single Fast Ethernet segment using copper cable can have a network diameter of only 205 meters. A full-duplex Fast Ethernet link can span 2,000 meters, as can an FDDI link. While suitable for even a large building or small campus, 2,000 meters isn't very far.

To connect geographically separate LANs, WAN links are used. These are usually provided by a local telephone company, such as one of the baby Bells, or one of the major long-distance companies, such as AT&T, MCI, or Sprint. In the 1970s and 1980s, WAN links were very slow and very expensive. Only large companies could justify their expense. In the early 1990s, the cost of WAN links started to drop as technology advanced and demand started to grow.

In 1995 and 1996 the need to connect remote and home offices to a parent office, and the desire to connect companies to the Internet created a huge new market for routers and WAN links. This market has ballooned as networking has become more pervasive and the structure of companies has started changing from monolithic groups at a single site to organizations distributed over a wide geographic area. Chances are you will need to connect your Fast Ethernet system to a WAN link.

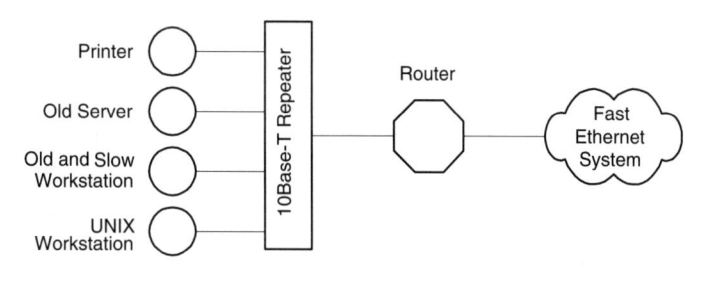

Figure 13.4
Shielding old and slow devices.

All WAN links have one thing in common: They provide point-to-point connections between two devices, one at each end of the link. Usually, the device at each end of a WAN link is a router. Many bridges and even some switches support WAN links as well, but bridging and WAN links have one big problem: broadcasts. WAN links are almost always much slower than the LAN to which they are connected via a bridge or router. If a bridge is connected to a WAN link, it must transmit all broadcasts it receives on its LAN ports to the WAN link. These broadcasts are a huge waste of WAN bandwidth, as the device that needs to respond to a broadcast is rarely on the other side of a WAN link.

Once again, routers are the solution to this problem, since they do not propagate broadcast frames. Routers send traffic over only the WAN link that must cross it. This uses the link most efficiently. Some routers can even use compression to squeeze more data through a link.

To connect a Fast Ethernet system to a WAN link, and then to other networks, a router requires two ports—one Fast Ethernet port and one WAN port. The WAN link connects to a router at the other end of the link. There are many different types of WAN links, from a simple dial-up modem at 28.8Kb baud to OC12 links at 622Mbps. Some common WAN links in the United States are listed in the following:

Type	Data Rate	Notes
Modems	28.8Kb, 33.6Kb, 56Kb	Regular modems over voice telephone lines
ISDN BRI	2 Channels at 64Kb each	Both channels can be *bonded* together to form one 128Kb channel
ISDN PRI	24 Channels at 64Kb each	Runs over a T1/DS1 line
Frame Relay	From 128Kbs to 1.544Mbps	Often runs over a T1; multiple FR circuits can share a T1-style line
T1/DS1	1.544 Mbps	The *standard* WAN link
T1C/DS1C	3.152 Mbps	2 T1 lines
T2/DS2	6.312 Mbps	4 T1 lines
T3/DS3	44.736 Mbps	28 T1 lines
802.3u	**100Mbps**	**Fast Ethernet (here for reference)**
T4/DS4	274.176 Mbps	177 T1 lines
OC3	155.52 Mbps	Used for ATM WAN links
OC12	622.08 Mbps	Used by MCI, AT&T, and Sprint for their Internet backbones

A WAN link can connect offices or sites across town, across the country, or in most major cities, around the world. Routers used for WAN links often have only two ports, one for the LAN connection, and one for the WAN link. However, it is common practice for routers to have several of both types of ports. Many companies will have a central set of routers at one or two sites that do all of the routing for their remote offices and sites in what is often called a **data center**. All the WAN links for a company will go from a remote site to a data center. This allows sites to communicate with each other and to a set of central servers. Centralization like this is very advantageous when companies have large databases that must be used by many sites. Companies that have large point-of-sale systems, such as a department store chain, or large databases, such as an insurance company, often use the data-center model.

Another common use for WAN links is to connect small and home offices to their parent offices. Many vendors make routers specifically designed for this. These routers have one LAN interface, typically for Ethernet or Fast Ethernet, and several modular WAN interfaces. A modular WAN interface can be plugged into a slot in a chassis. Some chassis-based devices are router specific, but many can support not only WAN cards, but repeater and switch cards as well. Many routers are specifically designed for remote access routing, and support only plug-in WAN ports. For example, an Internet service provider may have routers that support literally hundreds of dial-up modems. Other devices are designed for low-cost remote office applications. A typical remote office router in a parent office may look like the one shown in Figure 13.5.

In this case the router is attached directly to a Fast Ethernet backbone switch via a 10Mbps Ethernet link. The router supports modems for dial-up users, and could support salespeople who need to dial in for e-mail or to check prices and availability. It also supports three ISDN BRI lines for small remote and home offices, a dedicated T1 line to a large remote office, and a frame relay link to an Electronic Data Interchange provider.

There are also very small routers for the small remote or home office. These are usually small, two-port devices that often cost less than $1,000

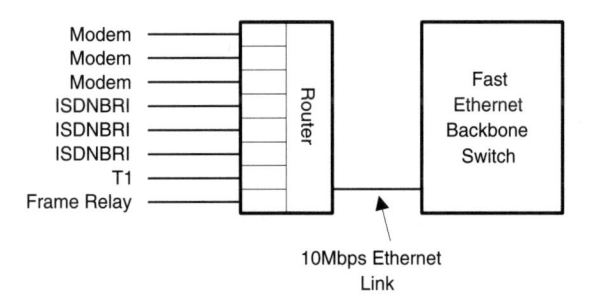

Figure 13.5
A modular WAN router.

and easily connect a small remote office via an ISDN or frame relay link. ISDN, frame relay, and T1 routers that are plug-in cards for PC servers and workstations are also available.

Remote office routers come in a dizzying array of sizes, types, port counts, and costs. Vendors have been wildly creative in building devices that meet very specific needs. New devices are coming to market regularly that have more features and higher performance at a lower price than the devices on the market today.

Integration with Other LAN Technologies

Often a company will need to connect a Fast Ethernet system to other types of networks. Routers offer a great solution for connecting a Fast Ethernet system to Token Ring, FDDI, ARCNet, and 100VG AnyLAN. Essentially, a router can connect all network technologies. Routers take care of big differences, such as those between media access methods and frame type. For example, Token Ring allows frame sizes up to 4Kb, and FDDI up to 64Kb. Ethernet allows frames of up to only 1,500 bytes. For the IP protocol, a router can fragment a large IP datagram from a Token Ring or FDDI LAN into multiple frames on an Ethernet LAN. This is called **IP fragmentation** and allows the routed system to use the larger, more efficient frame size of Token Ring or FDDI, and still communicate with a Fast Ethernet or Ethernet LAN.

Routers can also help manage the speed difference between slower technologies such as Token Ring and ARCNet. Routers can often buffer large amounts of data, helping to prevent congestion as data flows from a Fast Ethernet LAN to a slower LAN.

Connecting to the Internet

Connecting to the Internet is not much different from connecting to a remote office. Both are done via a WAN link, and most small or medium-size companies use an Internet service provider just as an individual does. However, instead of a dial-up modem or ISDN line that is only up or connected when in use, a company will purchase a WAN link that is up all the time. Of course, this costs a little more but it ensures that employees have access to the Internet, allowing e-mail to come and go, and ensuring customers always have access to the company's Web page.

Small companies might use an ISDN line at 128Kb or a frame relay link at 512Kb for their connection. Medium-size to larger companies often use a dedicated T1 link. This isn't really different from any other kind of

Figure 13.6
A firewall.

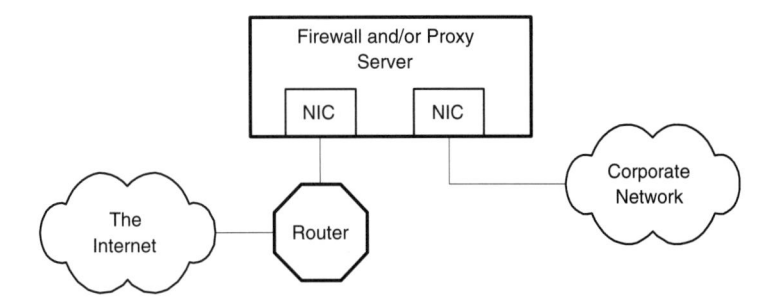

WAN routing. What is usually different is the kind of equipment that a company has at its end of the link.

Any company that is connected to the Internet is well advised to do so using a **firewall** or **proxy server**. These are devices that help prevent criminals from gaining access to your private corporate resources, while allowing your employees access to the Internet. (Note that we didn't use the term *hacker*, because it is a term that has been misused. Hackers are usually good guys that give us all kinds of free software. The first Web browser, Mosaic, was written by a hacker named Marc Andreessen, now CIO of Netscape, and given away for free.) Firewalls and proxy servers are usually just regular computers, though fast ones, that have two network adapters in them, one that connects to a router and then the Internet, and another that connects to your corporate network (see Figure 13.6).

The corporate network is said to be **inside the firewall** and is protected from intrusion by criminals. A firewall or proxy server can do this because it watches and filters *all* traffic going to and from the Internet. It can both detect and prevent all kinds of attacks from outside the corporate network. A proxy sever can also completely isolate corporate users from the Internet while still providing them access to the Web, FTP, and other Internet resources.

Firewalls and proxy servers can make a corporate network almost invulnerable to criminal attack, but they are not perfect. They are only part of a security plan that includes protecting servers with passwords, educating users, and all kinds of other measures. Connecting to the Internet is straightforward and can be extremely safe. However, to be safe it must be done right. We recommend that any company wanting to connect directly to the Internet take security extremely seriously.

CHAPTER 14

Using Network Management

Several other chapters have talked about metrics, or measures of network performance, such as network utilization, the number of broadcast frames per second, and the number of dropped frames on switch ports. Gathering and analyzing this kind of data is essential to keeping a Fast Ethernet network running well. This is especially true for networks that rely on switches for departmental and backbone connectivity. When using switches, a network manager must constantly be on the lookout for recurring congestion problems and problems with excessive broadcasts.

Network statistics and control information cannot be of any use to a network manager if they cannot be easily retrieved, and network management using the SNMP protocol is really the only way to accomplish this. Many devices support proprietary interfaces and sometimes even special protocols for controlling the device and gathering statistics. These methods are sometimes nifty, but they are very nonstandard. No matter how smart, a device is considered to be **managed** only if it supports the SNMP protocol. Any SNMP-managed device can be accessed using a Network Management Station (NMS), with which a network manager can fully control the device and read all its statistics. NMS software runs on PCs or workstations, and communicates with agents in order to gather statistics and control devices.

Managed devices often support many different MIBs. (For more information on MIBs and the Simple Network Management Protocol, see Chapter 6.) Often these are standard MIBs and are defined by the IETF standards body. Most devices also support enterprise MIBs or proprietary MIBs to provide extra information and control capabilities not provided for in standard MIBs. Often the data in an enterprise MIB is complementary to or gives added detail to the data in a standard MIB. For Fast Ethernet nodes, switches, and repeaters, the two most important MIBs are MIB-II from RFC1213, and the RMON MIB from RFC1757. There are also MIBs for specific types of devices: for switches, the Bridge MIB from RFC1493 (these MIBs are available from our Web page at www.wiley.com/FastEthernet), and for Ethernet and Fast Ethernet repeaters, the MAU MIB from RFC1368.

MIB-II was defined in May, 1990, and is supported by almost every single managed device on the planet. MIB-II is so common because it describes data objects that are specific to one or more network interfaces. In other words, if a device has even one network interface, it can (and should) support MIB-II.

In contrast, the RMON MIB contains information about an entire segment. For example, using MIB-II, the number of broadcast frames transmitted and received by a port on a switch can be retrieved. Using the RMON MIB, the number of broadcast frames transmitted for an entire network can be retrieved. For Fast Ethernet and Ethernet, RMON gathers data on a single collision domain.

Using MIB-II Interface-Based Management

MIB-II is the most universal and perhaps the most useful MIB in common use. It describes data about a device itself and all the network interfaces in a device, and is divided into groups that contain data specific to different aspects of a network interface, as shown in the following:

Group	Description
System group	Describes information about the device itself. For example, the device can be assigned a name, description, and location.
Interfaces group	Describes information about each interface in the device.
Address Translation group	Exists only to provide compatibility with MIB-I, the predecessor to MIB-II, information that is now provided by other groups in MIB-II.
IP Group	Provides information about the IP protocol and the network interfaces that use it.
ICMP group	Contains information about ICMP messages sent and received on an interface.

TCP group	Provides information about the TCP protocol used in this device.
Transmission group	Contains sub-MIBs that pertain to specific network technologies, such as Fast Ethernet or Token Ring.
SNMP group	Contains information about the SNMP protocol used to manage this device.

All of these groups have important and useful information. For the purpose of measuring network performance, data from the System group and Interfaces group are the most useful. Data gathered from a switch port using these two groups can be used to measure network utilization and discover congestion and broadcast-rate problems.

Usually, the MIB-II data gathered by a regular device, such as a server or workstation, describes the statistics for only a single network interface. By itself, this isn't enough to calculate network utilization and the other information in which we are interested. For example, you couldn't take the MIB-II data gathered from a network interface in a server, and calculate network utilization.

However, a switch port is a different animal. It operates in promiscuous mode and therefore *sees* all traffic on every collision domain to which it is connected. Therefore, using MIB-II statistics from switch ports, performance information can be easily calculated. This is even more useful when you consider that all managed switches support MIB-II on all their ports.

There are many other useful data objects in MIB-II, but the following values, when gathered from a switch port, are what are needed to calculate network utilization and make an approximation of network utilization by broadcast frames:

Object Name	Description	Clarification
sysUpTime	The time (in hundredths of a second) since the network management portion of the system was last reinitialized.	When the switch starts up (or is reset), this counter is reset to zero and then incremented every 1/100 second.
ifSpeed	An estimate of the interface's current bandwidth in bits per second. For interfaces that do not vary in bandwidth, or for those for which no accurate	This is the interface's baud rate—for Ethernet, 10,000,000; for Fast Ethernet, 100,000,000.

Object Name	Description	Clarification
	estimation can be made, this object should contain the nominal bandwidth.	
ifInOctets	The total number of octets received on the interface, including framing characters.	This value is a count of bytes generated by all the nodes on the collision domain connected to the switch port. Note that this *includes* broadcast and unicast frames.
ifInUcastPkts	The number of subnetwork-unicast packets delivered to a higher-layer protocol.	This value is a count of unicast frames generated by all the nodes on the collision domain connected to the switch port.
ifInNUcastPkts	The number of nonunicast (i.e., subnetwork-broadcast or subnetwork-multicast) packets delivered to a higher-layer protocol.	This value is a count of both broadcast and multicast frames generated by all the nodes on the collision domain connected to the switch port.
ifInDiscards	The number of inbound packets that were chosen to be discarded even though no errors had been detected to prevent their being deliverable to a higher-layer protocol. One possible reason for discarding such a packet could be to free up buffer space.	This value is a count of the received frames from the collision domain that were dropped by the switch due to congestion.
ifOutOctets	The total number of octets transmitted out of the interface, including framing characters.	This value is a count of the bytes transmitted on the collision domain by the switch. This is all data coming from other collision domains. Note that this *includes* broadcast and unicast frames.

ifOutUcastPkts	The total number of packets that higher-level protocols requested be transmitted to a subnetwork-unicast address, including those that were discarded or not sent.	This value is a count of the unicast frames bridged from other collision domains.
ifOutNUcastPkts	The total number of packets that higher-level protocols requested be transmitted to a non-unicast (i.e., a subnetwork-broadcast or subnetwork-multicast) address, including those that were discarded or not sent.	This value is a count of the broadcast and multicast frames transmitted on the collision domain that come from all other collision domains.
ifOutDiscards	The number of outbound packets that were chosen to be discarded even though no errors had been detected to prevent their being transmitted. One possible reason for discarding such a packet could be to free up buffer space.	This value is a count of the frames that could not be transmitted on the collision domain by the switch due to congestion in the switch.

Perhaps the most important value used to calculate anything from MIB-II is the **sysUpTime** value. This object is how a device measures time, and no meaningful data can be calculated without it. The reason for this is that all the counters in MIB-II and most other MIBs are just that, counters. For example, the **ifInUcastPkts** counter keeps track of the number of frames received by a network interface. Let's say the **ifInUcastPkts** counter for a switch port contains the value 168,284,917. What does this mean? Is this the number of frames in the last five minutes? The last hour? In short, using the counter value alone doesn't convey any time-based information.

Another issue with these MIB-II counters is that they are 32 bits in size. This means they can count only to 2^{32}, which is 4,294,967,296 (about 4.3 billion). At Fast Ethernet frame rates on a very busy LAN, a frame counter could easily roll back over to zero in about 14 hours.

At Fast Ethernet speeds the maximum throughput (and utilization) counters that measure bytes (octets) transferred can roll over in as little as 5.8

minutes. (1,518 bytes per frame at 8127.44 frames per second is 12,337,454 bytes per second. A 32-bit counter can contain a maximum value of 4,294,967,296. At this rate, a 32-bit counter will roll over every 348 seconds.)

NMS software solves this seemingly intractable problem by a process called **sampling**. When you tell an NMS to measure network utilization, it first reads the counters it needs, along with the value of **sysUpTime**, and remembers them. Over the duration of the measurement, the NMS will periodically sample the counters and **sysUpTime** until the desired time interval has passed. For example, for a measurement duration of five minutes, or 30,000 **sysUpTime** ticks, an NMS may sample the necessary data once every five seconds.

If you tell an NMS to measure network utilization over the next five minutes, it may first sample a **sysUpTime** value of 1,025,882,373. It will then periodically read data from the device until the **sysUpTime** value is *equal to or greater than* 1,025,912,373, or 30,000 time ticks after the value for **sysUpTime** was initially read. For any measurement using counters, an NMS must use this procedure.

All 32-bit statistics counters and the **sysUpTime** value are subject to rollover. Fortunately, this is a problem for which an NMS can easily compensate. All it must do is ensure that its sampling rate is shorter than the shortest possible rollover time for a particular counter. For Fast Ethernet, this is about five minutes. If an NMS samples often enough, it can always detect a counter rollover and thus keep track of the event counts that have occurred.

For example, to calculate network utilization, the **ifInUcastPkts** counter must be read. If the NMS reads a value for **ifInUcastPkts** that is *less than* the previous value read, then it knows the counter has rolled over. For example, the first time the counter is read, it may contain the value 4,292,824,677 only 2,142,619 counts from rolling over. On the next read of the counter, it might read a value of 2,785. The number of counts that has passed since the first read is simply calculated as follows:

Counter Rollover Calculation

$$counts = (2^{32} - V_1) + V_2$$

Where 2^{32} is the maximum counter value

V_1 is the first counter value

V_2 is the second counter value

2,145,404 = (4,294,967,296 − 4,292,824,677) + 2,785

In this case, the counter has increased by 2,145,404 counts. All 32-bit values must be checked for rollover even if their periods are long. For example, the **sysUpTime** timer counter can roll over as well, but it takes 11,930 hours, or 497 days, to do so. This is a long time but it is not inconceivable that a device such as a repeater powered by a UPS would be up for this long.

For a Fast Ethernet segment connected to a switch, the In and Out octet counters and the value of **sysUpTime** are used to measure the network utilization for a specified period of time. The **ifInOctets** counter on a switch port measures the octets removed from the attached segment—in other words, the number of bytes transmitted by all the nodes on the attached segment. A switch port's **ifOutOctets** counter holds the value of all the bytes forwarded to the attached segment from all the other segments in the broadcast domain. The total number of bytes that have been transmitted on the attached segment is calculated by adding these two values together. To calculate the network utilization for a switch port, an NMS uses the following formula:

Utilization Calculation

$$utilization\% = \frac{8 \times totalOctets}{(Delta(t_1, t_0)/100) \times ifSpeed} \times 100$$

Fast Ethernet has an ifSpeed of 10^8 which simplifies this equation to:

$$utilization\% = \frac{8 \times totalOctets}{Delta(t_1, t_0) \times 10{,}000}$$

The total number of octets transferred on the LAN is calculated as:

$$totalOctets = \begin{array}{l} Delta(ifInOctets_{t0}, ifInOctets_{t1}) + \\ Delta(ifOutOctets_{t0}, ifOutOctets_{t1}) \end{array}$$

The function **delta(later, earlier)** computes the difference between the value sampled later and the value sampled earlier. The delta function also takes into account counter rollover. The counters at t_0 and t_1 are the values at the beginning and end of the measurement period, respectively.

What this means in English is that the network utilization for a Fast Ethernet or Ethernet segment connected to a switch port is the total number of bits transmitted on the collision domain in nonerror frames, divided by the total number of bits of bandwidth available over that time period. For example, data sampled by an NMS for a five-minute period on a segment might look like that shown in Table 14.1.

Note that the value of **sysUpTime** is 187 time ticks greater than the 30,000 time ticks that span a five-minute interval. This is due to the

Table 14.1 Counter Readings

Counter	At t_0	At t_1	Delta
sysUpTime	283,549,192	283,579,379	30,187
ifInOctets	4,292,824,677	339,375,738	341,518,357
ifOutOctets	629,285,482	1,127,573,734	498,288,252
Total Octets			839,806,609

polling nature of the NMS software. In this case, the NMS read the first values when **sysUpTime** was at a t_0 value of 283,549,192. It then began polling every five seconds or so (by its time clock), and quit reading when at least 30,000 **sysUpTime** ticks had passed. Because of latencies, timer inconstancies, and other differences between the two systems, an NMS can't read values at exact time periods. It must take this into account in its calculations by using the actual difference between the sampled **sysUpTime** values t_0 and t_1, and not the specified time interval of 30,000 time ticks. After the last sample, the NMS will use the formula to calculate the network utilization. If we plug the values from Table 14.1 into the utilization equation we get the following calculation:

The Actual Calculation

$$23.26\% = \frac{8 \times 839{,}806{,}609}{(283{,}579{,}379 - 283{,}549{,}192) \times 10{,}000}$$

An interesting twist to calculating network utilization comes into play with full-duplex switch links. For full-duplex links, the formula in the *Utilization Calculation* equation must be modified a little by changing the value of **ifSpeed** from 100,000,000 to 200,000,000, because data can be flowing in each direction simultaneously. For full-duplex links, the formula becomes:

Full-duplex Network Utilization

$$utilization\% = \frac{8 \times totalOctets}{Delta(t_1, t_0) \times 20{,}000}$$

This same sampling technique can be used to calculate other values from a switch port's MIB-II data, such as:

- Broadcast frames per second transmitted by the nodes on a segment
- Broadcast frames per second forwarded from other segments to a segment
- Unicast frames per second generated by a segment

- Unicast frames per second forwarded to a segment
- Bytes per second generated by a segment

Often, these kinds of rates are calculated as per-second values, but a sample time of several minutes is usually used to gather the data. For example, using the data from Table 14.1 we can calculate the average throughput, in bytes per second, like this:

Calculation of Average Throughput

$$throughput_{Bps} = \frac{totalOctets}{Delta(t_1, t_0)/100}$$

Then, plugging in the actual values gives us:

Full-duplex Network Utilization

$$2{,}782{,}014_{Bps} = \frac{839{,}806{,}609}{30{,}187/100}$$

Using MIB-II data from switch ports is a great way to calculate some very useful network statistics. There are also a lot of other goodies in MIB-II, such as the number of error frames received and the MAC address for each interface. This data can be sampled and combined with network utilization and other statistics to get a very clear picture of how a network is operating.

Some NMS software is very sophisticated and will graph data over time and keep historical records. Most can keep running calculations of values. For example, values can be recalculated every sample time, yielding graphs that closely track what is actually happening.

MIB-II Extensions

MIB-II is a very well-designed MIB, which has contributed to its longevity. However, it's not perfect. In 1994, RFC1573, commonly called the Interface Extensions MIB, which describes many improvements to MIB-II, was released. The two most significant of these improvements are: support for 64-bit counters, and the separation of multicast and broadcast counters.

64-bit counters are really helpful for supporting new high-speed networking. For Fast Ethernet they are very helpful and mean that an NMS can monitor values over a period of hours, and sample only every 10 or 15 minutes. This is important not because the counters roll over less often, but because it reduces network management traffic. On large enterprise networks with many managed devices, an NMS may need to monitor and poll literally hundreds of devices. If polling is required frequently, a significant portion of bandwidth can be used up by SNMP traffic. It's also a lot of work for the NMS, and can limit the number of devices that a single NMS can monitor. This polling traffic can be an even bigger problem when the device being monitored is on the other side of one or more slow WAN links. Like broadcast traffic, SNMP traffic can be a somewhat wasteful use of expensive WAN bandwidth.

By using 64-bit counters, an NMS's poll cycles to a managed device can be very far apart, easily every 15 or 30 minutes even for important statistics. Polling every hour or two is adequate for normal monitoring. A 64-bit counter can hold numbers up to 18,446,744,073,709,600,000, which is really huge, but even 64-bit counters can overflow. On Fast Ethernet LAN, the shortest time in which a 64-bit counter can overflow is about 142 days, which is usually plenty of time. However, as we move to Gigabit Ethernet, which is 10 times faster than Fast Ethernet, the worst-case rollover time shrinks to just 14 days, and this is not the fastest network link available. An OC48 SONET wide area network operates at 2.448 gigabits per second.

For superfast networking speeds, 64-bit counters are not a luxury but a necessity. The following details the 64-bit counters in the MIB-II Interface extensions:

Object Name	Description	Clarification
InOctets	The total number of octets received on the interface, including framing characters. This object is a 64-bit version of **ifInOctets**.	For a switch port, this is the total number of bytes transmitted by nodes on the attached segment.
InUcastPkts	The number of packets delivered by this sublayer to a higher (sub)layer, which were not addressed to a multicast or broadcast address at this sublayer. This object is a 64-bit version of **ifInUcastPkts**.	For a switch port, this is the total number of unicast frames transmitted by nodes on the attached segment.
InMulticastPkts	The number of packets delivered by this	This is a counter expressly for multicast

	sublayer to a higher (sub)layer, which were addressed to a multicast address at this sublayer. For a MAC layer protocol, this includes both group and functional addresses. This object is a 64-bit version of **ifInMulticastPkts**.	frames and does not count frames with a destination address equal to the *all ones* broadcast address. For a switch port, this is the total number of multicast frames transmitted by nodes on the attached segment.
InBroadcastPkts	The number of packets delivered by this sublayer to a higher (sub)layer, which were addressed to a broadcast address at this sublayer. This object is a 64-bit version of **ifInBroadcastPkts**.	This is a counter expressly for broadcast frames and counts only frames with a destination address equal to the *all ones* broadcast address. For a switch port, this is the total number of broadcast frames transmitted by nodes on the attached segment.
OutOctets	The total number of octets transmitted out of the interface, including framing characters. This object is a 64-bit version of **ifOutOctets**.	For a switch, this is the total number of bytes forwarded from other segments in the broadcast domain to the attached segment.
OutMulticastPkts	The total number of packets that higher-level protocols requested be transmitted, and which were addressed to a multicast address at this sublayer, including those that were discarded or not sent. For a MAC layer protocol, this includes both group and	For a switch port, this counter tracks all the multicast frames forwarded to the attached segment from all the other segments in the broadcast domain.

Object Name	Description	Clarification
	functional addresses. This object is a 64-bit version of **ifOutMulticastPkts**.	
OutBroadcastPkts	The total number of packets that higher-level protocols requested be transmitted, and which were addressed to a broadcast address at this sublayer, including those that were discarded or not sent. This object is a 64-bit version of **ifOutBroadcastPkts**.	For a switch port, this counter tracks all the broadcast frames forwarded to the attached segment from all the other segments in the broadcast domain.

The interface extensions MIB also has separate counters for multicast and broadcast frames in contrast to MIB-II, which lumped this information into one counter for nonunicast traffic. Actually counting these frames differently provides one frame counter for each kind of IEEE address.

Ethernet-Specific MIB

All of the MIB-II data objects previously discussed are not specific to either Fast Ethernet or Ethernet, and can be applied (one way or another) to many other network technologies, such as FDDI, Token Ring, and 100VG AnyLAN. This is another of the design features of MIB-II that make its use so widespread. Valuable as this is, the designers of MIB-II knew that it would be valuable to have MIBs that were specific to individual technologies such as Ethernet and Fast Ethernet. This is what the Transmission group of MIB-II is for.

RFC1650 is a set of Definitions of Managed Objects for the Ethernet-like Interface Types, and describes a set of data objects that are specific to the CSMA/CD media access rules. There are some useful counters in this MIB that correspond directly to the events and errors that can happen during the CSMA/CD process. The following lists some of the more useful counters from this MIB:

Object Name	*Description*
AlignmentErrors	A count of frames received on a particular interface that are not an integral number of octets in length, and do not pass the FCS check. The count represented by an instance of this object is incremented when the alignment error status is returned by the MAC service to the LLC (or other MAC user). Received frames for which multiple error conditions obtained are, according to the conventions of IEEE 802.3 Layer Management, counted exclusively according to the error status presented to the LLC.
FCSErrors	A count of frames received on a particular interface that are an integral number of octets in length but do not pass the FCS check. The count represented by an instance of this object is incremented when the **frameCheckError** status is returned by the MAC service to the LLC (or other MAC user). Received frames for which multiple error conditions obtain are, according to the conventions of IEEE 802.3 Layer Management, counted exclusively according to the error status presented to the LLC.
SingleCollisionFrames	A count of successfully transmitted frames on a particular interface for which transmission is inhibited by exactly one collision. A frame that is counted by an instance of this object is also counted by the corresponding instance of either the **ifOutUcastPkts, ifOutMulticastPkts,** or **ifOutBroadcastPkts**, and is not counted by the corresponding instance of the **MultipleCollisionFrames** object.
MultipleCollisionFrames	A count of successfully transmitted frames on a particular interface for which transmission is inhibited by more than one collision. A frame that is counted by an instance of this object is also counted by the corresponding instance of either the **ifOut-**

Object Name	Description
	UcastPkts, **ifOutMulticastPkts**, or **ifOutBroadcastPkts**, and is not counted by the corresponding instance of the **SingleCollisionFrames** object.
LateCollisions	The number of times that a collision is detected on a particular interface later than 512 bit times into the transmission of a packet; 512 bit times corresponds to 5.12 microseconds on a 100 Mbit/s system. A (late) collision included in a count represented by an instance of this object is also considered as a (generic) collision for purposes of other collision-related statistics.

The most useful of these counters are the three collision counters. The single and multiple collision frame counters can be used to accurately gauge how well your network is performing when utilization is high. As network utilization climbs, the number of single-frame collisions will climb also, but usually not as much. As network utilization starts to peak, the number of multiple collision frames will start to climb.

Note that these collision counters are useful for only a single interface. Even on a switch or bridge port, these counters count only the collisions that that interface has, and cannot count the collisions between two other nodes on a segment. For example, if a collision occurs between nodes **A** and **B** on a switch port, the switch cannot detect it and the collision event will not be counted in the switch port's counters, only in **A** and **B**'s counters.

Another thing to keep in mind about collision counters is that *collisions are supposed to happen*. Collisions and detecting them are how a Fast Ethernet LAN controls access to the media. Many people assume that if collisions are happening then something must be bad. When cars collide this is a bad thing, so frames colliding must be equally bad. This just isn't the case.

The number or rate of collisions on a network interface attached to a Fast Ethernet or Ethernet segment is also relatively unimportant. The number of collisions per second can fluctuate wildly, especially when measured over a long period of time, while network utilization remains relatively constant or changes smoothly.

Last, the **LateCollisions** counter on any network interface should always be zero. Late collisions are *always bad* and mean that the network diameter of a segment is too big. As mentioned before, late collisions can cause all kinds of network problems. If your network has them, stop what you are doing, find the segments that are too long, and fix them.

Measuring Switch Congestion

Two of the most useful statistical values for switches are also right in MIB-II: **ifOutDiscards** and **ifInDiscards**. These objects count the number of frames dropped by a switch for a given port. The **ifInDiscards** object counts the number of frames received by a port that could not be processed due to congestion; the **ifOutDiscards** object counts the number of frames that needed to be forwarded from other segments to the port's segment but couldn't due to congestion.

Monitoring these two counters can be invaluable in detecting congestion problems in a switch. Normally, these counters should be very low. In some switched environments they will almost never be incremented. In other systems, the ratio of dropped frames to total frames should normally be less than 1 percent.

It is important to note that many switches do not become congested at a specific port, but internally. Because of this, frames dropped due to congestion in the switching engine itself may not show up in the MIB-II counters. Most switches have counters in their enterprise MIB that monitor this type of congestion, so one of the things to look for when purchasing a managed switch is how easy it is to detect congestion with MIB objects. A switch should have a discard counter for each place internally where frames can be dropped. Often, a salesperson will not be able to tell you this, and you must look at the MIBs themselves to find this information.

Using RMON Network-Based Management

RMON stands for **Remote Network Monitoring**, and is designed to monitor an entire network and not just a single network interface such as MIB-II. This MIB is defined in RFC1757, released in February 1995, and is an update of RFC1271.

RMON is a network-specific MIB and gathers statistics about an entire network segment—in contrast to MIB-II, which gathers statistics about only a single network interface and can partially be used only to gather segment statistics when a network interface runs in promiscuous mode.

The data in the RMON MIB are gathered by a device called an **RMON probe**, which can be implemented in any kind of device, such as a switch or repeater, that has access to all of the frames on a Fast Ethernet or Ethernet segment. RMON probes were initially dedicated devices and were expensive, often costing $5,000 to $10,000. Many early RMON probes attached to only a single LAN segment, although some expensive probes could monitor multiple segments from one box. Now, like many other features, even low-cost devices support RMON monitoring. RMON probes are also often built into switches and repeaters, an approach that is becoming more and more popular.

While MIB-II and its associated MIBs are extremely useful, they still must be polled to gather data, and this polling can be problematic. It is essentially a waste of network bandwidth and doesn't scale well. A single NMS console can actively poll only so many devices before it runs out of horsepower.

RMON probes help solve these polling related problems by doing the polling and data recording in the device itself. An RMON probe does this periodically by sampling statistics and recording them in buckets. All this happens independently of an NMS, which can configure an RMON probe to record data and then not communicate with the probe again until statistics need to be gathered. This can radically cut down on the amount of traffic needed to gather network-level statistics.

RMON is split up into groups. Implementation in a probe of each RMON group is optional. RFC1757 describes the groups as follows:

Group 1: Ethernet Statistics Group

"The Ethernet Statistics group contains statistics measured by the probe for each monitored Ethernet interface on this device. This group consists of the **etherStatsTable**. In the future, other groups will be defined for other media types, including Token Ring and FDDI. These groups should follow the same model as the Ethernet statistics group."

Group 2: History Control Group

"The History Control group controls the periodic statistical sampling of data from various types of networks. This group consists of the **historyControlTable**."

Group 3: Ethernet History Group

"The Ethernet History group records periodic statistical samples from an Ethernet network and stores them for later retrieval. This group consists of the **etherHistoryTable**. In the future, other groups will be defined for other media types, including Token Ring and FDDI."

Group 4: Alarm Group

"The Alarm group periodically takes statistical samples from variables in the probe and compares them to previously configured thresholds. If the monitored variable crosses a threshold, an event is generated. A hysteresis mechanism is implemented to limit the generation of alarms. This group consists of the **alarmTable**, and requires the implementation of the event group."

Group 5: Host Group

"The Host group contains statistics associated with each host discovered on the network. This group discovers hosts on the network by keeping a list of source and destination MAC addresses seen in good packets promiscuously received from the network. This group consists of the **hostControlTable**, the **hostTable**, and the **hostTimeTable**."

Group 6: HostTopN Group

"The **hostTopN** group is used to prepare reports that describe the hosts that top a list ordered by one of their statistics. The available statistics are samples of one of their base statistics over an interval specified by the management station. Thus, these statistics are rate based. The management station also selects how many such hosts are reported. This group consists of the **hostTopNControlTable** and the **hostTopNTable**, and requires the implementation of the host group."

Group 7: Matrix Group

"The Matrix group stores statistics for conversations between sets of two addresses. As the device detects a new conversation, it creates a new entry in its tables. This group consists of the **matrixControlTable**, the **matrixSDTable**, and the **matrixDSTable**."

Group 8: Filter Group

"The Filter group allows packets to be matched by a filter equation. These matched packets form a data stream that may be captured or may generate events. This group consists of the **filterTable** and the **channelTable**."

Group 9: Packet Capture Group

"The Packet Capture group allows packets to be captured after they flow through a channel. This group consists of the **bufferControlTable** and the **captureBufferTable**, and requires the implementation of the filter group."

Group 10: Event Group

"The Event group controls the generation and notification of events from this device. This group consists of the **eventTable** and the **logTable**."

The most common implemented RMON groups are 1, 2, 3, 4, and 10, often called the basic RMON groups, which are much easier to implement than groups 5 through 9, sometimes called the Advanced groups. The basic groups deal only with statistics, much like MIB-II. In modern devices, these statistics are almost always gathered by hardware, and can be tracked with very little CPU power. On the other hand, the information gathered by the Advanced group must be collected by physically examining each frame that is transmitted on a segment. For 10Mbps Ethernet this isn't too hard, but at Fast Ethernet speeds, the task can be daunting.

Group 1: Ethernet Statistics

Group 1, the Ethernet Statistics group, keeps interface-specific statistics, much like MIB-II does. An RMON probe will have one or more network interfaces. For example, a 16-port Fast Ethernet switch that supports RMON will collect RMON Ethernet statistics for all 16 ports. While similar to the MIB-II statistics, the RMON information is significantly different. The following lists these statistics:

Object Name	Description
Octets	Total number of octets of data (including those in bad packets) received on the network (excluding framing bits but including FCS octets).
Pkts	Total number of packets (including bad packets, broadcast packets, and multicast packets) received.
BroadcastPkts	Total number of good packets received that were directed to the broadcast address. Note that this does not include multicast packets.
MulticastPkts	Total number of good packets received that were directed to a multicast address. Note that this number does not include packets directed to the broadcast address.
CRCAlignErrors	Total number of packets received that had a length (excluding framing bits but including FCS octets) of between 64 and 1,518 octets, inclusive, but had either a bad frame check sequence (FCS) with an integral number of octets (FCS error) or a bad FCS with a non-integral number of octets (alignment error).
UndersizePkts	Total number of packets received that were less than 64 octets long (excluding framing bits but including FCS octets) and were otherwise well formed.

OversizePkts	Total number of packets received that were longer than 1,518 octets (excluding framing bits but including FCS octets) and were otherwise well formed.
Fragments	Total number of packets received that were less than 64 octets in length (excluding framing bits but including FCS octets) and had either a bad frame check sequence (FCS) with an integral number of octets (FCS Error) or a bad FCS with a nonintegral number of octets (alignment error). Note that it is entirely normal for **etherStatsFragments** to increment, because it counts both runts (which are normal occurrences due to collisions) and noise hits.
Jabbers	Total number of packets received that were longer than 1,518 octets (excluding framing bits but including FCS octets), and had either a bad frame check sequence (FCS) with an integral number of octets (FCS Error) or a bad FCS with a nonintegral number of octets (alignment error). Note that this definition of jabber is different than the definition in IEEE-802.3 section 8.2.1.5 [10Base-5] and section 10.3.1.4 [10Base-2]. These documents define jabber as the condition where any packet exceeds 20ms. The allowed range to detect jabber is between 20ms and 150ms.
Collisions	Best estimate of the total number of collisions on this Ethernet segment. The value returned will depend on the location of the RMON probe. Section 8.2.1.3 (10Base-5) and section 10.3.1.3 (10Base-2) of IEEE standard 802.3 states that a station must detect a collision, in the receive mode, if three or more stations are transmitting simultaneously. A repeater port must detect a collision when two or more stations are transmitting simultaneously. Thus a probe placed on a repeater port could record more collisions than a probe connected to a station on the same segment. Probe location plays a

Object Name	Description
	much smaller role when considering 10Base-T. 14.2.1.4 (10Base-T) of IEEE standard 802.3, which defines a collision as the simultaneous presence of signals on the DO and RD circuits (transmitting and receiving at the same time). A 10Base-T station can detect collisions only when it is transmitting. Thus probes placed on a station and a repeater should report the same number of collisions. Note also that an RMON probe inside a repeater should ideally report collisions between the repeater and one or more other hosts (transmit collisions as defined by IEEE 802.3), plus receiver collisions observed on any coax segments to which the repeater is connected.
Pkts64Octets	Total number of packets (including bad packets) received that were 64 octets in length (excluding framing bits but including FCS octets).
Pkts65to127Octets	Total number of packets (including bad packets) received that were between 65 and 127 octets in length, inclusive (excluding framing bits but including FCS octets).
Pkts128to255Octets	Total number of packets (including bad packets) received that were between 65 and 127 octets in length, inclusive (excluding framing bits but including FCS octets).
Pkts128to255Octets	Total number of packets (including bad packets) received that were between 128 and 255 octets in length, inclusive (excluding framing bits but including FCS octets).
Pkts256to511Octets	Total number of packets (including bad packets) received that were between 256 and 511 octets in length, inclusive (excluding framing bits but including FCS octets).
Pkts512to1023Octets	Total number of packets (including bad packets) received that were between 512 and 1,023 octets in length, inclusive (excluding framing bits but including FCS octets).
Pkts1024to1518Octets	Total number of packets (including bad packets) received that were between 1,024

and 1,518 octets in length, inclusive (excluding framing bits but including FCS octets).

The first nine statistics are similar to the data gathered by MIB-II and its associated MIBs. However, the last seven are counters that track the number of individual frames of a particular size, and are not found in any other standard MIBs.

The collision statistic is an interesting value and one that bears some discussion. As mentioned in the preceding list, and in Chapter 3, a node on a Fast Ethernet network can detect a collision only when it is transmitting. Nodes that are not transmitting cannot detect collisions between two or more other nodes. This makes the RMON collision counters in a switch or stand-alone RMON probe less than useful, because they can never be really accurate, only close approximations. This isn't too bad, since an RMON probe isn't totally blind to collisions because it can count runt frames. A collision will usually result in runt frame unless it happens in the last eight octets of the frame (after the 480th bit).

On the other hand, a Class-I repeater is the perfect place for an RMON probe. A probe in a repeater can see all collisions and thus count them accurately. How this works is also discussed in Chapter 3. A repeater detects any collision for any node that is connected to it. This is another advantage of a Class-I repeater over a Class-II repeater, especially when Class-I stackables are used. The requirement that there be only one Class-I repeater in a Fast Ethernet collision domain means that an RMON probe in a Class-I repeater can *accurately* count collisions.

Groups 2 and 3: History Groups

Although Group 1 is useful, it isn't the purpose of the RMON MIB; data recording is. Groups 2 and 3 allow an RMON probe to record data over time, which can later be collected by an NMS. RMON can sample data at any interval from once a second to once an hour (sample times longer than one hour are not allowed). Each time an RMON probe samples data from an interface, it places that data into a bucket. When an RMON probe is configured, the NMS tells the probe how many buckets should be allocated and how often the data should be sampled and placed in a bucket. The number of allocated buckets and the sample time determine the span of time over which a probe gathers data.

Each time a sample is taken, the following data is read from an interface and is stored in a bucket. These counters are taken directly from the Ethernet Statistics group for an interface being monitored:

Octets
Pkts
BroadcastPkts
MulticastPkts
CRCAlignErrors
UndersizePkts
OversizePkts
Fragments
Jabbers
Collisions

In addition to the preceding counters, two other pieces of information are stored in each bucket. They are:

Object Name	Description
DropEvents	Total number of events in which packets were dropped by the probe due to lack of resources during this sampling interval. Note that this number is not necessarily the number of packets dropped; it is just the number of times this condition has been detected.
Utilization	Best estimate of the mean physical layer network utilization on this interface during this sampling interval, in hundredths of a percent.

The **DropEvents** is an interesting value and, for switches or repeaters with RMON probes, will usually be zero. This value is necessary because not all RMON probes can keep up with maximum network traffic levels. This was especially true for older probes that did not have statistics that were gathered in hardware. These early probes often could not keep up with high levels of network traffic for extended periods of time (exactly when the information from an RMON probe is most useful). This problem was a barrier to the earlier adoption of RMON probes. Modern-day probes that provide only the basic groups will never (or almost never) drop frames, as all their information is gathered by hardware, not by a CPU, which examines each frame.

The utilization value is even more interesting, especially given its extremely vague definition in the RMON specification. However, most RMON probes provide a quite accurate measure of network utilization, which is probably the major reason to use an RMON probe. Without it, a basic RMON is only marginally useful.

Graphing network utilization combined with the other historical statistics can provide a very clear picture of how a network is running. Most Network Management Console packages that know how to use an RMON probe can display RMON data in a very wide and useful array of formats, including graphs and reports. Often recent data can be compared to historical data on-screen in graphical format. This is really useful for baselining.

Groups 4 and 10: Alarm and Event Groups

The Alarm and Event groups are usually considered to be part of any basic RMON implementation, and provide a monitoring mechanism that can alert a network manager to specific conditions. For example, it might be useful to be alerted when the number of broadcasts per second or the number of network errors exceeds a threshold.

The alarm group provides a mechanism that allows any MIB variable supported in the device, even those in a MIB besides RMON, to be monitored. An alarm is programmed into an RMON probe by setting several values:

Object Name	*Description*
Interval	Interval in seconds over which the data is sampled and compared with the rising and falling thresholds. Note that the sampling time should be short enough that the RMON probe can detect a counter rollover.
Variable	The OID of the particular variable to be sampled. An OID is the unique name of a MIB data object.
SampleType	Method of sampling the selected variable and calculating the value to be compared against the thresholds. If the value of this object is **absoluteValue(1)**, the value of the selected variable will be compared directly with the thresholds at the end of the sampling interval. If the value of this object is **deltaValue(2)**, the value of the selected variable at the last sample will be subtracted from the current value, and the difference compared with the thresholds.
Value	Value of the statistic during the last sampling period. For example, if the sample type is **deltaValue**, this value will be the difference between the samples at the beginning and end of the period. If the sample type is **absoluteValue**,

Object Name	Description
	this value will be the sampled value at the end of the period. This is the value that is compared with the rising and falling thresholds. The value during the current sampling period is not made available until the period is completed, and will remain available until the next period completes.
StartupAlarm	Alarm that may be sent when this entry is first set to valid. If the first sample after this entry becomes valid is greater than or equal to the **risingThreshold**, and **alarmStartupAlarm** is equal to **risingAlarm(1)** or **risingOrFallingAlarm(3)**, then a single rising alarm will be generated. If the first sample after this entry becomes valid is less than or equal to the **fallingThreshold**, and **alarmStartupAlarm** is equal to **fallingAlarm(2)** or **risingOrFallingAlarm(3)**, then a single falling alarm will be generated.
RisingThreshold	Threshold for the sampled statistic. When the current sampled value is greater than or equal to this threshold, and the value at the last sampling interval was less than this threshold, a single event will be generated. A single event will also be generated if the first sample after this entry becomes valid is greater than or equal to this threshold, and the associated **alarmStartupAlarm** is equal to **risingAlarm(1)** or **risingOrFallingAlarm(3)**. After a rising event is generated, another such event will not be generated until the sampled value falls below this threshold and reaches the **alarmFallingThreshold**. This object may not be modified if the associated **alarmStatus** object is equal to **valid(1)**.
FallingThreshold	Threshold for the sampled statistic. When the current sampled value is less than or equal to this threshold, and the value at the last sampling interval was greater than this threshold, a single event will be generated. A single event will also be generated if the first sample after this entry becomes valid is less than or equal to this threshold, and the associated **alarmStartupAlarm** is equal to **fallingAlarm(2)** or **risingOrFallingAlarm(3)**. After a falling event is generated, another such event will not be generated until the sampled value rises above this threshold and reaches the **alarmRisingThreshold**.

RisingEventIndex Index of the **eventEntry** that is used when a rising threshold is crossed. The **eventEntry** identified by a particular value of this index is the same as identified by the same value of the **eventIndex object**. If there is no corresponding entry in the **eventTable**, then no association exists. In particular, if this value is zero, no associated event will be generated, as zero is not a valid event index.

As you can see, alarms are very flexible. You can program an alarm to occur on just about anything that can be counted or measured in a managed device. Most often, alarms are set up as rate of change, or delta, alarms that watch for the rates of specific counters to change; for example, broadcasts per second.

There is another important component to alarms, and that is events. When an alarm occurs, an event is **triggered**. When an event is triggered by an alarm, one of four things can happen:

- Nothing
- Send an SNMP trap message
- Record the event in a log
- Send a trap and record the event in a log

An SNMP trap is a message that is transmitted by an agent that is not specifically requested by an NMS, such as a normal SNMP GET, GET NEXT or SET command. In general, traps are messages to an NMS that indicate something has occurred in an agent. Many MIBs define traps that occur when certain events occur. RMON traps indicate that an alarm triggered an event, and tell which one occurred. Traps are always sent to a specific NMS, and are not broadcast. When the NMS receives a trap it can beep, display an error message, count the event, record it in a log, or even e-mail someone or call someone's pager. In fact, many modern NMSs can do most of these things. Usually traps are used to indicate errors or problems, but not always; sometimes traps are used just to inform a network manager that normal events have occurred.

Traps have one problem: They are sent only once by an agent. An NMS does not respond to a trap in any way. Often, especially on busy or large networks, traps can easily be lost. This can happen due to congestion, network errors, or merely the fact that the NMS for which the trap is destined is not running.

This problem is solved by the event logging mechanism. When an event is logged it is stored in a table in the probe, which can later be read by an NMS. RMON probes can usually store many log entries, up to several hundred for high-end RMON probes. Logs are very useful and allow an NMS to read traps that they may have missed.

Alarms and events can be really helpful, especially for large networks. However, it can be easy to set up alarms that happen too often. Fortunately, this is an easy problem to detect when it occurs. You'll know, because you'll get them frequently and will need to figure out why. A few days or a couple of weeks playing with alarms will quickly tell you which ones are useful and which are just noise.

Group 5: Host Group

The Host group is part of the advanced RMON groups, and is not implemented on most RMON probes in switches and repeaters. It is often implemented in dedicated probes and very high-end switches. The Host group is used for a process called **automatic node discovery** or sometimes just **autodiscovery**. The idea is to automatically discover every node connected to a network. The first question most people ask when they hear about this feature is, Why? I know what's connected to my network! Well, do you? Are you really sure?

In all but the smallest networks, it can be really hard to know what is really connected. Users can add computers, printers, and other equipment pretty easily. This is a frequent occurrence. Most of the time, a new computer can be added to a network with no involvement from a network manager. Users can simply plug in one and go. People usually do this for reasons that are quite legitimate, such as:

- Connecting their laptop computer to transfer files to and from their main machine
- Adding a local printer
- Giving a guest from another corporate office or division a temporary network connection while visiting
- Connecting a new computer alongside an old one; many people use their old computers for e-mail and simple tasks
- Requiring two, three, or more machines to work; this is true for engineers (especially programmers) and these requirements can frequently change

How the Host group does this is best described by the text from the RMON RFC itself: Bear in mind that the term *host* is the same as the term *node*. The RMON RFC also uses the word *packet* the way this book uses the term *frame:*

The Host group discovers new hosts on the network by keeping a list of source and destination MAC addresses seen in good packets. For each of these addresses, the Host group keeps a set of statistics. The **hostControlTable** controls on which interfaces this function is performed, and contains some information about the process. On behalf of each **hostControlEntry**, data is collected on an interface and placed in both the **hostTable** and the **hostTimeTable**.

If the monitoring device finds itself short of resources, it may delete entries as needed. It is suggested that the device delete the least recently used entries first. The **hostTable** contains entries for each address discovered on a particular interface.

Each entry contains statistical data about that host. This table is indexed by the MAC address of the host, through which a random access may be achieved. The **hostTimeTable** contains data in the same format as the **hostTable**, and must contain the same set of hosts but is indexed using **hostTimeCreationOrder** rather than **hostAddress**. The **hostTimeCreationOrder** is an integer that reflects the relative order in which a particular entry was discovered and thus inserted into the table. As this order, and thus the index, is among those entries currently in the table, the index for a particular entry may change if an (earlier) entry is deleted. Thus the association between **hostTimeCreationOrder** and **hostTimeEntry** may be broken at any time.

The **hostTimeTable** has two important uses. The first is the fast download of this potentially large table. Because the index of this table runs from 1 to the size of the table, inclusive, its values are predictable. This allows very efficient packing of variables into SNMP PDUs, and allows a table transfer to have multiple packets outstanding.

These benefits increase transfer rates tremendously. The second use of the **hostTimeTable** is the efficient discovery by the management station of new entries added to the table. After the management station has downloaded the entire table, it knows that new entries will be added immediately after the end of the current table. It can thus detect new entries there and retrieve them easily.

Because the association between **hostTimeCreationOrder** and **hostTimeEntry** may be broken at any time, the management station must monitor the related **hostControlLastDeleteTime** object. When the management station thus detects a deletion, it must assume that any such associations have been broken, and invalidate any it has stored locally. This includes restarting any download of the **hostTimeTable** that may have been in progress, as well as rediscovering the end of the **hostTimeTable** so that it may detect new entries. If the management station does not detect the broken association, it may continue to refer to a particular host by its **creationOrder** while unwittingly retrieving the data associated with another host entirely. If this happens while downloading the host table, the management station may fail to download all of the entries in the table.

In simpler terms, this means that an RMON probe runs in promiscuous mode, and keeps track of every MAC address that it sees. An NMS can then keep a list of which nodes are on which segments. The probe keeps some useful statistics for each MAC address it detects. They are:

Object Name	Description
InPkts	Number of good packets transmitted to this address since it was added to the **hostTable**
OutPkts	Number of packets, including bad packets, transmitted by this address since it was added to the **hostTable**
InOctets	Number of octets transmitted to this address since it was added to the **hostTable** (excluding framing bits but including FCS octets), except for those octets in bad packets
OutOctets	Number of octets transmitted by this address since it was added to the **hostTable** (excluding framing bits but including FCS octets), including those octets in bad packets
OutErrors	Number of bad packets transmitted by this address since this host was added to the **hostTable**
OutBroadcastPkts	Number of good packets transmitted by this address that were directed to the broadcast address since this host was added to the **hostTable**
OutMulticastPkts	Number of good packets transmitted by this address that were directed to a multicast address since this host was added to the **hostTable** (note that this number does not include packets directed to the broadcast address)

The preceding host statistics can be really useful when trying to find bandwidth problems. For example, a network may be running well until one afternoon when everyone starts to complain that it's slow and klunky. A quick scan through the hosts table might indicate a node that is transmitting a very large number of error or broadcast frames.

Data from the host statistics can also be used to detect changes in users' habits. For example, when migrating to a new client/server database, it could be very helpful to monitor a few of the early users to see how much more bandwidth they require than users who are not using the new tool. Data about these users' bandwidth usage could also be compared to data from before the client/server upgrade. This kind of technique can be very effective when trying to determine what kind of network resources a new tool or application may require.

Group 6: Host Top N Group

This group works with the Host group to generate information about hosts sorted by one of the host's statistics. For example, you could generate a report of which nodes generated the most broadcast traffic, or which nodes generate the most network traffic. The RFC describes this group as follows:

> The Host Top N group is used to prepare reports that describe the hosts that top a list ordered by one of their statistics. The available statistics are samples of one of their base statistics, over an interval specified by the management station. Thus, these statistics are rate based. The management station also selects how many such hosts are reported.
>
> The **hostTopNControlTable** is used to initiate the generation of such a report. The management station may select the parameters of such a report, such as which interface, which statistic, how many hosts, and the start and stop times of the sampling. When the report is prepared, entries are created in the **hostTopNTable** associated with the relevant **hostTopNControlEntry.** These entries are static for each report after it has been prepared.

For example, you could tell the probe: Generate a list of the top 25 nodes, sorted by **OutOctets,** over the next hour. At the end of the hour, you will have a list of the 25 nodes that generated the most network traffic, sorted by their amount transmitted data.

The Top N group works by monitoring the Host group for a specified duration of the report. At the end of the report duration, it sorts its information from highest to lowest, based on the required statistic. This group can sort nodes based on the following values:

- InPkts
- OutPkts
- InOctets
- OutOctets
- OutErrors
- OutBroadcastPkts
- OutMulticastPkts

The Top N group is not as useful as some of the other groups primarily because it is impractical to generate data for more than a handful of nodes. Usually, the big traffic generators for the packet and octet statistics will be such devices as servers and routers. Likewise, switches and bridges will be the biggest sources of broadcast and multicast frames.

Generating a report on **OutErrors** can be helpful in finding bad network cards, cables, and other components that may not be working well. For example, running a Top-10 **OutErrors** report once a week or so could help find some problems before users start to complain.

Group 7: Matrix Group

The Matrix group also collects data based on MAC addresses, but instead of data about a single node, the Matrix group collects data about the traffic that flows between any two network nodes, such as a server and a workstation. This group keeps a table indexed by both source and destination MAC addresses. For example, for a specific workstation (node **A**) and a server (node **B**), there will be two table entries. One table entry will contain statistics for frames transmitted by **A** with a destination of **B**, and the other table entry will be for frames going in the other direction. Each pair of table entries is sometimes called a **conversation**. The Matrix group also keeps single table entries for frames with broadcast and multicast addresses as their destination addresses.

The Matrix Group keeps only three statistics for each conversation:

Object Name	Description
Pkt	Number of packets transmitted from the source address to the destination address (this number includes bad packets)
Octets	Number of octets (excluding framing bits but including FCS octets) contained in all packets transmitted from the source address to the destination address
Errors	Number of bad packets transmitted from the source address to the destination address

Like the Top N group, the Matrix group has minimal value, and most network managers will not find it to be a primary network management tool, because the vast majority of the conversations in most networks will be between workstations and servers, or workstations and routers. Likewise, most of the statistics for conversations, including broadcast and multicast addresses, will involve bridges and switches.

The Matrix group really runs into problems when there is a lot of peer-to-peer traffic and switched systems of any size at all, because the amount of memory needed to keep track of a large combination of source and address pairs is simply too big. The Matrix group must share memory resources with the other RMON groups, which aren't exactly frugal. Most devices use memory for other items as well. This means that for many RMON probes, the amount of memory available to store matrix tables is limited. If memory fills up and new conversations are detected, the data about oldest conversations are deleted. There is also no way to control this. Unlike the Top N group, where the number of hosts can be specified, there is no way to tell the Matrix group which conversations to record data about. This means that the data about a conversation that is important could easily be deleted to make room for a conversation that is inconsequential.

Lots of broadcast traffic and peer-to-peer traffic just make this problem worse. Broadcast traffic is a sizable problem, but one that could possibly be managed even for a few hundred nodes. For this kind of traffic, the matrix table will keep one table entry for every source MAC address it sees in a broadcast frame. This means one entry for each node in the attached broadcast domain, not just the attached collision domain. For high-end RMON probes with lots of memory, this might work, but for large switched networks this is probably impractical.

For networks with any amount of peer-to-peer traffic the Matrix group can easily be overwhelmed. Even for small peer-to-peer networks, the total number of combinations can become quite large and easily require many megabytes of memory. For example, a matrix entry can take up about 28 bytes of memory. At this size, the conversation matrix statistics for 250 nodes takes up 1,743,000 bytes. For a workstation or server, this is nothing. However, for such devices as repeaters, switches, and RMON probes, 4 megabytes of memory is considered huge and only a fraction of this is available for such uses as matrix tables.

Groups 8 and 9: Filter and Packet Capture Groups

The Filter and Packet Capture groups are used to actually record packets from the network in the probe's memory for later analysis by an NMS. To do this, a probe sets aside some buffer memory for packet storage. As packets are received by the probe, it applies a filter to the frames. If a packet matches a filter pattern, it is then saved in a buffer. An NMS is used to configure a probe for packet capture, and then to read and analyze the captured packets.

The problem with the RMON packet capture group is that it takes huge amounts of memory to do anything useful, especially at Fast Ethernet frame rates. The maximum frame size for Fast Ethernet is 1,518 bytes. This means that each packet buffer must be 1,518 bytes in size, plus a little overhead.

Most protocols attempt to send large frames for data transfers, as this is most efficient. So, a large percentage of packets on a Fast Ethernet LAN is usually 1,518 bytes in size. For conversation's sake, let's say that the average frame size on a LAN is one-half the maximum; that is, 759 bytes in size. Just to save one second of data when network utilization is 10 percent would take about 2.4 megabytes of memory.

If a packet capture filter is set up correctly, only the frames that are interesting will be captured. If these frames don't happen too often, then this RMON feature can be useful. However, with today's Fast Ethernet LANs, the RMON packet capture feature isn't very useful, because the RMON probe can't contain enough memory.

This is especially true when compared to today's modern network analyzers. For example, Microsoft has a software package, called Network Monitor, that runs on Windows NT or 95, and can put any adapter in promiscuous mode and capture packets. Since it runs on a PC, it can easily use many, many megabytes of RAM for frame storage. Not only will Network Monitor capture frames, but it will analyze them too. Microsoft's Network Monitor can also be remotely controlled. For example, a network manager could control a PC with Network Monitor installed remotely, capturing frames on a remote segment and analyzing them on his PC, just like RMON is supposed to do.

There are other software-only packages available too, such as LANalyzer from Novell. This is an excellent program that works extremely well, especially when used in conjunction with Novell servers. The only problem with software-based analyzers is they can't keep up with wire-speed traffic; for example, the maximum frame rates of Fast Ethernet. On normally loaded networks, they do fine; but when things are really busy, they can drop frames.

Some companies, such as Shomiti, make hardware-assisted network analyzers that implement packet capture and filtering using hardware. These devices can capture huge amounts of Fast Ethernet traffic even at full wire speed without dropping a single frame.

In short, the RMON Packet Capture MIB was a good idea in 1991, when it was published. However, modern-day network analyzing tools perform much better and have many more capturing and analysis features than an RMON, often at a lower price.

RMON: The Reality

RMON is a great tool, especially the basic groups, 1, 2, 3, 4, and 10. Many managed Fast Ethernet repeaters and switches now come standard with these basic RMON groups. The data can be gathered for these groups by hardware, and are easy to implement even in low-cost devices.

However, the advanced groups, 5, 6, 7, 8, and 9, are much less useful and can take huge amounts of CPU horsepower and memory to implement in a fashion that is actually useful. This is especially true for Fast Ethernet, which can move data at better than 12 megabytes per second.

> Most of the literature you see will talk about 9 group RMON, not 10, because most devices still support the RMON specified by RFC1271, which was published in November 1991. This is in contrast to RMON described by RFC1757, which was published in February of 1995. The RFC1271 version has only 9 groups. In this version, the History Control and Ethernet History groups are one group, called simply the History group. The problem with this is that it made it hard to implement RMON on anything but Ethernet-like FDDI or Token Ring. So, RFC1757 split this into the History Control and Ethernet History groups. This allows an RMON implementation for another network technology like FDDI to have a history group.
>
> For RFC1271 RMON, the basic groups are 1 through 3, and 9, with the advanced groups being 4 through 8.

Many vendors claim that their devices support all the RMON groups. Be very wary of this claim. Most switches and repeaters just don't have the internal processing power to properly implement groups 5 through 9, because the cost of adding this CPU horsepower and RAM is simply too great. Even doing some RMON processing in an ASIC doesn't help the cost situation much because of the RAM required to do these groups correctly. Adding proper support for the advanced RMON groups to a switch or repeater could easily add at least $1,000 to its sales price.

On the other hand, the basic RMON groups can be implemented quite inexpensively, as many devices already have hardware that collects the necessary statistics. For example, most switches that support RMON support the basic groups on all their ports. This allows a switch to gather huge amounts of data about a network very easily.

Most switches that support the advanced groups do so for only a single port at a time. The port that is activated for the advanced RMON groups can be changed. This is called a **roving** RMON probe. If there are enough resources to support the advanced groups, this can be very effective.

Another problem with RMON is on the Network Management Station side. Most MIBs, such as MIB-II, are very simple and can be directly accessed by a human using software called a **MIB browser**, which is a software tool that lets a user directly examine or change MIB objects in a managed device. This simplicity also makes it relatively easy to write very nice and usable graphical windows-based software that gathers and displays data from these MIBs.

In contrast, the MIB objects in RMON are *not* designed to be manipulated by a human. The RMON RFC says:

> The objects defined in this document are intended as an interface between an RMON agent and an RMON management application, and are not intended for direct manipulation by humans. While some users may tolerate the direct display of some of these objects, few will tolerate the complexity of manually manipulating objects to accomplish row creation. These functions should be handled by the management application.

An RMON-aware NMS or RMON Management Application is a very complex thing to develop, and hard to do well. In fact, most RMON-aware NMSs do a poor job of both configuring an RMON probe and displaying the resultant data. The few that do it well are unfortunately very expensive, as much as $10,000 to $50,000 for a single user licensee. This is really the biggest problem with RMON. While RMON agents are available in many low-cost devices, most people who buy it can't use it because the inexpensive console software is so bad that they can't justify buying the better NMS software.

This problem is magnified by the fact that many repeater and switch vendors are now giving away Network Management Console software for free. Much of this software is quite good and provides users with relatively sophisticated network management. Many of these packages manage the products from only a single vendor, but they're *free*. Some of them have built-in MIB browsers that will allow you to poke around on any managed device. An excellent example of this is the Compaq Network Management Software (CNMS) that comes with all Compaq's Nettelligent devices. Unfortunately, most of these free NMS packages, while very useful, simply don't do RMON well or at all!

In summary, RMON is great if, and only if, you have NMS software that makes it usable. If you don't have this kind of software, or don't want to pay for it, then you shouldn't pay any more for a box that acts as an RMON agent. This isn't to say, Don't buy boxes with RMON agents; just that you shouldn't pay any more for them than for boxes that don't have it. This is especially true for agents that claim to support the advanced groups.

Baselining and Network Performance

We asked a network manager what was the best measure he had to indicate his Fast Ethernet and Ethernet systems were running well. He said, "When my voice-mail light is out, and my e-mail box is empty."

In truth, this is really the best measure of network health and performance. If users aren't complaining, then everything is probably okay. The real job for a network manager is to keep it that way. This is done by maintaining a network's performance level and robustness.

A network's robustness is pretty straightforward and is discussed early in Chapter 8. Its simple definition is when a network functions well in the face of unpredicted change. A network that never had to change would be easy to design and keep running, but that's not the situation for most networks.

Performance is a much more difficult topic to define. The reason for this is that *performance is relative.* There is no absolute measure for network performance. Yes, we know that Fast Ethernet can transfer a maximum of 12,191,157 bytes per second, and twice that for full-duplex links, but this really doesn't mean much because it can't do this all the time, only for very short periods. A network that has high performance is one that meets its users' needs, in contrast to one that is simply the fastest one that can be built.

Every network will reach full utilization and saturation at different offered loads. These points can even differ over time for the same network. There is no way to directly measure offered load, or to find a network's full utilization point or level at which it will saturate. It is possible, however, to watch your network, understand it, and monitor various metrics for change over time.

> The best way to measure and analyze network performance is by baselining—a process in which the performance characteristics of a network are measured, recorded, and subsequently compared to a known baseline. A **baseline** is a collection of certain performance metrics that are measured when a networked system is working properly under normal loads, preferably right at its full utilization point.

The best time to gather data for a baseline is when a network is running in its normal, busiest state. This is usually during the busiest part of a normal day, often between 9:30 and 11:45 in the morning, and 2:00 to 4:00 in the afternoon. Of course, these are only typical times for a 9-to-5 office environment. Many networks will be busiest at other times. For example, for a network that serves a manufacturing line the busiest time may start one hour into a shift and last for many hours, with shifts beginning at 7:00 A.M., 3:00 P.M., and 11:00 P.M.

Any metric, or measure, can be used to create a baseline. Some are more useful than others. Many provide little value unless used with other metrics. However, probably the most common and useful ones are:

- Network utilization
- Broadcasts per second
- Frames per second
- Gross throughput (bytes per second)

These are not the only metrics to use, only what we feel are the most useful ones. Like optimizing any kind of process, it is wise to work with the items that affect 80 percent of a process before working on the other 20 percent. For example, the number of collisions a node has, on a per-second basis or as a percentage of frames transmitted, is really of little value. As a mater of fact, this is probably the single, worst statistic to use. We advise against using a collision statistic as a baseline metric. These kinds of statistics simply do not mean much.

Network utilization, on the other hand, is a very good statistic, as it is a measure of how much bandwidth is being used on a LAN. Most of the other metrics should be baselined in combination with network utilization.

The first thing to do in order to baseline your network is to find its busy times. This is easily done by tracking network utilization for 15-minute periods during normal, everyday operation when the network configuration is stable. Recording utilizations for a week or two should give you a good idea when the busiest times are. After that, baselining is easy. Just measure the statistics in which you are interested during three or four consecutive busy times, and take an average. You then have a baseline.

Once you have a baseline, you can track it and judge other metrics in its context. You can also modify your baseline as network configurations, user habits, and applications change. Many statistics can then be measured and analyzed in the context of the baseline information.

Collision counters are excellent examples of this. While almost useless by themselves and poor baseline metrics, the number of collisions a station has over a period of time can be quite telling when judged in the context of a network utilization baseline. This technique can be used to detect if your network is overloaded.

This is often accomplished by graphing collision counts on key network nodes against utilization. Good nodes for which to measure collisions are servers and routers, as most or all of the nodes on a LAN will communicate with them. RMON probes in Class-I repeaters are also good sources for collision statistics.

Collision counters can be graphed with utilization to look for overloading and saturation. For example, a network that is overloaded will often see curves like those shown in Figure 14.1, which shows the busy period of a LAN. Network utilization rises to a normal level, then suddenly drops off for a short time. The problem is indicated because collisions went way up during that interval. In other words, lots of nodes were contending for access to the network at the *same time*. We know that nodes were contending at the same time because collisions went up. In this case, the LAN was probably operating at close to its saturation point. If it had saturated, collisions would have shot up very high, and utilization would have dropped off to almost nothing.

If this scenario happens just every now and then, or even more frequently, but for merely short periods, there is generally not a problem. However, if you start to see trends like this occurring more frequently or lasting for longer periods of time, you may want to ask users if they are experiencing any slowdowns or other network problems, such as lost connections. Asking them before they think there is a problem might pleasantly surprise them and your boss, especially if you then act to avoid any problems.

Baselining also has another advantage, for it allows you to justify requests to purchase equipment with hard data. Convincing upper management that you need a new, expensive Fast Ethernet backbone switch can be made much easier when you can prove it's needed.

Baselining is a technique that can be used to monitor and compare many different statistics. It is a powerful tool that is easy to use, and is generally very effective even if only using MIB-II data. When combined with information from RMON probes, and advanced data from proprietary MIBs, baselining is often the best tool to help you keep your Fast Ethernet LAN robust and running at peak performance.

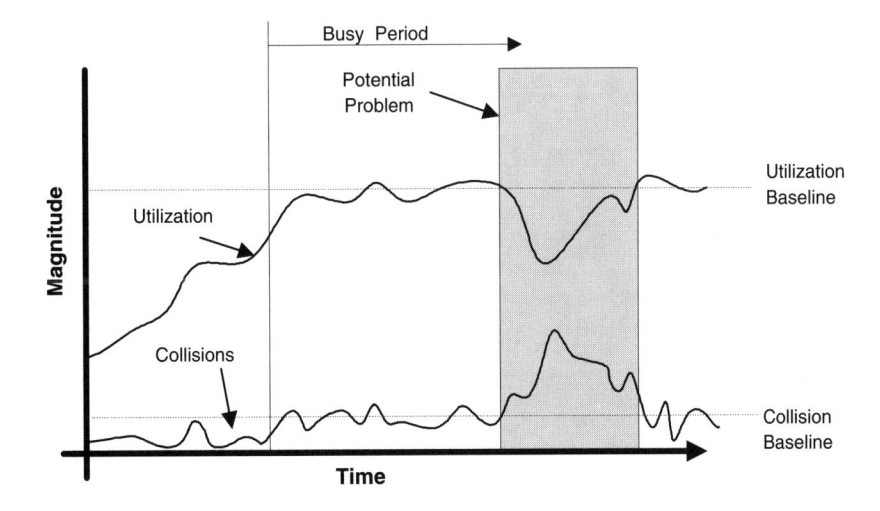

Figure 14.1
Potential network overload.

MIB Browsers

Accessing MIB data is usually done with a Network Management Station. An NMS usually provides a graphical view of a device, hiding the nature of the MIB from the user. Often users are presented with a picture of a device on the screen, with LEDs that blink, displays that mirror those on the actual device, and clickable hot spots. For example, to control a repeater port, the user can just double-click on the port to bring up a window displaying statistics and other information about that port (see Figure 14.2).

This kind of interface is sometimes called a **product specific interface** or a **management interface module.** These kinds of interfaces are extremely useful and easy for a user to understand and manipulate. A good device GUI can display information in different formats, such as tables, graphs, and pie charts. They can often be configured to generate automatic reports.

However, not all devices come with a graphical interface. Often these must be purchased separately and function only with a large, expensive NMS system, such as Hewlett Packard's OpenView. In these cases, a MIB browser can be used to access the data in the device.

MIB browsers work by reading a MIB file and communicating directly with a device, using SNMP to read the data objects described by the MIB. While not as pretty or easy to use as a graphical device interface, a MIB browser does allow a user to access all the MIB elements in a device. This can be useful for looking at simple MIBs, such as MIB-II or basic device MIBs provided by an equipment manufacturer. Figure 14.3 shows a MIB browser looking at the MIB-II data for a Fast Ethernet switch port.

As you can see, the MIB and its data are fully exposed. The MIB browser shows the Object IDs, object names, values, and descriptions for each object in the MIB.

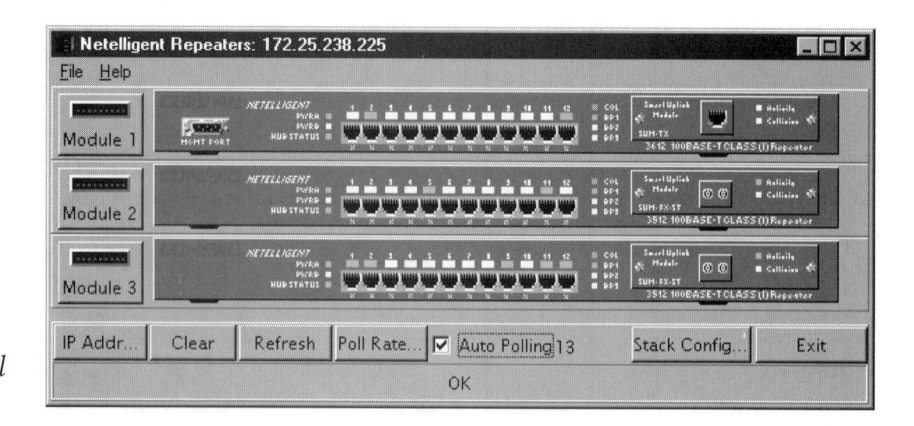

Figure 14.2
An NMS graphical interface.

Figure 14.3
A MIB browser.

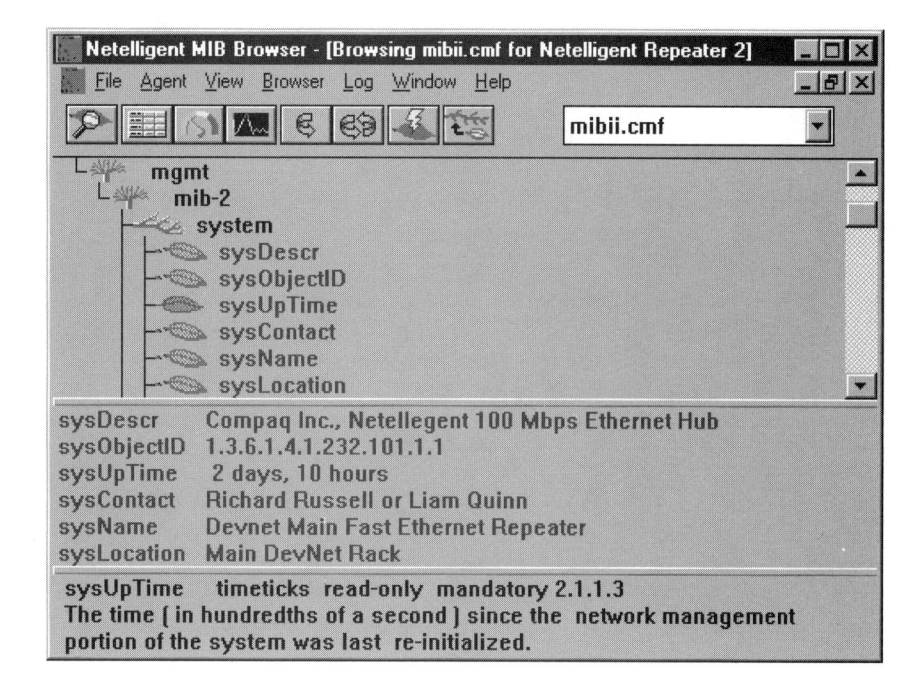

```
Netelligent MIB Browser - [Browsing mibii.cmf for Netelligent Repeater 2]
File  Agent  View  Browser  Log  Window  Help

                                                          mibii.cmf

    mgmt
      mib-2
        system
          sysDescr
          sysObjectID
          sysUpTime
          sysContact
          sysName
          sysLocation

sysDescr       Compaq Inc., Netellegent 100 Mbps Ethernet Hub
sysObjectID    1.3.6.1.4.1.232.101.1.1
sysUpTime      2 days, 10 hours
sysContact     Richard Russell or Liam Quinn
sysName        Devnet Main Fast Ethernet Repeater
sysLocation    Main DevNet Rack

sysUpTime    timeticks  read-only  mandatory 2.1.1.3
The time ( in hundredths of a second ) since the network management
portion of the system was last re-initialized.
```

A MIB browser is a great tool to have in your network management tool box. They often come bundled with many of the free product-specific interfaces that come with repeaters and switches. All network management systems also have built-in MIB browsers. Unfortunately, there is no shareware MIB browser of which we are aware. If one becomes available, you'll be able to find it on our Web site.

APPENDIX A

Ethernet and Fast Ethernet Compared

One major reason for the widespread acceptance of Fast Ethernet in the marketplace is its strong similarity to Ethernet. Lots of people say that Fast Ethernet is just like Ethernet, just 10 times faster. This is only partly true. While Fast Ethernet is very similar to Ethernet, there are some very big differences.

Fast Ethernet is almost always compared to 10Base-T Ethernet because they both can use the same kinds of cable and require the use of repeaters. In this regard, Fast Ethernet looks a lot like 10Base-T Ethernet. The biggest difference between Ethernet and Fast Ethernet is speed. Ethernet runs at 10Mbps, and Fast Ethernet runs at 100Mbps—10 times faster. All of the differences between the two systems result from their magnitude difference in speed. However, that is where the similarity stops.

Fast Ethernet has a much smaller maximum network diameter. When only copper cable (100Base-TX) is used, the longest cable distance between any two nodes on a Fast Ethernet segment is 205 meters, in contrast to a 10Base-T network, which can span up to 500 meters. Using coaxial cable to link 10Base-T repeaters allows a 10Mbps Ethernet segment to span even larger distances. When *only* fiberoptic cable is used, a Fast Ethernet segment can span up to 320 meters, still less than the 500 meters of a copper-only Ethernet segment. Overcoming these topology limits is generally accomplished most with switches or routers.

Fast Ethernet cannot run over coaxial cable. Unlike Ethernet, which can run over several types of coaxial cable, Fast Ethernet can run only over UTP or STP copper cable and fiberoptic cable. There are no standards for operating Fast Ethernet over coaxial cable.

The topology rules for Fast Ethernet are very different from 10Base-T. A Fast Ethernet segment can have only one or two repeaters (see Chapter 3), while a 10Base-T Ethernet segment can have many repeaters as long as there are no more than four repeaters between any two nodes on the segment.

Fast Ethernet uses completely different signaling methods than 10Base-T. Both 10Base-T and Fast Ethernet can run over Cat-3, -4, and -5 cable. However, Fast Ethernet uses very different PHYs than 10Base-T does. For all three cable types, 10Mbps Ethernet uses the same 10Base-T PHY. However, Fast Ethernet uses the 100Base-T4 PHY for Cat-3, -4, and -5 cable, and the 100Base-TX PHY for Cat-5 cable. Both 100Mbps PHYs use completely different signaling techniques than the 10Base-T PHY and are incompatible with one another. Note that some dual-speed 100Base-TX PHYs, which can operate in two completely different manners, can detect when they are connected to a 10Base-T PHY, and will operate in that mode; but these do not provide compatibility between 100Base-TX and 10Base-T. The 10Mbps fiber PHYs (10Base-FP) and the 100Base-FX PHYs also use different signaling methods.

Fast Ethernet costs more than Ethernet. Ethernet technology has been around a long time and has been optimized and cost reduced by engineers and manufacturers over a period of many years. This is especially true for 10Base-T Ethernet, which has extremely wide market acceptance and is installed in tens of millions of computers. This has made 10Base-T an extremely low-cost commodity item. In late 1996 it was possible to purchase a 10Base-T ISA bus card for as little as $20; 10Base-T repeaters are available for as little as $30 a port. As of late 1996, Fast Ethernet NICs and repeaters were still significantly more expensive than 10Base-T components, but only by a factor of 3 or so. For example, low-cost PCI Fast Ethernet NICs were available for about $95, and repeater ports were going for about $80 dollars a port. As shipments of Fast Ethernet increase in volume, the cost of this equipment will come down radically. This actually happened in early 1997, when NIC prices dropped from $225 to the $100 range. Repeaters also had a similar price drop during this time.

While 10Mbps Ethernet and 100Mbps Fast Ethernet are quite different, in two key areas they are the same:

- **Both use exactly the same frame format.** All frames can be between 64 bytes and 1,518 bytes in size, and have destination and source address fields, a length/type field, a variable length data field, and a frame check sequence field. This allows software, such as protocols, to operate over Ethernet and Fast Ethernet in exactly the same way.

Because they use exactly the same frame format, any protocol or other software that will run over Ethernet will also run over Fast Ethernet.

- **Both use the same CSMA/CD access method.** While some of the timings are not exactly identical, the algorithm is *exactly* the same for both. This allows the MII interface between the PHY and the MAC to be simply *scaled up* from 10 to 100Mbps. The following illustrates the characteristics that are the same or different:

Value	*Ethernet*	*Fast Ethernet*
Baud Rate	10Mbps	100Mbps
Interframe Gap	9.60μs	0.960μs
Bit Time	100μs	10μs
Slot Time	512 bits	512 bits
TransmitAttemptLimit	16	16
Back-Off Limit	10	10
Jam Size	32 bits	32 bits
Maximum Frame Size	1,518 bytes	1,518 bytes
Minimum Frame Size	64 bytes	64 bytes
Address Size	48 bits	48 bits

10Base-T, 100Base-TX, and 100Base-FX can operate in full-duplex mode. All three of these low-level datalinks are inherently full duplex and support the full-duplex media access rules. Note that full-duplex operation is *not* part of the 802.3 standard and not supported by all devices. However, implementing it is very easy, as the collision detection mechanism is simply disabled, allowing both nodes to transmit simultaneously. This makes it easy for full-duplex-capable devices from different manufacturers to interoperate well without the force of a standard to ensure compliance. Note that 100Base-T4 and other forms of Ethernet cannot operate in full-duplex mode. Also note that only node-to-node (also called point-to-point) links can operate in full-duplex mode. A node-to-repeater connection always operates in CSMA/CD mode.

APPENDIX B

Fast Ethernet Topology Rules

There are two sets of rules, called transmission models, which specify how the components of a single Fast Ethernet collision domain may be connected together. The Model-1 rules are the simpler rules and can be used for most LANs. The Model-2 rules are more complex and are to be used only when a Fast Ethernet LAN needs to be built at the limit of the maximum network diameter.

The Model-1 rules assume that all components have worst-case but reasonable propagation delays. For example, they assume that the Nominal Value of Propagation for Category-5 cable is 0.6, 5.7ns/m (nanoseconds per meter), or 0.570 BT/m (bit times per meter). Almost all Cat-5 cable you can buy today has a much better NVP. If you build a Fast Ethernet segment using the Model-1 rules, you will be guaranteed that its collision window is no greater than the slot time, which is the maximum allowed value. The Model-2 rules are much more flexible but also significantly more complex to use. They require that the actual propagation delays for all components on the segment be measured or known. These values are used to determine the worst-case path delay value on the segment. If this is less than or equal to the slot time, then the configuration is a legal Fast Ethernet LAN and will function properly.

Model-1 Rules

The Model-1 rules define a set of three configurations that can be used for a Fast Ethernet collision domain. For all three configurations, some absolute maximums must be met.

- Length of all copper cable runs, Cat-5, Cat-4, or Cat-3, must not exceed 100 meters.
- Length of all fiber multimode or single-mode fiber segments must not exceed 412 meters.
- For devices with modular PHYs, the connection between the MAC and the PHY (the MII cable, or connection) must not exceed 0.5 meters.

The first configuration is when two nodes are connected directly together without a repeater, as shown in Figure B.1. This is usually called a **DTE-to-DTE connection**. A node is anything except a repeater, such as a workstation, printer, switch port, or router port.

The maximum lengths for the media link **A** are shown in the following:

Media	Max Length for Link A
Any copper media	100 Meters
Fiber half duplex	412 meters
Fiber full duplex	2,000 meters

The second configuration is when a Fast Ethernet segment has only one Class-II or Class-I repeater, as shown in Figure B.2.

Figure B.1
Node-to-node.

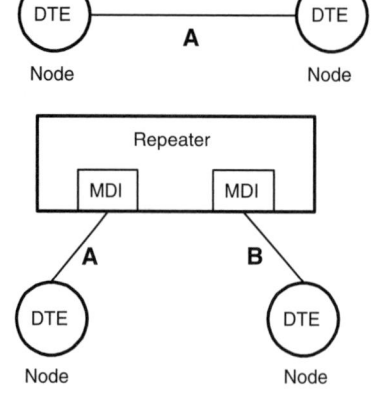

Figure B.2
Nodes and one repeater.

The following list shows the maximum lengths for the possible combinations of media for links **A** and **B**:

Link A Media	Link B Media	Repeaters	Max A	Max B	MaxDiameter
Cat-5, -4, -3 (TX, FX)	Cat-5, -4, -3 (TX, FX)	Class I or II	100	100	200
Cat-5 (TX)	Fiber (FX)	Class I	100	160.8	260.8
Cat-3 or -4 (T4)	Fiber (FX)	Class I	100	131	231
Fiber (FX)	Fiber (FX)	Class I	136	136	272
Cat-5 (TX)	Fiber (FX)	Class II	100	208.8	308.8
Cat-3 or -4 (T4)	Fiber (FX)	Class II	100	204	304
Fiber (FX)	Fiber (FX)	Class II	160	160	320

The third configuration is when a segment is built using two Class-II repeaters, as shown in Figure B.3, which shows two Class-II repeaters, the uplink that connects them, and two nodes. It's important to note that the transmission Model-1 rules assume that the uplink (link **C**) will always be copper and will never exceed five meters in length. This is assumed in the following:

Link A Media	Link B Media	Max A	Max B	Max Diameter
Cat-5, -4, -3 (TX, FX)	Cat-5, -4, -3 (TX, FX)	100	100	200
Cat-5 (TX)	Fiber (FX)	100	116.2	216.2
Cat-3 or -4 (T4)	Fiber (FX)	100	136.3	236.3
Fiber (FX)	Fiber (FX)	114	114	272

Note that the maximum lengths for all the copper links in both preceding lists are 100 meters, but the lengths of the fiber segments vary with the type of PHY used to drive the copper (TX or T4) and the type of

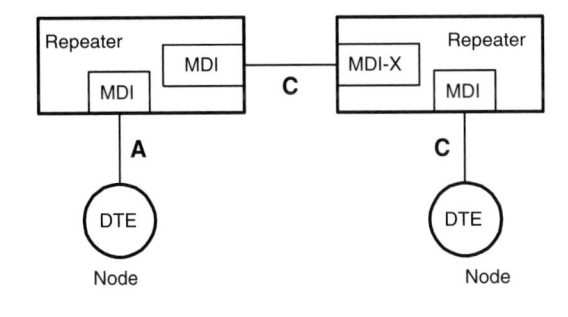

Figure B.3
Two Class-II repeaters.

repeater. Copper links are limited to 100 meters in length, not due to propagation delay but by the characteristics of the TX and T4 PHYs, which are guaranteed to drive up to only 100 meters of copper cable. The 100Base-FX PHY for fiberoptic cable can drive up to 2,000 meters of cable. This means that the upper limit on fiber cable for configuration 2 is limited by the path delay values of the other components. An interesting side effect of this is that fiber runs can be longer than those shown in the second list if the longest copper cable run is less than 100 meters in length. For every meter that the maximum copper run is less than 100 meters, the maximum fiberoptic run can be increased by 1.19 meters. For example, if all the copper runs in a TX/FX network using a Class-I repeater (row 2) were 75 meters or less, then there could be one fiber link that was 160.75 meters in length.

The same thing applies for any segment that is made up of only fiberoptic cable runs. Rows 5 and 8 in the first list, and row 4 in the second list, assume that both fiber runs are the same length. However, for every meter that link A is shortened, length B can be lengthened by one meter. For example, if there were a segment using a Class-I repeater (row 4) where all the links were fiber, and all but one were 50 meters, then one (and only one) link could be 222 meters. Note that this still keeps maximum network diameter under 272 meters.

Another interesting note about the two configurations with repeaters is that row 6 in the first list, and row 3 in the second list will probably never occur. In other words, a Class-II repeater that supports both T4 and FX/TX connections is practically impossible to build due to timing constraints. However, this is included in the list for completeness, as the 802.3u spec does cover it.

Model-2 Rules

The physical size and the number of repeaters in a Fast Ethernet collision domain are limited by the maximum length of copper links (100 meters) and the worst-case round-trip collision delay, also called the **collision window**. The maximum-size collision window, called the **slot time**, is 512 bit times. The Model-2 rules are a method by which the collision window for a segment is calculated. If it does not exceed 512 bit times, then the segment has a legal collision window size. In other words, its network diameter is not too big.

Like the Model-1 rules, the Model-2 rules can be applied to the three possible Fast Ethernet segment configurations. However, instead of just knowing the cable lengths, we must know the propagation delays in bit times (1 bit time is equal to 10 nanoseconds [$1E10^{-8}$ seconds]) for the *cable links*, the *network interfaces*, and the *repeater or repeaters* that make up the segment. If you can find the delay values of the network components on a segment, then the Model-2 rules are fairly easy to use. Figure B.4 shows the same configurations shown in the previous section but with more detail.

For the NICs and the repeaters, the propagation delays are usually provided by the manufacturer of the device. Unfortunately only a few vendors provide these numbers in the product literature. This is especially true for NICs. If this information is not available in the documentation you receive with the product, then the manufacturer must be contacted to obtain them. If the propagation delay values for a particular component are not available, then you can assume the following worst-case delay values, which are specified in bit times:

Device	Delay in BT
Class-I repeater	70
Class-II repeater (all T4)	33.5
Class-II repeater (T4 TX/FX combo)	46
TX or FX NIC	25
T4 NIC	34.5

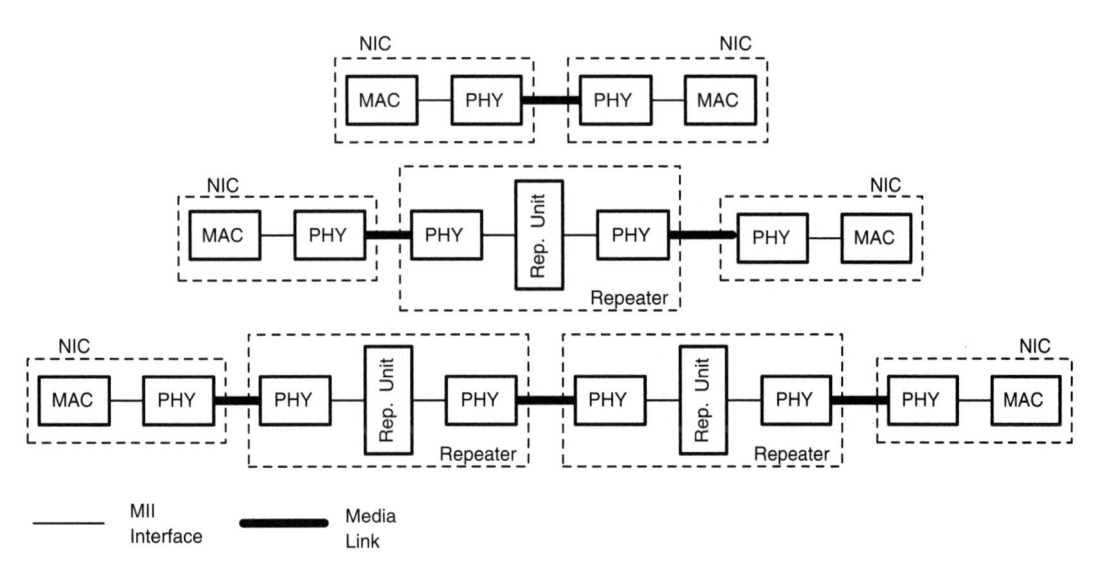

Figure B.4
Component detail.

For cables, the propagation delays in BT and the cables lengths can be measured directly using a cable tester. Usually a cable installer will make these measurements when the newly installed cable plant is tested, and will provide a report listing both the length and propagation delay of each run. If you do not have a cable tester but know the length of each cable run, you can calculate the propagation delay of the run using the Nominal Value of Propagation (NVP) for the cable. This value can be obtained from the manufacturer of the cable, and is a percentage of the speed of light in a vacuum. The length of the cable is usually measured when the cable is installed, and is easy to do by hand without a cable tester. However, measurements by hand must be done accurately. If a cable's length and or propagation delay value is unknown, then the transmission Model-2 rules cannot be used. To calculate a cable's bit time delay using its NPV value and length, use the following formula:

$$Delay_{BT} = 0.355/NPV \times Length_{meters}$$

Like repeaters and network interfaces, if the delay values for cable cannot be measured or calculated, but if the length is known, then worst-case values can be assumed. The following lists the worst-case values for cable:

Cable Type	Delay in BT per Meter
Category-3 and -4 cable	0.57
Category-5 and shielded twisted-pair cable	0.556
Fiberoptic cable	0.5

Note that it is important to include the patch cables at each end of the cable drop. Most cable plants are installed using patch panels and wall jacks. Repeaters are usually connected to the patch panel using a patch cable. Workstations or other nodes are usually connected to the wall jack using another patch cable. It is essential to include the lengths of these patch cables in your calculations. Figure B.5 illustrates typical connections.

The most difficult part of using the Model-2 rules is finding the worst-case delay values for your cable plant. These will be the values for the longest two cable runs in use. However, using patch cables can make these two runs a little difficult to find. It is sometimes necessary to measure several cable runs to find the longest two.

Once the delay values for the components and the longest two cable drops are found, they are plugged into the following formula to compute the worst-case, round-trip propagation delay of the segment:

Figure B.5
Typical connections.

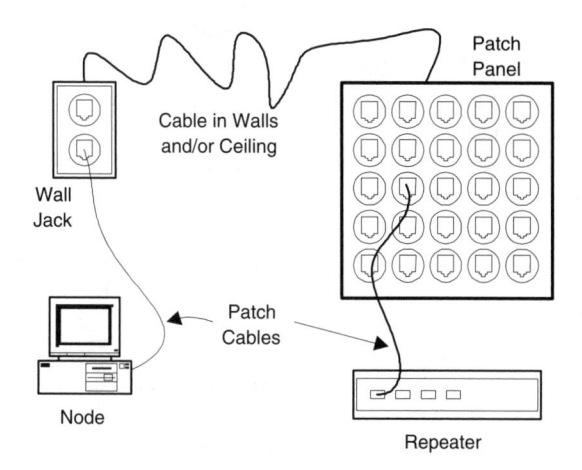

$$PDV = 2\,(\Sigma\,LDV + \Sigma\,RDV + DTED_1 + DTED_2) + Margin$$

The values in the equation are as follows:

Value	Description
LDV	**Link Delay Value.** The total of all the cable delays between the nodes on the longest two cable runs, including patch cables, cable in the walls and ceiling, and any uplink cables between Class-II repeaters.
RDV	**Repeater Delay Value.** The delays of all the repeaters on the segment.
DTED-1	**DTE Delay for Node 1.** The delay value for the NIC on one of the longest two cable runs.
DTED-2	**DTE Delay for Node 2.** The delay value for the NIC on the other of the longest two cable runs.
Margin	**Safety Margin.** A value between 0 and 4 bit times is recommended by the 802.3u specification. A value of 4 is considered the best value to use, and accounts for long patch cables in the wiring closet and office, and other miscellaneous delays and measurement errors.
PDV	**Calculated Path Delay Value.** This is synonymous with the segment's collision window size.

If the value of the PDV calculated does not exceed 512, then everything is okay and the Fast Ethernet segment will operate properly. If not, then the segment must be reconfigured.

Two interesting facts are not readily apparent from the preceding list and equation: Using the Model-2 rules, more than two Class-II repeaters can be used; and there can be more than five meters of cable between two Class-II repeaters.

The Model-1 rules specify that only two Class-II repeaters can be used and only five meters of cable can be between them in order to make things simple. This may sound great, but using more than two Class-II repeaters has a big drawback: It radically limits the physical network diameter of a segment. For example, if the NPV of the cable you are using is 0.72, for a delay of 0.465 bt/m, then adding a second Class-II repeater with a delay of 38 (slightly better than the assumed worst case) on a 1-meter uplink cable will mean that the maximum copper cable distance will drop by 81.7 meters to 18.3 meters. This is tiny and illustrates why using more than two Class-II repeaters, while possible, is just not practical.

The transmission Model-2 rules are not very useful when using copper cable; they really come into play in designing segments using fiberoptic cable, as fiber does not have the 100-meter limit. Using these rules, it is possible to safely create large fiberoptic segments that are at the limits of the maximum network diameter.

APPENDIX C

Online Resources

In the past two years, the use of the Internet, and the World Wide Web in particular, has radically changed the distribution of technical information, making it easier to access, easier to update, and most of all easier to find. There is a huge amount of information online about Fast Ethernet and networking in general. This online information is changed and added to on almost a daily basis. Instead of listing a large number of related sites in this appendix, John Wiley & Sons and the authors maintain a Fast Ethernet Web site at:

http:\\www.wiley.com\compbooks\fastethernet

Here, we keep updated links to online information regarding Fast Ethernet, updates to the contents of this book, contact information for the authors, and other interesting information about Fast Ethernet and related networking topics.

APPENDIX D

Performance RFCs

RFCs 1242 and 1944 are very important in understanding switch performance and how it is measured. While relatively easy to find on the Web, and directly accessible from our Web site, they are included on the following pages for those people who do not have easy access to the Web.

```
Network Working Group                                   S. Bradner, Editor
Request for Comments: 1242                              Harvard University
                                                                July 1991


               Benchmarking Terminology for Network Interconnection Devices

Status of this Memo

   This memo provides information for the Internet community. It does
   not specify an Internet standard. Distribution of this memo is
   unlimited.

Abstract

   This memo discusses and defines a number of terms that are used in
   describing performance benchmarking tests and the results of such
   tests. The terms defined in this memo will be used in additional
   memos to define specific benchmarking tests and the suggested format
   to be used in reporting the results of each of the tests. This memo
   is a product of the Benchmarking Methodology Working Group (BMWG) of
   the Internet Engineering Task Force (IETF).

1. Introduction

   Vendors often engage in "specsmanship" in an attempt to give their
   products a better position in the marketplace. This usually involves
   much "smoke & mirrors" used to confuse the user. This memo and
   follow-up memos attempt to define a specific set of terminology and
   tests that vendors can use to measure and report the performance
   characteristics of network devices. This will provide the user
   comparable data from different vendors with which to evaluate these
   devices.

2. Definition format

        Term to be defined. (e.g., Latency)

        Definition:
             The specific definition for the term.

        Discussion:
             A brief discussion about the term, it's application
             and any restrictions on measurement procedures.

        Measurement units:
             The units used to report measurements of this
             term, if applicable.

        Issues:
             List of issues or conditions that effect this term.

        See Also:
             List of other terms that are relevant to the discussion
             of this term.
```

3. Term definitions

3.1 Back-to-back

    Definition:
        Fixed length frames presented at a rate such that there is the minimum legal separation for a given medium between frames over a short to medium period of time, starting from an idle state.

    Discussion:
        A growing number of devices on a network can produce bursts of back-to-back frames. Remote disk servers using protocols like NFS, remote disk backup systems like rdump, and remote tape access systems can be configured such that a single request can result in a block of data being returned of as much as 64K octets. Over networks like ethernet with a relatively small MTU this results in many fragments to be transmitted. Since fragment reassembly will only be attempted if all fragments have been received, the loss of even one fragment because of the failure of some intermediate network device to process enough continuous frames can cause an endless loop as the sender repetitively attempts to send its large data block.

        With the increasing size of the Internet, routing updates can span many frames, with modern routers able to transmit very quickly. Missing frames of routing information can produce false indications of unreachability. Tests of this parameter are intended to determine the extent of data buffering in the device.

    Measurement units:
        Number of N-octet frames in burst.

    Issues:

    See Also:

3.2 Bridge

    Definition:
        A system which forwards data frames based on information in the data link layer.

    Discussion:

    Measurement units:
        n/a

    Issues:

    See Also:
        bridge/router (3.3)
        router (3.15)

3.3 bridge/router

    Definition:
        A bridge/router is a network device that can selectively function as a router and/or a bridge based on the protocol of a specific frame.

    Discussion:

```
            Measurement units:
                    n/a

            Issues:

            See Also:
                    bridge (3.2)
                    router (3.15)

3.4  Constant Load

            Definition:
                    Fixed length frames at a fixed interval time.

            Discussion:
                    Although it is rare, to say the least, to encounter
                    a steady state load on a network device in the real
                    world, measurement of steady state performance may
                    be useful in evaluating competing devices. The
                    frame size is specified and constant. All device
                    parameters are constant. When there is a checksum
                    in the frame, it must be verified.

            Measurement units:
                    n/a

            Issues:
                    unidirectional vs. bidirectional

            See Also:

3.5  Data link frame size

            Definition:
                    The number of octets in the frame from the first octet
                    following the preamble to the end of the FCS, if
                    present, or to the last octet of the data if there
                    is no FCS.

            Discussion:
                    There is much confusion in reporting the frame
                    sizes used in testing network devices or network
                    measurement. Some authors include the checksum,
                    some do not. This is a specific definition for use
                    in this and subsequent memos.

            Measurement units:
                    octets

            Issues:

            See Also:

3.6  Frame Loss Rate

            Definition:
                    Percentage of frames that should have been forwarded
                    by a network device under steady state (constant)
                    load that were not forwarded due to lack of
                    resources.

            Discussion:
                    This measurement can be used in reporting the
                    performance of a network device in an overloaded
                    state. This can be a useful indication of how a
                    device would perform under pathological network
```

```
                       conditions such as broadcast storms.

           Measurement units:
                   Percentage of N-octet offered frames that are dropped.
                   To be reported as a graph of offered load vs frame loss.

           Issues:

           See Also:
                   overhead behavior (3.11)
                   policy based filtering (3.13)
                   MTU mismatch behavior (3.10)

    3.7   Inter Frame Gap

           Definition:
                   The delay from the end of a data link frame as defined
                   in section 3.5, to the start of the preamble of the
                   next data link frame.

           Discussion:
                   There is much confusion in reporting the between
                   frame time used in testing network devices. This
                   is a specific definition for use in this and subsequent
                   memos.

           Measurement units:
                   Time with fine enough units to distinguish between
                   2 events.

           Issues:
                   Link data rate.

           See Also:

    3.8   Latency

           Definition:
                   For store and forward devices:
                   The time interval starting when the last bit of the
                   input frame reaches the input port and ending when
                   the first bit of the output frame is seen on the
                   output port.

                   For bit forwarding devices:
                   The time interval starting when the end of the first
                   bit of the input frame reaches the input port and
                   ending when the start of the first bit of the output
                   frame is seen on the output port.

           Discussion:
                   Variability of latency can be a problem.
                   Some protocols are timing dependent (e.g., LAT and IPX).
                   Future applications are likely to be sensitive to
                   network latency. Increased device delay can reduce
                   the useful diameter of net. It is desired to
                   eliminate the effect of the data rate on the latency
                   measurement. This measurement should only reflect the
                   actual within device latency. Measurements should be
                   taken for a spectrum of frame sizes without changing
                   the device setup.

                   Ideally, the measurements for all devices would be from
                   the first actual bit of the frame after the preamble.
                   Theoretically a vendor could design a device that
                   normally would be considered a store and forward
                   device, a bridge for example, that begins transmitting
```

a frame before it is fully received. This type of
device is known as a "cut through" device. The
assumption is that the device would somehow invalidate
the partially transmitted frame if in receiving the
remainder of the input frame, something came up that
the frame or this specific forwarding of it was in
error. For example, a bad checksum. In this case,
the device would still be considered a store and
forward device and the latency would still be
from last bit in to first bit out, even though the
value would be negative. The intent is to treat
the device as a unit without regard to the internal
structure.

Measurement units:
Time with fine enough units to distinguish between
2 events.

Issues:

See Also:
link speed mismatch (3.9)
constant load (3.4)
back-to-back (3.1)
policy based filtering (3.13)
single frame behavior (3.16)

3.9 Link Speed Mismatch

Definition:
Speed mismatch between input and output data rates.

Discussion:
This does not refer to frame rate per se, it refers to
the actual data rate of the data path. For example,
an Ethernet on one side and a 56KB serial link on the
other. This is has also been referred to as the "fire
hose effect". Networks that make use of serial links
between local high speed networks will usually have
link speed mismatch at each end of the serial links.

Measurement units:
Ratio of input and output data rates.

Issues:

See Also:
constant load (3.4)
back-to-back (3.1)

3.10 MTU-mismatch behavior

Definition:
The network MTU (Maximum Transmission Unit) of the
output network is smaller than the MTU of the input
network, this results in fragmentation.

Discussion:
The performance of network devices can be significantly
affected by having to fragment frames.

Measurement units:
Description of behavior.

Issues:

See Also:

```
3.11  Overhead behavior

      Definition:
            Processing done other than that for normal data frames.

      Discussion:
            Network devices perform many functions in addition
            to forwarding frames. These tasks range from internal
            hardware testing to the processing of routing
            information and responding to network management
            requests. It is useful to know what the effect of
            these sorts of tasks is on the device performance.
            An example would be if a router were to suspend
            forwarding or accepting frames during the processing
            of large routing update for a complex protocol like
            OSPF. It would be good to know of this sort of
            behavior.

      Measurement units:
            Any quantitative understanding of this behavior is by
            the determination of its effect on other measurements.

      Issues:
            bridging and routing protocols
            control processing
            icmp
            ip options processing
            fragmentation
            error processing
            event logging/statistics collection
            arp

      See Also:
            policy based filtering (3.13)

3.12  Overloaded behavior

      Definition:
            When demand exceeds available system resources.

      Discussion:
            Devices in an overloaded state will lose frames. The
            device might lose frames that contain routing or
            configuration information. An overloaded state is
            assumed when there is any frame loss.

      Measurement units:
            Description of behavior of device in any overloaded
            states for both input and output overload conditions.

      Issues:
            How well does the device recover from overloaded state?
            How does source quench production effect device?
            What does device do when its resources are exhausted?
            What is response to system management in overloaded
            state?

      See Also:

3.13  Policy based filtering

      Definition:
            Filtering is the process of discarding received
            frames by administrative decision where normal
            operation would be to forward them.
```

```
        Discussion:
                Many network devices have the ability to be
                configured to discard frames based on a number
                of criteria.  These criteria can range from simple
                source or destination addresses to examining
                specific fields in the data frame itself.
                Configuring many network devices to perform
                filtering operations impacts the throughput
                of the device.

        Measurement units:
                n/a

        Issues:
                flexibility of filter options
                number of filter conditions

        See Also:

3.14  Restart behavior

        Definition:
                Reinitialization of system causing data loss.

        Discussion:
                During a period of time after a power up or
                reset, network devices do not accept and forward
                frames.  The duration of this period of unavailability
                can be useful in evaluating devices.  In addition,
                some network devices require some form of reset
                when specific setup variables are modified.  If the
                reset period were long it might discourage network
                managers from modifying these variables on production
                networks.

        Measurement units:
                Description of device behavior under various restart
                conditions.

        Issues:
                Types:
                        power on
                        reload software image
                        flush port, reset buffers
                        restart current code image, without reconfuration
                Under what conditions is a restart required?
                Does the device know when restart needed (i.e., hung
                        state timeout)?
                Does the device recognize condition of too frequent
                        auto-restart?
                Does the device run diagnostics on all or some resets?
                How may restart be initiated?
                        physical intervention
                        remote via terminal line or login over network

        See Also:

3.15  Router

        Definition:
                A system which forwards data frames based on
                information in the network layer.

        Discussion:
                This implies "running" the network level protocol
                routing algorithm and performing whatever actions
                that the protocol requires.  For example, decrementing
```

```
                        the TTL field in the TCP/IP header.

           Measurement units:
                 n/a

           Issues:

           See Also:
                 bridge (3.2)
                 bridge/router (3.3)

    3.16  Single frame behavior

           Definition:
                 One frame received on the input to a device.

           Discussion:
                 A data "stream" consisting of a single frame can
                 require a network device to do a lot of processing.
                 Figuring routes, performing ARPs, checking
                 permissions etc., in general, setting up cache entries.
                 Devices will often take much more time to process a
                 single frame presented in isolation than it would if
                 the same frame were part of a steady stream. There
                 is a worry that some devices would even discard a single
                 frame as part of the cache setup procedure under the
                 assumption that the frame is only the first of many.

           Measurement units:
                 Description of the behavior of the device.

           Issues:

           See Also:
                 policy based filtering (3.13)

    3.17  Throughput

           Definition:
                 The maximum rate at which none of the offered frames
                 are dropped by the device.

           Discussion:
                 The throughput figure allows vendors to report a
                 single value which has proven to have use in the
                 marketplace. Since even the loss of one frame in a
                 data stream can cause significant delays while
                 waiting for the higher level protocols to time out,
                 it is useful to know the actual maximum data
                 rate that the device can support. Measurements should
                 be taken over a assortment of frame sizes. Separate
                 measurements for routed and bridged data in those
                 devices that can support both. If there is a checksum
                 in the received frame, full checksum processing must
                 be done.

           Measurement units:
                 N-octet input frames per second
                 input bits per second

           Issues:
                 single path vs. aggregate
                 load
                 unidirectional vs bidirectional
                 checksum processing required on some protocols

           See Also:
```

```
                    frame loss rate (3.6)
                    constant load (3.4)
                    back-to-back (3.1)

   4. Acknowledgements

      This memo is a product of the IETF BMWG working group:

             Chet Birger, Coral Networks
             Scott Bradner, Harvard University (chair)
             Steve Butterfield, independant consultant
             Frank Chui, TRW
             Phill Gross, CNRI
             Stev Knowles, FTP Software, Inc.
             Mat Lew, TRW
             Gary Malkin, FTP Software, Inc.
             K.K. Ramakrishnan, Digital Equipment Corp.
             Mick Scully, Ungerman Bass
             William M. Seifert, Wellfleet Communications Corp.
             John Shriver, Proteon, Inc.
             Dick Sterry, Microcom
             Geof Stone, Network Systems Corp.
             Geoff Thompson, SynOptics
             Mary Youssef, IBM

Security Considerations

      Security issues are not discussed in this memo.

Author's Address

      Scott Bradner
      Harvard University
      William James Hall 1232
      33 Kirkland Street
      Cambridge, MA 02138

      Phone: (617) 495-3864

      EMail: SOB@HARVARD.HARVARD.EDU
      Or, send comments to: bmwg@harvisr.harvard.edu.
```

```
Network Working Group                                         S. Bradner
Request for Comments: 1944                            Harvard University
Category: Informational                                        J. McQuaid
                                                             Bay Networks
                                                                May 1996


              Benchmarking Methodology for Network Interconnect Devices

Status of This Memo

   This memo provides information for the Internet community.  This memo
   does not specify an Internet standard of any kind.  Distribution of
   this memo is unlimited.

Abstract

   This document discusses and defines a number of tests that may be
   used to describe the performance characteristics of a network
   interconnecting  device.  In addition to defining the tests this
   document also describes specific formats for reporting the results of
   the tests.  Appendix A lists the tests and conditions that we believe
   should be included for specific cases and gives additional
   information about testing practices.  Appendix B is a reference
   listing of maximum frame rates to be used with specific frame sizes
   on various media and Appendix C gives some examples of frame formats
   to be used in testing.

1. Introduction

   Vendors often engage in "specsmanship" in an attempt to give their
   products a better position in the marketplace.  This often involves
   "smoke & mirrors" to confuse the potential users of the products.

   This document defines a specific set of tests that vendors can use to
   measure and report the performance characteristics of network
   devices.  The results of these tests will provide the user comparable
   data from different vendors with which to evaluate these devices.

   A previous document, "Benchmarking Terminology for Network
   Interconnect Devices" (RFC 1242), defined many of the terms that are
   used in this document.  The terminology document should be consulted
   before attempting to make use of this document.

2. Real world

   In producing this document the authors attempted to keep in mind the
   requirement that apparatus to perform the described tests must
   actually be built.  We do not know of "off the shelf" equipment
   available to implement all of the tests but it is our opinion that
   such equipment can be constructed.

3. Tests to be run

   There are a number of tests described in this document.  Not all of
   the tests apply to all types of devices under test (DUTs).  Vendors
   should perform all of the tests that can be supported by a specific
   type of product.  The authors understand that it will take a
   considerable period of time to perform all of the recommended tests
   nder  all of the recommended conditions.  We believe that the results
   are worth the effort.  Appendix A lists some of the tests and
   conditions that we believe should be included for specific cases.

4. Evaluating the results
```

Performing all of the recommended tests will result in a great deal
of data. Much of this data will not apply to the evaluation of the
devices under each circumstance. For example, the rate at which a
router forwards IPX frames will be of little use in selecting a
router for an environment that does not (and will not) support that
protocol. Evaluating even that data which is relevant to a
particular network installation will require experience which may not
be readily available. Furthermore, selection of the tests to be run
and evaluation of the test data must be done with an understanding of
generally accepted testing practices regarding repeatability,
variance and statistical significance of small numbers of trials.

5. Requirements

In this document, the words that are used to define the significance
of each particular requirement are capitalized. These words are:

* "MUST" This word, or the words "REQUIRED" and "SHALL" mean that
the item is an absolute requirement of the specification.

* "SHOULD" This word or the adjective "RECOMMENDED" means that there
may exist valid reasons in particular circumstances to ignore this
item, but the full implications should be understood and the case
carefully weighed before choosing a different course.

* "MAY" This word or the adjective "OPTIONAL" means that this item
is truly optional. One vendor may choose to include the item because
a particular marketplace requires it or because it enhances the
product, for example; another vendor may omit the same item.

An implementation is not compliant if it fails to satisfy one or more
of the MUST requirements for the protocols it implements. An
implementation that satisfies all the MUST and all the SHOULD
requirements for its protocols is said to be "unconditionally
compliant"; one that satisfies all the MUST requirements but not all
the SHOULD requirements for its protocols is said to be
"conditionally compliant".

6. Test set up

The ideal way to implement this series of tests is to use a tester
with both transmitting and receiving ports. Connections are made
from the sending ports of the tester to the receiving ports of the
DUT and from the sending ports of the DUT back to the tester. (see
Figure 1) Since the tester both sends the test traffic and receives
it back, after the traffic has been forwarded but the DUT, the tester
can easily determine if all of the transmitted packets were received
and verify that the correct packets were received. The same
functionality can be obtained with separate transmitting and
receiving devices (see Figure 2) but unless they are remotely
controlled by some computer in a way that simulates the single
tester, the labor required to accurately perform some of the tests
(particularly the throughput test) can be prohibitive.

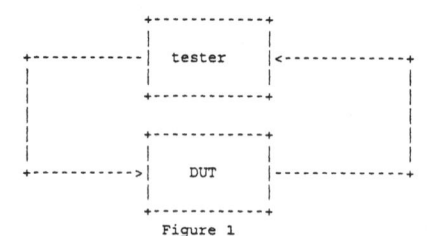

```
                      +-------------+
                      |             |
         +------------|   tester    |<-------------+
         |            |             |              |
         |            +-------------+              |
         |                                         |
         |            +-------------+              |
         |            |             |              |
         +----------->|    DUT      |--------------+
                      |             |
                      +-------------+
                          Figure 1
```

```
        +--------+      +------------+      +----------+
        |        |      |            |      |          |
        | sender |------>|    DUT    |------>| receiver |
        |        |      |            |      |          |
        +--------+      +------------+      +----------+
                           Figure 2
```

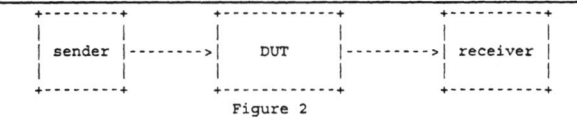

6.1 Test set up for multiple media types

Two different setups could be used to test a DUT which is used in
real-world networks to connect networks of differing media type,
local Ethernet to a backbone FDDI ring for example. The tester could
support both media types in which case the set up shown in Figure 1
would be used.

Two identical DUTs are used in the other test set up. (see Figure 3)
In many cases this set up may more accurately simulate the real
world. For example, connecting two LANs together with a WAN link or
high speed backbone. This set up would not be as good at simulating
a system where clients on a Ethernet LAN were interacting with a
server on an FDDI backbone.

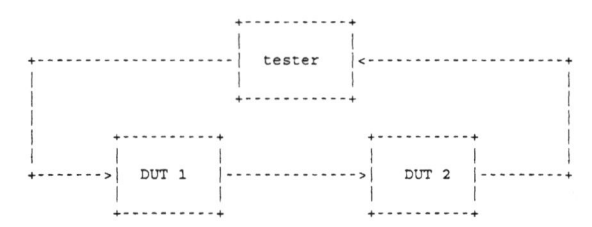

```
                       +------------+
                       |            |
          +------------|   tester   |<---------------------+
          |            |            |                      |
          |            +------------+                      |
          |                                                |
          |        +----------+        +----------+        |
          |        |          |        |          |        |
          +------->|  DUT 1   |------->|  DUT 2   |--------+
                   |          |        |          |
                   +----------+        +----------+

                            Figure 3
```

7. DUT set up

Before starting to perform the tests, the DUT to be tested MUST be
configured following the instructions provided to the user.
Specifically, it is expected that all of the supported protocols will
be configured and enabled during this set up (See Appendix A). It is
expected that all of the tests will be run without changing the
configuration or setup of the DUT in any way other than that required
to do the specific test. For example, it is not acceptable to change
the size of frame handling buffers between tests of frame handling
rates or to disable all but one transport protocol when testing the
throughput of that protocol. It is necessary to modify the
configuration when starting a test to determine the effect of filters
on throughput, but the only change MUST be to enable the specific
filter. The DUT set up SHOULD include the normally recommended
routing update intervals and keep alive frequency. The specific
version of the software and the exact DUT configuration, including
what functions are disabled, used during the tests MUST be included
as part of the report of the results.

8. Frame formats

The formats of the test frames to use for TCP/IP over Ethernet are
shown in Appendix C: Test Frame Formats. These exact frame formats
SHOULD be used in the tests described in this document for this
protocol/media combination and that these frames will be used as a
template for testing other protocol/media combinations. The specific
formats that are used to define the test frames for a particular test
series MUST be included in the report of the results.

9. Frame sizes

All of the described tests SHOULD be performed at a number of frame
sizes. Specifically, the sizes SHOULD include the maximum and minimum
legitimate sizes for the protocol under test on the media under test
and enough sizes in between to be able to get a full characterization
of the DUT performance. Except where noted, at least five frame
sizes SHOULD be tested for each test condition.

Theoretically the minimum size UDP Echo request frame would consist
of an IP header (minimum length 20 octets), a UDP header (8 octets)
and whatever MAC level header is required by the media in use. The
theoretical maximum frame size is determined by the size of the
length field in the IP header. In almost all cases the actual
maximum and minimum sizes are determined by the limitations of the
media.

In theory it would be ideal to distribute the frame sizes in a way
that would evenly distribute the theoretical frame rates. These
recommendations incorporate this theory but specify frame sizes which
are easy to understand and remember. In addition, many of the same
frame sizes are specified on each of the media types to allow for
easy performance comparisons.

Note: The inclusion of an unrealistically small frame size on some of
the media types (i.e. with little or no space for data) is to help
characterize the per-frame processing overhead of the DUT.

9.1 Frame sizes to be used on Ethernet

    64, 128, 256, 512, 1024, 1280, 1518

    These sizes include the maximum and minimum frame sizes permitted
    by the Ethernet standard and a selection of sizes between these
    extremes with a finer granularity for the smaller frame sizes and
    higher frame rates.

9.2 Frame sizes to be used on 4Mb and 16Mb token ring

    54, 64, 128, 256, 1024, 1518, 2048, 4472

    The frame size recommendations for token ring assume that there is
    no RIF field in the frames of routed protocols. A RIF field would
    be present in any direct source route bridge performance test.
    The minimum size frame for UDP on token ring is 54 octets. The
    maximum size of 4472 octets is recommended for 16Mb token ring
    instead of the theoretical size of 17.9Kb because of the size
    limitations imposed by many token ring interfaces. The reminder
    of the sizes are selected to permit direct comparisons with other
    types of media. An IP (i.e. not UDP) frame may be used in
    addition if a higher data rate is desired, in which case the
    minimum frame size is 46 octets.

9.3 Frame sizes to be used on FDDI

    54, 64, 128, 256, 1024, 1518, 2048, 4472

    The minimum size frame for UDP on FDDI is 53 octets, the minimum
    size of 54 is recommended to allow direct comparison to token ring
    performance. The maximum size of 4472 is recommended instead of
    the theoretical maximum size of 4500 octets to permit the same
    type of comparison. An IP (i.e. not UDP) frame may be used in
    addition if a higher data rate is desired, in which case the
    minimum frame size is 45 octets.

9.4 Frame sizes in the presence of disparate MTUs

    When the interconnect DUT supports connecting links with disparate

MTUs, the frame sizes for the link with the *larger* MTU SHOULD be
used, up to the limit of the protocol being tested. If the
interconnect DUT does not support the fragmenting of frames in the
presence of MTU mismatch, the forwarding rate for that frame size
shall be reported as zero.

For example, the test of IP forwarding with a bridge or router
that joins FDDI and Ethernet should use the frame sizes of FDDI
when going from the FDDI to the Ethernet link. If the bridge does
not support IP fragmentation, the forwarding rate for those frames
too large for Ethernet should be reported as zero.

10. Verifying received frames

The test equipment SHOULD discard any frames received during a test
run that are not actual forwarded test frames. For example, keep-
alive and routing update frames SHOULD NOT be included in the count
of received frames. In any case, the test equipment SHOULD verify
the length of the received frames and check that they match the
expected length.

Preferably, the test equipment SHOULD include sequence numbers in the
transmitted frames and check for these numbers on the received
frames. If this is done, the reported results SHOULD include in
addition to the number of frames dropped, the number of frames that
were received out of order, the number of duplicate frames received
and the number of gaps in the received frame numbering sequence.
This functionality is required for some of the described tests.

11. Modifiers

It might be useful to know the DUT performance under a number of
conditions; some of these conditions are noted below. The reported
results SHOULD include as many of these conditions as the test
equipment is able to generate. The suite of tests SHOULD be first
run without any modifying conditions and then repeated under each of
the conditions separately. To preserve the ability to compare the
results of these tests any frames that are required to generate the
modifying conditions (management queries for example) will be
included in the same data stream as the normal test frames in place
of one of the test frames and not be supplied to the DUT on a
separate network port.

11.1 Broadcast frames

In most router designs special processing is required when frames
addressed to the hardware broadcast address are received. In
bridges (or in bridge mode on routers) these broadcast frames must
be flooded to a number of ports. The stream of test frames SHOULD
be augmented with 1% frames addressed to the hardware broadcast
address. The frames sent to the broadcast address should be of a
type that the router will not need to process. The aim of this
test is to determine if there is any effect on the forwarding rate
of the other data in the stream. The specific frames that should
be used are included in the test frame format document. The
broadcast frames SHOULD be evenly distributed throughout the data
stream, for example, every 100th frame.

The same test SHOULD be performed on bridge-like DUTs but in this
case the broadcast packets will be processed and flooded to all
outputs.

It is understood that a level of broadcast frames of 1% is much
higher than many networks experience but, as in drug toxicity
evaluations, the higher level is required to be able to gage the
effect which would otherwise often fall within the normal
variability of the system performance. Due to design factors some

test equipment will not be able to generate a level of alternate frames this low. In these cases the percentage SHOULD be as small as the equipment can provide and that the actual level be described in the report of the test results.

11.2 Management frames

Most data networks now make use of management protocols such as SNMP. In many environments there can be a number of management stations sending queries to the same DUT at the same time.

The stream of test frames SHOULD be augmented with one management query as the first frame sent each second during the duration of the trial. The result of the query must fit into one response frame. The response frame SHOULD be verified by the test equipment. One example of the specific query frame that should be used is shown in Appendix C.

11.3 Routing update frames

The processing of dynamic routing protocol updates could have a significant impact on the ability of a router to forward data frames. The stream of test frames SHOULD be augmented with one routing update frame transmitted as the first frame transmitted during the trial. Routing update frames SHOULD be sent at the rate specified in Appendix C for the specific routing protocol being used in the test. Two routing update frames are defined in Appendix C for the TCP/IP over Ethernet example. The routing frames are designed to change the routing to a number of networks that are not involved in the forwarding of the test data. The first frame sets the routing table state to "A", the second one changes the state to "B". The frames MUST be alternated during the trial.

The test SHOULD verify that the routing update was processed by the DUT.

11.4 Filters

Filters are added to routers and bridges to selectively inhibit the forwarding of frames that would normally be forwarded. This is usually done to implement security controls on the data that is accepted between one area and another. Different products have different capabilities to implement filters.

The DUT SHOULD be first configured to add one filter condition and the tests performed. This filter SHOULD permit the forwarding of the test data stream. In routers this filter SHOULD be of the form:

   forward input_protocol_address to output_protocol_address

In bridges the filter SHOULD be of the form:

   forward destination_hardware_address

The DUT SHOULD be then reconfigured to implement a total of 25 filters. The first 24 of these filters SHOULD be of the form:

   block input_protocol_address to output_protocol_address

The 24 input and output protocol addresses SHOULD not be any that are represented in the test data stream. The last filter SHOULD permit the forwarding of the test data stream. By "first" and "last" we mean to ensure that in the second case, 25 conditions must be checked before the data frames will match the conditions that permit the forwarding of the frame. Of course, if the DUT reorders the filters or does not use a linear scan of the filter rules the effect of the sequence in which the filters are input is properly lost.

The exact filters configuration command lines used SHOULD be included with the report of the results.

11.4.1 Filter Addresses

Two sets of filter addresses are required, one for the single filter case and one for the 25 filter case.

The single filter case should permit traffic from IP address 198.18.1.2 to IP address 198.19.65.2 and deny all other traffic.

The 25 filter case should follow the following sequence.

```
deny aa.ba.1.1 to aa.ba.100.1
deny aa.ba.2.2 to aa.ba.101.2
deny aa.ba.3.3 to aa.ba.103.3
 ...
deny aa.ba.12.12 to aa.ba.112.12
allow aa.bc.1.2 to aa.bc.65.1
deny aa.ba.13.13 to aa.ba.113.13
deny aa.ba.14.14 to aa.ba.114.14
 ...
deny aa.ba.24.24 to aa.ba.124.24
deny all else
```

All previous filter conditions should be cleared from the router before this sequence is entered. The sequence is selected to test to see if the router sorts the filter conditions or accepts them in the order that they were entered. Both of these procedures will result in a greater impact on performance than will some form of hash coding.

12. Protocol addresses

It is easier to implement these tests using a single logical stream of data, with one source protocol address and one destination protocol address, and for some conditions like the filters described above, a practical requirement. Networks in the real world are not limited to single streams of data. The test suite SHOULD be first run with a single protocol (or hardware for bridge tests) source and destination address pair. The tests SHOULD then be repeated with using a random destination address. While testing routers the addresses SHOULD be random and uniformly distributed over a range of 256 networks and random and uniformly distributed over the full MAC range for bridges. The specific address ranges to use for IP are shown in Appendix C.

13. Route Set Up

It is not reasonable that all of the routing information necessary to forward the test stream, especially in the multiple address case, will be manually set up. At the start of each trial a routing update MUST be sent to the DUT. This routing update MUST include all of the network addresses that will be required for the trial. All of the addresses SHOULD resolve to the same "next-hop". Normally this will be the address of the receiving side of the test equipment. This routing update will have to be repeated at the interval required by the routing protocol being used. An example of the format and repetition interval of the update frames is given in Appendix C.

14. Bidirectional traffic

Normal network activity is not all in a single direction. To test
the bidirectional performance of a DUT, the test series SHOULD be run
with the same data rate being offered from each direction. The sum of
the data rates should not exceed the theoretical limit for the media.

15. Single stream path

   The full suite of tests SHOULD be run along with whatever modifier
   conditions that are relevant using a single input and output network
   port on the DUT. If the internal design of the DUT has multiple
   distinct pathways, for example, multiple interface cards each with
   multiple network ports, then all possible types of pathways SHOULD be
   tested separately.

16. Multi-port

   Many current router and bridge products provide many network ports in
   the same module. In performing these tests first half of the ports
   are designated as "input ports" and half are designated as "output
   ports". These ports SHOULD be evenly distributed across the DUT
   architecture. For example if a DUT has two interface cards each of
   which has four ports, two ports on each interface card are designated
   as input and two are designated as output. The specified tests are
   run using the same data rate being offered to each of the input
   ports. The addresses in the input data streams SHOULD be set so that
   a frame will be directed to each of the output ports in sequence so
   that all "output" ports will get an even distribution of packets from
   this input. The same configuration MAY be used to perform a
   bidirectional multi-stream test. In this case all of the ports are
   considered both input and output ports and each data stream MUST
   consist of frames addressed to all of the other ports.

   Consider the following 6 port DUT:

   ```
                    ---------------
            ---------| in A   out X|--------
            ---------| in B   out Y|--------
            ---------| in C   out Z|--------
                    ---------------
   ```

   The addressing of the data streams for each of the inputs SHOULD be:

   ```
   stream sent to input A:
      packet to out X, packet to out Y, packet to out Z
   stream sent to input B:
      packet to out X, packet to out Y, packet to out Z
   stream sent to input C
      packet to out X, packet to out Y, packet to out Z
   ```

   Note that these streams each follow the same sequence so that 3
   packets will arrive at output X at the same time, then 3 packets at
   Y, then 3 packets at Z. This procedure ensures that, as in the real
   world, the DUT will have to deal with multiple packets addressed to
   the same output at the same time.

17. Multiple protocols

   This document does not address the issue of testing the effects of a
   mixed protocol environment other than to suggest that if such tests
   are wanted then frames SHOULD be distributed between all of the test
   protocols. The distribution MAY approximate the conditions on the
   network in which the DUT would be used.

18. Multiple frame sizes

   This document does not address the issue of testing the effects of a
   mixed frame size environment other than to suggest that if such tests

are wanted then frames SHOULD be distributed between all of the
listed sizes for the protocol under test. The distribution MAY
approximate the conditions on the network in which the DUT would be
used. The authors do not have any idea how the results of such a test
would be interpreted other than to directly compare multiple DUTs in
some very specific simulated network.

19. Testing performance beyond a single DUT.

    In the performance testing of a single DUT, the paradigm can be
    described as applying some input to a DUT and monitoring the output.
    The results of which can be used to form a basis of characterization
    of that device under those test conditions.

    This model is useful when the test input and output are homogenous
    (e.g., 64-byte IP, 802.3 frames into the DUT; 64 byte IP, 802.3
    frames out), or the method of test can distinguish between dissimilar
    input/output. (E.g., 1518 byte IP, 802.3 frames in; 576 byte,
    fragmented IP, X.25 frames out.)

    By extending the single DUT test model, reasonable benchmarks
    regarding multiple DUTs or heterogeneous environments may be
    collected. In this extension, the single DUT is replaced by a system
    of interconnected network DUTs. This test methodology would support
    the benchmarking of a variety of device/media/service/protocol
    combinations. For example, a configuration for a LAN-to-WAN-to-LAN
    test might be:

    (1) 802.3-> DUT 1 -> X.25 @ 64kbps -> DUT 2 -> 802.3

    Or a mixed LAN configuration might be:

    (2) 802.3 -> DUT 1 -> FDDI -> DUT 2 -> FDDI -> DUT 3 -> 802.3

    In both examples 1 and 2, end-to-end benchmarks of each system could
    be empirically ascertained. Other behavior may be characterized
    through the use of intermediate devices. In example 2, the
    configuration may be used to give an indication of the FDDI to FDDI
    capability exhibited by DUT 2.

    Because multiple DUTs are treated as a single system, there are
    limitations to this methodology. For instance, this methodology may
    yield an aggregate benchmark for a tested system. That benchmark
    alone, however, may not necessarily reflect asymmetries in behavior
    between the DUTs, latencies introduce by other apparatus (e.g.,
    CSUs/DSUs, switches), etc.

    Further, care must be used when comparing benchmarks of different
    systems by ensuring that the DUTs' features/configuration of the
    tested systems have the appropriate common denominators to allow
    comparison.

20. Maximum frame rate

    The maximum frame rates that should be used when testing LAN
    connections SHOULD be the listed theoretical maximum rate for the
    frame size on the media.

    The maximum frame rate that should be used when testing WAN
    connections SHOULD be greater than the listed theoretical maximum
    rate for the frame size on that speed connection. The higher rate
    for WAN tests is to compensate for the fact that some vendors employ
    various forms of header compression.

    A list of maximum frame rates for LAN connections is included in
    Appendix B.

21. Bursty traffic

It is convenient to measure the DUT performance under steady state load but this is an unrealistic way to gauge the functioning of a DUT since actual network traffic normally consists of bursts of frames. Some of the tests described below SHOULD be performed with both steady state traffic and with traffic consisting of repeated bursts of frames. The frames within a burst are transmitted with the minimum legitimate inter-frame gap.

The objective of the test is to determine the minimum interval between bursts which the DUT can process with no frame loss. During each test the number of frames in each burst is held constant and the inter-burst interval varied. Tests SHOULD be run with burst sizes of 16, 64, 256 and 1024 frames.

22. Frames per token

Although it is possible to configure some token ring and FDDI interfaces to transmit more than one frame each time that the token is received, most of the network devices currently available transmit only one frame per token. These tests SHOULD first be performed while transmitting only one frame per token.

Some current high-performance workstation servers do transmit more than one frame per token on FDDI to maximize throughput. Since this may be a common feature in future workstations and servers, interconnect devices with FDDI interfaces SHOULD be tested with 1, 4, 8, and 16 frames per token. The reported frame rate SHOULD be the average rate of frame transmission over the total trial period.

23. Trial description

A particular test consists of multiple trials. Each trial returns one piece of information, for example the loss rate at a particular input frame rate. Each trial consists of a number of phases:

a) If the DUT is a router, send the routing update to the "input" port and pause two seconds to be sure that the routing has settled.

b) Send the "learning frames" to the "output" port and wait 2 seconds to be sure that the learning has settled. Bridge learning frames are frames with source addresses that are the same as the destination addresses used by the test frames. Learning frames for other protocols are used to prime the address resolution tables in the DUT. The formats of the learning frame that should be used are shown in the Test Frame Formats document.

c) Run the test trial.

d) Wait for two seconds for any residual frames to be received.

e) Wait for at least five seconds for the DUT to restabilize.

24. Trial duration

The aim of these tests is to determine the rate continuously supportable by the DUT. The actual duration of the test trials must be a compromise between this aim and the duration of the benchmarking test suite. The duration of the test portion of each trial SHOULD be at least 60 seconds. The tests that involve some form of "binary search", for example the throughput test, to determine the exact result MAY use a shorter trial duration to minimize the length of the search procedure, but the final determination SHOULD be made with full length trials.

25. Address resolution

The DUT SHOULD be able to respond to address resolution requests sent
by the DUT wherever the protocol requires such a process.

26. Benchmarking tests:

Note: The notation "type of data stream" refers to the above
modifications to a frame stream with a constant inter-frame gap, for
example, the addition of traffic filters to the configuration of the
DUT.

26.1 Throughput

Objective:
To determine the DUT throughput as defined in RFC 1242.

Procedure:
Send a specific number of frames at a specific rate through the
DUT and then count the frames that are transmitted by the DUT. If
the count of offered frames is equal to the count of received
frames, the rate of the offered stream is raised and the test
rerun. If fewer frames are received than were transmitted, the
rate of the offered stream is reduced and the test is rerun.

The throughput is the fastest rate at which the count of test
frames transmitted by the DUT is equal to the number of test
frames sent to it by the test equipment.

Reporting format:
The results of the throughput test SHOULD be reported in the form
of a graph. If it is, the x coordinate SHOULD be the frame size,
the y coordinate SHOULD be the frame rate. There SHOULD be at
least two lines on the graph. There SHOULD be one line showing
the theoretical frame rate for the media at the various frame
sizes. The second line SHOULD be the plot of the test results.
Additional lines MAY be used on the graph to report the results
for each type of data stream tested. Text accompanying the graph
SHOULD indicate the protocol, data stream format, and type of
media used in the tests.

We assume that if a single value is desired for advertising
purposes the vendor will select the rate for the minimum frame
size for the media. If this is done then the figure MUST be
expressed in frames per second. The rate MAY also be expressed in
bits (or bytes) per second if the vendor so desires. The
statement of performance MUST include a/ the measured maximum
frame rate, b/ the size of the frame used, c/ the theoretical
limit of the media for that frame size, and d/ the type of
protocol used in the test. Even if a single value is used as part
of the advertising copy, the full table of results SHOULD be
included in the product data sheet.

26.2 Latency

Objective:
To determine the latency as defined in RFC 1242.

Procedure:
First determine the throughput for DUT at each of the listed frame
sizes. Send a stream of frames at a particular frame size through
the DUT at the determined throughput rate to a specific
destination. The stream SHOULD be at least 120 seconds in
duration. An identifying tag SHOULD be included in one frame
after 60 seconds with the type of tag being implementation
dependent. The time at which this frame is fully transmitted is
recorded (timestamp A). The receiver logic in the test equipment
MUST recognize the tag information in the frame stream and record

the time at which the tagged frame was received (timestamp B).

The latency is timestamp B minus timestamp A as per the relevant definition frm RFC 1242, namely latency as defined for store and forward devices or latency as defined for bit forwarding devices.

The test MUST be repeated at least 20 times with the reported value being the average of the recorded values.

This test SHOULD be performed with the test frame addressed to the same destination as the rest of the data stream and also with each of the test frames addressed to a new destination network.

Reporting format:
The report MUST state which definition of latency (from RFC 1242) was used for this test. The latency results SHOULD be reported in the format of a table with a row for each of the tested frame sizes. There SHOULD be columns for the frame size, the rate at which the latency test was run for that frame size, for the media types tested, and for the resultant latency values for each type of data stream tested.

26.3 Frame loss rate

Objective:
To determine the frame loss rate, as defined in RFC 1242, of a DUT throughout the entire range of input data rates and frame sizes.

Procedure:
Send a specific number of frames at a specific rate through the DUT to be tested and count the frames that are transmitted by the DUT. The frame loss rate at each point is calculated using the following equation:

((input_count - output_count) * 100) / input_count

The first trial SHOULD be run for the frame rate that corresponds to 100% of the maximum rate for the frame size on the input media. Repeat the procedure for the rate that corresponds to 90% of the maximum rate used and then for 80% of this rate. This sequence SHOULD be continued (at reducing 10% intervals) until there are two successive trials in which no frames are lost. The maximum granularity of the trials MUST be 10% of the maximum rate, a finer granularity is encouraged.

Reporting format:
The results of the frame loss rate test SHOULD be plotted as a graph. If this is done then the X axis MUST be the input frame rate as a percent of the theoretical rate for the media at the specific frame size. The Y axis MUST be the percent loss at the particular input rate. The left end of the X axis and the bottom of the Y axis MUST be 0 percent; the right end of the X axis and the top of the Y axis MUST be 100 percent. Multiple lines on the graph MAY used to report the frame loss rate for different frame sizes, protocols, and types of data streams.

Note: See section 18 for the maximum frame rates that SHOULD be used.

26.4 Back-to-back frames

Objective:
To characterize the ability of a DUT to process back-to-back frames as defined in RFC 1242.

Procedure:
Send a burst of frames with minimum inter-frame gaps to the DUT

and count the number of frames forwarded by the DUT. If the count
of transmitted frames is equal to the number of frames forwarded
the length of the burst is increased and the test is rerun. If
the number of forwarded frames is less than the number
transmitted, the length of the burst is reduced and the test is
rerun.

The back-to-back value is the number of frames in the longest
burst that the DUT will handle without the loss of any frames.
The trial length MUST be at least 2 seconds and SHOULD be
repeated at least 50 times with the average of the recorded values
being reported.

Reporting format:
The back-to-back results SHOULD be reported in the format of a
table with a row for each of the tested frame sizes. There SHOULD
be columns for the frame size and for the resultant average frame
count for each type of data stream tested. The standard deviation
for each measurement MAY also be reported.

26.5 System recovery

Objective:
To characterize the speed at which a DUT recovers from an overload
condition.

Procedure:
First determine the throughput for a DUT at each of the listed
frame sizes.

Send a stream of frames at a rate 110% of the recorded throughput
rate or the maximum rate for the media, whichever is lower, for at
least 60 seconds. At Timestamp A reduce the frame rate to 50% of
the above rate and record the time of the last frame lost
(Timestamp B). The system recovery time is determined by
subtracting Timestamp B from Timestamp A. The test SHOULD be
repeated a number of times and the average of the recorded values
being reported.

Reporting format:
The system recovery results SHOULD be reported in the format of a
table with a row for each of the tested frame sizes. There SHOULD
be columns for the frame size, the frame rate used as the
throughput rate for each type of data stream tested, and for the
measured recovery time for each type of data stream tested.

26.6 Reset

Objective:
To characterize the speed at which a DUT recovers from a device or
software reset.

Procedure:
First determine the throughput for the DUT for the minimum frame
size on the media used in the testing.

Send a continuous stream of frames at the determined throughput
rate for the minimum sized frames. Cause a reset in the DUT.
Monitor the output until frames begin to be forwarded and record
the time that the last frame (Timestamp A) of the initial stream
and the first frame of the new stream (Timestamp B) are received.
A power interruption reset test is performed as above except that
the power to the DUT should be interrupted for 10 seconds in place
of causing a reset.

This test SHOULD only be run using frames addressed to networks
directly connected to the DUT so that there is no requirement to

```
         delay until a routing update is received.

         The reset value is obtained by subtracting Timestamp A from
         Timestamp B.

         Hardware and software resets, as well as a power interruption
         SHOULD be tested.

         Reporting format:
         The reset value SHOULD be reported in a simple set of statements,
         one for each reset type.

   27. Security Considerations

      Security issues are not addressed in this document.

   28. Editors' Addresses

      Scott Bradner
      Harvard University
      1350 Mass. Ave, room 813
      Cambridge, MA 02138

      Phone +1 617 495-3864
      Fax +1 617 496-8500
      EMail: sob@harvard.edu


      Jim McQuaid
      Bay Networks
      3 Federal Street
      Billerica, MA 01821

      Phone +1 508 436-3915
      Fax: +1 508 670-8145
      EMail: jmcquaid@baynetworks.com

Appendix A: Testing Considerations

A.1 Scope Of This Appendix

   This appendix discusses certain issues in the benchmarking
   methodology where experience or judgment may play a role in the tests
   selected to be run or in the approach to constructing the test with a
   particular DUT. As such, this appendix MUST not be read as an
   amendment to the methodology described in the body of this document
   but as a guide to testing practice.

   1. Typical testing practice has been to enable all protocols to be
      tested and conduct all testing with no further configuration of
      protocols, even though a given set of trials may exercise only one
      protocol at a time. This minimizes the opportunities to "tune" a
      DUT for a single protocol.

   2. The least common denominator of the available filter functions
      should be used to ensure that there is a basis for comparison
      between vendors. Because of product differences, those conducting
      and evaluating tests must make a judgment about this issue.

   3. Architectural considerations may need to be considered. For
      example, first perform the tests with the stream going between
      ports on the same interface card and the repeat the tests with the
      stream going into a port on one interface card and out of a port
      on a second interface card. There will almost always be a best
      case and worst case configuration for a given DUT architecture.

   4. Testing done using traffic streams consisting of mixed protocols
```

has not shown much difference between testing with individual protocols. That is, if protocol A testing and protocol B testing give two different performance results, mixed protocol testing appears to give a result which is the average of the two.

5. Wide Area Network (WAN) performance may be tested by setting up two identical devices connected by the appropriate short- haul versions of the WAN modems. Performance is then measured between a LAN interface on one DUT to a LAN interface on the other DUT.

The maximum frame rate to be used for LAN-WAN-LAN configurations is a judgment that can be based on known characteristics of the overall system including compression effects, fragmentation, and gross link speeds. Practice suggests that the rate should be at least 110% of the slowest link speed. Substantive issues of testing compression itself are beyond the scope of this document.

Appendix B: Maximum frame rates reference

(Provided by Roger Beeman, Cisco Systems)

Size (bytes)	Ethernet (pps)	16Mb Token Ring (pps)	FDDI (pps)
64	14880	24691	152439
128	8445	13793	85616
256	4528	7326	45620
512	2349	3780	23585
768	1586	2547	15903
1024	1197	1921	11996
1280	961	1542	9630
1518	812	1302	8138

```
Ethernet size
 Preamble 64 bits
 Frame 8 x N bits
 Gap   96 bits

16Mb Token Ring size
   SD              8 bits
   AC              8 bits
   FC              8 bits
   DA             48 bits
   SA             48 bits
   RI             48 bits ( 06 30 00 12 00 30 )
   SNAP
     DSAP          8 bits
     SSAP          8 bits
     Control       8 bits
     Vendor       24 bits
     Type         16 bits
   Data 8 x ( N - 18) bits
   FCS            32 bits
   ED              8 bits
   FS              8 bits

Tokens or idles between packets are not included

FDDI size
   Preamble      64 bits
   SD             8 bits
   FC             8 bits
   DA            48 bits
   SA            48 bits
   SNAP
     DSAP         8 bits
     SSAP         8 bits
```

```
        Control       8 bits
        Vendor       24 bits
          Type       16 bits
    Data 8 x ( N - 18) bits
           FCS       32 bits
            ED        4 bits
            FS       12 bits
```

Appendix C: Test Frame Formats

This appendix defines the frame formats that may be used with these tests. It also includes protocol specific parameters for TCP/IP over Ethernet to be used with the tests as an example.

C.1. Introduction

The general logic used in the selection of the parameters and the design of the frame formats is explained for each case within the TCP/IP section. The same logic has been used in the other sections. Comments are used in these sections only if there is a protocol specific feature to be explained. Parameters and frame formats for additional protocols can be defined by the reader by using the same logic.

C.2. TCP/IP Information

The following section deals with the TCP/IP protocol suite.

C.2.1 Frame Type.
An application level datagram echo request is used for the test data frame in the protocols that support such a function. A datagram protocol is used to minimize the chance that a router might expect a specific session initialization sequence, as might be the case for a reliable stream protocol. A specific defined protocol is used because some routers verify the protocol field and refuse to forward unknown protocols.

For TCP/IP a UDP Echo Request is used.

C.2.2 Protocol Addresses
Two sets of addresses must be defined: first the addresses assigned to the router ports, and second the address that are to be used in the frames themselves and in the routing updates.

The network addresses 192.18.0.0 through 192.19.255.255 are have been assigned to the BMWG by the IANA for this purpose. This assignment was made to minimize the chance of conflict in case a testing device were to be accidentally connected to part of the Internet. The specific use of the addresses is detailed below.

C.2.2.1 Router port protocol addresses
Half of the ports on a multi-port router are referred to as "input" ports and the other half as "output" ports even though some of the tests use all ports both as input and output. A contiguous series of IP Class C network addresses from 198.18.1.0 to 198.18.64.0 have been assigned for use on the "input" ports. A second series from 198.19.1.0 to 198.19.64.0 have been assigned for use on the "output" ports. In all cases the router port is node 1 on the appropriate network. For example, a two port DUT would have an IP address of 198.18.1.1 on one port and 198.19.1.1 on the other port.

Some of the tests described in the methodology memo make use of an SNMP management connection to the DUT. The management access address for the DUT is assumed to be the first of the "input" ports (198.18.1.1).

C.2.2.2 Frame addresses
Some of the described tests assume adjacent network routing
(the reboot time test for example). The IP address used in the
test frame is that of node 2 on the appropriate Class C
network. (198.19.1.2 for example)

If the test involves non-adjacent network routing the phantom
routers are located at node 10 of each of the appropriate Class
C networks. A series of Class C network addresses from
198.18.65.0 to 198.18.254.0 has been assigned for use as the
networks accessible through the phantom routers on the "input"
side of DUT. The series of Class C networks from 198.19.65.0
to 198.19.254.0 have been assigned to be used as the networks
visible through the phantom routers on the "output" side of the
DUT.

C.2.3 Routing Update Frequency

The update interval for each routing protocol is may have to be
determined by the specifications of the individual protocol. For
IP RIP, Cisco IGRP and for OSPF a routing update frame or frames
should precede each stream of test frames by 5 seconds. This
frequency is sufficient for trial durations of up to 60 seconds.
Routing updates must be mixed with the stream of test frames if
longer trial periods are selected. The frequency of updates
should be taken from the following table.

```
IP-RIP  30 sec
IGRP    90 sec
OSPF    90 sec
```

C.2.4 Frame Formats - detailed discussion

C.2.4.1 Learning Frame
In most protocols a procedure is used to determine the mapping
between the protocol node address and the MAC address. The
Address Resolution Protocol (ARP) is used to perform this
function in TCP/IP. No such procedure is required in XNS or
IPX because the MAC address is used as the protocol node
address.

In the ideal case the tester would be able to respond to ARP
requests from the DUT. In cases where this is not possible an
ARP request should be sent to the router's "output" port. This
request should be seen as coming from the immediate destination
of the test frame stream. (i.e. the phantom router (Figure 2)
or the end node if adjacent network routing is being used.) It
is assumed that the router will cache the MAC address of the
requesting device. The ARP request should be sent 5 seconds
before the test frame stream starts in each trial. Trial
lengths of longer than 50 seconds may require that the router
be configured for an extended ARP timeout.

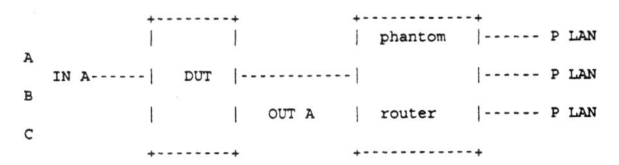

```
                   +--------+           +------------+
         A         |        |           |  phantom   |------ P LAN
              IN A-|  DUT   |-----------|            |------ P LAN
         B         |        | OUT A     |  router    |------ P LAN
         C         +--------+           +------------+
```

Figure 2

In the case where full routing is being used

C.2.4.2 Routing Update Frame

If the test does not involve adjacent net routing the tester must supply proper routing information using a routing update. A single routing update is used before each trial on each "destination" port (see section C.24). This update includes the network addresses that are reachable through a phantom router on the network attached to the port. For a full mesh test, one destination network address is present in the routing update for each of the "input" ports. The test stream on each "input" port consists of a repeating sequence of frames, one to each of the "output" ports.

C.2.4.3 Management Query Frame

The management overhead test uses SNMP to query a set of variables that should be present in all DUTs that support SNMP. The variables for a single interface only are read by an NMS at the appropriate intervals. The list of variables to retrieve follow:

```
sysUpTime
ifInOctets
ifOutOctets
ifInUcastPkts
ifOutUcastPkts
```

C.2.4.4 Test Frames

The test frame is an UDP Echo Request with enough data to fill out the required frame size. The data should not be all bits off or all bits on since these patters can cause a "bit stuffing" process to be used to maintain clock synchronization on WAN links. This process will result in a longer frame than was intended.

C.2.4.5 Frame Formats - TCP/IP on Ethernet

Each of the frames below are described for the 1st pair of DUT ports, i.e. "input" port #1 and "output" port #1. Addresses must be changed if the frame is to be used for other ports.

C.2.6.1 Learning Frame

ARP Request on Ethernet

```
-- DATAGRAM HEADER
offset  data (hex)              description
00      FF FF FF FF FF FF       dest MAC address send to broadcast address
06      xx xx xx xx xx xx       set to source MAC address
12      08 06                   ARP type
14      00 01                   hardware type Ethernet = 1
16      08 00                   protocol type IP = 800
18      06                      hardware address length 48 bits on Ethernet
19      04                      protocol address length 4 octets for IP
20      00 01                   opcode request = 1
22      xx xx xx xx xx xx       source MAC address
28      xx xx xx xx             source IP address
32      FF FF FF FF FF FF       requesting DUT's MAC address
38      xx xx xx xx             DUT's IP address
```

C.2.6.2 Routing Update Frame

```
-- DATAGRAM HEADER
offset  data (hex)              description
00      FF FF FF FF FF FF       dest MAC address is broadcast
06      xx xx xx xx xx xx       source hardware address
12      08 00                   type
```

```
          -- IP HEADER
          14      45                      IP version - 4, header length (4
          byte units) - 5
          15      00                      service field
          16      00 EE                   total length
          18      00 00                   ID
          20      40 00                   flags (3 bits) 4 (do not
          fragment),
                                          fragment offset-0
          22      0A                      TTL
          23      11                      protocol - 17 (UDP)
          24      C4 8D                   header checksum
          26      xx xx xx xx             source IP address
          30      xx xx xx                destination IP address
          33      FF                      host part = FF for broadcast

          -- UDP HEADER
          34      02 08                   source port 208 = RIP
          36      02 08                   destination port 208 = RIP
          38      00 DA                   UDP message length
          40      00 00                   UDP checksum

          -- RIP packet
          42      02                      command = response
          43      01                      version = 1
          44      00 00                   0

          -- net 1
          46      00 02                   family = IP
          48      00 00                   0
          50      xx xx xx                net 1 IP address
          53      00                      net not node
          54      00 00 00 00             0
          58      00 00 00 00             0
          62      00 00 00 07             metric 7

          -- net 2
          66      00 02                   family = IP
          68      00 00                   0
          70      xx xx xx                net 2 IP address
          73      00                      net not node
          74      00 00 00 00             0
          78      00 00 00 00             0
          82      00 00 00 07             metric 7

          -- net 3
          86      00 02                   family = IP
          88      00 00                   0
          90      xx xx xx                net 3 IP address
          93      00                      net not node
          94      00 00 00 00             0
          98      00 00 00 00             0
          102     00 00 00 07             metric 7

          -- net 4
          106     00 02                   family = IP
          108     00 00                   0
          110     xx xx xx                net 4 IP address
          113     00                      net not node
          114     00 00 00 00             0
          118     00 00 00 00             0
          122     00 00 00 07             metric 7

          -- net 5
          126     00 02                   family = IP
          128     00 00                   0
          130     00                      net 5 IP address
```

```
133    00                        net not node
134    00 00 00 00               0
138    00 00 00 00               0
142    00 00 00 07               metric 7

-- net 6
146    00 02                     family = IP
148    00 00                     0
150    xx xx xx                  net 6 IP address
153    00                        net not node
154    00 00 00 00               0
158    00 00 00 00               0
162    00 00 00 07               metric 7
```

C.2.4.6 Management Query Frame

   To be defined.

C.2.6.4 Test Frames
       UDP echo request on Ethernet

```
       -- DATAGRAM HEADER
       offset  data (hex)          description
       00      xx xx xx xx xx xx   set to dest MAC address
       06      xx xx xx xx xx xx   set to source MAC address
       12      08 00               type

       -- IP HEADER
       14      45                  IP version - 4 header length 5 4
       byte units
       15      00                  TOS
       16      00 2E               total length*
       18      00 00               ID
       20      00 00               flags (3 bits) - 0 fragment
       offset-0
       22      0A                  TTL
       23      11                  protocol - 17 (UDP)
       24      C4 8D               header checksum*
       26      xx xx xx xx         set to source IP address**
       30      xx xx xx xx         set to destination IP address**

       -- UDP HEADER
       34      C0 20               source port
       36      00 07               destination port 07 = Echo
       38      00 1A               UDP message length*
       40      00 00               UDP checksum

       -- UDP DATA
       42      00 01 02 03 04 05 06 07    some data***
       50      08 09 0A 0B 0C 0D 0E 0F
```

* - change for different length frames

** - change for different logical streams

*** - fill remainder of frame with incrementing octets,
repeated if required by frame length

Values to be used in Total Length and UDP message length fields:

```
       frame size   total length   UDP message length
            64         00 2E            00 1A
           128         00 6E            00 5A
           256         00 EE            00 9A
           512         01 EE            01 9A
           768         02 EE            02 9A
          1024         03 EE            03 9A
          1280         04 EE            04 9A
          1518         05 DC            05 C8
```

APPENDIX E

Fast Ethernet Media Specifications

The Fast Ethernet standard defines three media types that have been specified for the transmission of 100Mbps Ethernet signals over a number of different media types. The choice of media types was based on derivative work done in the FDDI media standards for fiberoptic cable and Category-5 unshielded twisted-pair cable. A new specification was developed in order to provide support for those cable plant installations that did not have Category-5 cable, but a lower-grade UTP wire, such as Category-3 or -4. In addition, the Fast Ethernet standard also provides guidelines for the use of Type-1 shielded twisted-pair cable, which is the standard cable traditionally used with Token Ring networks. The support and recommendations for using Fast Ethernet with STP provide a migration path to Fast Ethernet for customers with STP cabling plant installations.

The Fast Ethernet specification also includes an Autonegotiation mechanism that allows the node port to automatically detect and adjust to either 10Mbps or 100Mbps data rate based on a series of packet exchanges with the hub or switch port. The Autonegotiation mechanism is a software algorithm run between the station node and the attached repeater/switch port. The cables used are:

- 100Base-TX, which uses two pairs of wires and is based on the data-grade twisted-pair physical medium standard developed by ANSI (American National Standards Institute). The data-grade twisted-pair cable may be either unshielded twisted-pair cable or shielded twisted pair cable. More complete descriptions for each type are given later in this section.

- 100Base-FX, which uses two pairs of fiberoptic cable based on the fiberoptic physical medium standard developed by ANSI. The 100Base-TX and the 100Base-FX media specifications are based on the same physical medium standard developed by ANSI, and use the same signaling method. These two media specifications are known as 100Base-X. Because they are both developed from the same physical medium standard, it is easier to integrate these two media types in the same collision domain using repeaters.

100Base-T4 is a new specification developed by the IEEE 803u committee. It is based on a twisted-pair link segment, and uses four pairs of telephone-grade twisted-pair cable commonly known as Category-3 UTP cable.

100Base-TX Media

The 100Base-TX media specification is based on the ANSI TP-PMD physical medium standard. The 100Base-TX media interface operates over two pairs of twisted-pair cables, with one pair used for transmit data and one pair used for receive data. Since the ANSI TP-PMD specification includes both shielded twisted-pair cable and unshielded twisted-pair cable, the 100Base-TX media interface supports two pairs of data-grade unshielded twisted-pair cable or two pairs of Type-1 shielded twisted-pair cable.

MDI Connector

The medium-dependent interface for a 100Base-TX link may be one of two types. For unshielded twisted-pair cabling, the MDI connector must be a Category-5-capable eight-pin RJ45 connector, the same connector as is used for 10Base-T, which ensures backward compatibility for existing Category-5 cable plant installations. For shielded twisted-pair applications, the MDI connector must be an IBM Type-1 STP connector, which uses a shielded DB9 style connector. This type of connector is commonly used with Token Ring installations.

Category-5 UTP

The 100Base-TX UTP media interface uses two pairs of wires of the MDI connector to carry Ethernet signals to and from the network medium. This means that four pins out of the eight in the RJ45 connector are taken up. To minimize crosstalk and possible signal distortion, the other four wires

Table E.1 100Base-TX UTP MDI Connector

Pin Number	Signal Name	Cable Code
1	Transmit +	White/Orange
2	Transmit −	Orange/White
3	Receive +	White/Green
4	Unused	
5	Unused	
6	Receive −	Green/White
7	Unused	
8	Unused	

should not be used to carry any other signals. The transmit and receive signals for each pair are polarized, with one wire carrying the positive (+) signal and the other carrying the negative (−) signal. The cable color code for 100Base-TX connection is also shown for each pin position in Table E.1. Although the 100Base-TX PHY was modeled after the ANSI TP-PMD standard, the pin numbers used in the eight-pin RJ45 connector for 100Base-TX were changed to conform to the wiring scheme already in use for the 10Base-T standard. The ANSI TP-PMD standard uses pins 7 and 9 for receive data, while 100Base-TX uses pins 3 and 6, the same as 10Base-T. This change in the wiring standard ensures that 100Base-TX adapters may be used in place of 10Base-T adapters, and be plugged into the same Category-5 wiring plant without making any wiring changes. For an RJ45 connector, the correct wiring pair assignments are pins [1, 2] and pins [3, 6]. Every effort should be made to use the correct color-coded wire pairs for the MDI pin assignments, but color-code substitution, if it is consistent on both ends of the cable, has no electrical impact on the link segment performance. However, never split wire pairs apart.

Type 1 STP

The 100Base-TX standard also supports shielded twisted-pair cabling with characteristic impedance of 150 ohms. This type of cable is not as widely deployed as unshielded twisted-pair cable, and is typically found in plants and buildings wired for Token Ring networks. Shielded twisted-pair cables use a nine-pin D-Type connector and are wired according to the ANSI TP-PMD specification for shielded twisted-pair cabling. On a DB-9 connector the correct wiring pair assignments are pins [1, 6] and pins [5, 9]. If the NIC does not have a DB-9 connector, then the STP cable must be reterminated using an RJ45 connector. It is important to use only a Category-5 RJ45 connector for the cable termination and any cross-connect equipment (see Table E.2).

Table E.2 100Base-TX 9-Pin STP MDI Connector

Pin Number	Signal Name	Cable Code
1	Receive +	Orange
2	Unused	
3	Unused	
4	Unused	
5	Transmit +	Red
6	Receive –	Black
7	Unused	
8	Unused	
9	Transmit –	Green
10	Chassis	Cable Sheath

100Base-TX Crossover Wiring

When two nodes are connected together over a segment, the transmit pair from one MDI connector is wired to the receive pair of the MDI on the second station. For stand-alone applications where two stations are connected together, an external crossover cable must be provided by wiring the transmit pins on the eight-pin RJ45 connector at one end of the cable to the receive pins on the eight-pin RJ45 connector at the other end of the crossover cable. In practice where multiple stations are connected to a repeater or switch ports, the crossover wiring is done inside the ports of the repeater or switch (see Figure 3.13).

This allows a straight-through cable to be used between each station and the repeater or switch port. This eliminates any ambiguity of whether the cables in the segment or patch panel are crossed over (see Table E.3).

Table E.3 100Base-TX Crossover Pin Assignments

	Category-5 UTP Cable		Type-1 STP Cable	
Pin Number	No Crossover Signal Name	Crossover Signal Name	No Crossover Signal Name	Crossover Signal Name
1	Transmit +	Receive +	Receive +	Transmit +
2	Transmit –	Receive –	Unused	Unused
3	Receive +	Transmit +	Unused	Unused
4	Unused	Unused	Unused	Unused
5	Unused	Unused	Transmit +	Receive +
6	Receive –	Transmit –	Receiver –	Transmit –
7	Unused	Unused	Unused	Unused
8	Unused	Unused	Unused	Unused
9	N/A	N/A	Transmit –	Receive –
Shell	N/A	N/A	Chassis	Chassis

Table E.4 100Base-TX Cable Distance Rules

100Base-TX—Network Diameter	
Physical Model	*Copper Cable*
DTE to DTE	100m (328 ft)
One Class-I Repeater	200m (656 ft)
One Class-II Repeater	200m (656 ft)
Two Class-II Repeaters	205m (672 ft)

The 100Base-TX standard recommends this method, and specifies that each port of the hub that is internally crossed over should be clearly marked with an X.

100Base-TX Cable Configuration Guidelines

Cable plant installation for LANs, and especially new cable plant installations for Fast Ethernet, should conform to the EIA/TIA-568 standard, which specifies the exact cable length between the wiring closet and the network node. This length of cable is called the segment and is defined as the link segment in the Ethernet specification (see Table E.4). A link segment is formally defined as a point-to-point medium that connects two and only two MDIs. The 100Base-TX specification supports a maximum link segment up to 100m.

The 100Base-TX specification allows a segment of up to 100m in length for a point-to-point link segment between two DTEs or a DTE and a switch port. If a single Class-I repeater or a single Class-II is used, then two 100m link segments may be used between two DTEs for a maximum distance of 200m. Two Class-II repeaters may be connected together in a single collision domain with a maximum of 5m between the two Class-II repeaters. This provides a maximum collision domain of 200m using a Class-I repeater, or 205m using two Class-II repeaters.

100Base-FX Media

Fiberoptic cable is one of the supported media types specified for 100Base-FX, and is extremely easy to install because of its light weight, size, and flexibility. Because it does not conduct electricity and is free from EMI interference, it is easier to place and route fiberoptic cable than any other copper-based cable. It may be buried directly in the ground or enclosed in PVC pipes to protect it from frost, water, and seepage.

Fiberoptic cables may also be installed along traditional telephone poles or power lines. The primary consideration for these types of installations are environmental, such as high winds, frost, ice storms, and the physical tension placed on the cable. The type of installation depends on the complexity of the installation, and the cost of burying the cable versus stringing it on existing telephone or power lines.

If the fiberoptic cable is installed entirely within a building, additional factors must be considered when planning the physical installation of the network installation. Most indoor cable installations are placed in cable trays or conduits. This rule does not apply to fiberoptic cable, since it is immune from EMI and electrical interference, allowing the placement of fiberoptic cable in the same ducts as high-voltage cables without the special insulation required by copper cables. The one area where fiberoptic cable is not recommended (or allowed in some states) is in the air-conditioning ducts. If there should be a fire, the outer jackets of the cables could burn and produce toxic fumes. For this reason it is best to route fiberoptic cable (or any other type of cable) outside of air-conditioning ducts. The advantages of fiberoptic cable over twisted-pair cable are as follows:

Bandwidth

The applications being used by today's power users are a driving force for increased bandwidth in the network medium. The greater the bandwidth of the medium, the greater the potential to send more and more data at faster speeds along the network. The frequency of light is several orders of magnitude above that of radio waves, and the invention of the laser and its ability to use light as a carrier opened up the possibility to use fiberoptic cable as a high-bandwidth network medium. The upper limit of fiberoptic cable is about 1THz, which is not close to being exploited by Fast Ethernet or even Gigabit Ethernet. Installing fiber for major cable segments on a Fast Ethernet LAN allows upgrading to faster technologies without pulling new cable.

Low Signal Power Loss

While cable bandwidth is a good indication of the rate at which information can be sent, the term **loss** indicates how far the information can be sent along the cable medium. As a signal travels along a transmission path, the signal loses strength (known as **signal attenuation**). With copper-based cable the signal attenuation increases with the transmission frequency. In optical-fiber cable the signal attenuation is flat, with signal loss being the same over a wide range of frequencies up to a certain upper band of frequencies. The loss at very high frequencies in the fiberoptic cable medium does not result from attenuation of the light, but a loss of information as it travels along the fiberoptic cable. The main advantage of using fiberoptic cable is that the speed of the light source is increased, so fewer repeaters are required.

Security

It has long been known that by using a sensitive antenna, EMI from copper-based media can easily be detected and decoded. This cannot happen with fiberoptic cable, since it does not radiate EMI, which makes it a requirement for such institutions as the military and Government as well as numerous businesses determined to keep company secrets and data out of the hands of competitors. Fiberoptic cable is a highly secure transmission medium, and it is extremely difficult to tap a fiber cable without being detected.

Safety and Size

Fiberoptic cable is much smaller in diameter than copper-based cables. It is also extremely flexible and easy to handle and install. Fiberoptic cable is also very light compared to copper-based cable, an important factor in some areas of application. This makes fiberoptic cable an attractive choice for applications where space and size are a premium, such as in aircraft, ships, submarines, computer rooms, and underground conduits. Fiberoptic cable is dielectric and therefore does not carry or conduct electricity. It is not a fire hazard, does not present a spark, does not attract lightning, and therefore cannot cause fires or explosions, which can happen with copper-based cable. These features allow fiberoptic cable to be used in areas and applications where copper-based cable cannot be used or is prohibited.

Electromagnetic Immunity

Unlike copper-based cables, such as UTP or STP, fiberoptic cables do not radiate or pick up electromagnetic radiation. Cables are the main source of EMI emission, and they also behave as well-defined antennas, picking up EMI from other external sources and carrying it into the equipment where it can cause a whole range of problems, from the annoying to serious disruption or expensive damage or destruction. Since fiberoptic cables do not radiate or receive electromagnetic interference, they are the ideal media for networks where EMI is a concern. Fiberoptic cable in a networked application is used in noisy environments with heavy motorized or industrial equipment, and may also be used in proximity to high-voltage lines where copper-based cable cannot be run.

MDI Connector

The medium-dependent interface for a 100Base-FX link may be one of three types of fiberoptic connectors. The popular media interface connector (MIC) is used on FDDI networks. These connectors are keyed as A, B, M, and S to ensure that the FDDI cabling is installed correctly. The key name denotes whether they connect to a node or to particular ports on the FDDI concentrator.

If an FDDI MIC is used as a 100Base-FX MDI, the IEEE specification states that it must be keyed as an M type connector. The FDDI MIC is pushed into the receptacle and forms the connection automatically. The ST (straight twist) connector is the same as the one used on a 10Base-FL link, and it features a spring-loaded bayonet-type connector that is keyed similarly to an oscilloscope connector. A connection is formed by lining up the connector and pushing against the spring mechanism until the connector is pushed onto the receptacle, then twisting the outer casing to lock the connector in place.

The duplex SC (straight connector) is the third type of fiberoptic connector, and is the one officially recommended by the IEEE committee for use with 100Base-FX Fast Ethernet. Pushing the SC into the receptacle automatically forms the connection.

Fiberoptic Cable Medium

The 100Base-FX standard is designed to support fiber segments up to 412m in length. The standard specifies two strands of multimode fiber, one for transmit data and one for receive data, which can run over 2Km when the workstation's NIC is operating at full-duplex mode. The fiberoptic cable can be divided into two categories: multimode and single mode.

Multimode Fiber

This type of fiberoptic cable uses a 62.5 micron fiber core and a 125 micron outer cladding, and is typically specified as 62.5/125 micron multimode fiberoptic cable. Multimode fiber uses an LED-based transceiver to launch a light signal with a wavelength of 820nm into the fiber, while single-mode fiber uses a laser-based transceiver to launch the light signals into the fiber cable. The maximum distance supported by Fast Ethernet using multimode fiber is 2Km when it is connected between two switch ports configured in full-duplex mode.

Single-Mode Fiber

Single-mode fiber has a smaller core diameter than multimode fiber, and propagates only one mode (wavelength) efficiently over longer distances. The point at which a single-mode fiber propagates only one mode depends on the wavelength of the light signal, and for single-mode fiber this is when the wavelength approaches the core diameter or 1,300nm, which is known as the zero-dispersion wavelength. There is no modal dispersion or loss of signal power with single-mode fiber, and this allows the single-mode fiber to carry light signals over greater distances than multimode fiber.

100Base-FX Crossover Wiring

The crossover of the fiber cable in the link segment between the node and the repeater port is part of the physical connection of the fiber cable. There are no requirements to build crossover cables when connecting two nodes together, and there is no crossover connection inside 100Base-FX repeaters or switches. When installing a 100Base-FX NIC, the user may use an external crossover cable connector to run external loopback diagnostics. These connectors are commercially available for MIC, SC, and ST type connectors.

100Base-FX Cable Configuration Guidelines

Cable plant installation for LANs, and especially new cable plant installations for Fast Ethernet, should conform to the EIA/TIA-568 standard, which specifies the exact cable length between the wiring closet and the network node (see Table E.5). This length of cable is called the segment and is defined as the link segment in the Ethernet specification. A link segment is formally defined as a point-to-point medium that connects two and only two MDIs connected together. The 100Base-FX standard speci-

Table E.5 100Base-FX Cable Distance Rules

100Base-FX Fiber Cable—Network Diameter	
Physical Model	All Fiber
DTE to DTE	412m
One Class-I Repeater	272m
One Class-II Repeater	320m
Two Class-II Repeaters	228m

fies a maximum distance of 412m in length for a single fiber point-to-point link segment, which will be less when either a Class-I or Class-II repeater is used between two DTEs. If a single Class-I repeater is used to link fiber segments, the maximum distance between two DTEs linked with all fiber segments is limited to 272m. If a single Class-II repeater is used to link fiber segments, the maximum distance between two DTEs is 320m. If two Class-II repeaters are used to link fiber segments, the maximum distance between two DTEs is 228m. Half-duplex 100Base-FX networks support a maximum lobe length of 400m, while a full-duplex link supports a length of 2Km. The network diameter for 100Base-FX networks depends on the combination of half- and full-duplex segments in the collision domain, as well as the combination of fiber cable and UTP segments serviced by the same 100Base-T/FX hub. There is no practical limit on the network diameter using all full-duplex link segments.

100Base-T4 Media

100Base-T4 is the only completely new PHY standard within the 100Base-T standard, since 100Base-TX and 100Base-FX were developed using the ANSI FDDI standards. The 100Base-T4 standard was developed to facilitate those users who had Category-3 or -4 UTP cable already installed. The 100Base-T4 specification encourages that Category-5 patch cables, jumper cables, and equipment cables be used where possible. This helps to ensure better signal quality when the inside wall wiring is Category-3 or -4 UTP cable.

MDI Connector

The medium-dependent interface for a 100Base-T4 link is based on Category-3, -4, or -5 unshielded twisted-pair cable. The 100Base-T4 standard uses four pairs of wires, which means all eight pins of a standard eight-pin RJ45-style connector are used. The RJ45 connector used for 10Base-T may also be used for 100Base-T4. One of the four pairs is used for transmit data, one pair is used for receive data, and two pairs are used as bidirectional data pairs. Three of the four pairs are used to transmit data at one time, while the fourth pair is used for collision detection. Each pair is polarized with one wire of each pair carrying the positive (+) signal and the other wire of the pair carrying the negative (−) signal. Since all four pairs are used and there are no dedicated transmit and receive pairs, then full-duplex operation is not possible with 100Base-T4. While every effort should be made to use the correct color-coded wire pairs for the MDI pin assignments, color-code substitution, if it is consistent on both ends of the cable, has no electrical impact on the link segment performance. However, never split wire pairs apart (see Table E.6).

100Base-T4 Crossover Wiring

When two stations are connected together over a segment, the transmit pair from one MDI connector is wired to the receive pair of the MDI on the second station. For stand-alone applications where two stations are connected together, an external crossover cable must be provided by wiring the transmit pins on the eight-pin RJ45 connector at one end of the cable to the receive pins on the eight-pin RJ45 connector at the other end of the crossover cable. In practice where multiple stations are connected to a repeater or switch ports, the crossover wiring is done inside the ports of the repeater or switch (see Figure 3.13).

This allows a straight-through cable to be used between each station and the repeater or switch port. This eliminates any ambiguity of whether the cables in the segment or patch panel are crossed over. The 100Base-T4 standard recommends this method, and specifies that each port of the hub that is internally crossed over should be clearly marked with an X (see Table E.7).

100Base-T4 Cable Configuration Guidelines

The 100Base-T4 specification allows a maximum link segment of up to 100m. The EIA/TIA-568 cabling standard recommends a maximum of 90m between the wall plate and the punch-down block in the wiring

Table E.6   100Base-T4 UTP MDI Pin Assignments

Pin Number	Signal Name	Cable Code
1	TX_D1 +	White/Orange
2	TX_D1 –	Orange/White
3	RX_D2 +	White/Green
4	BI_D3 +	Blue/White
5	BI_D3 –	White/Blue
6	RX_D2 –	Green/White
7	BI_D4 +_	White/Brown
8	BI_D4 –	Brown/White

Table E.7 100Base-T4 Crossover Pin Definition

Pin Number	Signal Name	Pin Number	Signal Name
1	TX_D1 +	1	RX_D2 +
2	TX_D1 –	2	RX_D2 –
3	RX_D2 +	3	TX_D1 +
4	RX_D2 –	4	TX_D1 –
5	BI_D3 +	5	BI_D4 +
6	BI_D3 –	6	BI_D4 –
7	BI_D4 +	7	BI_D3 +
8	BI_D4 –	8	BI_D3 –

closet. This leaves 5m to connect the end station to the wall plate, and 5m to connect the repeater or switch port to the punch-down block. The 100Base-T4 specification allows a segment of up to 100m in length for a point-to-point link segment between two DTEs or a DTE and a switch port. If a single Class I or Class II repeater is used, two 100m link segments may be used between two DTEs for a maximum distance of 200m. Two Class-II repeaters may be connected together in a single collision domain, with a maximum of 5m between them. This provides a maximum collision domain of 200m using a Class-I repeater, or 205m using two Class-II repeaters (see Table E.8).

Clause 23 of the IEEE 802.3u standard defines the 100Base-T4 Physical Coding Sublayer (PCS), the 100Base-T4 Physical Medium Attachment (PMA) sublayer, and the 100Base-T4 Medium Dependent Interface (MDI). In combination the PCS and the PMA layers comprise the 100Base-T4 Physical Layer (PHY).

PCS

The 100Base-T4 PCS couples the Media Independent Interface (MII) to the PMA sublayer. The PCS accepts data nibbles from the MII, encodes

Table E.8 100Base-T4 Cable Distance Rules

Physical Model	Copper
DTE to DTE	100m
One Class-I Repeater	200m
One Class-II Repeater	200m
Two Class-II Repeaters	205m

these nibbles using an 8B6T coding scheme, and passes the resulting ternary symbols to the PMA. In the receive direction, the PMA sends received ternary symbols to the PCS, where they are decoded into octets. These octets are then passed one nibble at a time up to the MII.

8B6T Coding Scheme

Effectively the 8B6T coding algorithm maps each eight-bit data octet into a six-bit ternary symbol called a 6T code group, hence the term 8B6T. The 6T code groups are fanned out to the three transmission pairs, with the effective data rate carried on each pair being one-third the 100Mbps data rate or 33.33 Mbps. The ternary symbol transmission rate on each pair is 6/8 times 33.3 Mbps, or exactly 25MHz, which is the same rate as the MII clock, thereby eliminating the requirement for a PLL in the 100Base-T4 PHY. The ternary symbols transmitted on each pair can have three levels, unlike binary signals, which have two levels.

8B6T Coding Scheme

> Using 8B6T, each octet of data assembled by the PCS is converted into six ternary (three levels) symbols, according to the 8B6T coding table. The three signal levels used are +V, 0, and –V. With six ternary symbols, 729 (3^6) possible groups or code words are available to represent the 256 (2^8) groups required to represent the complete set of eight-bit octet combinations. The code words used are selected to best achieve DC balance and ensure all code words have at least two signal transitions within each. This allows the receiver to maintain clock synchronization with the transmitter, and allows the use of inexpensive transformer coupling in the MDI interface, since no DC restoration is required.

PMA Sublayer

The PMA sublayer provides a link between the PCS and the MDI interface. It couples messages from the PMA service interface onto the twisted-pair physical medium, and it provides communication at 100Mbps over four pairs of twisted-pair wiring up to 100m in length. The PMA incorporates the ternary transmit and receive functions that generate the physical signaling of the ternary symbols from the PCS sublayer. The PMA transmit function consists of three independent ternary data transmitters. Each transmitter output driver has a ternary output, meaning that the output waveform can assume any one of three values, corresponding to the transmission of defined ternary symbols called CS0, CS1, or CS-1. The PMA transmit function drives data on pairs 1, 3, and 4. The PMA receive function comprises three independent ternary data receivers that are responsible for acquiring the clock in the received data stream, detecting the Start of Stream Delimiter (SSD) on each channel, acting as data equalizers, and providing data to the PCS. The PMA receiver and equalizer blocks receive data on pairs 2, 3, and 4. The PMA sublayer also contains functions for PMA carrier sense and link integrity.

100Base-T4 Data Coding

100Base-T4 encodes the data before it is transmitted onto the cable medium. The primary reasons for coding the data are to lower the symbol transmission rate in order to pass EMI regulation standards. Coding also generates a signaling rate on each media pair equal to the MII clock rate of 25MHz, thereby eliminating the requirement for a Phase Locked Loop (PLL) in the receive path of the PHY.

The 100Base-T4 transmission algorithm uses three pairs for transmission, leaving the fourth pair open for collision detection. This method reduces the 100Base-T4 signaling rate to 33.3 Mbps for each of the three pairs. This translates to a clock rate of 33MHz, which is above the 30MHz set for UTP cabling. To overcome this, 100Base-T4 uses a three-level ternary code called 8B6T (8 Binary, 6 Ternary), in place of traditional two-level binary encoding. All collision detection functions are accomplished using the unidirectional pairs TX_D1 and RX_D2. This leaves three pairs in each direction free for data transmission using the 8B6T coding algorithm (see Tables E.9 and E.10).

Table E.9 100Base-T4 MDI Signals Transmitted by the PHY

Signal	Allowed Pair	Description
CS1	TX_D1 B1_D3	A waveform that conveys ternary symbol 1. Nominal voltage level +3.5V
CS1	TX_D1 B1_D3 B1_D4	A waveform that conveys ternary symbol 1. Nominal voltage level +3.5V.
CS0	TX_D1 B1_D3 B1_D4	A waveform that conveys ternary symbol 0. Nominal voltage level 0V.
CS-1	TX_D1 B1_D3 B1_D4	A waveform that conveys ternary symbol −1. Nominal voltage level −3.5V.
TP-IDL-100	TX_D1	Idle signal, indicates transmitter is currently operating at 100Mbps.

Table E.10 100Base-T4 MDI Signals Received by the PHY

Signal	Allowed Pair	Description
CS1	RX_D2 B1_D3 B1_D4	A waveform that conveys ternary symbol 1. Nominal voltage level +3.5V.
CS0	RX_D2 B1_D3 B1_D4	A waveform that conveys ternary symbol 0. Nominal voltage level 0V.
CS-1	RX_D2 B1_D3 B1_D4	A waveform that conveys ternary symbol −1. Nominal voltage level −3.5V.
TP-IDL-100	RX_D2	Idle signal, indicates transmitter is currently operating at 100Mbps.

APPENDIX F

EIA/TIA Twisted-Pair Cable Specifications

The Electronic Industries Association/Telecommunications Industries Association (EIA/TIA) is a U.S. standards body that has developed a series of standards for communications and telecommunications systems. The EIA/TIA specifies LAN cables in terms of *categories*, according to the cable specifications, and in 1991 the EIA/TIA 568 standard for Commercial Building Telecommunications wiring was published. The purposes of the standard are as follows:

- Form a generic telecommunications standard that will support a multivendor environment
- Enable the planning and installation of a structured wiring system for commercial buildings
- Establish performance and technical guidelines for various cabling configurations

It is an open standard that allows multiple cable vendors to develop and produce cable products that meet specific categories of the EIA/TIA 568 standard. This standard also describes both the performance specifications of the cable, and the components of a structured wiring scheme for unshielded twisted-pair cable. These components include horizontal (single-floor) and backbone cable plant installations, and the specifications of the type of cable to use in each case. In summary, the EIA/TIA standard:

- Specifies minimum requirements for telecommunications cabling within the office area
- Recommends a standard cabling topology with cable distances specified
- Specifies media parameters, such as attenuation and loss factors, which determine performance
- Defines the MDI connector and pin assignments to ensure interoperability
- States that a structured cabling topology should have a life greater than 10 years, with 25 years desired

EIA/TIA Standard Choices

The EIA/TIA 568 standard lists a number of cabling choices that may be used in a building wiring plant. It specifies that two cables be run to each wall outlet: one for voice, and one for data. One of the two cables must be four-pair UTP for voice; the other cable is used for data and may be either UTP or coaxial. If fiber cable is also run to the wall outlet, it cannot displace the UTP data cable. Currently there are three cable choices for Fast Ethernet, with several choices of cable categories within the unshielded twisted-pair and fiberoptic groupings. However, the EIA/TIA 568 specification covers only unshielded twisted-pair wiring and installation, and this standard was chosen by the IEEE as the basis for the 802.3u Fast Ethernet standard.

Category 1

This category of cable is not covered by the EIA/TIA 568 standard. This cable is typically untwisted 22 AWG (American Wire Gauge) or 24 AWG wire with a broad range of impedance and attenuation values. It is typically used for voice and low-speed data transmission, and is not recommended for use with signaling speeds over 1Mbps.

Category 2

This type of cable is similar to Category 1, and derived from the IBM Type-3 specification, and uses 22 AWG or 24 AWG solid wire in twisted pairs. It is tested to a maximum bandwidth of 1MHz, but is not tested for near-end crosstalk.

Category 3

This type of cable uses 24 AWG solid wire in twisted pairs and is tested for performance, attenuation, and near-end crosstalk through a maximum bandwidth of 16MHz. It has a typical impedance of 100 ohms, and is the minimum recommended UTP cable for 10Base-T Ethernet. Category-3 cable is also known as voice-grade cable.

Category 4

This type of cable uses 22 AWG or 24 AWG solid wire in twisted pairs and is tested for performance, attenuation, and near-end crosstalk through a maximum bandwidth of 20MHz. It has a typical impedance of 100 ohms and meets the specification for 10Base-T Ethernet and 100Base-T4 Fast Ethernet. It is not recommended for new installations, and generally has been displaced by Category-5 UTP cable in all new installations.

Category 5

This type of cable uses 22 AWG or 24 AWG solid wire in twisted pairs and is tested for performance, attenuation, and near-end cross-talk through a maximum bandwidth of 100MHz. It has a typical impedance of 100 ohms, and can carry data signaling rates under specified conditions of 100Mbps. Category-5 UTP cable, also known as data-grade cable, is the recommended choice for all new cable plant installations, and is the required minimum UTP cable for 100Base-TX Fast Ethernet. It is the highest-quality UTP cable available today and is also the predominant cable used in new installations. The quality and widespread use of Category-5 UTP cable have effectively made Category-4 UTP cable installation obsolete (see Figure F.1).

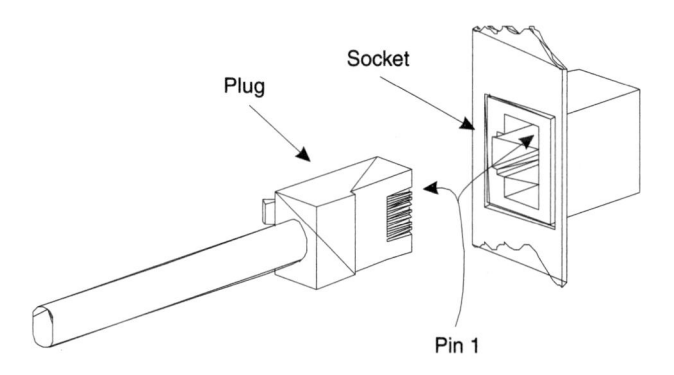

Figure F.1
RJ45 pin out.

Other Fast Ethernet Cabling

As an alternative to the EIA/TIA categories, the following sections focus on two other types of cabling.

IBM Type-1 STP Cable

Type-1 shielded twisted-pair cable has two shielded twisted-pair cables of type-22 AWG. It is the most common and best known of the IBM cable specifications. The pairs have an impedance of 150 ohms, with each shielded twisted pair being encased inside an external aluminum-foil or woven-copper shield that helps to reduce electrical noise interference. Type-1 cable combines the attributes of coaxial cable and twisted-pair cable, which explains the higher cost and difficulty in working with STP cable. IBM specifies two types of connectors for their STP cable: a Type-1 data connector and a DB9 connector for NICs (see Figure F.2). For this reason the IEEE 802.3u committee included support for IBM Type-1 wiring in the 100Base-TX media specification. The Type-1 data connector is not part of the IEEE specification, but the DB9 connector may be used with Type-1 STP cable.

Fiberoptic Cable

The fiber cable specified for 100Base-FX uses two strands of multimode (62.5/125 μm) or single-mode fiber cabling, although the exact cabling distance for single-mode fiber has not been specified. When multimode fiber is used, the recommended cable distance between a node and a DTE is 412 meters, but this can be extended to up to 2Km in full-duplex mode when running between two DTEs, such as two switch ports or a switch port and a router port. The 100Base-FX standard recommends three different styles of connectors for use with the fiber

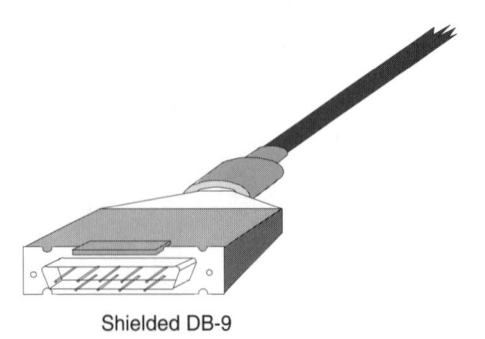

Figure F.2
DB9 connector.

Shielded DB-9

cable. The MIC (media interface connector) used in FDDI networks is a spade-type device and is categorized by port type, depending on where it is used in the network. These are very expensive and are not generally recommended for use in cost-conscious Fast Ethernet applications. The second type of connector is the ST or straight-twist connector (see Figure F.3). The ST connector has been used with the 10Base-F, and also as a low-cost connector for FDDI applications. It is a spring-loaded, bayonet-type connector keyed similarly to an oscilloscope probe that is secured in place by twisting the outer shielded cover over a retaining nut located in the mating connector on the NIC or the cross-connection device. The third and recommended connector is the SC or straight-connect type. This is a lower-cost connector than the other two, and it supports easy insertion and removal of the fiber cable to the NIC or cross-connect device. Fiber cable is recommended for backbone applications, building risers, or campus-type connectivity, and in areas where the use of STP or UTP cable is not suitable (see Figures F.3 and F.4).

Installation and Maintenance

All cable plant installations should be installed under the guidelines of the EIA/TIA 568 Commercial Building Telecommunications Wiring Standard, as well as local building, fire, and safety codes. Once the network is installed and commissioned, regular maintenance of the network must be implemented in order to provide a cost-effective, reliable system for the installed users. A properly installed UTP cable plant will have all the proper color codes matched between the wall outlet termination unit and the incoming cable pair from the office PC. In existing site installations, examine the termination behind each wall plate to

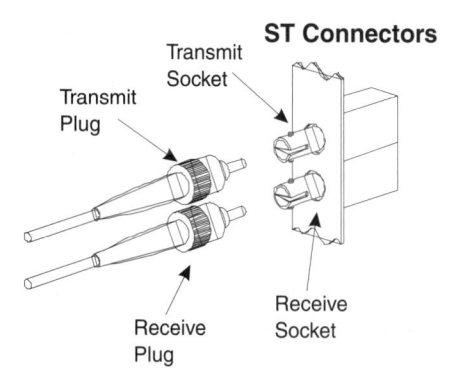

Figure F.3
ST connectors.

Figure F.4
SC connectors.

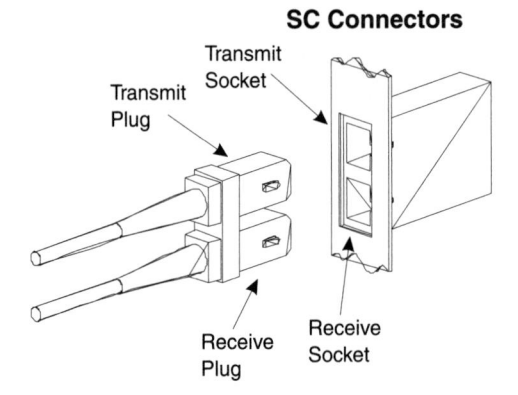

check for excess wear, and reterminate cables where necessary with new hardware.

Cables coming into the wiring closet or equipment rooms should be neatly bundled using tie wraps, and should not be pulled too tightly. Check for loose connections at the punch-down blocks, and reterminate or replace the punch-down blocks where necessary. Bad connections behind the wall plate or in the equipment room can cause the link segment to drop packets or to initiate jabber packets on the network. UTP cables should have less than one-half inch of untwist in the cable at the point of termination, in order to meet the near-end cross-talk (**NEXT**) specifications.

Near-End Cross-Talk is the term used when signals from one twisted pair couple to an adjacent twisted pair. This has the undesirable effect of causing data corruption in both cable pairs. The term *near-end* indicates that the coupling happens at the end where transmission originates. Several components and installation factors contribute to NEXT:

- UTP cable itself: Check to see if it is low quality or routed in an electrically noisy environment.
- RJ45 connectors: Specify Cat-5 connector where possible.
- Patch panels: Check the quality of the patch cable and the patch connectors.
- Punch-down blocks: Check the quality of the punch-down block and the robustness of the wire termination.
- Wall plates: Check the termination behind the plate and the quality of the RJ45 connector.
- Crossed pairs in the wiring closet, or at the wall plate.
- Excessive amount of untwist in the cable or patch cable pairs at the RJ45 connectors.

- Cables damaged due to sharp bends and twists.
- Cables damaged by being pulled too tightly.

EIA/TIA Wiring Guidelines

The EIA/TIA-568 cabling standard specifies the exact cable length of the horizontal, vertical, and campus cable. The horizontal cable length between the end node and the wiring closet is limited to 100m. It recommends a maximum of 90m between the wall plate and the punch-down block in the wiring closet. This leaves 5m to connect the end station to the wall plate, and 5m to connect the repeater or switch port to the punch-down block. Following are the guidelines for the EIA/TIA link segment lengths:

Source	Destination	Maximum Length	Description
Network node	Wall plate	W1*	Node equipment cord
Wall plate	Punch-down block	90m	Horizontal wiring
Cross-connect	Cross-connect	W2*	Cross-connect cable
Cross-connect	Network hub	W3*	Equipment cord
Total segment length		100m	Segment or link

*W1 + W2 + W3 must be less than or equal to 10 meters. This combined length of all cabling from the wiring-closet equipment port to the end-station port must not exceed 100 meters. This rule of thumb requires that the wall cable from the work area wall plate to the punch-down block should not exceed 90 meters.

The EIA/TIA recommends a maximum distance of 2Km between wiring closets for fiberoptic cable, and 800m for UTP backbone cable. These recommended numbers by the EIA/TIA are independent of technology, and are general guidelines for structured cable-plant design. In all cases where there are conflicts with the IEEE standard for Fast Ethernet, the IEEE standards will supersede those of the EIA/TIA wiring standard. Thus, for Fast Ethernet, the maximum distance between wiring closets using fiberoptic cable is 2Km when the link segment is configured in full-duplex mode. The 2Km link segment must be between two switches, or a switch port and a DTE port.

Cable Plant Testing

A number of sophisticated wire and cable testers are available on the market today. These are used to analyze the cable plant for connectivity, robustness of the cables, and other factors, such as attenuation and crossed or split pairs. For 100Base-TX networks, Category-5 cable is required throughout the cable plant in order to provide high-speed, reliable, and optimized performance on the network. The EIA/TIA standard also recommends using Category-5 components and cabling wherever possible on 100Base-T4 installations. As part of the cable plant design and installation, a requirement should be in place to certify the cable plant before the contract is signed and the contractor leaves the premises. The reliability, dependability, and performance of the network depend greatly on the quality of the material and installation of the cable plant itself.

After the cable plant has been tested and certified to be in compliance with the design and the EIA/TIA specifications, a baseline reference model should be recorded. This model can then be used as a reference for future cable plant inspections, to determine if there is degradation in performance or reliability due to a bad cable termination in the work area or wiring closet.

Other factors that may degrade the cable plant reliability are cables being stressed or damaged due to new infrastructure equipment changes and upgrades, damaged connectors, oxidation of punch-down block terminators, or loose cables behind the wall plate or in the wiring closet.

GLOSSARY

100 Mbps Ethernet   100Base-T Fast Ethernet (IEEE 802.3u standard) or 100VG-AnyLAN (IEEE 802.12 standard).

100Base-FX   The Fast Ethernet PHY standard for 100Mbps CSMA/CD operation over single-mode fiberoptic cable. Note that 100Base-FX will also run over multimode fiber but is still limited to 2,000 meters.

100Base-T   A generic term for the three Fast Ethernet PHY standards, 100Base-TX, 100Base-T4, and 100Base-TX.

100Base-T4   The Fast Ethernet PHY standard for 100Mbps CSMA/CD operation over Category-5 cable. It uses four pairs of Category-3, -4, or -5 UTP cable or STP, and supports the CSMA/CD access method.

100Base-TX   The Fast Ethernet PHY standard for 100Mbps CSMA/CD operation over Category-5 cable. It uses two pairs of Category-5 UTP or STP, and supports the CSMA/CD access method.

100Base-X   A generic term for the two Fast Ethernet PHYs standards, 100Base-TX and 100Base-FX. These two PHYs are almost identical and are derived from the FDDI PHY, with which they share line-level signaling techniques and formats. Note that 100Base-T4 is completely different from 100Base-X in its use of cable pairs, signaling, and cable requirements, so it is usually considered separately.

10Base-T   10Mbps Ethernet that runs over Cat-3, -4, and -5 cable using repeaters. This is the most popular form of Ethernet.

80/20 Rule   One of the most common networking rules of thumb. Segmenting an Ethernet system with bridges is effective when there is more, usually much more, local-segment traffic than off-segment traffic. The 80/20 rule says a network system should be designed and built so that at least 80 percent of the traffic is local-segment traffic. Of course this leaves 20 percent as off-segment traffic. When the rule is met, bridges are very effective. Meeting the rule is usually accomplished simply by putting the servers that users use most on the same segment as the users.

802.3   IEEE standard specification for 10Base-T Ethernet.

802.3u IEEE standard specification for 100Base-T Ethernet. 802.3u covers 100Base-TX, 100Base-T4, and 100Base-FX topologies.

Abstract Syntax Notation 1 Abbreviated ASN.1. A formal syntax used to describe data objects and their hierarchy. See *Management Information Base*.

Adaptive Switching The ability of some switches to operate in both cut-through mode and store-and-forward mode.

Address Learning The process used by a bridge or switch to learn which network interfaces are connected to each port of the device. During this process, a switch or bridge builds its MAC address table. The process is often called *learning* for short.

Adds, Moves, and Changes The process of adding devices, moving devices, and changing network configurations; it is the activity that consumes the bulk of a network manager's time.

Age Limit When a bridge learns an address, it records two things: the address itself and the inbound port number. It also sets the age of the MAC address to zero. Once per second, the age of the addresses in the table is incremented. If the age value gets to a certain value, called the age limit, the entry for that MAC address will be erased. This process is called aging. A MAC address' age field is reset to zero any time the bridge sees a frame with that source address. This process keeps the addresses for active nodes in the table while automatically discarding address that are no longer in use. All bridges have a maximum size for their MAC address table. If the address table fills up, then no new address can be added to it. The aging process ensures that if a node is disconnected from its segment, its entry is removed from the table. This also ensures that bridges will properly relearn the addresses of nodes when they are moved from one segment to another. The 802.1d specification for bridges recommends the default aging time of 300 seconds (5 minutes).

Agent The program that runs in a device that collects statistics for transfer to an NMS, and receives commands from an NMS. An agent communicates to an NMS using the SNMP protocol.

Aggregate Forwarding Rate The maximum number of frames a bridge can forward for all ports. For example, a four-port Ethernet bridge may have a maximum forwarding rate of 14,800 frames per second (the highest it can get), but have an aggregate forwarding rate of only 18,000 frames per second. This means that it cannot handle full packet rates on all its ports, but just on two.

Aging The process of monitoring a MAC address age in a bridge or switch. See *Age Limit* for more information.

Alias Prevention A type of data link-level security that prevents criminals from breaching the security of a network by changing the MAC address that his node uses to access the LAN.

ANSI The American National Standards Institute. The main group representing the U.S. in the ISO (International Standards Organization).

API Application Programming Interface. A well-defined set of function calls that a program uses to access the functions and features of another subsystem. For example, most applications, such as Web browsers and e-mail programs communicate over a LAN using an API called WinSock.

Application Level Protocols Client/server and peer-to-peer applications communicate using application-level protocols. Hundreds, if not thousands, of application protocols are in use today. Some, such as HTTP and FTP, are well documented and understood; many others are proprietary and used only by the software from a single vendor. The key element about these application-specific protocols is that they are designed for a narrow purpose. They have detailed, specialized, and often private rules and semantics. Common examples of client software are Web browsers such as Netscape Navigator, e-mail programs such as Microsoft Mail, and client programs for online services such as CompuServe and America Online. These clients have corresponding server software, such as Netscape Enterprise Server, Microsoft Back Office, and the huge programs that run on CompuServe and America Online's giant computers. These applications each support one or more application-specific protocols. Application-level protocols are usually transported over network-level protocols.

Application-Specific Integrated Circuit (ASIC) A chip that is specifically designed for a particular application. All modern switches are based on ASICs that are designed for switching. ASICs allow very complex, fast, and powerful electronic designs to be implemented as low-cost, high-density chips. Ever wonder why electronics (especially computers) get more powerful and less expensive at the same time? Remember when a 300 baud modem cost $1,200? ASICs are a big part of the reason for the ever increasing capability at lower and lower costs. ASICs are designed by a hardware engineer a lot like software is written by a software engineer. All of the logic design is done on a computer using a high-level language. In the past, custom electronic chips were designed at the transistor level, which was a detailed, complex, and time-consuming process. To test one of these designs, the device actually had to be built. This was often very expensive. If any problems were found (and they usually were), the process had to start all over again. The advent of ASICs changed all of that. ASICs are designed not at the transistor level but at the logic level, using special hardware design languages. ASIC designs can also be thoroughly tested by simulation on a computer before a single physical device is created.

ASIC See *Application Specific Integrated Circuit*.

ASN.1 See *Abstract Syntax Notation 1*.

Asymmetric Load Describes the condition when the offered load to a device is not distributed evenly across all its ports. This is the kind of load usually placed on bridges, switches, and routers. These devices will usually handle normal asymmetric loads well. Larger asymmetric loads that persist over a long period of time will cause congestion.

Attenuation The amount of signal energy lost while traveling down a cable. For fiberoptic cable this is the amount of optical power lost as the light signal travels from the transmitter to the receiver. This loss is expressed in decibels (dB).

Automatic Node Discovery   A process of monitoring a LAN in order to automatically discover all the nodes connected to it, often called autodiscovery.

Back-Off Time   The random period of time that a MAC waits before retransmitting a frame corrupted by a collision. A MAC will retransmit 16 times before giving up.

Backplane Segment   A network segment provided by the backplane of a chassis-based device. One or more plug-in repeater, bridge, switch, or router cards can plug into a chassis and be connected to a backplane segment. Most chassis backplanes support four or more segments.

Backbone   A high-speed network used to interconnect lower-speed networks.

Back Pressure   A method used by a switch to control incoming traffic on ports when there is congestion in the switch. There are two ways to do this: by generating collisions with a 64-byte frame when incoming frames are received, or by sending a jabber (an endlessly long frame) as long as congestion is present in the switch.

Balanced Signals   In a balanced signal the signal traveling over one of the wires of the pair is the opposite of the signal traveling over the other wire. Balanced signals over twisted-pair wire are very immune to noise, can travel long distances, and are necessary to meet the 100-meter distance requirement for copper cable. Many unbalanced signals, like those used for RS232 serial ports, are useful at distances from only 50 to 100 feet.

Bandwidth   The amount of data that can be transmitted over a channel; measured in bits per second.

Baseline   A baseline is a collection of performance metrics that are measured when a networked system is working properly under normal loads, preferably right at its full utilization point. Once a baseline is gathered, future data can be compared to it in order to find network problems or determine when a network's configuration needs to change in order to maintain peak performance.

Baseband   The frequency occupied by a single signal in its original form.

Bit Time   The time it takes to transmit one bit of information: for Ethernet, 100μs; for Fast Ethernet, 10μs. (One μs, or microsecond is one millionth of a second.) The bit time is the reciprocal of the technology's baud rate, which is 10Mbps for Ethernet, and 100Mbps for Fast Ethernet.

BNC   British Naval Connector. Used for 10Base-2 (Cheapernet) Ethernet connections.

Boot ROM   A boot ROM is installed on a NIC and allows the host computer to boot itself over the network. This means that the host computer does not need a hard disk drive or even a floppy drive.

BPDU   See *Bridge Protocol Data Unit*.

Bridge   A device that operates at level 2 (data link layer) of the seven-layer OSI model, and is used to connect LAN networks or segments that use the same protocol.

Bridge Loop   In a bridge loop there is more than one *active* bridged path from a node on one segment to a node on another segment.

Bridge Protocol Data Unit (BPDU)   A message used by bridges and switches to communicate to each other. BPDUs are used to discover the network topology and to eliminate bridged loops.

Broadband   Systems that carry multiple frequencies in a channel, typically requiring more than 50Mbps channel capacity.

Broadcast   See *Broadcast Address*.

Broadcast Address   A special destination address placed in a frame. For 48-bit IEEE, which is used by all LAN technologies except ARCNet, the broadcast address is an address with all 48 bits set to a 1 value. Any node can transmit a broadcast frame on a LAN. All broadcast frames are copied from the LAN by the MACs on all network interfaces. In other words, broadcast frames are received and processed by *all* nodes on a LAN. Also see *Multicast Address* and *Individual or Group Address Flag*.

Broadcast Domain   The set of all nodes connected in a switched or bridged network, which will receive each other's broadcasts. A single collision domain or segment is a broadcast domain, but a broadcast domain can be made up of one or more segments.

Broadcast Frame   Any frame with the destination address set to the IEEE 48-bit broadcast address.

Broadcast Storm   When a bridge loop causes bridges to endlessly forward broadcast and/or multicast frames.

Brouter   A device that supports both bridging and routing.

Buffering   In buffering, information (in this context, usually frames) is stored in memory. Frames are usually buffered while waiting to be forwarded, transmitted, or processed in some way.

Byte   A group of eight bits. See *Octet*.

Cable Plant Wiring Topology   The physical way a cable plant is installed in a building or campus. The EIA/TIA Commercial Building Wiring Standard recommends a three-level cable-plant wiring topology. This is basically a three-level star wiring topology designed to cover all aspects of network configuration, such as Ring, Star, and Bus type networks.

Carrier Sense   When a node or a repeater detects that data is being received. For example, when a PHY detects receive data, it asserts the carrier sense signal to its attached MAC or repeater over the MII interface.

Carrier Sense Multiple Access with Collision Detection   Abbreviated CSMA/CD. These are the media access rules for both Fast Ethernet and Ethernet, and are defined in the IEEE 802.3 specification.

Category-3 Cable   Voice-grade UTP cable used for digital telephones and LANs.

Category-4 Cable   Data-grade UTP cable used for LANs.

Category-5 Cable   The top grade of UTP cable used for LANs.

Chipsets   A chipset is a single chip or set of two or three chips that implements a specific function. Many companies sell chipsets that implement an entire NIC in one or two chips. This allows even low-tech companies to build NICs.

Cladding   The material that surrounds the core of an optical fiber, causing the transmitted light beam to travel down the core.

Class-I Repeater   A Class-I repeater is one of the two types of repeaters defined by the 802.3u spec for use in a Fast Ethernet collision domain. The other type is a Class-II repeater. Only one Class-I repeater can be used in a Fast Ethernet collision domain. Class-I repeaters may not be uplinked to other repeaters, but this limitation is overcome by the use of stackable repeaters.

Class-II Repeater   One of the two types of repeaters defined by the 802.3u spec for use in a Fast Ethernet collision domain. The other type is a Class-I repeater. Only one or two Class-II repeaters can be used in a Fast Ethernet collision domain when using the transmission Model-1 topology rules. A Class-II repeater may be uplinked to another Class-II repeater, but not to a Class-I repeater.

Client/Server Networking   Client/server applications require two pieces of software: a client application and a server application. Client software makes requests for information or services, and server software satisfies these requests (an extremely broad definition but one that works very well). Clients and servers tend to be on different computers and communicate over a network using application-level protocols. Common examples of client software are Web browsers such as Netscape Navigator, e-mail programs such as Microsoft Mail, and client programs for online services such as CompuServe and America Online. These clients have corresponding server software, such as Netscape Enterprise Server, Microsoft Back Office, and the huge programs that run on CompuServe and America Online's giant computers. These applications each support one or more application-specific protocols, such as HTTP, FTP, POP, SMTP, and NNTP.

Collapsed Backbone   When a large enterprise-level chassis is used as the backbone. In other words, a backbone is collapsed into a single box.

Collision   When two or more network interfaces transmit a frame at the same time. A collision corrupts the colliding frames. The MAC in a network interface detects collisions and will resend any frames that are corrupted due to a collision.

Collision Domain   The set of nodes that share a LAN by using the CMSA/CD media access rules. A single Fast Ethernet or Ethernet LAN or segment.

Collision Frame   Any frame that results from a collision. Note that this isn't a widely used or accepted term, just one we made up, but we like it anyway. Most people just use the term runt frame in the same way. However, while all runt frames are the result of a collision, not all collisions result in a runt frame.

Collision Percentage   The ratio of the number of frames successfully transmitted to the number of collisions that have occurred over some period of time. This value is usually less than 100 percent but can be greater if the number of collisions that have occurred over a period of time is greater than the number of frames successfully transmitted.

Collision Window   The worst-case Path Delay Value on the collision domain. The collision window is the time between when a MAC transmits the first bit of a frame and when it can detect a collision with *any node* on the LAN. A Fast Ethernet segment's collision window depends on the segment's network diameter: the bigger the network diameter, the bigger the maximum propagation delay between any pair of nodes. The Fast Ethernet specification defines the maximum allowable collision window (called the slot time) for Fast Ethernet as 512 bit times. A configuration of Fast Ethernet components that has a collision window larger than the slot time is an invalid configuration and will not function properly. This rule can also be stated like this: The worst-case SPD on a Fast Ethernet must not be more than half the slot time. A synonym for collision window is round-trip delay time.

Concentrator   A term used to describe a wiring hub in an FDDI network. A concentrator connects to the FDDI backbone, and may be single-concentrator or dual attached. Concentrators support dual homing connectivity to an FDDI backbone by providing redundant paths.

Congestion   Congestion occurs in a switch or router when there are not enough resources inside the device to handle the load offered to the device. The result of congestion is that a device must discard or drop frames, which means that a frame that would normally be received and properly processed by the device isn't.

Contention   When two or more nodes transmit at the same time and a collision occurs, the nodes are said to be contending for the network. Contention is partially how the CSMA/CD media access rules arbitrate transmission rights to nodes on a LAN.

Copying (or Frame Copying)   Copying is similar to forwarding but is the specific case when a MAC on a node's network interface transfers a frame received from the LAN, and passes it to the node for processing.

CPU Utilization   The amount of CPU horsepower being used for a particular task. For example, a good measure of NIC performance is how much CPU utilization it has when at a maximum load (the lower the better).

Cross-Bar Matrix   A device that can provide multiple paths for connecting ports in a switch to each other.

Crossover Cable   Often called an X cable or a null repeater cable. This is the *opposite* of a straight-through cable. An X cable is wired so that the pairs in the cable are crossed. This allows two devices with MDI ports or MDI-X ports to be connected together. See *Straight-Through Cable*.

Cross-Connect   A device typically located within the wiring closet and used to terminate the horizontal and backbone cabling in a network. Cross-connect devices provide an easy cable management mechanism.

Crossover Cable Wiring   For 10Base-T Ethernet and 100Base-TX Fast Ethernet, dedicated pin positions on the data connector are allocated for the transmit and receive pairs for both the client and the hub. In the standard pin allocation the client has the transmit pairs allocated to pins 1 and 2 of the data connector, and the receive pairs allocated to pins 3 and 6 of the data connector. The pin connection at the hub is complementary to that of the client, with the receive pair connected to pins 1 and 2 of the data connector, and the transmit pair connected to pins 3 and 6 of the data connector. Inside the hub, the wires are crossed over so that the receive pair connects to the receive logic, and the transmit pair connects to the transmit logic. A wiring crossover link is required in every connection between a DTE and a DCE, with the hub, switch, or repeater being the preferred location for the crossover function. When two DTEs are connected together in a point-to-point configuration, a crossover cable is required to form the link. Similarly, whenever a connection is formed between two hub ports, an explicit external crossover cable must be used to form the link. It is important to clearly label the crossover cables, since they look the same as straight-through connected cables. Doing this avoids confusion and long periods of troubleshooting the network.

Cross-Talk   The undesired voice-band energy transferred from one medium to another, most commonly found in unshielded twisted-pair cable.

Cut-Through Switching   A cut-through switch begins to forward frames before they have been completely received by the switch. Also see *Runt-Free Cut-Through* and *Store-and-Forward Switching*.

DAS   Dual attached station. An FDDI station that has two connections to the FDDI dual counter-rotating rings.

Data Center   A central installation where most or all of an organization's servers are located. Other network resources are often located in the data center.

Data-Grade Cable   See *Category-4 Cable*.

Data Link-Level Security   This kind of security depends on processing frames at layer 2 of the OSI model, which consists mostly of processing a frame's destination address at the repeater or switch level. There are three types of data link-level security: eavesdropping prevention, identity enforcement, and alias prevention.

Data Packet   See *Datagram*.

Data Terminal Equipment (DTE)   In the context of Fast Ethernet a DTE device is a node with a network interface. Note that for copper cable, the RJ45 plug on a DTE device is usually wired in the MDI configuration.

Datagram   The lowest level of network protocol encapsulation. For Ethernet and Fast Ethernet, datagrams are encapsulated in frames.

DB15   A standardized 15-pin connector used in Ethernet AUI connections.

DB9   A standardized 9-pin connector used in Token Ring connections.

Desktop Switch   A switch that supports only one to four MAC addresses per port. This requires that single nodes or a small number of nodes be connected to each port.

Device Controller   The microprocessor (e.g., in a repeater) that operates a device. The device controller is often responsible for running a network management agent.

Directed Frame   See *Unicast Frame*.

Directed Packet   See *Directed Frame* and *Unicast Frame*.

Distribution Frame   A stand-alone rack used to hold patch panels, cross-connect panels, and other wiring-closet equipment. It may be fixed to the floor or placed in a specified location within the wiring closet.

DMA   Direct Memory Access. A memory access method that is independent of the host CPU. This feature is found in high-performance adapters, and allows direct memory transfer cycles between the adapter module and the host memory.

Drive Mapping or Sharing   A technique used by PC-based operating systems that support peer-to-peer networking. One person could make drive letter K: access the disk drive on someone else's computer. For example, if Bob's K: drive were connected to Karen's computer, when Bob saved a word processing file to his K: drive it would actually be written to the disk drive in Karen's computer. The important thing to note is that this occurs without any other computers being involved; Karen's and Bob's computers communicate directly with each other. Drive mapping can also occur in a client/server fashion between workstations and servers. For example, Bob might connect his drive M: to \\Bilbo\documents to access the document partition on the server Bilbo.

DTE   See *Data Terminal Equipment*.

Dual Connectivity   When a workstation or server is connected to two different and otherwise independent LANs not connected by a router or a bridge.

Eavesdropping Prevention   A type of data link-level security, often called *intrusion prevention and detection*, that prevents criminals from snooping the traffic on a network by connecting a device that operates in promiscuous mode. Snooping allows criminals to capture data from the LAN, such as passwords, files, e-mail, and other data.

EIA   Electronic Industries Association. A trade organization representing a large portion of the industry that focuses on developing hardware interface standards.

EISA   Extended Industry Standard Architecture.

Equipment Rack   An enclosed version of the distribution panel is used to secure network equipment within the wiring closet or in the workgroup area.

Ether Types   The values of the Length/Type field in an Ethernet frame. These values are tracked by Xerox. For more information see our Web site at www.wiley.com/FastEthernet.

Ethernet   Network topology defined by IEEE specification 802.3. Ethernet networks use the CSMA/CD media access protocol and transmit data at 10Mbps over UTP, COAX, and fiberoptic cable media.

Ethernet Collapse As the offered load starts to increase from 0, network utilization will rise correspondingly. At some point, the LAN will reach full utilization. If the offered load continues to increase, network utilization on the LAN will drop due to contention. If the load increases even further, the LAN will reach its saturation point and utilization will fall off sharply. This is called Ethernet collapse.

Fast Ethernet An extension of Ethernet running at 100Mbps over Category-3, -4, and -5 UTP, STP, and fiberoptic media.

FDDI Fiber Distributed Data Interface. A high-speed specification for fiberoptic networks, based on a timed Token Ring protocol, that operates at 100Mbps over a dual pair of fiberoptic cables. Primarily used in backbone applications, it also supports operation over Category-5 UTP cable.

Field Programmable Gate Array (FPGA) A device consisting of a large number of logic devices (gates) that can be connected together in an almost infinite number of ways by loading an FPGA program into the device. To test an ASCI design, it is converted into an FPGA program and loaded into an FPGA that is part of an actual device, such as a switch. It can then be tested more rigorously, proving the ASIC design. The drawback to FPGAs is that they are expensive—a large FPGA can cost $10,000 or more. Many ASIC designs can be bigger than a single FPGA, and an ASIC design that might fit into $30,000 worth of FPGAs can cost as little as $10 or $12 for the final ASIC chip.

Filtering Many devices, such as bridges, switches, or routers, filter—that is, receive a frame on one port and decide *not* to forward (transmit) it out of another port. The MAC on a network interface also filters frames that it receives. On a Fast Ethernet or Ethernet LAN, every network interface connected to the LAN receives all the frames transmitted on that LAN by all the other network interfaces. When the MAC receives a frame, it compares the frame's destination address with its MAC address. If they do not match, and the address is not a multicast or unicast address, then the frame is filtered. In other words, it is not copied from the LAN to the node for processing.

Firewall A firewall is a device that is connected to the internet on one port, and an organization's internal network on one or more other ports. The firewall can block many criminal attacks. Also see *Proxy Server.*

Flooding When a frame is forwarded to all the ports on a bridge or switch except the inbound port. Also see *Spraying.*

Forwarding In forwarding, a device (such as a bridge, a switch, or a router) receives a frame on one port and decides to transmit it out of another port (also see *Filtering*). The rules that decide whether a frame is filtered or forwarded are called *forwarding rules*. The forwarding rules for bridges are defined in the 802.1d specification. The rules for routers depend on the protocol being routed. For example, the IPX and IP protocols have different (though similar) rules. These rules are not defined by the IEEE: The IETF defines the rules for IP, and Novell and Xerox have defined the rules for IPX.

Forwarding Decision   The decision a switch or bridge makes about what to do with a received frame. Routers also make forwarding decisions but in a way very different from a switch or bridge.

Forwarding Latency for Bridges and Switches   From RFC 1242, "The time interval starting when the last bit of the input frame reaches the input port, and ending when the first bit of the output frame is seen on the output port. Variability of latency can be a problem."

Forwarding Latency for Repeaters   From RFC 1242, "The time interval starting when the end of the first bit of the input frame reaches the input port, and ending when the start of the first bit of the output frame is seen on the output port."

FPGA   See *Field Programmable Gate Array*.

Frame   The basic level of communication on any LAN. Each LAN technology defines a frame format that is used to transfer data between nodes. Fast Ethernet and Ethernet share the same frame format, as does 100VG AnyLAN; the frame formats for FDDI, Token Ring, and ARCNet are different.

Frame Cloning   When a bridge loop causes a bridge to duplicate unicast frames.

Frame Switch   See *Switch*.

Frame Type   The way the data portion of a frame is structured. There are basically four Ethernet frame types: 802.3, SNAP, Ethernet-II (or DIX), and Raw format.

Framing Error   Framing errors are detected when a packet is received that is not an integral number of octets in length. Frames are made up of octets (bytes); therefore, the number of bits in the frame must be evenly divisible by 8. If some bits are lost during the transmission of the frame, then the frame would be evenly divisible by 8. Note that the CRC will almost always catch framing errors, but the MAC both detects and counts framing errors separately.

Full Duplex   This is accomplished for Ethernet and Fast Ethernet using a switch to establish a point-to-point connection between LAN nodes that allows simultaneous sending and receiving of data packets. Full-duplex performance is twice that of half-duplex performance. For Ethernet, full-duplex performance is capable of 20Mbps data rates. A full-duplex 100Base-TX or 100Base-FX network is capable of 200Mbps throughput.

Full-Duplex Link   A link that is inherently full duplex. In other words, it supports simultaneous data flow in two directions.

Full-Duplex Mode   An operational mode between two Ethernet or Fast Ethernet nodes where collision detection is disabled, which means that both nodes can transmit data to each other simultaneously. This is possible only over 10Base-T, 100Base-TX, and 100Base-FX links, which are inherently full-duplex links.

Full Utilization   A network is operating in full utilization when both its offered load and network utilization are high. A good way to quantify this is as the point at which utilization no longer rises with increasing offered load.

Functional Address See *Multicast Address*.

Gateway The access point to a WAN link. See *WAN*.

Group Address See *Multicast Address*.

Half Duplex In half duplex, network traffic is moving in one direction at a time in between two DTEs, either sending or receiving, but not both directions at the same time.

Hierarchy A system of network components, usually software, that are arranged in an ordering from top to bottom. Lower-level, LAN technology-dependent parts are at the bottom, and higher-level, application-specific parts are at the top. The OSI reference model describes such a hierarchy.

Host Number The part of a network address that identifies the individual node on a LAN. See *Network Address*.

Hub A network device that connects nodes on a network segment.

Hyper Text Transport Protocol (HTTP) The protocol used by Web browsers to communicate with Web servers.

I/G Flag See *Individual or Group Address Flag*.

Identity Enforcement A type of data link-level security that prevents a criminal from breaching the security of a network by allowing only network interfaces with well-known MAC addresses access to the network.

IEEE The Institute of Electrical and Electronics Engineers, the world's largest technical professional society and a nonprofit organization. You can find out more about them by visiting their Web page at www.ieee.org.

IEEE Address A 48-bit value used to identify a single network interface, a set of interfaces, or all interfaces. These addresses consist of four fields, the individual or group address flag, the universal or local administration flag, the organizationally unique identifier and the organizationally unique addresses.

Incoming Port The port on a device on which a frame or packet is received.

Individual or Group Address Flag (I/G Flag) Bit 47 (the first bit) in a 48-bit IEEE address, used to indicate if the address is an individual or group address. Individual addresses are assigned to one, and only one, interface (or node) on a network. Addresses with the I/G bit set to zero are usually called MAC addresses or node addresses. These addresses are always unique to one, and only one, network interface on a LAN. When the I/G bit is set to one, the address is a group address. These are usually called multicast addresses, or sometimes functional addresses. A group address is one that can be assigned to one or more network interfaces on a LAN. Frames sent to a group address are received, or copied, by all the network interfaces on a LAN with that group address. Multicast addresses allow a frame to be sent to a subset of nodes on a LAN. If the I/G bit is a 1, then all the bits 46 through 0 are treated as the multicast address. If bits 46 through 0 are all 1s, then the address is the broadcast address.

Interim Cut-Through   Synonym for runt-free cut-through. Another synonym is modified cut-through.

Internet Protocol   A protocol for carrying datagrams in the TCP/IP protocol suite (see *TCP/IP*).

Interoperate   Two (or more) devices are said to interoperate when they work together properly in the context of a formal or informal specification, or accepted way of doing things. The goal of such specifications as the 802.3 Ethernet and Fast Ethernet documents is to describe in clear, unambiguous, and complete detail how a technology works so that different manufacturers can build equipment that interoperates.

Intersegment Traffic   Network traffic that is forwarded by a switch or router between two segments, sometimes called off-segment traffic.

Intrasegment Traffic   Network traffic from a segment that is not forwarded by a switch or router to another segment, sometimes called local segment traffic.

Intrusion Prevention and Detection   See *Eavesdropping Prevention*.

IP Fragmentation   The breaking up of IP datagrams into smaller datagrams so they can be forwarded from a LAN to another LAN that supports only smaller frame sizes. For example, FDDI can support frames up to 64,000 bytes in size. If such a datagram needs to be forwarded to a Fast Ethernet LAN, it must be fragmented.

IPG   InterPacket Gap. The quiet time between transmitted Ethernet frames, 9.6μs for Ethernet, and 960ns for Fast Ethernet.

IPX/SPX   Abbreviation for Internet Packet Exchange/Sequenced Packet Exchange. The core protocol used by both Novell's NetWare and Microsoft's Windows 95 and Windows NT. All three of these operating system products can use other protocols. For example, all of them use TCP/IP equally well, and the Microsoft products also support a protocol called NetBEUI.

IRQ   Abbreviation for Interrupt ReQuest. The method by which hardware devices request processor attention to service a request.

ISA   Industry Standard Architecture.

ISO   The International Standards Organization is the international organization that creates networking standards.

Jabber   The term used to denote continuous transmission of corrupted or random data onto a network, usually caused by faulty cabling or a faulty NIC.

Jam   If a station is transmitting on the network and it receives a collision, it sends out a jam frame so that all other stations will also see the collision. When a repeater detects a collision on any port, it sends out a jam packet on all other ports, thereby causing a collision to occur on those segments that are transmitting, and forcing any nontransmitting stations to wait before transmitting.

Jitter   A change in a signal relative to phase or time, which can cause errors or loss of synchronization in networks.

LAN See *Local Area Network*.

Latency The length of time required for a NIC to access the server and receive the requested data.

Learning See *Address Learning*.

Learning Bridge A learning bridge monitors MAC layer addresses on both segments, and determines which addresses are on each segment. Packets received with source and destination addresses on one side are not forwarded. If the bridge receives a packet with an unknown address, it is forwarded to the other side by default.

Length Errors Length errors are detected when the Length/Type (L/T) field does not agree with the physical length of the frame. Length errors can be used only if the node is set up to handle 802.3-type frames. If the node is using Ethernet-II frames, then the L/T field cannot be used to look for errors.

LLC Logical link control is the layer-2 protocol for transmission, also referred to as the IEEE 802.2 standard.

Local Area Network (LAN) A system for directly connecting multiple computers. LANs are local because they are designed to connect computers over a small area, such as an office, a building, or small campus. LANs are *systems* because they are made up of several components, such as cable, repeaters, network interfaces, nodes, and protocols. All of these elements work together and function as a LAN. If any one of these elements is missing, the system is not a LAN. LANs provide *connectivity*, or a way for computers to exchange information and/or data. A LAN imposes no restrictions on the type of data that nodes can exchange except that it be in digital form. A LAN also directly connects *multiple* (two or more) nodes. Any two nodes on a LAN can *directly* communicate with each other without having to explicitly communicate with or be aware of any intermediate devices.

Local Segment Traffic This term is easier to use and understand than intrasegment traffic but means the same thing. Also see intersegment traffic and off segment traffic, which have the same relationship.

Locally Administered Address An IEEE address with the U/L flag set to a 1. This means that someone besides the network interface's manufacturer sets the address. For example, an organization could set the MAC address on a network interface to a value of its own choosing by setting the U/L bit to a 1, and then setting bits 2 through 47 to some value. Of course, that organization would have to keep track of them. Since all network interfaces come with a universally administered address, locally administered addresses are rarely used. No modern networking protocols or other software in wide use require you to set network addresses by hand. Actually, we are not aware of *anything* that requires, or that is even helped by, using locally administered addresses. There is generally a way to override the UAA of a network interface. Usually, this is an entry in a configuration file or registry. This method is often obscure and poorly documented, or undocumented altogether.

Loop See *Bridge Loop*.

Glossary

MAC Address   Each network interface on a Fast Ethernet, Ethernet, Token Ring, or FDDI LAN has a unique, 48-bit address. This address is programmed into the interface's MAC, and is thus called the MAC address. Every network interface manufactured has a unique MAC address. In other words, no two network interfaces manufactured for any technology have the same MAC address. See also *Universal or Local Administration Flag* and *Universally Administered Address*.

MAC Address Security   See *Alias Prevention* and *Identity Enforcement*.

MAC Address Table   The table inside a bridge or switch that maps ports to MAC addresses, and holds address aging information. This table is built during the address learning process.

MAC Frame   A synonym for packet.

Main Distribution Frame (MDC)   The central point of focus for all vertical or backbone wiring in a network. Vertical cables from each wiring closet are brought to the cross-connect panel in the MDC. In large campus-type environments or high-rise buildings, intermediate distribution frames may be used to avoid excessive cabling between the floor and the MDC.

Managed   Any device that can communicate using the SNMP protocol is said to be managed.

Management Information Base (MIB)   An ASCII text file that describes data objects and structures in a networking device or component running an agent. The descriptions of the data objects in the MIB are in the Abstract Syntax Notation 1, or ASN.1 format. A device or component's data objects and structures can be retrieved and/or modified using the SNMP protocol. When a device supports data described by a MIB and the SNMP protocol, it is said to be managed.

Management Interface Module   Synonym for product interface.

Max Throughput Test   A switch and bridge test that generates symmetric, steady-state loads at wire speed with the maximum frame size of 1,518 bytes (12,144 bits).

Max Traffic Test   A switch and bridge test that generates symmetric, steady-state loads at wire speed with the minimum frame size of 64 bytes (512 bits).

Maximum Forwarding Rate   The maximum number of packets per second that can be forwarded from one port to another. On bridges with more than two ports, this is usually measured on two ports only while the other ports are idle. Most Ethernet bridges have a forwarding rate lower than the maximum frame rate of Ethernet, which means that while providing connectivity, bridges can be a performance bottleneck between nodes on different segments. Some high-speed bridges have a forwarding rate that can keep up with the maximum Ethernet frame rates. One of the big differences between bridges and switches is that switches almost always support the maximum forwarding rate on all ports.

Maximum Network Diameter   The maximum allowable network diameter for a CSMA/CD LAN is determined by the slot time. A segment's network diameter must be small enough so that a signal can start from one MAC and travel to any other MAC and back, within the slot time. Components with shorter SPDs will allow for a larger maximum network diameter.

MDI Port A normal network interface port on an Ethernet or Fast Ethernet interface. On an MDI port, pair 3 of the RJ45 plug is connected to the PHY's receiver, and pair 1 to the transmitter. Also see *MDI, DTE,* and *Uplink.*

MDI-X Port A normal repeater port on an Ethernet or Fast Ethernet repeater. On an MDI-X port, pair 1 of the RJ45 plug is connected to the PHY's receiver, and pair 3 to the transmitter. Also see *MDI, DTE,* and uplink.

Media Access Controller (MAC) The device on a network interface controller that implements the media access rules for the node. For Ethernet and Fast Ethernet, these are the CSMA/CD rules. A MAC is connected to the LAN's media using a PHY. MACs are usually implemented in a single chip. These MAC chips are often responsible for other functions as well, such as the interface to the node via a host bus, such as ISA, EISA, or PCI. MAC chips often control LED indicators and provide interface for boot ROMs and other network adapter features.

Media Access Rules The rules for a LAN technology that govern when a network interface can transmit and/or receive frames from the LAN. The media access rules for a given LAN technology are almost always its distinguishing characteristics. Fast Ethernet and Ethernet share the same media access rules, called CSMA/CD. Token Ring, FDDI, 100VG AnyLAN, and ARCNet all have different rules.

Media Independent Interface (MII) The interface between the MAC and the PHY, which allows the MAC to operate completely independently of the type of media to which the network interface is attached. The PHY takes care of any media-dependent operation.

Meshed Network A network that has multiple routed connections between its LANs. For example, a meshed network can have multiple active traffic paths between any two connected LANs.

MIB See *Management Information Base.*

Modified Cut-Through Synonym for runt-free cut-through. Another synonym is interim cut-through.

Monitor Mode See *Promiscuous Mode.*

Multicast Address One of the 48 IEEE addresses that are very similar to broadcast addresses except that multicast frames can be received by none, one, some, or all the nodes on a LAN. A multicast address is one with the first bit set to a 1, and where at least one of the other bits is a 0. If all the other bits were a 1, then it would be a broadcast address. A node can elect to listen for and copy frames addressed to only certain multicast addresses. In this way, a node can listen for multicast frames in which it is interested, and copy only these frames. The filtering or copying of multicast frames is done by the MAC. Also see *Broadcast Address.*

Multicast Frame Any frame with the destination address set to an IEEE 48-bit multicast or unicast address, or any multicast address.

Multiheaded NIC   A single adapter card with multiple network interfaces. Cards with two or four interfaces are common.

NetBEUI   NetBIOS Enhanced User Interface. An enhancement of the NetBIOS interface and protocol. Note that this user interface is really an API and has nothing to do with a user interface in the traditional sense.

NetBIOS   Network Basic Input Output System. NetBIOS is both a protocol and application programming interface (API) developed by IBM in the mid-1980s, and adopted (unfortunately) by Microsoft for use in MS-DOS and, later, Microsoft Windows.

Network Adapter   Synonymous with network interface card. See *Network Interface*.

Network Address   An address that identifies a node on a routed network. These addresses are made up of two parts, a host number and a network number.

Network Diameter   The maximum cable distance between any two nodes on a LAN. Note that there can be several *hops* through repeaters to get from one node to another.

Network Interface   A network interface, often called a network interface controller, connects a node to a LAN (see the definition of *Node*). A NIC can be built into a device, such as a PC motherboard or printer, or it can be on a separate card. NIC can also mean network interface card. The term *network interface card* or *network adapter* is usually used to refer to a network interface that is provided on a plug-in card.

Network Interface Card (NIC)   See *Network Interface*. A NIC often provides more functionality than a basic network interface, which only connects a node to a LAN. A NIC may provide other features, such as boot ROMs, buffer memory, dedicated I/O Controllers, LED indicators, automatic configuration utilities in ROM, built-in diagnostics, and other advanced features.

Network Interface Controller   A hardware plug-in module for a workstation or server that physically connects the host to the LAN. The NIC is the hardware communication medium and is supported by specialized network software called drivers, which run under the host operating system.

Network-Level Protocols   The standard rules by which applications communicate using application-level protocols to each other over a network. These protocols are like standard English, German, or French. They are extremely standardized, documented, common, and well understood. There are a huge number of application-level protocols but only a handful of commonly used network protocols, and only two are really in widespread use: TCP/IP and IPX/SPX. Network-layer protocols define the message formats and rules by which nodes communicate with each other over a LAN using frames. All of these protocols, especially TCP/IP, can be transported using an extremely wide variety of networking technologies. TCP/IP can be transported over traditional networks, such as Ethernet or Token Ring, and new technologies, such as Fast Ethernet. TCP/IP is also easily transmitted over serial links on PCs, satellite links, radio links, and just about anything else that will transport digital data. One of the key features about protocols is that they are transport independent, which means that an application using TCP/IP or IPX/SPX operates independently of the networking technology used. This allows general-purpose applications to work over any network technology that supports these protocols. For example, you can upgrade your Ethernet LAN to Fast Ethernet, and all your applications will continue to work as before—but much faster.

Network Management Station (NMS)   Usually an application that runs on a workstation that gathers data from and controls device agents using the SNMP protocol. The data that is transferred between the NMS and an agent is defined by a MIB. An NMC knows what data objects are available from an agent by reading a MIB.

Network Number   The part of a network address that identifies the LAN of the connected device. See *Network Address*.

Network Utilization   The ratio of data bits transmitted on a LAN over a period of time to the maximum possible number of bits that could have been transmitted. This value is usually expressed as a percentage and will always be less than 100 percent.

NIC   Network Interface Controller or just Network Interface.

NMS   See *Network Management Station*.

Node   Any device that is connected to a LAN. A node is connected to a LAN via a Network Interface. Nodes can be almost anything—a workstation, printer, router, switch, bridge, fax machine, or terminal. A node can have multiple network interfaces and be connected to multiple LANs. However, a network interface is part of only a single node.

Node Address   Synonym for MAC address. Note that a node may have multiple network interfaces and thus multiple node addresses. However, those addresses will still be unique to that node, because each network interface is manufactured with a unique MAC address.

NOS   Network Operating System.

Octet   A group of eight bits. See *Byte*.

Off-Segment Traffic   This term is easier to use and understand than intersegment traffic but means the same thing. Also see *Intrasegment Traffic* and *Local Segment Traffic*, which have the same relationship.

Offered Load   The amount of data, or frames, that the network is being asked to carry. Another way to look at it is that the offered load is the demand for throughput that the users are currently placing on the LAN, or simply how much traffic *needs* to travel over a LAN. This is in contrast to network utilization, which is a measure of how much traffic is actually traveling over a LAN. It's important to realize that these two things are entirely different. It is also important to note that there is no way to directly measure this value.

On-Band Communications Communication to a device controller's agent over the LAN or networks to which it is connected, in contrast to out-of-band communications.

Organizationally Unique Address (OUA) The part of the 48-bit IEEE address that is assigned to a network interface by the manufacturer of the device. It is in bits 23 through 0 of the address.

Organizationally Unique Identifier (OUI) The basic tool that the IEEE uses to administer MAC or node addresses. The IEEE assigns one or more OUIs to each manufacturer of network interfaces. The OUI is in bits 45 through 24 of a 48-bit IEEE address. By using OUIs, the IEEE has to track only a few (often just one) numbers per manufacturer, not individual node addresses. Twenty-two bits of OUI allow for just over four million OUIs. Each manufacturer is then responsible for keeping track of the organizationally unique addresses (OUAs) that it assigns to each node it manufactures. The 24 bits in the OUA allow a manufacturer to build over 16 million network interfaces before it needs another OUI.

OSI Open systems interconnection is the seven-layer protocol stack for data communication defined by the ISO standards organization.

OUA See *Organizationally Unique Addresses.*

OUI See *Organizationally Unique Identifier.*

Out-of-Band Communications Communication to a device controller's agent over a path other than the LAN or networks to which it is connected, in contrast to in-band communications.

Outgoing Port The port on a device out which a frame or packet will be (or is) transmitted.

Overload A CSMA/CD LAN is overloaded if it operates much past its full utilization point more than 20 percent of the time.

Oversubscribed When a bridge or switch does not have an aggregate forwarding rate equal to its number of ports, times the maximum data rate on its ports, it is said to be oversubscribed. For example, most bridges have a lower aggregate forwarding rate than the sum of the bandwidth of the segments to which they are connected. These bridges are called oversubscribed. However, most switches are not oversubscribed and support an aggregate forwarding rate equal to the sum of the bandwidth of the segments to which they are connected.

Packet How a frame is transmitted by a PHY onto a LAN's media. In other words, frames are encapsulated in, or transmitted inside of, packets.

Pad Data Often a protocol or application will need to transmit a datagram that is shorter than 64 bytes in length. In this case the data portion of the frame must be padded so that the frame is the minimum frame size of 64 bytes. This data is called the pad data. The value of the pad data is arbitrary and not defined by the 802.3 standard.

Partitioning   In the context of Fast Ethernet and Ethernet, partitioning consists of dividing one collision domain or segment into two or more segments using switches or bridges. This is usually done for performance reasons, or to overcome topology limitations when the configuration of a segment needs to be changed. The word is also used in another context: A repeater may temporarily partition a port when an excessive number of errors occur on that port, which means that the port is disconnected from the repeater unit.

Path Delay Value (PDV)   The time difference, in terms of propagation delay, between two particular nodes on the Fast Ethernet LAN. Each pair combination of nodes on a Fast Ethernet LAN has a PDV. The PDV for two particular nodes is calculated simply by adding up the individual propagation delays of each component between the MAC at each node to get the *Simple Path Delay* (SPD) time, then multiplying the SPD by 2. The PDV is twice the SPD because it is a measure of the *round-trip* time between two nodes, or the time it takes for a signal to get from the MAC at one node to another MAC and back again.

PDU   See *Protocol Data Unit*.

PDV   See *Path Delay Value*.

Peer-to-Peer Networking   In a peer-to-peer network the same software programs running on two different nodes communicate to each other. A good example of this is Windows 95 and Windows NT workstation. These operating systems can communicate directly with each other to share resources. For example, you could share the disk drive or CD-ROM on your workstation with someone else on the network without going through a server. Another good example of peer-to-peer software is Internet telephone applications. People using the same type of software can talk to each other over the Internet. Once again, this occurs without using a server as an intermediary.

PI   See *Product Interface*.

Point-to-Point Link   A link that is between only two devices. In other words, a link with a single device at each end.

Product Interface (PI)   A user interface for a network management station that is specifically designed to provide an interface for a particular product or series of products.

Promiscuous Mode   A special mode in which a network interface's MAC can operate. When a MAC is in promiscuous mode it will *copy* all received frames, regardless of a frame's destination address, to the network interface's node. This is often called *monitor mode*, as this mode is used by network analyzers to monitor and record all received network traffic.

Propagation Delay   The time it takes for an electrical or optical signal to travel through a component. In human terms, electrical (or optical) signals travel instantaneously, essentially at the speed of light. However, at the speeds at which electronic network equipment operates, the time it takes for a signal to travel through a component is not only measurable, but significantly long.

Glossary

Protocol   A set of rules governing how computers communicate. This is a broad definition but an accurate one. Generally, protocols are divided into two categories, application-level protocols and network protocols.

Protocol Data Unit (PDU)   A single SNMP message. In other words, SNMP commands and other data are encoded into PDUs.

Protocol Implementation Conformance Statement (PICS)   The 802.3u specification provides a set of tests that any suppliers of Fast Ethernet components must pass before they can say they meet the specification. These are called PICS.

Proxy Server   A device that is connected to the Internet on one port and an organization's internal network on one or more other ports, and acts as a firewall to block many criminal attacks. Also see *Firewall*.

Punch-Down Blocks   Punch-down blocks are used to terminate the cable plant entering the wiring closet. A punch-down block is so named because of the act of using a special spring-loaded hand tool to punch or push a shielded wire down between the jaws of a retaining clip. As the wire is forced between the jaws of the retaining clip, it slices the outer PVC covering of the wire, thereby making electrical contact with the wire. These punch-down blocks have been used for years by the telephone companies, and have migrated to the LAN wiring closet.

Read Only Memory (ROM)   ROM devices store data and/or programs that do not need to be changed.

Receive CRC   The CRC value for a frame calculated by a MAC when the frame is received. This value is compared to the last 4 bytes in the frame (the frame's FCS). If these values are different, then the frame was corrupted on its way from the source to the destination, and should be discarded. If they match, then the frame is valid and can be processed further by the MAC and/or node.

Remote Bridge   This type of bridge has an Ethernet segment on one side and a serial interface on the other side. It connects to a similar device on the other side of the serial line, and is commonly used in a WAN link application where it is impractical to provide a network connection. A leased line or modem is used to connect the two remote bridges.

Remote Network Monitoring (RMON)   A MIB that describes statistics used for monitoring an entire LAN segment.

Repeater   In the context of Fast Ethernet and Ethernet, a repeater is a device that receives data from individual nodes (via their network interface), and repeats that data to all the other nodes. A good analogy is a conference call with more than two people on the line. When you are on such a call, the telephone company takes whatever you say and repeats it to all the other listeners. In this way, everyone hears what you say. A Fast Ethernet or Ethernet repeater does the same thing for the nodes connected to it, but with encoded serial bit streams. A repeater functions on the electrical level to connect LAN segments. It receives, amplifies, reshapes, and retimes the electrical signals between nodes.

Glossary

Repeater Hub A device that acts as both a wiring hub (a central point at which many cable runs come together in a star configuration) and a packet-level repeater. All Ethernet and Fast Ethernet repeaters are also wiring hubs.

RJ45 An eight-wire connector used for connecting networks and digital telephones running over UTP cable. Token Ring, Ethernet, and Fast Ethernet networks use RJ45 connectors.

RMON See *Remote Network Monitoring*.

RMON Probe A device that implements the RMON MIB in a device agent.

ROM See *Read Only Memory*.

Root Bridge The master bridge in a switched or bridged network.

Round-Trip Delay Time Synonym for collision window.

Routing A method of forwarding frames received on one port on a device to another port using layer-3 protocol information. This is in contrast to bridges and switches, which use layer-2 frame information to make forwarding decisions.

Run-On Frame Any frame that is longer than 1,518 bytes (12,144 bits). Run-on frames are always errors. It doesn't matter if the CRC is good, no MAC should ever transmit a frame that is longer than 1,518 bytes. These are almost always caused by a faulty network interface; however, a buggy driver could also cause this problem.

Runt Frame Often just runt. Any frame less than 64 bytes (512 bits) in size. Runt frames are always caused by a collision.

Runt-Free Cut-Through A type of frame switching that prevents runt frames from being forwarded. This is a type of cut-through switching. Synonyms are *modified cut-through* and *interim cut-through*.

SAS Single Attached Station. An FDDI station that has a single connection that connects to an FDDI concentrator.

Segment In the context of Fast Ethernet and Ethernet, a segment is a single collision domain or single LAN.

Segment Switch A switch that can hold enough MAC addresses in its table to support attaching repeaters to its ports.

Segmentation The division of bandwidth into multiple LANs to overcome performance bottlenecks.

Segmenting Synonym for partitioning.

Server Message Block (SMB) A datagram format used by the application-level protocols in Microsoft networking products. When Windows 95 or NT workstations access an NT server, they exchange SMB datagrams.

Shared Media Any LAN technology where nodes physically or logically are connected to and share the same media. All modern LAN technologies—including

Fast Ethernet, Ethernet, FDDI, 100VGAnyLAN, Token Ring, and ARCNet—are shared media technologies. Most of these (except ARCNet) can be used in either a partially or fully switched environment, in contrast to ATM (asynchronous transfer mode) networking, which is fully switched and never runs over shared media.

Simple Network Management Protocol (SNMP)   The protocol that network management stations (NMSs) and agents use to communicate to each other. SNMP is an application-level protocol that is used to transfer data between an NMS and an agent in a machine-independent manner. It is a standard protocol and is defined by the IETF.

Simple Path Delay (SPD)   The SPD for two particular nodes is simply calculated by adding up the individual propagation delays of each component between the MAC at each node.

Slot Time   The maximum allowable size of a collision window for a Fast Ethernet or Ethernet segment. For both technologies, this is 512 bit times.

SNAP   SubNetwork Access Protocol.

SNMP   See *Simple Network Management Protocol*.

SNMP Agent   Synonym for agent.

SPD   See *Simple Path Delay*.

Spraying   When a frame is forwarded to more than one of the ports on a bridge or switch except the inbound port. Very similar to flooding.

Stackable Hubs   Also called a stackable repeater. A special type of repeater that can be combined or stacked with other stackable hubs to form a single repeater. This is done by connecting together the repeater units internal to the hubs directly over a digital bus or direct digital link, in contrast to how 10Base-T hubs or Class-II Fast Ethernet repeaters are connected together using uplinks. Uplink connections are made using regular PHYs and are subject to the rules of the associated standard.

Start-of-Packet Propagation Delay   For a repeater, the time delay between when a signal is received on one port and is retransmitted on another port.

Steady-State Load   A load that is constant over time. See *Symmetric Load*.

Store-and-Forward Switching   A store-and-forward switch receives and stores entire frames before they are forwarded. Also see *Cut-Through Switching* and *Runt-Free Cut-Through*.

STP   Shielded twisted-pair cable. This is 18- to 26-gauge wire used for LANs, such as Fast Ethernet 100Base-TX, 100Base-T4, and Ethernet. It features a metal shield to protect it from external electrical interference, which allows it to be used over longer distances than UTP cable.

Straight-Through Cable   This kind of cable is called straight-through because connector pins 1 through 8 on one end of a cable are connected to their corresponding pins on the other end. This is accomplished by terminating both ends of the cables with RJ45 plugs the same way on each end of the cable. A straight-through cable is used to connect one device with an MDI port (usually a node) to another device's MID-X port (usually a repeater). See *Crossover Cable*.

Switch   A multiport learning bridge that is extremely fast. Unlike a plain bridge, a switch can process multiple frames at one time, and effectively has multiple paths over which to forward frames. A switch can also effectively make multiple forwarding decisions at one time. Switches are built using ASICs.

Symmetric Load   When the offered load to a device is distributed evenly across all its ports. These kinds of loads are usually used in a steady-state fashion in order to test a device and determine its maximum possible throughput.

TCP/IP   Transmission Control Protocol/Internet Protocol. One of the two most commonly used protocols today (the other is IPX/SPX), TCP/IP is the basis for the Internet, and is used to transfer everything from Web pages and files to real-time voice and video.

Throughput   The number of bytes transferred per second. This can be over some media, through a device, or across a LAN.

TIA   Telecommunication Industries Association.

Token Ring   A network topology defined by the IEEE 802.5 specification. Token Ring networks are deterministic, since they use a token-passing access protocol, in which each station must wait to receive the token before it can transmit to the network. Token Ring supports a ring topology at speeds of 4Mbps or 16Mbps.

Too Many Collisions Error   This error occurs after a MAC attempts to retransmit a frame 16 times due to collisions.

Topology Rules   A set of rules that dictate how the components of a network are physically connected to one another. These rules often dictate maximum cable lengths and the number of certain components, such as repeaters, that can be present on a network. All network technologies have topology rules, and the rules for each technology differ greatly. The rules for a particular technology may be a big advantage or a disadvantage when compared to other technologies. For example, the rules for Fast Ethernet are very restrictive when compared to those for other high-speed technologies, such as FDDI and 100VGAnyLAN.

Transceiver   Part of a PHY. The device that is responsible for translating between the electrical signals that travel on the media, and digital signals used internally by the device.

Transmission Errors   Errors that happen due to physical problems with the media or equipment, such as random bit errors (these happen very rarely), bad cables, flaky network interfaces or repeaters, and electrical interference (noise).

Transmission Model 1   One of two transmission models used by the 802.3u specification to describe the topology rules for Fast Ethernet. The other set contains the transmission Model-2 rules.

Transmission Model 2   One of two transmission models used by the 802.3u specification to describe the topology rules for Fast Ethernet. The other set contains the transmission Model-1 rules.

Glossary

U/L Flag   See *Universal or Local Administration Flag*.

UAA   See *Universally Administered Address*.

Unicast Address   One of 48 IEEE addresses that are MAC addresses. In other words, a unicast address identifies a single node on a LAN. Frames with a destination address that is a unicast address will be received by only a single node on a LAN. A unicast address is one with the first bit set to a 0. All the other bits can be a 1 or a 0.

Unicast Frame   A frame with a destination address that is a unicast address. A synonym for unicast frame is *directed frame*.

Universal or Local Administration Flag (U/L Flag)   Bit 46 in a 48-bit IEEE address, this flag indicates whether the address is locally administered or globally administered. If both the I/G individual or group address flag and the U/L bits are zero, then the address is a 48-bit number that is *unique* to a single network interface. It is universal because the address was assigned to the network interface by a combination of the IEEE and the manufacturer of the device. It is unique because it is assigned to a single network interface at manufacture time. If the I/G bit is a 0 and the U/L bit is a 1, then the address is one that was assigned by the local network administrator, and is not administered by the IEEE. If the I/G is a 0 and the U/L bit is a 1, then the address is a locally administered address.

Universally Administered Address (UAA)   The IEEE term for MAC address.

Uplink Cable   Any cable used to connect two 10Base-T repeaters or two 100Base-T Class-II repeaters. It is attached to an MDI-X, or uplink port, on one repeater, and a normal (MDI) port on the other repeater.

Uplink Port   A special port on a 10Base-T repeater or Fast Ethernet Class-II repeater that is used to connect to another repeater. An uplink port is connected to the PHY backward from a normal MDI-X repeater port, and is usually labeled as an MDI port. This allows a standard straight-through cable to connect the two PHYs so that packets can flow between them.

UTP   Unshielded twisted-pair cable. Insulated 18- to 26-gauge wire used for LANs and telephones. There are three primary grades of UTP cable. It does not have metal shielding to protect it from external electrical noise or interference.

WAN   See *Wide Area Network*.

Wide Area Network (WAN)   A system for connecting nodes or LANs together over a wide area, such as a city, region, country, or across the world. WAN links are almost always point-to-point, and connect two devices in different geographical locations (the wide area). The two devices are generally called gateways and usually also function as bridges or routers. Many devices on one end of a WAN link communicate to other devices on the other end of the link via the gateways at each end. WANs differ from LANs in their point-to-point nature and the distances they cover. WAN link equipment, such as gateways, is usually designed to optimize and efficiently utilize the often expensive link between them, in contrast to LANs, in which the physical media is very inexpensive and the primary focus is on high throughput.

Wire Speed When a steady stream of frames is transmitted on a CSMA/CD LAN, with only the IPG time between them. In other words, a series of frames is transmitted as fast as possible. Note that the frame rate depends on the size of the frames being transmitted. The wire speed rate for 64-byte frames (the minimum size) is 148,809.52 frames per second. For 1,518-byte frames (the maximum size), it is 8,127.44 frames per second.

Index

Abstract Syntax Notation 1 (ASN.1), 18, 104
Access, in and out of band, 103–104
Accounts Payable (AP) groups, 161–162
Adapter(s), 192. *See also* PCI bus
Adapter cards, 95
Address(es), in frames, 9–10
Address learning, 113, 115–116
  problems with, 119
Agents, 105, 301–302. *See also* RMON agents
Aging process, 115
  and forwarding, 117
Alarm(s), types of, 299–301
Alarm group (Group 4), 292, 299–302
Alias prevention, 239–240
American National Standards Institute (ANSI) standards, *see* FDDI
APIs (application programming interfaces), 18, 25, 30
Application(s), 24–26
  transport independence of, 27
Application layer, 19
Application Programming Interfaces, *see* APIs
Application-specific integrated circuits, 124–125
Applications software, 24–26
ARCNet, 58
ASICs, 124–125
Asymmetric load, 136–137
Attempt counter, 93
Attenuation signal, 366–367
Autodiscovery, 302
Automatic node discovery, 302

Autonegotiation, 35, 53–55, 202–203, 361–362
Autopartitioning, 7, 9
Autosensing, in NICs, 202–203

Backbone(s), 156, 168–170. *See also* EIA/TIA 568 standard
  collapsed, 172
  switches for, 246, 253
  vertical, 213, 219–220
Back-off time, 93
Backplane segments, 231
Back pressure, 263–264
Bandwidth:
  and broadcasting, 260–262
  and congestion, 137
  and fiberoptic cable, 366
  future use of, 157
Baselining, 100
Bit time, 37
  delay, 326
BOOTP, 236
Boot ROM, 191
Bradner, Scott, 254
Bradner tests, 254
Bridge(s), 11, 110–122
  and loops, 118–121
  and network interfaces, 113
  operation of, 114
  performance measures of, 122–123
  in promiscuous mode, 113
  and routers, comparison, 141–142
  and switches, comparison, 123–124
  transparency of, 111, 118
Bridge MIB, 107

Bridge protocol data units (BPDUs), 120–121
Broadcast address, 11, 61
Broadcast domain, 116, 144
Broadcast frames, 60, 62–63. *See also* Broadcasting; Traffic
Broadcasting, 260–262
  limits on, 265
Broadcast storms, 118–119
Brouters, 267
Buckets, 297–298
Buffering, 33, 259–260
Buffer memory, 191–192
  of switches, 132–133
Building entrance, cabling of, 213–215
Bulletin boards, for technical support, 180
Bus(es):
  digital, 8
  topology, 6, 213
  transfer modes, 199–201
Bus-mastering DMA data transfer, 189, 200

Cable:
  bit time delay, 326
  Category-3, 16, 379
  Category-5, *see* Category-5 cable
  coaxial, 317–318
  copper, 32–33, 80
  cost of, 45
  cross-connect, 221
  crossover, 51
  distribution systems for, 217–218
  and the EIA/TIA 568 standard, 81, 210, 377–384
  for Fast Ethernet, 8, 16

411

Index

Cable *(Continued)*:
  for horizontal cabling, 220–221
  labeling of, 218
  for NIC media interfaces, 205
  null repeater, 51
  propagation delays, 326
  signal speed through, 76–77
  straight through, 48–49, 364
  termination of, 221
  twisted pair, 8
  uplink, 32
Cable trays, 217
Cabling plant, *see also* Cable; EIA/TIA 568 standard
  certification of, 212
  designing, 209–226
  elements of, 213–222
  installation, 381–383
  maintenance, 381–383
  media selection, 224–226
  and network growth, 224
  and network services, 223
  security, design for, 222–223
  testing of, 384
  topology of, 212–213
Campus wiring, 213, 219–220
CardBus standard, 198–199
Carrier sense, 37. *See also* CSMA/CD
Carrier Sense Multiple Access with Collision Detection, *see* CSMA/CD
Category-3 cable, 16, 379
Category-5 cable, 16, 379. *See also* Cabling plant
  and collision windows, 80–81
  for new networks, 211–212
  NVP of, 77, 321
  for 100Base-TX links, 362–363
Chassis, 230
Chassis-based devices, 253
  with WAN card support, 273
Chipsets, 190
Class-I repeaters, 31–33, 43–44, 227–230
  propagation delays of, 77
Class-II repeaters, 31–33, 41–43, 234
  connections of, 48
  propagation delays of, 77
Client/server applications, 24–25
Clouds, 270
Coaxial cable, 317–318

Code, downloadable, 235
Collision(s), 73, 74, 76, 77–92. *See also* CSMA/CD
  excessive, 40
  and full-duplex links, 138–140
  late, 85–86, 290
  and partitioning, 38
  reasons for, 76–86
  and runt frames, 91–92, 94
Collision counters, 290, 312–313
Collision delay, 42, 43
Collision detection, 92–94
Collision domains, 74
  segmentation of, 247–248
Collision frames, 91–92
Collision percentage, 99
Collision recovery, 93–94
Collision sense, 35. *See also* CSMA/CD
Collision statistics, 297
Collision windows, 77–82, 324
  and network performance, 89–91
  and slot time, 86–87
Communication, any-to-any, 5
Compaq, NICs and drivers of, 28–29
Concentrators, 9
Concurrency, 194
Conduits, 217
Congestion, 135–138
  for cut-through switches, 129–130
  of SUMs, 243
  in switches, 136–137, 259, 263–264, 291
Connectivity, 4, 269–270. *See also* Router(s)
Connectors, 35, 47–48, 216, 218, 381–382
Consoles, 105
Contention, 76
Controllers, 103
Conversations, 306
Copper cable:
  limiting factors for, 80
  and Model-1 rules, 32–33
Counters:
  in MIB-II, 279–281
  rollover calculation for, 282
CPUs:
  and congestion, 137
  and network management, 103
  NIC utilization of, 176–177, 184

CRCs, 66
  and JAMs, 80
Crossbar matrix switches, 125–127
CSMA/CD, 10, 16, 69–74
  access methods of, 319
  and full-duplex links, 138–140
  and RFC1650, 288

Dark fiber, 224–225
Data:
  digital, 4
  and NICs, 28
  pad, 65
  transmitting, 9–11, 20, 28–30, 37, 199–201. *See also* Frame(s); Repeater(s)
Data centers, 273
Data field, 65
Datagrams, 142–143
Data Link layer, 20
  security of, 237
Data translation services, 19
DEC, and Ethernet as a standard, 63
Denial of service attacks, 240
Departments, 156
  networks for, 166–168
  switches for, 252
Designing networks, 211
Desktop Management Interface (DMI), 183
Destination address, 57
Device(s):
  managed, 18, 104, 277–278. *See also* MIB
  SNMP, reading with, 104–106
Device controllers, 103
DHCP, 236
Diagnostics, and promiscuous mode, 11
Direct Memory Access (DMA) data transfer, 189, 198, 200
Discovery, 11
  and broadcast frames, 62
Diskless workstations, 62
  boot ROM of, 191
Disk space, 158
DIX Blue Book, 63
DIX frames, 65
DIX group, 63
DMA, 189, 200
  PC Card support of, 198

Index

Drive mapping, 5–6
Driver(s) for NICs, 178–180
Driver software interfaces, 29
Drive sharing, 5–6
DTE ports, 48
DTE-to-DTE connection, 322
Dual connectivity, 163

Eavesdropping prevention, 237–238

EIA/TIA 568 standard, 81, 210, 377–384
   cable choices of, 378–381
   wiring guidelines, 383–384
8B6T coding algorithm, 373
802.3 frames, 65
EISA bus, 195–196
   and ISA, compatibility, 196–197
Engineering group, 162–163
Enterprise needs, determining, 156–157
Enterprise networks, 170–173
Equipment room, cabling of, 215
Error handling, 38–39
   with FCS field, 66
   MAC-level, 66–67
Ethernet:
   and Fast Ethernet, comparison, 317–319
   simplicity of, 71
   10Base-T, 8
   10Base-2, 6–7
   thin net, 6–7
Ethernet collapse, 102
Ethernet History group (Group 3), 292, 297–299
Ethernet Statistics group (Group 1), 292, 294–297
Ethernet 10+100 workgroup switches, 252
Ethernet-II frames, 65
Ether Types, 64
Event group (Group 10), 293, 299–302
Event logging, 301–302
Excessive collision errors (ECEs), 40

False carrier events (FCEs), 30–40
Fast Ethernet, 3, 6
   baud rate of, 39
   cable for, 16. See also Cable; Cabling plant

components of, 14–18
costs of, 45, 318
efficiency of, 97
and Ethernet, comparison, 317–319
media types for, 361–374
online information about, 329
and small offices, 164–166
speed of, 95–98
100Base-T, 8
planning installation, 149–152
repeaters of, 33. See also Repeater(s)
standardizing, 53. See also IEEE 802.3u
upgrading to, 224–226
FDDI, 52–53
Fiberoptic cable, 16, 362, 365–370, 380–381. See also 100 Base-FX
   advantages of, 224–225
   and Model-1 rules, 32–33
   and Model-2 rules, 87–88
   and propagation delay, 81
   and security, 223
Field programmable gate arrays (FPGAs), 124–125
FIFO memory, 200
File(s):
   opening, 12
   reading, 13
File Transfer Protocol, 25
Filter group (Group 8), 293, 307–308
Filtering, 11, 112, 116
Firewalls, 275
Flooding, 116
Forwarding, 112, 116
   decision to, 117, 128
   latency of, 128, 131, 132
   rates of, 122–123
Frame(s), 9–11, 14
   address of, 58–61
   and bridges, 110–122
   cloning of, 119
   collision, 91–92
   copying, 11
   CRC of, 66
   format of, 318–319
   and packets, 36
   pending, 72
   run-on, 66–67
   runt, 91–92, 94, 129–131

size of, 57, 86
transmission rates, 97–98
types of, 63–65
Frame Check Sequence (FCS), 57, 65–66
Frame switching, 18, 109–110, 122–130. See also Bridges
Framing errors, 67
FTP, 25
Full-duplex mode, 46, 138–140, 163, 319
   and network utilization calculations, 284–285
   and switches, 248–249
Functional address, 59
Funnel problem, 258–260
FX, see 100Base-FX

Gateways, 5
   routers as, 18
GET command, 106
GET NEXT command, 106
Gigabit Ethernet, 265
Graphical interfaces, 314
Group addresses, 60, 61

Half-duplex systems, 46. See also CSMA/CD
Hierarchy, 14
History Control group (Group 2), 292, 297–299
Horizontal wiring, 213, 220–221. See also EIA/TIA 568 standard
Host group (Group 5), 292, 302–305
Host Top N group (Group 6), 293, 305–306
HTTP (Hyper Text Transport Protocol), 13
Hub(s), 4, 8–9
   chassis-based, 230–234
   repeaters, 8, 9, 228
Hub and Spoke topology, 6
Hub cards, 232
Hyper Text Transport Protocol, 13

Identity enforcement, 239
Idle state, 37
IEEE address, 59–60
IEEE 802.3u standard, 2, 44–45
I/G bit (individual or group address flag), 59–61

Index

Intel:
   and Ethernet as a standard, 63
   and the PCI bus, 193
Interfaces, 23, 25
   product-specific, 314
Internet, 18, 170
   connecting to, 157, 268, 274–275
Internet Telephones, 4
Interoperability and Autonegotiation, 53–55
Interpacket gap (IPG), 72–73
   timers for, 79
Intrusion prevention, 239
I/O address space, 197
IP addresses, 143, 236
IP fragmentation, 274
IPX (Internet Packet Exchange):
   addresses, 144
   repeater support of, 236
IPX/SPX (Internet Packet Exchange/ Sequenced Packet Exchange), 26–27
ISA bus, 195–196
   and EISA, compatibility, 196–197

Jabber, 35, 38, 40–41, 264
JAM, 38–40, 80
JAM propagation delay, 42, 43
JEIDA, 197

Kalpana frame switch, 122

LAN(s) (Local Area Networks), 3–6, 156. *See also* Networks
   diameter of, 33
   and media access rules, 71
   media independence of, 44
   and routers, 146–147
LAN(s), virtual, 265
LAN(s), workgroup, 160–166
LANanalyzer (Novell), 308
Laptop computers and PC Cards, 197
Latencies, low access, 194
Layer-2 devices:
   bridges, 111–112
   SUMs, 242–243
   switches, 125
Layer-3 devices, routers, 142, 267–275. *See also* Router(s)
LEDs, 202
Legacy applications, 26

Length errors, 67
Length/Type (L/T) field, 57, 63–65
   errors in, 67
Linear bursts, 194
Links:
   configuring with Autonegotiation, 54
   integrity of, 9
   problems with, 38–39
   status of, 35
LINK UNSTABLE state, 40
Loops in bridged networks, 118–120

MAC(s), 69–70
   and collision recovery, 94
   frame transmission, 36–37
   functions of, 69
   and runt frames, 91
MAC address(es), 9, 58–61
   aliasing, 240
   format of, 58–59
   security of, 240
MAC address table, 113, 115–118
Magic packet, 204–205
Management, out-of-hand, 235
Management Information Base, 18. *See also* MIB
Management interface module, 314
Marketing group, 164
Mastering, 194
Matrix group (Group 7), 293, 306–307
MAU (Media Access Unit), 9
MAX tests, 254–257
MDI connector:
   and NIC interface, 201
   for 100Base-FX links, 368
   for 100Base-T4 links, 370–371
   for 100Base-TX links, 362
MDI ports, 48
MDI-X port, 47–48
Media Access Rules, 10, 69
Media interface connector (MIC), 381
Media modules, 252
Media types, 361–375. *See also* 100Base-FX; 100Base-T4; 100Base-TX
   and PHY, 44–50
Memory address space, 196
Message formats and network protocols, 26–27

MIB, 104–108
MIB browser, 309, 314–315
MIB-II, 107, 278
   Ethernet-specific, 288–290
   extensions to, 285–288
   information groups of, 278–281
   switch congestion, measures of, 291
Microseconds, 39
Microsoft operating systems and NDIS, 29
MII, 205–206
Model-1 rules, 1, 32, 321–324
   and PDVs, 81–82
Model-2 rules, 2, 32–33, 324–328
   and network diameter, 87–88
   and PDVs, 82
Multicast address, 59, 61, 62
Multicast frames, 116
Multimode fiber, 368

Nanoseconds, 39
NDIS, 29
Near-End Cross-Talk (NEXT), 382–383
NetBEUI protocol, 13
Network(s), 4–5, 156
   backbone, 156, 168–170
   bussed, 6–8
   cabling for, *see* Cabling plant
   departmental, 166–168
   enterprise, 170–172
   flat, 168
   growth, designing for, 157–158, 224
   layers of, 16–18
   meshed, 141
   planning setup, 149–152, 154–155
   problems, isolating, 7
   reliability of, 159–160, 223
   routed, 145. *See also* Router(s)
   sizing, 155
Network Adapters, 15
Network addresses, 141, 143
Network analyzer, 237–238, 308
Network configuration:
   and bridges, 111–112
   categorizing, 155–156
Network diameter, 33
   and collision window, 78, 80, 84–86
   of Fast Ethernet, 317

Index

and slot time, 87–88
and switches, 246
Network Driver Interface Specification, 29
Networking standard, 100Mbps, 52–53
Network interface, 5, 15, 27–28, 113
Network Interface Cards, *see* NICs
Network interface drivers, 28–29
Network layer, 20
Network management, 18, 103–108, 277–315
  enterprise-level, 172–173
  MIB browsers for, 314–315
  of performance, 247–248
  plan for, 158–159
  and stackable repeaters, 228–229
Network Management Console, 310
Network Management Station (NMS), 105–108, 277, 282–284
Network Monitor (Microsoft), 308
Network number, 143–144
Network performance:
  baselining of, 310–313
  and collision windows, 89–91
  and drivers, 28
  and FIFO memory size, 200
  and full-duplex links, 140
  and network utilization, 99–100
  and offered load, 100–103
  and switching problems, 258–264
Network Plan, 211
Network protocols, 26–27
Network services, 19
Network traffic, *see* Traffic
Network utilization, 98–100, 102
  for baselining, 312
  calculating, 279, 283–285
  and the RMON probe, 298–299
NICs (Network Interface Cards), 15, 27–28, 175–176
  architecture of, 189–192
  Autonegotiation and, 54, 202–203
  boot ROM of, 191
  and buffer memory, 191–192
  certification of, 207–208
  chipsets of, 190
  client, 186–187
  CompactPCI, 188–189
  drivers of, 28–29, 178–180
  dual-speed, 202

  ease of installation, 181–182
  embedded, 187–188
  features of, 206
  interface with MDI connector, 201
  LEDs of, 202
  media flexibility of, 205
  mobile, 188
  multithreaded or multiport, 184
  and network management, 183
  power management by, 204–205
  price/performance ratio, 176–178
  propagation delays of, 325
  server-based, 184–186
  technical support for, 180–181
  voltages of, 203–204
  warranty of, 182–183
  workstation, 186–187
NMS, 105–108, 277
  network utilization, measuring, 282–284
Node(s), 113
  acquiring the network, 89–90
  back-off time, calculating, 93–94
  and collision detection, 92
  components of, 23–24
  connecting, 50–52
  and data transmission, 4, 9–11, 145
  jabbering of, *see* Jabber
  MAC addresses for, 9
  and media access rules, 72
  and network interfaces, 15
  PDV of, 77–78
Node address, 58. *See also* MAC address(es)
Noise, electrical, 38
Nominal Velocity of Propagation (NVP), 76–77
Novell Netware, ODI drivers for, 29
NWAY Autonegotiation scheme, 53–55, 185–186

Octets, 57, 143
Offered load, 100–103
100Base-FX, 16, 34–35, 224–225, 362, 365–370
  crossover wiring of, 369
  PHY for, 49
100Base-T, 8
100Base-T2, 45
100Base-T4, 16, 34–35, 45, 53, 225–226, 370–375

  connection of, 49–50
  crossover wiring of, 371
100Base-TX, 16, 34–35, 44, 45, 225–226, 361–365
  connections with, 46–47
  crossover wiring of, 364, 365
100Base-X, 362
Online information, address for, 329
Open command, 12
Open Data Link Interface (ODI) specification, 29
Open response, 12
Organizationally unique identifier (OUI), 59
OSI Reference Model, 14, 19–21, 23
Overhead, of data transmission, 96
Overload, 103
Oversubscribed switches, 256

Packet(s), 33
  dropping, 263
  size of, 86–87
  transmission of, 36–37
  transmission rate, 96–97
Packet Capture group (Group 9), 293, 307–308
Partition function, 38
Partitioning, 7, 9, 39–41, 110
Password capture programs, 237
Patch cables, 221
Patch panels, 216, 382
Path Delay Value (PDV), 77–78
PC Cards, 197–199
PCI (Peripheral Component Interconnect) bus, 192–195
  voltages of, 203–204
  width of, 195
PCMCIA interface, 188. *See also* PC Cards
PCS, of 100Base-T4, 372–373
PDUs, 106
Peer-to-Peer (PTP) Networking, 5
Performance bottlenecks of bridges, 122–123
PHYs, 34–36, 201
  MACs of, 70
  media dependence of, 44–50
  in NICs, 190–191
  propagation delay of, 77
Physical layer, 21
Planning networks, 211

Index

Plug-and-play operation and Autonegotiation, 54
Plugs, 35
PMA sublayer, 373–374
Point-to-point links, 138. *See also* Full-duplex mode
Polling, 292
Port(s):
  backup, 234–235
  control of, with repeaters, 235
  crossbar matrix connections of, 125–127
  density of, 232
  linking of, 34
  modular, 265
  partitioning of, 38–39
  segmentation of, 265
Power consumption, of computer systems, 204–205
Power down modes, 204
Power outages, 219
Presentation layer, 19
Probes, RMON, 11, 107–108, 291–292
Product interfaces, 108
Programmed Input/Output (PIO) data transfer, 189, 201
Promiscuous mode, 11, 113
Propagation delay:
  and contention, 76–77
  and network diameter, 87–88
  and the PHY, 77
Protocol(s), 12–14
  application-level, *see* SNMP
  command/response pattern of, 12–13
  network, 26–27. *See also* IPX/SPX; TCP/IP
  SNMP, 104–106. *See also* SNMP
  transparency to, 16
  vendor-specific, 26
Protocol data units, 106
Protocol Implementation Conformance Statement (PICS) tests, 36
Protocol software interfaces, 29–30
Proxy servers, 275
PTP software, 25
Punch-down blocks, 215–216, 382

Raised floors, 217–218
Read command, 12–13
Read response, 12–13

Received event handling, 37–38
Receive jabber function, 38
Redundancy, 150
Remote access and routers, 273–274
Remote Network Monitoring, *see* RMON
Repeater(s), 4, 7–9, 14–15, 31, 227–243
  Class-II, 234
  and collision detection, 92
  features of, 234–236
  function of, 33–43
  and packets, 111–112
  propagation delays of, 325
  requirements of, 37–38
  and RMON probes, 297
  security features of, 236–241
  and Smart Uplink Modules, 242–243
  stackables, 227–230
  topology rules for, 31–33
Repeater hubs, 7–8. *See also* Hub(s)
Repeater MIB, 107
Repeater PHY, 34–36
Requirements analysis, 153–173
RFC 1067, 104
RFC 1098, 104
RFC 1157, 104
RFC 1242, 254, 331–340
RFC 1271, 291
RFC 1650, 288
RFC 1757, 291
RFC 1944, 254, 321, 341–360
Ring topology, 6, 213
RJ45 connectors, 216, 382
  labeling of, 218
RJ45 socket, 47–48
RMON, 309–310
  repeater support of, 235
RMON agents, 183
RMON MIB, 107–108, 278, 291–310
RMON probes, 11, 107–108, 291–292. *See also* RMON MIB
roving, 309
Root bridge, 145
Router(s), 5, 8, 110–111, 140–147, 267–275
  congestion of, 137
  for connectivity, 147, 269–270
  edge, 270
  for enterprise networks, 170–172

functions of, 146–147, 268, 274
  for shielding devices, 270
  and WAN links, 171–172
Runt frames, 91–92, 94
  forwarding of, 129–131

Sampling, 282
Scalability:
  of routed networks, 268–269
  of switched LANs, 260–263
Security, 159–160
  and boot ROM, 191
  and cabling design, 222–223, 367
  and Internet connections, 275
  repeater features for, 236–241
Segment(s), 18, 74
  length of, 383
  performance of, 247–248
  switches for, 251. *See also* Switch(es)
Segmenting, 110, 112–113
Server(s):
  applications, 24
  and full-duplex links, 249
  NICs for, 184–186
  slot numbers of, 193
Server Message Block (SMB) protocol, 13
Session layer, 19–20
SET command, 106
Shared media technology, 5
Shared memory architecture, 200–201
Shared memory data transfer, 189
Shielded twisted pair (STP) wire, 45–46, 226, 380. *See also* Cable
Signal(s), balanced, 47
Signaling methods of Fast Ethernet, 318
Signal restoration, 37–38
Simple Network Management Protocol, *see* SNMP
Simple Path Delay (SPD), 77
Single-mode fiber, 369
Site survey, for network installation, 210, 211
Slot time, 82–83, 324
  and collision windows, 86–87
  and network diameter, 87–88
Small offices, and Fast Ethernet, 164–166

Index

Smart back pressure for switches, 264
Smart Uplink Modules (SUMs), 242–243
SNMP, 18, 104–106, 183
 device independence of, 106
 device management of, 277
 trap messages, 301
SNMP agents, 105
Sockets, 35
Sound card(s), 4
Source address, 57
Spanning tree algorithm, 120–121
Spanning tree switches, 264–265
Spraying, 116
Stackables, 227–230
Start of frame delimiter (SFD), 37
Start-of-packet propagation delay, 33–34, 128
Star topology, 6, 44, 213
Switch(es), 11, 18, 109–110, 245–266. *See also* Bridge(s)
 ASICs of, 124–125
 backbone, 253
 and bridges, comparison, 123–124
 congestion of, 136–137, 263–264, 291
 department, 252
 desktop, 250–252
 enterprise, 253
 features of, 264–266
 forwarding rates of, 123
 full-duplex mode, 138–140, 248–249
 internal design of, 125–127
 layer-3, 267
 oversubscribed, 256
 performance of, 253–258
 problems with, 258–264
 and scalability, 260–263
 segment, 251
 techniques of, 127–134
 10/100 workgroup, 252
 topology limitations, overcoming, 245–247
 workgroup, 250
Switched LAN (SLAN), 18
Switching, *see also* Frame switching
 cut-through, 128–130

 hybrid designs, 134–135
 interim cut-through, 130–131
 store-and-forward, 132–134

TCP/IP, 16, 26–27
 interface for, 30
Telecommunications room, cabling of, 215–216
Telnet, 103
 repeater support of, 236
10Base-2 Ethernet, 6–7
10Base-T Ethernet, 8
10/100 adapters, 202
10/100 workgroup switches, 252, 265
Terminators, 6
Thick net, 7
Thin net, 6–7
Throughput:
 calculation for, 285
 maximum, for Fast Ethernet, 96–98
Thunder LAN devices, 28
Time delays in repeaters, 33–34
T-LAN chips, 28
Token Ring networks, 71
Tolly Group, 254
Topology rules, 6
 for Fast Ethernet, 318, 321–328
 limitations of, 245–247
Traffic, 100, 112
 cabling plant design for, 223
 and the 80/20 rule, 112–113
 and the matrix table, 307
 wire-speed, 255
Traffic generator, 254–255
Transceivers, *see also* PHYs
 for 100Base-TX, 47
Transmission errors, 65–66
Transmission models, *see* Model-I rules; Model-II rules
Transmit attempts counter, 93
Transport layer, 20
Traps, 301
Truncated binary exponential back off, 93
TX, *see* 100Base-TX
Type-1 STP cable, 361, 363, 380. *See also* Cable

U/L bit (universal or local administration flag), 59–61
Unicast addresses, 60–62
Unicast frames, *see also* Frame(s)
 cloning of, 119–120
 forwarding of, 116–117, 126
 scrambling of, 238
Uninterruptible power supplies (UPSs), 219
Universally administered address (UAA), 59–60
Unshielded twisted-pair (UTP) wire, 44, 77. *See also* Cable; EIA/TIA 568 standard
Uplink(s):
 gigabit, 265
 modular, 265
 ports, 41–43, 48
Users:
 habits of, 304–305
 needs of, 154–156

Video teleconferencing, 25

Wall plate outlet, 221, 382
WANs, 3
 connections to, 215
 gateways of, 5
 links to, 171–172, 265, 270–274
Web sites, for technical support, 181
Wide Area Networks, *see* WANs
WinSock, 30
WinSock 2.0, 20
Wire speed frame rates, 97
Wiring, *see also* Cable; Cabling plant; EIA/TIA 568 standard
 types of, 213
Wiring closet, 215–219. *See also* EIA/TIA 568 standard
Work area, cabling of, 221–222
Workgroups, 156
 configuring for, 160–166
 segmentation of, 247–248
 switches for, 246–248, 250–252
Workstations, diskless, 62, 191

Xerox and Ethernet as a standard, 63